Political Economy
of Development

Recent Titles in the
CAROLINA ACADEMIC PRESS
AFRICAN WORLD SERIES
Toyin Falola, Series Editor

Africa, Empire and Globalization: Essays in Honor of A. G. Hopkins
Edited by Toyin Falola and Emily Brownell

*The African Civil Service Fifty Years after Independence: With Case Studies
from Cameroon, Ghana, Kenya and Nigeria*
Edited by Emmanuel M. Mbah and Augustine E. Ayuk

African Humanity: Creativity, Identity and Personhood
Abimbola Asojo and Toyin Falola

Against the Predators' Republic: Political and Cultural Journalism, 2007–2013
Biodun Jeyifo

Authority Stealing: Anti-Corruption War and Democratic Politics in Post-Military Nigeria
Wale Adebanwi

*Conflict Resolution in Africa: Language, Law, and Politeness
in Ghanaian (Akan) Jurisprudence*
Samuel Gyasi Obeng

Contentious Politics in Africa: Identity, Conflict, and Social Change
Edited by Toyin Falola and Wanjala S. Nasong'o

*Creative Incursions: Cultural Representations of Human Rights in Africa
and the Black Diaspora*
Edited by Abikal Borah, Bisola Falola, and Toyin Falola

Decolonizing the University, Knowledge Systems and Disciplines in Africa
Edited by Sabelo J. Ndlovu-Gatsheni and Siphamandla Zondi

Democracy in Africa: Political Changes and Challenges
Edited by Saliba Sarsar and Julius O. Adekunle

Democradura: *Essays on Nigeria's Limited Democracy*
N. Oluwafemi Mimiko

*Diaspora and Imagined Nationality: USA-Africa Dialogue and
Cyberframing Nigerian Nationhood*
Koleade Odutola

Èsù: Yoruba God, Power, and the Imaginative Frontiers
Edited by Toyin Falola

Ethnicities, Nationalities, and Cross-Cultural Representations in Africa and the Diaspora
Edited by Gloria Chuku

Falolaism: The Epistemologies and Methodologies of Africana Knowledge
Abdul Karim Bangura

Gendering African Social Spaces: Women, Power, and Cultural Expressions
Edited by Toyin Falola and Wanjala S. Nasong'o

*Horror in Paradise: Frameworks for Understanding the Crises of
the Niger Delta Region of Nigeria*
Edited by Christopher LaMonica and J. Shola Omotola

Ifá in Yorùbá Thought System
Omotade Adegbindin

The Indigenous African Criminal Justice System for the Modern World
Olusina Akeredolu

Intercourse and Crosscurrents in the Atlantic World:
Calabar-British Experience, 17th–20th Centuries
David Lishilinimle Imbua

Issues in African Political Economies
Edited by Toyin Falola, Jamaine Abidogun

Julius Nyerere, Africa's Titan on a Global Stage: Perspectives from Arusha to Obama
Edited by Ali A. Mazrui and Lindah L. Mhando

The Muse of Anomy: Essays on Literature and the Humanities in Nigeria
Femi Osofisan

Narratives of Struggle: The Philosophy and Politics of Development
John Ayotunde Isola Bewaji

Nigeria and the Politics of Everybody: Social Media, Idealism, and Activism
Toyin Falola

Nollywood: Popular Culture and Narratives of Youth Struggles in Nigeria
Paul Ugor

Pan-Africanism in Ghana: African Socialism, Neoliberalism, and Globalization
Justin Williams

Perspectives on the Religious Landscape in Africa
Edited by Lady Jane Acquah and Toyin Falola

The Philosophy of Nimi Wariboko: Social Ethics, Economy, and Religion
Edited by Toyin Falola

Political Economy of Development: Public Policy Alternatives
and Progressive Ideas in Nigeria
Tayo Oke

Satires of Power in Yoruba Visual Culture
Yomi Ola

The United States' Foreign Policy in Africa in the 21st Century: Issues and Perspectives
Edited by Adebayo Oyebade

Urban Challenges and Survival Strategies in Africa
Edited by Adeshina Afolayan and Toyin Falola

The Vile Trade: Slavery and the Slave Trade in Africa
Edited by Abi Alabo Derefaka, Wole Ogundele, Akin Alao, and Augustus Babajide Ajibola

Women, Gender, and Sexualities in Africa
Edited by Toyin Falola and Nana Akua Amponsah

Yoruba Creativity: Cultural Practices of the Modern World
Bessie House-Soremekun

The Yoruba in Brazil, Brazilians in Yorubaland: Cultural Encounter, Resilience,
and Hybridity in the Atlantic World
Edited by Niyi Afolabi and Toyin Falola

Political Economy of Development

Public Policy Alternatives and Progressive Ideas in Nigeria

Tayo Oke

PRINCIPAL, ASIKO CHAMBERS [FINANCIAL AND ECONOMIC LAW]
SENIOR LECTURER, AFE BABALOLA UNIVERSITY, ADO-EKITI, NIGERIA

CAROLINA ACADEMIC PRESS
Durham, North Carolina

Copyright © 2024
Tayo Oke
All Rights Reserved

Library of Congress Cataloging-in-Publication Data

Names: Oke, Tayo, author.
Title: Political economy of development : public policy alternatives and
  progressive ideas in Nigeria / by Tayo Oke.
Description: Durham : Carolina Academic Press, 2023. | Includes index.
Identifiers: LCCN 2022057121 (print) | LCCN 2022057122 (ebook) | ISBN
  9781531026509 (paperback) | ISBN 9781531026516 (ebook)
Subjects: LCSH: Political planning–Nigeria. | Nigeria–Economic
  conditions–21st century. | Nigeria–Politics and government–21st
  century.
Classification: LCC JQ3089.5.P64 O54 2023 (print) | LCC JQ3089.5.P64
  (ebook) | DDC 320.609669–dc23/eng/20221128
LC record available at https://lccn.loc.gov/2022057121
LC ebook record available at https://lccn.loc.gov/2022057122

CAROLINA ACADEMIC PRESS
700 Kent Street
Durham, North Carolina 27701
(919) 489-7486
www.cap-press.com

Printed in the United States of America

Contents

Series Editor's Foreword	xi
Acknowledgments	xiii
Foreword	xv
Introduction	xvii
Chapter Synopsis	xxiii

Chapter One · Economy	3
1.01 Nigeria's Interest Rates/Forex Quagmire (1)	3
1.02 Nigeria's Interest Rates/Forex Quagmire (II)	5
1.03 Easing Nigeria Out of Recession	8
1.04 A Note on Foreign (Direct) Investment in Nigeria	11
1.05 Can Nigeria Ever Stop Importing Rice?	13
1.06 Diversifying or Decentralising Nigerian Economy?	16
1.07 AMCON's Dubious Economic Function	19
1.08 DMO and the Paradox of 'Debt Management'	22
1.09 The Elusive Quest for Tax Revenue	25
1.10 Crippling Cost of Borrowing; Who Cares?	27
1.11 First Law of Development	30
1.12 9Mobile: How (Not) to Resurrect Business Failure	33
1.13 Parallel Universe of the IMF and Nigerian Government	35
1.14 NNPC/Multinational Oil Contracts: Grand Bargain or Grand Larceny?	39
1.15 NNPC, FAAC, Minister of Finance, and the Missing Billions	42
1.16 High Inflation as a By-Product of High-Level Corruption	45
1.17 Nigerian Workers Deserve Living (Not Minimum) Wage	47
1.18 When a Country's Debt Becomes a 'Crisis'	50
1.19 Why Companies Go Public (I)	53

1.20	Why Companies Go Public (II)	55
1.21	Why Companies Go Bust	58
1.22	Nigeria's Unabated Stagflation: Why it Matters	62

Chapter Two · Finance/Capital Markets — 67

2.01	Sovereign Wealth Fund: Cui bono?	67
2.02	FRCN, Corporate Governance and Regulatory Overreach (I)	70
2.03	FRCN, Corporate Governance and Regulatory Overreach (II)	73
2.04	FRCN, Corporate Governance and Regulatory Overreach (III)	75
2.05	We've Had Pro-Democracy Activists, Why not Activist Investors?	78
2.06	SEC's Tepid Response to Market Infractions	80
2.07	Forex: CBN Governor's Parallel Universe	83
2.08	Forex: Nigerian Banks in the Dock	86
2.09	Budget 2017 Through the Lens of Capital Markets	88
2.10	Rise and Fall of Nigeria's Banking Services	90
2.11	Nigeria's Financial 'Intelligence' at the Crossroads	94
2.12	Stock Exchange and the Mechanics of Markets	96
2.13	US Dollar: The Power and the Glory (I)	99
2.14	US Dollar: The Power and the Glory (II)	102
2.15	US Dollar: The Power and the Glory (III)	105
2.16	Why Banks Fail	107
2.17	SEC's New "Derivatives" Platform	110
2.18	SEC's Litany of Corporate Governance Lapses	113
2.19	Painful Lesson for 9Mobile Shareholders	116
2.20	Nigeria's $2.5bn Currency 'Swap' with China	118
2.21	Combating Corporate Greed Through Corporate Governance	122
2.22	China: Generous Lender or Loan Shark?	125
2.23	Rise of Non-Interest (Islamic) Banking	128
2.24	Bureaux de Change, Banks, and Economic Saboteurs	131

Chapter Three · Economic and Financial Crime — 135

3.01	EFCC, Courts, Stolen Funds, and Legal Technicality	135
3.02	EFCC, Transparency International, and the Game of Numbers	138
3.03	EFCC's Persistent Failure at Criminal Assets Forfeiture	141
3.04	Kleptocracy Assets Recovery Initiative: Dog that Bites!	144
3.05	Between White Collar Crime and Business Efficacy	146
3.06	EFCC and PEPs: Caught in a Cobweb of Legalism	149

CONTENTS ix

Chapter Four · Education 153
  4.01 Why Nigerian Universities are Graduating Illiterates 153
  4.02 Should Academics Be Moral Agents? 156
  4.03 Why "VC" Position Is Keenly Contested in Nigeria 158
  4.04 NUC: Assessing the Assessors 161

Chapter Five · Media 165
  5.01 Why Channels is in the Government's Crosshair 165
  5.02 Sorry, Servile, Supine State of Nigeria's Media 168
  5.03 Channels TV Interview (Sorry, Torture) of President Buhari 171
  5.04 Why Governments Love (and Loathe) Twitter 173

Chapter Six · Politics 177
  6.01 Why 'Vote Buying' Matters: Why it Does Not 177
  6.02 Transition Gap: A Looters' Charter 180
  6.03 Yes, Nigeria Needs a Revolution — of the Mind 182
  6.04 Nigeria: 'Tribalism' and the Nationality Question 185
  6.05 Buhari Should Lance the Boil of Separatism 188
  6.06 Round-Tripping Politicians: Blessing or Curse? 191
  6.07 APC, PDP in Disarray: Is There an Alternative? 193
  6.08 Taliban Victory: Morale Booster for Boko Haram 196
  6.09 Is Nigeria Worth Dying For? 199
  6.10 Nigeria: A Nation of Lions Led By Donkeys 202
  6.11 Why Millions Join Political Parties in Nigeria 205
  6.12 INEC and its 'Independence' Troubles . . . 208
  6.13 How Religion Enables Gender-Based Violence 210
  6.14 Dearth of Female Nigerian Leaders 213
  6.15 How #EndSARS Was Lost 216
  6.16 Imperative (and Myth) of Youth Representation 218
  6.17 Warning: Parliamentary System is Brutal and Vicious 221

Chapter Seven · Law 225
  7.01 "Panama papers": Lawyers' Ethical Dilemma 225
  7.02 SEC: Minister's Right to Suspend DG 227
  7.03 Why Nigerian Police Relish Parading Suspects 230
  7.04 Legality of P&ID/$9.6bn award 232
  7.05 Politics of P&ID $9.6bn Award 235
  7.06 Legality of Government's Raid on Pension Funds 238
  7.07 Malami's 'Open' Road to Anarchy 241

CONTENTS

Chapter Eight · Military   245
  8.01 Nigeria: Still Under Shadows of Military   245
  8.02 Nigerian Military's Conflict of Loyalties   248
  8.03 AFRICOM: Buhari's White Flag of Surrender   250
  8.04 Africa and the 'Corrective Coup' Syndrome   253

Chapter Nine · Intra-African Affairs   257
  9.01 Zimbabwe: An African Tragedy   257
  9.02 How Europe Underdeveloped Africa   260
  9.03 How 'African Time' Is Killing Africa   263
  9.04 New Scramble for Africa: Not the Chinese, Surely?   265
  9.05 Who's Afraid of Africa's Free Trade Bloc?   269
  9.06 Why We Celebrate (Not Jail) Corrupt Leaders In Africa (I)   272
  9.07 Why We Celebrate (Not Jail) Corrupt Leaders in Africa (II)   274
  9.08 What "Brexit" Means for Africa   277
  9.09 South Africa: False Narrative of Xenophobic Attacks   280
  9.10 Nigeria's Muddled Policy on Western Sahara   282
  9.11 Adesina's Re-election: Slap in the Face for America   285
  9.12 Africans Hiding Wealth in Offshore Accounts Are Traitors   288
  9.13 Thomas Sankara: Africa's Finest, Gunned Down Too Soon   291
  9.14 King Mswati III: Africa's Last Maximum Ruler   294

Chapter Ten · International Affairs   299
  10.01 Hypocrisy of Foreign Election Observers   299
  10.02 Why Trump Supporters Are So Wrong   302
  10.03 USA: Why Trump Must (and will) Be Defeated   305
  10.04 What Makes a Country 'Third World'?   307
  10.05 Why G7 Disavow 'Race to Bottom' Tax Incentive   310

Conclusion   315

Index   321

Series Editor's Foreword

The *Carolina Academic Press African World Series*, inaugurated in 2010, offers significant new works in the field of African and Black World studies. The series provides scholarly and educational texts that can serve both as reference works and as readers in college classes.

Studies in the series are anchored in the existing humanistic and the social scientific traditions. Their goal, however, is the identification and elaboration of the strategic place of Africa and its Diaspora in a shifting global world. More specifically, the studies will address gaps and larger needs in the developing scholarship on Africa and the Black World.

The series intends to fill gaps in areas such as African politics, history, law, religion, culture, sociology, literature, philosophy, visual arts, art history, geography, language, health, and social welfare. Given the complex nature of Africa and its Diaspora, and the constantly shifting perspectives prompted by globalization, the series also meets a vital need for scholarship connecting knowledge with events and practices. Reflecting the fact that life in Africa continues to change, especially in the political arena, the series explores issues emanating from racial and ethnic identities, particularly those connected with the ongoing mobilization of ethnic minorities for inclusion and representation.

Toyin Falola
University of Texas at Austin

Acknowledgments

This work is literally owed to dozens of friends, colleagues, and well-wishers all over the world who, in various ways, had badgered me for years, in some cases, about the need to assemble the essays on my column in a book form. It would be quite uncharitable of me to start mentioning individual names, as I am bound to leave out many for lack of space.

Special thanks, therefore, go to those who were instrumental in the actual task of putting the work together; my colleagues both in academia and in journalism. Professors Olukayode Amund, Vice-Chancellor, Elizade University, and Francis Iyoha, Chartered Accountant and Professor of Accounting, Covenant University, Nigeria deserve a special commendation for their encouragement and constant thumbs up for my write-ups. Dr Emeka Iloh, Department of International Relations and Diplomacy, Afe Babalola University, Ado-Ekiti for his painstaking review and expert comments on the manuscript. His breadth of knowledge and awareness of facts goes beyond his departmental brief.

Particular appreciation goes to my friends in the corridors of power in Abuja, the Federal Capital of Nigeria, and in the various states of the federation. Many of you have expressed preference to remain anonymous, including some captains of industry who communicate with me in private, and in confidence. I am grateful to you all. I am also equally encouraged by communications from a number of foreign diplomatic missions, as well as foreign media outlets who have been in touch at various points over the years, either to disprove or commend the stance taken in my write-ups, which directly affect their interests.

My most sincere appreciation must go to Aare Afe Babalola, Founder/Chancellor, Afe Babalola University, for not only being my foremost intellectual sparring partner in the university, but for having an unshakable belief in me, as a person with 'untapped' potential, which he has dedicated a considerable amount of his time to draw out. One of such potential is the writing of this book. Needless to say, Aare Babalola expects more. I pray God will grant us both the time and space to meet his expectations even halfway. "The price for excellence is even more hard work, and more burden on one's shoulders", he would often say. I totally agree.

Acknowledgment is also due to the anonymous reviewers of the manuscript, who all tried in their objective ways to contribute to its improvement. Every single comment, and remark has been taken into account for the final product. The biggest gratitude, however, must go to my editors, as well as the avid readers of my weekly column in PUNCH, from where the raw materials for this book have been harvested. It is nigh impossible to put a finger on the exact number of the readers, but it is safe to assume that they are in their thousands, if not millions in, and outside of Nigeria. My postbag is full of your reactions and responses to particular things you have read and understood or not understood, that surprised or calmed you, or that you were incredulous about. Big thanks to you all!

Finally, thanks to Femi Olowu, in the Department of Accounting, Afe Babalola University, for dealing effortlessly with the initial word processing and printing of the manuscript, Dr Jacinta Benjamin-Ohwodede, English and Literature Department, University of Benin, and Olabisi Atinmo, Before Books and Beyond (first and second proofreaders respectively), for an excellent proofreading job, and Manni Ochugboju, a lawyer and public policy and development analyst, for agreeing to an impromptu review of the manuscript, which he carried out substantially and diligently. It behoves me at this juncture to make clear that while all influences and inspirations for every chapter have contributed to the successful completion of this book, and have been duly acknowledged, responsibility for errors and omissions in the entire volume is solely mine.

Foreword

As the final outcome of the 2023 presidential election remains contested in Nigeria, the whole world is watching with bated breath as the political leaders in the country have not covered themselves in glory in terms of the way, and manner in which they have governed, or not governed since the return to civilian order in 1999. It has led many to start questioning the essence of democracy and the federal system of governance in operation in the country. The 1999 Constitution of the Federal Republic of Nigeria, Chapter II, Section 2 (b) and (c) state: "The Fundamental Objectives and Directive Principles of State Policy is that the security and welfare of the people shall be the primary purpose of government; and the participation by the people in their government shall be ensured in accordance with the provisions of this Constitution". This, in fact, is a universal principle, which forms the basis of the "social contract" between citizens and their governments in every democratic nation. By any yardstick, the political elites in Nigeria have failed to live up to any aspect of the fundamental objectives in the Constitution. That much is clear. What is less clear, however, is why. Probing into why successive Nigerian governments have failed in their obligations under the Constitution, not just since 1999, but generally since independence in 1960, is very much like sifting through a huge pile of shredded corn husk in search of a needle.

Some attribute the failure to the Constitution itself, especially the 1999 Constitution, which has never been affirmed by the people. It was a hotchpotch of ideas, hurriedly packaged and enacted by the departing military government and falsely stated as emanating from the people. Others see the incompetence and a lack of commitment by political leaders to nation-building. Philosophers, economists, political scientists, sociologists, lawyers, and several others in the field of social science and humanities have developed theories and assumptions purporting to give us an insight into the Nigerian 'problem'. Every angle, every account seems to have succeeded only in expanding the parameters of the 'problem', rather than narrowing it. It is therefore refreshing to see a book that is not designed to offer yet another pathway based on a set of theoretical assumptions, but one that is anchored on a panoramic view of the country as it is. It is a 'live' commentary on events as they happen, leaving the reader to draw his own conclusions. The ten chapters in the book feature 'events' covering every aspect of Nigeria's public life: economics, politics, law, capital markets, media, military, etc. They are designed to inform, elucidate, and educate the masses. They are also grounded in scholarship for the more inquiring mind. Every chapter is backed up by empirical evidence, scrupulously avoiding any hint of sweeping generalisations.

The choice of the title of the book, "Political Economy of Development", also gives the impression that it, too, is starting from a set of theoretical assumptions, but this is palpably not so. The author's choice of the title encapsulates the chequered journey of Nigeria towards development through aspects of its politics and economics. In his incisive commentaries on Nigeria that he presents here for his readers, Professor Tayo Oke succinctly deploys his in-depth knowledge and experience of living and working in some twenty countries-in-transition around the world. This experience spans over two decades as a consultant and field staff for notable international organisations such as the United Nations, the European Union, International Organisation for Migration, amongst others. Having been involved in post-conflict nation-building-related tasks in various locations across the globe, his methodological approach for this book can best be described as one of participant-observer. Rich in its breadth of analysis, unequivocal in its assertions, and evocative in its projections, each chapter in the book can best be described as a treasure trove of seminal pieces of writing that convey the socio-cultural jigsaw that Nigeria and its political economy constitute. This work is a masterful collection of writing by a committed scholar, journalist, and social science practitioner, whose experience in the global arena as a field worker, and detail-oriented lawyer, puts him a cut above the rest.

Aare Afe Babalola, BSc, LLB, LLD (London),
Senior Advocate of Nigeria
Founder/Chancellor, Afe Babalola University,
Ado-Ekiti, Nigeria
March 1st 2023

Introduction

This is a compilation of essays on a swathe of subjects: economics, politics, law, finance, education, media, military, and international relations, focusing on public policy in an emerging economy, in a key African state. Put together in one neat volume, they are as original as they are full of depth and breadth. The methodological approach to this collection was innovative in its design. It was based on a careful dissection of crucial aspects of public policy in their raw elements, and placed in the context of their conceptual and empirical groundings. It is bearing witness to a marriage between theory and practice. This is then used to critique policy choices, and proffer alternative options to fill the lacunae where necessary. The eclectic mix of theories deployed for analysis stands it out from the conventional approach seen in standard textbooks. No book on the market would have engaged with the effect of monetarism and supply-side economics versus public ownership and dependency logic; theories of democracy and pluralism versus militarism and dictatorship; distributive justice versus social justice and 'free and fair' election as a concept, as against 'substantial compliance' with legal requirements as the end results.

The intersection between theoretical assumptions and public policy is the mechanic's workshop for this book. The essays have been written to appeal to a wide audience across different socio-economic strata, but also carefully manicured by data to raise their essence beyond a passing interest in the subject matter, to one the reader will generally find arresting, and certainly illuminating. Rather than producing a single-subject standard text in a typically isolated fashion, the approach to this volume is deliberately multidisciplinary as it is multifaceted.

Perhaps what marks out this book the most from the others in the discipline is that it does not set out in the usual manner of providing 'the grand narrative' to a known 'problem'. Rather, it is a chronicle of events in real time. It unravels

xviii INTRODUCTION

a series of narratives for their effectiveness, and relevance to public policy alternatives in a major regional economy; it is a running commentary whose goal it is to deconstruct and reconstruct the differing narratives based on the evidence. It is primarily aimed at a general readership, some of whom will have no pre-conceived notion of the subject-matter, while others will already be well-informed on it. Others, still, will be specialists and experts in the field being provided with a new angle, and a new lens to wade through a familiar territory. In other words, the book is a 'one stop shop' for the less sophisticated as well as the highly sophisticated readership. In partnership with the publisher, and based on a sustained public interest, it should be updated as, and when subsequent events justify.

Africa, says Alao,[1] is a voice to be heard, not a problem to be solved. My approach to this book aligns with that thought. It categorically rejects the usual pathological approach to the study of Nigeria as a disease to be dissected, followed by swallowing the latest dose of remedial (if ineffectual) pills. All the known theories and ideas on the political economy of development in respect of Nigeria are tested in this work against actual policy output, then, subjected to public debate in a dedicated newspaper column in the PUNCH,[2] over a period of ten years. The outcome of that exercise is what is contained in this book. While efforts were made to preserve the original texts of the essays in this book as they first appeared in print, there have been minor editorial tweaks here and there for quality control, and the need to substantiate bold assertions with data. It stands to reason, therefore, that the essays have already been 'road tested', judging by the column's growing readership; domestic as well as international and by the numerous correspondence from ordinary readers, to top level individuals and various institutions, many of whom have, at one time or another, become the object of debate over the period covered in the book. Requests have, at various times, been received from interested parties to have aspects of the essays translated into Chinese, French, Spanish and other languages for additional world-wide readership. Although PUNCH provides the vehicle for publication of the essays, they are, almost invariably, gratuitously copied and pasted on rival media platforms as well as other institutions' platforms often within hours of release. This is surely an indication of the

---

1. See; A. Alao. "Africa: A Voice to be heard, not a problem to be solved". An inaugural lecture at King's College, University of London, 2016. Given the divergence of Africa's regional aspirations from Cape to Cairo, it should be emphasised that the 'voice' is not monosyllabic, it is multidimensional in essence.

2. PUNCH is the widest circulating newspaper in Nigeria, and by extension, West Africa.

INTRODUCTION

strong interest in them by various audiences; it is also a compelling case for having them in a book form to satisfy demand.

The essays have been written for public consumption for the past ten years. They number in their hundreds, although, only the last six years have been taken into account for this collection. Many have appeared and reappeared in unauthorised platforms, including private blogs in Nigeria and beyond. It has not been easy to reproduce and rewrite them in one volume of work of this nature. The essays cover mainly the last six years as a result of the need to make them contemporary and relevant to current discourse. There is no other book of the same genre on the market anywhere in Nigeria, or indeed, anywhere else, in the world.

The author has received numerous requests from top-level government functionaries, and captains of industry for the links to specific topics covered on the column at different times. Sadly, there is no ready-made audit of the four hundred or so essays published across a decade. Producing them in double volumes is probably what should have been done, but this one volume offers the best start. Nigeria, like many countries in Africa, does not have a well-established and practicable intellectual property protection law. Copyright is still a strange concept to many people engaged in lifting other people's work with reckless abandon. Producing a book of this nature is a good way of countering this endemic problem as it makes author identification easier, and more compelling.

After reading through many of the essays, repeatedly in some cases, a decision was made to group them under ten headings. The combined headings provide a good snapshot to the political economy of a key African state at a particular moment in time. They are "reflections" written from the vantage point of an academic with a trained eye on the specifics. In many ways, the book is a chronicle of events as they happened, how they ought to have happened, and how they may happen in the foreseeable future. The arguments presented are rich enough in their complexity to appeal to professionals in the field, yet, devoid of jargon enough to appeal to the curious mind, and the self-motivated in public policy. Many students of economics, political science, journalism, sociology, and accounting, have had cause to email the author, thanking him for simplifying a previously complex issue for them. One such correspondence came from an undergraduate accounting student who, having read a column on bonds and capital markets, wrote to express his relief that the issue had provided such a headache for him and his colleagues the whole year long, but they had finally been put out of their mystery by the write up.

Similarly, a postgraduate student in Ukraine once got in touch to clarify the treatment of 'hedge funds' and the global financial crisis. A lot more correspondence have also come in from university professors on the crisis of education and other hot-button issues of the day. Civil servants, legislators and many others have also had cause to engage with the column. One particular avid reader, an American expatriate living in Lagos, was so livid about the column's characterisation of America under President Donald Trump, that he got in touch, first with a five-page rebuttal of the column's stance on Trump, then, swiftly entered into a bet of one hundred dollars that he (Trump) would be re-elected, with the breakdown of the states he would carry, and the ones he would lose, and the final tally from the electoral college.

Since the column had made an impassioned analysis of why and how Trump would lose the election, the author was happy to double the bet to two hundred dollars. The expatriate hurriedly insisted on exchanging bank details in advance of the election of November 2020, because he was convinced that Trump's victory at the polls was a "slam dunk", and had expected his account to be credited immediately after the expected victory. Trump, of course, lost the election by a wide margin. Not to rub salt in his wound, the author politely declined the promised payment but advised him to re-examine his near fanatical belief in Trump going forward. To his credit, he declined, and would have none of that mollycoddling sentiment from him. He insisted on paying up, like the proud American that he was, and kept badgering the author until he reluctantly accepted, but, only if he would agree to meet him in person at a coffee shop for that purpose. He did, and he let go of his hard-earned, clean two hundred dollar bills with a broad grin on his face, a hand shake, and a bear hug.

Others from within Nigeria, from time to time, have also found reasons to send in copious notes on the column's "brilliant" or "fussy" facts and figures on the financial market or the economy and politics, amongst others. When analyses of the political economy of a country become a subject of everyday conversation, then the column and this book in particular could be said to have achieved their objective. The essence of publishing a book of this nature is to acquire readership and also to tap into their consciousness. It has not been plain sailing selecting the essays to include, and the ones to cut out. There were enough materials to create four volumes of this book in one go, but that would be stretching the reader's loyalty too far. The chapters have been carefully arranged to accommodate the titles under each heading. That too, was not always as exact as was intended. Efforts have been made to cut out the professional critique and profile of individuals in the public eye to avoid distraction from the central themes of the book. Where the office of an individual is attached to their person, for instance, the Attorney General of the Federation making changes to provisions of the law, it becomes inevitable that the minister is mentioned by name, by dint of his office, and his peculiar role as both the Attorney General and Minister of Justice.

The book consists of ten chapters, made up of ten areas of public policy, giving the reader a panoramic view of the subject-matter. Each chapter should, ideally, contain a similar number of essays, but there is an inevitable variation based on the issues, and the regularity in which they occurred during the period covered. For instance, the chapters on the economy contain the highest number of essays because the subject has been a dominant issue of governance in Nigeria as elsewhere, in the past three decades. The chapters on finance/capital markets, and politics are not too far behind. The others contain a minimum of five essays per chapter. The essays are approximately one thousand words in length each. The aim is to keep the overall length of the book within the agreed limit. The essays have been carefully selected from a bank of four hundred, all of which are pertinent to the book's mission of educating, illuminating, challenging old, as well as new assumptions for the reader. It was a wrench deciding which to include, and which to leave out. Consequently, except for the first essay on capital markets in Chapter Two (2013), all of them date from 2015 to 2021, the period covering the administration of President Muhammadu Buhari. The essays that made the final list for inclusion in the book are the ones that best exemplify the chapter and period in which they appear. Moreover, priority was given to particular essays that shed new light on contentious theories in the debate on the relevant subject. As stated earlier, this book does not set out to drive home a particular theoretical assumption about the country under study. It does not set out to propagate a particular 'solution' to the 'problem with Nigeria', or proffer definitive analytical remedies to previously intractable problems. In short, as stated earlier, the chapters in the book do not contain a 'grand narrative' to sell to the reader in the usual manner of books on the market. Instead, the chapters are an encounter with public policy in real time. Conventional assumptions and old theories are tested against the reality of policy as it happens, where necessary. In other areas, a direct critique of policy is provided in a historical context. This either reinforces an established understanding or throws light on a new angle in the debate.

Finally, the book should appeal to a broad spectrum of professionals: Cabinet ministers and their advisers, policy analysts, civil servants, media analysts, journalists, scholars, students and captains of industry. It should also appeal to professionals and individuals outside Nigeria seeking a comprehensive overview of the socio-political-economy of the country that is both technical and academic in substance, in one neat package. In addition, the book serves as a pointer to various angles for those keen on conducting research on Nigeria, as many topics covered in the chapters have the potential for expansion into journal articles singly or collectively, or even into a separate book or books. The author has been subjected to relentless prodding and goading by colleagues, friends and family for several years to undertake this rolling project. The task has now been accomplished. Over to you, the reader, to come along and enjoy.

Chapter Synopsis

Chapter One

Chapter One examines different aspects of economic policy, starting with the government's application of a Washington-inspired "supply-side economics" and monetarism in an emerging economy with a chronic problem of high interest rates. On this basis, a recession is never too far behind. Attracting Foreign Direct Investment (FDI) has become an article of faith for successive governments in Nigeria from the early 1990s. This is a major shift from the excessive bank borrowings of the 1970s and 1980s, which led to a pile of unpaid (and unpayable) loans. The shift in focus to FDI is therefore understandable. What is often lost in the discussion, however, is the fact that while a direct bank loan gives the borrower the latitude to spend the money as he pleases, usually based on the development priorities of his government, FDI does not allow for such luxury. The development aspiration of the host government is only incidental to the foreign investor's principal objective of maximising profit. Consequently, the foreign investment is willy-nilly channelled to the sectors that promise the maximum return at a minimal cost, and in the fastest time. Borrowing from banks is a good idea if the money so acquired was properly invested in the country's economy, but more often than not, the loans were frittered away on white elephant projects, and often used to line the pockets of corrupt public officials. FDI is a good viable option in many respects, but that too comes with a hefty price tag in form of various concessions the investor would extract from the host government: tax holidays, freedom to repatriate profits, supplying own personnel, reluctance to transfer technology, increase in environmental pollution from their production method,

xxiii

xxiv CHAPTER SYNOPSIS

to mention but a few. 'A Note on Foreign (Direct) Investment' critically engages with the conventional wisdom on this important aspect of economic policy and priorities.

The persistent problem of foreign exchange and the role of Nigerian banks in creating a 'parallel' market for its currency became a major public policy discourse, as much as the decision to close Nigeria's land borders in an attempt to stem the tide of importation (or smuggling) of foreign-manufactured rice. 'Can Nigeria Ever Stop Importing Rice'? This brought to the fore the industrial policy option of protectionism versus free trade by examining both the desirability and feasibility of discouraging rice importation when the country has still not built up sufficient capacity to absorb demand for the product. The argument dovetails with the wider debate about the need to diversify or decentralise the economy. State intervention and free market have always being a delicate balancing act even in the most advanced economies. The concept of 'too big to fail', occasioned by the financial crisis that started in the US in 2008, pushed Congress to pass legislation aimed at rescuing the financial institutions considered too big to fail. It has since been exported to the rest of the world. Nigeria's Assets Management Corporation of Nigeria (AMCON) and Debt Management Organisation (DMO) have come to symbolise this latest innovation at market intervention by stealth. In Nigeria, large corporations and banks found to be in 'distress' are taken over, their assets subjected to 'restructuring' or 'management' by AMCON, the toxic part of them are shipped over to DMO, and the company is then eased back into the private sector once the balance sheet becomes attractive enough to investors. This is a case of nationalising liability and privatising profit, it would seem. The 'elusive quest for tax revenue' and the 'crippling cost of borrowing' expatiate further on the Federal Government's ability to balance its books amidst mounting budget deficit. 'First Law of Development' postulates on who carries the burden of government's ever increasing public debt and wonders whether it is not disproportionately left on the shoulders of the have-nots . The issue of government intervention in business failure resurfaces again in the discussion on '9mobile' and attempts at saving it from collapse. These themes run through public debate for a considerable number of months when the issue of taking a company from private to public ownership comes to the fore mainly as a public education exercise. 'Why companies go bust' rounds up the chapter by exposing the reader to some aspects of company finance, especially the pivotal role of cash flow in keeping a company solvent.

Chapter Two

The teaching, coverage, and public discussion of capital markets, universally, have been somewhat esoteric for a very long time. The financial crisis of 2008 heightened interest in the subject worldwide, but it is still a little hard to grapple with in the atmosphere of an emerging economy, where shareholding is yet to move into the mainstream. Consequently, the aim of this chapter is to bring the subject matter into public discourse in a way that reflects the language and understanding of the ordinary person, while still being technically relevant to the professional in the field. What better way to kick off the debate than by a discussion of the Sovereign Wealth Fund (SWF). The idea of saving up for the proverbial rainy day is as old as the merchant banks, but a relatively new concept in an otherwise cash-strapped economy. Why would a struggling economy wish to save for the future generation, when the present generation is still underfed, and malnourished? SWF is a brilliant idea seen in other well-endowed (petrol-dollar) economies, but Nigeria is a pseudo petrol-dollar economy at best since the product accounts for less than 10% of the country's GDP. So, the question: "Sovereign Wealth Fund: Cui Bono?" was appropriately raised, and attracted volumes of correspondence right across the professional divide for years. This was followed by an attempt to simplify the logic of bonds and shares in the market, using real life examples. It is often the case that the rosier side of capitalism is understood, but not its uneven, seamier side. Another hot button topic of public concern in the financial sector is the issue of non-interest (Islamic) finance fronted in Nigeria by the country's indigenous Islamic bank, Jaiz Bank. Is it an attempt at an Islamic 'takeover' of society? Nothing could be further from the truth. It is just another instrument for raising funds, but few people, even highly qualified professionals, understand this very well. 'Why companies go public' came up as part of the continuous public education exercise by the column, and so was the issue of "derivatives" as an addition to Nigeria's capital markets. Derivatives are difficult to grapple with even in London, at the heart of Europe's financial market, talk less of an emerging economy. This too was followed up with a call for 'activist investors' in the capital markets. It is a matter for conjecture that if 'political activists' applied half of their energy and interest to the capital markets, the public would be much better served. The debate it provoked spurred other topics around the same theme for a few weeks more. Finally, a bold attempt was made to bring the use of the US dollar into the fray, as the Naira continued the downward spiral of depreciation against it. This is all the more important, given that the Naira was stronger than the dollar for a long period of time after independence. That said, other emerging economies have had their currencies

xxvi CHAPTER SYNOPSIS

suffer the same fate as the Naira, hence, the need to discuss the economic history of the reserved currency of international finance over the course of three weeks. The chapter concludes with a short essay on why banks fail.

Chapter Three

Economic and financial crime has been a prominent feature of public life in Nigeria at least since the 1980s. The agency set up to both deter and prosecute such crimes is the Economic and Financial Crimes Commission (EFCC). Its mandate has led the organisation into a continuing controversy in the sense that everyone agrees on the imperative of combating financial crime in official circles, but no one seems to agree on the best tactics to achieve that. The head of the EFCC is by necessity thrust into the spotlight from inception, especially when it comes to political influence to either (as some see it) 'back off' certain corrupt elements in government, or 'go after' some of the others outside government. EFCC is also used by outside observers (Transparency International and other international financial institutions) as a barometer on how steadfast Nigeria is in combating official corruption. The pressure on the organisation and its leadership is understandably immense. The pressure is not made any easier by the unsettled view of its 'independence' from, or 'subordination' to the country's Ministry of Justice in the use of its prosecutorial powers. EFCC is a statutory body. Technically, the appropriate government department for its oversight is the Ministry of Justice, but no Minister of Justice would wish to be seen as 'interfering' in the 'independence' of the EFCC by raising even the most innocuous query about the organisation's rationale on certain matters. Additionally, EFCC is erroneously seen by many as a body with untrammelled powers. It is seen as accuser, prosecutor, judge, jury, and jailer in cases within its purview. One of the highlights of the many tensions inside the organisation came to the fore when the column raised an issue on 'EFCC's Persistent Failure at Criminal Assets Forfeiture'. The following day, the column received a message from the EFCC threatening legal action over 'inaccuracies' in the piece. The Minister of Justice announced the suspension of its Chairman three days later, then, subjected him to an official probe. He was subsequently removed from office a couple of months afterwards. Coincidence? That is for the reader to judge.

Chapter Four

The chapter focuses on university education under the auspices of the National Universities Commission, the agency that regulates the sector. On independence in 1960, there was a universal embrace of the strategic need to

CHAPTER SYNOPSIS

boost graduate admissions. The departing colonial administration did not make university education a priority. The oil boom of the 1970s saw a spike in the national expenditure on education, which was quickly followed by a sharp drop amidst the late 1980s inflation, recession and Nigeria's rising debt profile. University education, like other sectors of the economy, has endured its share of government cuts. Negotiating over pay and conditions of its academic staff has been moved from the Ministry of Education to the Ministry of Labour, where a more stringent approach and emphasis is placed on 'productivity'. It is no surprise, therefore, that government and the Academic Staff Union of Universities (ASUU) are nearly always at loggerheads over pay and working conditions. Government insists on efficiency, while the union demands funding to upgrade dilapidating infrastructure. General standards have inevitably taken a turn for the worse. The emergence and proliferation of private universities has done much, but not enough to stem the tide of the decline in the university sector. More parents are opting to educate their children in private universities which do not have a unionised workforce, but there are question marks over academic standards in some of the private universities as well. The regimented approach to student discipline applied in private universities is alien to the pervasive liberal environment in the public-funded universities. The jury is still out on which will become dominant, as the debate continues.

Chapter Five

The Nigeria media is acknowledged to be relatively free by comparison with its peers across the African continent. Neither restricted nor free would be a fair assessment of where things are with the media. The prolonged military interregnum prior to a return to civilian governance in 1999 has embedded a culture of self-censoring across the media houses in Nigeria. There is a heightened awareness, on the part of journalists, of the need to pay attention to government sensitivities in media content. On its part, government (of all hues) often impose a burden on journalists to give credence to the 'national security' concerns of the state, and to refrain from doing things that could 'overheat' the polity. The regulatory agency, the National Broadcasting Commission (NBC), is on hand to monitor the broadcasters for compliance. The print media also broadly fall in line with the precepts of government, though, some of them stray beyond their permissible limits from time to time, leading to the occasional confrontation with the regulator. The essays in this chapter should be read with this background in mind.

Chapter Six

The study of contemporary Nigerian politics is tied to the return of the country to civil rule in 1999. The biggest political question until then was the feasibility and indeed, survival of Nigeria as one entity. The military that held power until 1999 was seen as a major roadblock to democracy, having annulled what was considered the fairest and freest election that voted for what was to be the civilian administration of Chief Moshood Abiola, from the Southwest region in 1993. The military leadership (dominated by the north) had disavowed the election, apparently, as it had not resulted in the victory of their preferred candidate. The sudden cancellation of the results as they were being announced plunged the country into turmoil with the real fear that Nigeria might disintegrate. It came as no coincidence, therefore, that major stakeholders of northern extraction embraced the idea that the President of the Federal Republic of Nigeria at the handover from the military should be a person from the Southwest, if only to pacify the region for the annulment of the 1993 election adjudged to have been won by one of their own, Chief Abiola, who mysteriously died while in the custody of the government headed then by the military strongman, General Sani Abacha in 1998. He himself had died a few weeks prior. The Presidency was thus 'zoned' to the Southwest, leading to the emergence of former military General, Olusegun Obasanjo, as a civilian President in the election of 1999, under the auspices of the hurriedly formed Peoples' Democratic Party (PDP), a coalition of conservative political bedfellows from across the ethnic divide. The party had remained in power for an unbroken sixteen years, until defeated by another coalition of political bedfellows, the All Progressives Congress, in 2015. If dousing the agitation for separatism was the raison d'etre of the PDP, it achieved its purpose, but left itself vulnerable to attack on other fronts, especially in the area of insecurity and rampant levels of official corruption. APC thus came into office under the mantra 'change', but did not define exactly what that meant. It was left for the voter to fill in the void. The period under review for this book falls neatly within the first five years of the 'change' mantra. For many people, it is more than just a slogan, it is a challenge to see if and how the country, Nigeria, could be re-envisioned. This is the premise upon which the write-ups in this chapter were based.

Chapter Seven

Certainly, the biggest concern with the judiciary in Nigeria since 1999 is the extent to which it has become politicised, and how to disentangle one of the great institutions of state from partisan politics. The term 'judiciary' is applied

CHAPTER SYNOPSIS xxix

in a liberal sense here to refer not only to the institutions, but also to everyone connected with it; lawyers, judges, and other functionaries. The main focus in this chapter is not so much the politics of the judiciary, but the application of the law in specific situations, and the logic and principles underlying the actions taken or not taken. Wider analysis about judicial corruption and its independence from political office holders is left for another assignment.

Chapter Eight

The military has played a prominent role in the running of government in Nigeria since the first coup that toppled the post-independence civilian government in 1963. The military has been in and out of power ever since. The 'pro-democracy' activism of the political elite that finally pushed them out of power in 1999 came as a relief to everyone in and outside Nigeria. Suspicion remains, however, whether at some point, they may stage a comeback. Upon departure from government administration, the military hierarchy wrote and enacted a military-style constitution which protected their interest, and which to a large extent guaranteed their continued influence on government. Many of the military top brass resigned their posts and contested for, and indeed, won various political positions in the newly constituted National Assembly. The incoming Head of State, Olusegun Obasanjo, was a General in the army, likewise Muhammadu Buhari, who was elected in 2015. The military no longer directly wields power, but its influence remains ubiquitous throughout the political echelons, and the fear of another putsch is neither too far-fetched, nor too far away.

Chapter Nine

Since independence, the ruling elites in Nigeria have convincingly propagated the idea that it is their country's 'manifest destiny' to lead Africa. The 1970s 'oil boom' and the frontline role the country played during the anti-apartheid struggle in South Africa gave credence to this conception. But since then, the internal crisis of governance that has plagued successive administrations in Nigeria has curtailed their ambition to take a more prominent role in the affairs of the continent. Other African leaders who might otherwise be sympathetic to a leadership role for Nigeria look at its internal problems both on the economic and political front, including the ineffectiveness of the military to deal with insurgency incidents, and choose to look the other way. It is to be noted that when it came to the major issue of African unity, Nigeria has been traditionally 'cautious' and difficult to convince. The latest continental trading initiative, the African Continental Free Trade

Area (AfCFTA) did not meet with the immediate approval of Nigeria, which held back on signing the agreement until one year after it came into force.

Chapter Ten

This chapter focuses on how international events played into Nigeria's political activity and vice-versa. Particular attention was to the USA and the UK; the first being a successful federal system of government that Nigeria likes to hold out as a good example to emulate, and the second, being the former colonial master that bequeathed a lot of political and legal legacies some of which remain relevant presently. One of the two major events that have impacted on the domestic politics in Nigeria was the election of President Donald Trump in America, who, despite his reported disdain for the continent, enjoyed plenty of admiration as a maverick politician who had assumed the mantle of leadership in his country apparently from 'nowhere', and who had little time for the establishment. Trump was seen as a breath of fresh air, the likes of whom Nigeria, indeed, Africa could benefit from. The contrary position of the column meant it was sailing against the prevailing wind for much of the period under review. The second event, the 'Brexit' debate and election in the UK was a subject that baffled and confused many people watching from Nigeria. A lot of column inches needed to be devoted to simplifying both the argument and its attendant conundrum.

Political Economy
of Development

Chapter One

Economy

1.01 Nigeria's Interest Rates/Forex Quagmire (1)

27 December 2016

A quagmire is "an area of soft, wet ground that you sink into if you try to work on it" (Cambridge dictionary). It is "a soft boggy area of land that gives way underfoot" (Oxford dictionary). It is " ... a predicament from which a skilful or graceful escape is impossible".[1] For our purposes, the latter definition sums up the previous two rather well. Several years of observing and analysing public policy in Nigeria as it concerns the issues of interest rates and foreign exchange (ever shifting) policies have led me to conclude, as I suspect, many people have also concluded, that the Nigerian economy is in a quagmire of lacerating interest rates[2] and a sliding currency that sheds its value by the day if not by the hour.[3]

Nowhere is this state of affairs more readily manifested than in the absurd attempt at targeting Nigerian students in various universities across the globe. One day, they could access maintenance funds, the next day, they could not. One day, maintenance funds were reinstated, the next day, they were drastically cut to more than half their previous value. One day, some banks freeze access to maintenance funds, the next day, they put a moratorium on them. One day, some banks cancel access to these funds; the next day, others announce al-

---

1. Vocabulary.com

2. The inter-bank rate as at November 2021 was 11.53% according to the Central Bank of Nigeria, but it can be as high as 20–35% in the real world. Even at the inter-bank rate, it is still rather punitive compared to rates in industrialised economies staying in single digits for the past ten years or more.

3. Naira exchanged for 257 to the dollar in 2016, when this piece first appeared. Now, in 2022, it is more than 500 (see www.xe.com, and www.ngnrates.com)

4 1 · ECONOMY

lowance of a rather paltry sum. It is almost approaching a Shakespearian tragedy: "To allow or not to allow ..."

The maintenance funds shambles had, at its core, the hallmarks of policy-making on the hoof. It was a spur-of-the-moment kind of idea emanating from the presidency. It was meant to tap into the public perception of schooling abroad as an elite privilege; hard to defend at a time of recession, but as it turned out, it was an absurdity. For a start, Nigeria does not have enough university places to satisfy demand. By way of a quick comparison, London alone, with a population of less than 10 million, has more universities per capita, than Nigeria with a population of almost 200 million. What someone palpably failed to mention to President Muhammadu Buhari when he was championing this policy was that students are a capital resource, and many studying abroad (like I did), do eventually come back home to put in their quota to national development. Those hardworking students (a lot of whose families are in fact on modest incomes) need to be encouraged and not be maligned for seeking to upgrade their skills wherever they choose. That said, when one is in a quagmire, one does pretty desperate things.

The above intertwines with the cost of borrowing (interest rates) policy in Nigeria. Let us focus on the interest rates on bank credits to the private sector. In Nigeria, this is mediated through the Nigerian Inter-Bank Offered Rate (otherwise called NIBOR). It is the rate at which the Central Bank of Nigeria lends to commercial banks, also known in common parlance as "the official rate". It follows, therefore, that once you designate something as "official", any other source of similar transaction becomes "the black market". Very often, when we enquire about any merchandise in this country, we are immediately given two different quotes; one price for the "original", and the other for the "Aba" or "Taiwan" equivalent. This is done even for medical products. Thus, it was the state; the Nigerian state, which created the black market in its currency, which it has sought, for a long time, to re-christen "the parallel market" as a way of removing the stigma attached to it.[4] Many people have long recognised the blindingly obvious: the "parallel market" rate is indeed the official rate in disguise. How then does the government get the convergence it desperately needs between these two? The CBN is "working on the elimination of arbitrage", the Minister of Finance, Kemi Adeosun, said.[5] Inter-switch Lim-

---

4. Many official transactions, even from the commercial banks themselves are routinely diverted to the "black market", which is now being referred to as the "parallel market".

5. https://www.reuters.com/article/nigeria-naira-idUSL5N1EF2Z4; https://businessday .ng/business-economy/article/central-bank-will-eliminate-forex-black-market-says-kemi -adeosun.

ited, which processes payments for banks, is the latest of a long line of corporations reluctant to list on the Nigerian Stock Exchange as a result of the fluctuation in the value of the naira and the restrictions on foreign exchange.[6]

One thing the CBN could do is to instruct the commercial banks to lend to its customers at a rate not higher than, say, three per cent of NIBOR. That would provide the Minister of Finance with the magic wand she needs if that were remotely possible. Commercial banks are in the market to make profits; they are not civil service departments that can be bossed around by ministers, nor should they. Lending rates in this country have been a lacerating (the word is carefully chosen) experience for business in this country for over 40 years. The average level of (official) interest rate in Nigeria between 1970 and 2014 is 15.18% according to the World Bank reports.[7] Of course, in the real world, it is much worse. Rates can be as high as thirty-five per cent and even more. Our nearest competitors fare a lot better: Egypt twelve per cent, India ten per cent, South Africa nine per cent, and Libya six per cent.[8] When cost of borrowing is so high as it is in Nigeria, the manufacturing sector cannot survive, so too the capital market, which will be starved of funds because it is a riskier investment option. By contrast, in order to get out of a prolonged recession, interest rates went down as low as one per cent in the UK and the USA for a considerable period of time, until now, in fact. Neither of these two large economies is anxious to hike the rates anytime soon. Under normal circumstances, it takes years for them to move it up by a single digit sometimes. So, why are we seemingly stuck in the miasma of high interest rates, high inflation, low growth and high unemployment in this country?

1.02 Nigeria's Interest Rates/Forex Quagmire (II)

3 January 2017

The naira has been trading at about three hundred and five to the dollar on the official interbank market in the second half of 2016, while it is being sold around 500 to the dollar in the black market. By the way, there is nothing 'black' about the black market since it operates in the open with even govern-

---

6. It finally agreed to list on the exchange in 2020: https://www.african-markets.com /en/stock-markets/ngse/interswitch-to-list-n30bn-bond-on-nigerian-stock-exchange.

7. https://data.worldbank.org/country/NG.

8. https://tradingeconomics.com/country-list/interest-rate?continent=africa.

ment officials and commercial banks actively taking part. The black market could be more appropriately described as the bleak market though, as it often knocks the wind off the sails of the economy, it is resilient and impervious to the government's macro-economic strategy in any economic cycle. Those privileged enough to remember when the naira sold for eighty kobo to the dollar, and the naira was on a par with the British pound sterling can only now look back with nostalgia and bewildering resignation. Yes, interest rates, then, was administratively fixed by government through the CBN. That worked well to correct the lopsidedness in the country's economy, but created its own snags: it encouraged a boom in consumer spending, which became worse in the 1970s. This was made worse by the Israeli-Arab conflict, the 'Yom Kippur' war in 1973, which sent the price of crude oil to stratospheric levels. Western banks, unable to lend to business in their countries because of the recession brought on by crippling energy prices, looked overseas for willing borrowers.[9]

It was during this time that Nigeria sowed the seeds for the economic disaster and the quagmire it finds itself today, for even though the country had so much money from the oil boom, economists at home and abroad still bizarrely prescribed huge government borrowing as a panacea for development. Hence the "Udoji Award" of 1977, which recommended huge salary increases for public sector employees, followed by scores of uncompleted mega infrastructural projects, many of which were later re-awarded and ultimately abandoned.[10] The agricultural sector was abandoned and farmers made their way to the cities to join in the bonanza, the floodgates to the importation of everything from toothpicks to toilet rolls opened and Nigerians rejoiced and basked in ostentatious display of Western consumer/luxury items. As Newton's law of gravity tells us, what goes up must surely come down. The oil boom ended at some point towards the end of the 1970s, by which time Nigeria had become indebted to Western financial agencies to the tune of billions of dollars. The high level of public debt became unsustainable.[11] More importantly though, the banks in the West that had lent too much to Nigeria and other Less Developed Countries (LDCs), many of who then got into trouble; were

---

9. For a general understanding of this see; Rurik Krymm. "The Economic Impact of Oil Prices" https://www.iaea.org/sites/default/files/publications/magazines/bulletin/bull16 -1/161_204006065.pdf

10. See; Usman D Umaru. "Assessment of the Implementation of 1972 Udoji and 2003 Obasanjo Public Service Reform in Nigeria: A Neo-Public Management Paradigm". 'Journal of Economics and Sustainable Development', Vol 7, No 10, 2016.

11. For a detailed trend analysis see; "Nigeria External Debt 1970–2022" https://www.macrotrends.net/countries/NGA/nigeria/external-debt-stock

1 · ECONOMY

under serious threat of insolvency as a result of what many saw as reckless lending to poor countries who could least afford to pay back. So, the banks needed bailing out as much as the LDCs who took the loans.

It was against this background that the Reagan/Thatcher "revolution"[12] came about in the early 1980s, with an evangelical zeal of "rolling back the frontiers of the state", massive privatization of hitherto public owned enterprises, "limited government", and freedom of "the individual". The neo-liberal policy agenda was going to be exported to the rest of the world, especially the LDCs. This came about in Nigeria through the Structural Adjustment Programme (SAP) of the International Monetary Fund (IMF). Nigeria was then forced into accepting the prescriptive formula for economic growth in which inflation constituted the main enemy to be defeated through monetary policy mechanism; interest rate. In an economy with the requisite forward-backward linkages, such as in the West, this was a novel idea, but in a lopsided economy like Nigeria, it was like being given a blood transfusion already contaminated with the HIV virus. The SAP did not ask Nigerian officials to negotiate the value of the currency, but simply handed down an instruction for which compliance was expected. Devaluation, historically, is a choice weapon in a trade war. Many advanced economies see the benefit of it at various stages of their economic growth. In modern times, however, it is used to boost export to countries with which there is a balance of trade deficit. What real benefit was currency devaluation in an economy that was 90% dependent on oil for its foreign exchange, and a product that is measured and sold in dollars anyway? The adoption and implementation of the SAP was when Nigeria lost its economic independence as a nation. That was what made the quagmire a present day reality for the country. The battle to regain some control of it is what the CBN and various finance ministers have been grappling with ever since.

It must be said, however, that the Nigerian public kicked against the SAP programme very forcefully at the time, but it was railroaded and shoved down their throats by military diktat under 'President' Ibrahim Babangida (IBB).[13] Having said that though, I do not believe Nigerians should in any way adopt the victim approach to their economic woes. The one positive consequence of the SAP's conditionalities is the opening up of the political space hitherto

---

12. This is in reference to the election of right-wing conservative leaders in the persons of Mrs Margaret Thatcher, Prime Minister of the UK (1979–1990), and Ronald Reagan, President of the United States, ((1981–1989)

13. General Ibrahim Babangida was the head of the military junta which appointed him 'President'

restricted to a select few. It is that space which is not being fully utilized to the people's economic benefit. The population are yet to learn how to make political office holders accountable for the bread and butter issues, as they do elsewhere. Former President, George Bush (Snr), for instance, was riding high in the opinion polls following a successful prosecution of the first Gulf War against the invasion of Kuwait by Saddam Hussein in 1990. His re-election was seen as a foregone conclusion until the then candidate, Bill Clinton, came up with the clarion call: "it's the economy, stupid!"[14] Bush lost the economic argument and the election. Similarly, at the just concluded 2016 US presidential election, the Republicans, under Donald Trump, managed to make the economy a major issue against the Democrats during the campaign and won, despite the fact that the Democrats, under President Obama, did in fact save the US recession from turning into a depression; enabling the creation of millions of jobs during his eight years in office.[15] Nigeria will come out of the current quagmire when, and only when, there is a more assertive electorate, willing and ready to exert retribution on people in power for economic failings. Political leaders should expect to have their feet routinely held much closer to the fire for their economic performance. The bottom line ought to be, that, regardless of which party created 'the mess', if you are privileged enough to be in office, you own the problem, here and now. The earlier a consensus is built around this view, the healthier the economic condition will be.

1.03 Easing Nigeria Out of Recession

31 January 2017

The "ease of doing business" in Nigeria remains one of the toughest in the world according to the latest World Bank Report for 2017.[16] It ranks the country 169 out of the 190 countries surveyed; a miniscule improvement from the 170 position for the year 2016. For an economy in recession, this ought to be a pretty grim news; capturing the attention of politicians and business leaders up and down the country. Instead, the report appears to have been

---

14. See; https://politicaldictionary.com/words/its-the-economy-stupid

15. See; "Final Tally: Obama Created 11.3 Million Jobs". CNN Report, January 2017, https://money.cnn.com/2017/01/06/news/economy/obama-over-11-million-jobs/index.html

16. See; "World Bank Group, 2016, Doing Business Economy Profile 2017: Nigeria, World Bank, Washington DC" https://openknowledge.worldbank.org/handle/10986/25592

1 · ECONOMY

shrugged off as another one of such negative write ups by outsiders. World Bank Economic Reports, however, are not known for frivolities; they collate and report on raw, objective data which the country's leadership can only dismiss at its own peril. More than that, the reports often form the basis upon which the sought-after foreign investors make the initial assessment of their investment destination.

As a Nigerian with a professional interest in these things, the report makes a painful reading if only for the fact that they contain, in many parts, statements of the obvious. However, in an interconnected world where business and trade are the vehicles driving economic development, the ease of doing business in a particular economy becomes an important indicator of its readiness for economic growth. Nigeria is (on paper at least), the largest economy in Africa endowed with huge human and natural resources. That the country is not ipso-facto a magnet for foreign investors is a puzzle even to the most well-meaning. The government would indeed be hard-pressed to find an average Nigerian who would want to take issues with the findings of the report. It is an uncomfortable reading, particularly in view of the fact that it is akin to having a self-inflicted injury to a team of players about to participate in a World Cup competition.

As a vivid demonstration of the elements of the report, on a personal level, very often I choose to travel from Abuja to Lagos on assignments by road, and the ease, or should I say the malaise of doing so can only be experienced to be believed. In case anyone is wondering why I choose travelling by road over flying, my response is travelling by road is the real life experience for over ninety per cent of Nigerians engaged in daily business in this country. The invaluable lesson drawn from that is what is reflected in this column. As you make your way out of Abuja via Gwagwalada, one feels relatively at ease on the trunk 'B' road until Lokoja, where all hell breaks loose; bumps, potholes, crates in the middle of the road, open sewage, falling trees, articulated lorries overturning, you name it, they are all on the road from Kogi State, right through to Lagos-Ibadan express way, where there is, once again, a semblance of a motorway (albeit) under construction. As if the road condition was not bad enough, the highways are littered with angry and (indeed) hungry looking 'law enforcement officers' all too ready to compound one's agony. They are there to do anything but ensure law and order as they openly solicit for gratification. Every uniformed personnel on the road feels entitled to ask for vehicle particulars. But it is often used merely as a bargaining chip for, if you present them with a neatly packaged papers, they then immediately think of what you might not have paid attention to, for instance, the red triangle, fire extinguisher or latterly, tinted permit; specifically, anything to put you on the defensive; to strengthen their hands and ultimately extort money.

By the time you finally arrive at your destination, the first thing you do is send your car to the mechanic for repairs, and give yourself time to recuperate from the ordeal of venturing out of your comfort zone. You don't even want to start calculating the financial loss you have incurred just trying to make your way from one part of the country to another. This is the daily routine for millions of Nigerians. It is thus amazing that the country is only ranked 138 for starting a business; the reports measure the paid-in minimum capital requirement, number of procedures, time and cost for a small-to-medium-sized limited liability company to operate. Accordingly, 180 for electricity, considering the procedure, time and cost required for a business to obtain a permanent electricity connection for a newly constructed warehouse; 182 for registering property and paying taxes (the reports examine steps time and cost involved in doing that) and 181 for trading across border. Some of the conclusions from the World Bank Reports are staggering even for the most ardent cynic: It is easier to obtain electricity connection in Afghanistan than it is in Nigeria! Even construction permits are easier to obtain in war-torn places like Iraq and Afghanistan. In terms of mandatory taxes and contributions payable by a medium sized company in a given year, the report records up to fifty-nine of such contributions for Nigeria compared to seven for South Africa, 33 for Ghana and Liberia, 25 for India and 29 for Egypt.

Getting out of the current recession is obviously the Federal Government's number one priority, but so too should be the ease with which business is done in the country. Admittedly, government does not have a magic wand with which to eliminate recession in one fell swoop; it is the individual business person who will do the heavy lifting before this translates into an influx of foreign investors into the country. So, given the scale of the hurdle from number 169 on the World Bank chart, how ambitious should the current administration be? To jump up the ranking to, say, 100 in the world by the time of the next election? No, let us set the bar pretty low for the administration in order not to get too carried away. Let us hope Nigeria will have moved up a notch to 168 by the time of the next election. Anything more than that will be hailed as a spectacular success by the administration and the APC leadership. Mind you, though, at this rate, it will take Nigeria the next 100 years to be in the top 10 of countries in which to do business with ease.

1.04 A Note on Foreign (Direct) Investment in Nigeria

7 February 2017

The correlation between the "ease of doing business" in a country and the inflow of foreign (direct) investment is so palpable as not to be even worth mentioning, yet Nigeria advertises her fervent desire for foreign investment almost in oblivion of the presence of numerous difficulties of conducting business in the country, which are anathema to investors, foreign or otherwise.[17] As of July 2016, according to the latest reports, net inflow of foreign direct investment into the country stands at a lowly USD3.45bn,[18] meanwhile, the economy again contracts for the third quarter, key interest rate remains unchanged at 14%, and the dreaded inflation remains at an all-time high at almost 19%. Capital expenditure in the 2016 budget is up to 1.8 trillion naira or 30% of the budget, meanwhile, the Federal Government is running a deficit of 2.2 trillion naira. In other words, money for infrastructure, exploration, reconstruction, manufacturing, science, engineering etc. has to come from somewhere: foreign investors (not lenders).[19] Foreign investment is so crucial, yet not so easy to come by in this globalised, dog-eat-dog world of international finance. That said, Nigeria is not alone in seeking to attract foreign investors; every member of the World Trade Organisation (WTO), 164 countries in all, is reliant in some way on foreign investors to bridge their budget gap. No wonder then that these elusive foreign investors are treated like royalty whenever and wherever they pitch their tent.

As much as we want foreign investors to invest in our economy in this country, we also benefit from Nigerian citizens investing their money in other countries' economy; Dangote Cement, Globacom and Oando are three prominent cases with considerable investment in the Nigerian economy.[20] This is also be-

---

17. Ease of doing business is an annual rating by the World Bank that measures the difficulties and 'ease' of doing business in a particular country. The latest report shows an improvement to 131 out of 190 countries. It was 146 in 2018. It is not the ranking the government would have preferred given the Buhari administration's avowed desire to record a significant achievement on that score. https://tradingeconomics.com/nigeria/ease-of-doing-business

18. https://www.macrotrends.net/countries/NGA/nigeria/foreign-direct-investment

19. For a breakdown of the figures, see; https://www.pwc.com/ng/en/assets/pdf/nigeria-2016-budget-analysis-and-insights.pdf

20. Dangote Cement for example; https://www.bloomberg.com/news/articles/2021-04-23/africa-s-top-cement-maker-boosts-capacity-to-meet demandsurge#:~:text=In%202020 %20Dangote%20Cement%20sales,and%20BUA%20Group%20the%20remainder. Globacom

cause foreign investment is not a free lunch; not something for nothing, but something for something really big. Foreign investors invest their money to make more money. Their primary concern is not to help anyone bridge their budget gap or to aid their host country's development aspiration; their primary and secondary concern is reaping maximum returns for their shareholders. Not all foreign investments are *direct*, however, some (indeed, a lot) are indirect. Indirect investment normally occurs through what is called foreign (portfolio) investment, which refers to acquisition of shares and equities in listed companies. Whereas a foreign direct investor has physical presence in the host country, a foreign portfolio investor can do so from anywhere in the world, and that is not surprising in the world of fast digital and electronic communications. Moreover, while it is mandatory for a foreign direct investor to register a Nigerian company,[21] a foreign portfolio investor has no such obligation.

Prior to the expansion of international trade through globalisation, Nigeria, like South Korea in the 1960s, ran a somewhat 'closed' economy under heavy reliance on the state to regulate and even invest in what the countries considered strategic industries. Thus, there was the Nigerian Enterprises Promotion Decree promulgated after the civil war in the late 1970s.[22] South Korea was also run under a benevolent authoritarian regime. The country does not have the level of natural resources available to Nigeria; so, it focused mainly on what analysts considered prudential investment, technological acquisition, education and science. It is one of the most technologically advanced economies in the world,[23] while Nigeria has stagnated by comparison. Even South Africa, a country that Nigeria used to champion the cause of liberation from its debilitating Apartheid rule and a country that had its first democratic elections only in 1994, managed to attract USD1958.00 million in the same year. The lingering question is, what does a country like South Korea have that Nigeria does not? (It also has its fair share of ethno-linguistic/cultural difficulties prevalent in this country). The answer, surely, is visionary leadership. It is abundant in one, and lamentably in short supply in the other. That apart, and in spite of the leadership vacuum, the creative energy of Nige-

---

is the second largest telecom provider in Nigeria https://www.statista.com /statistics/1177697/market-share-of-mobile-telecommunication-operators-in-nigeria, Oando has a bourgeoning market capitalisation of over 62bn naira https://simplywall.st/stocks /ng/energy/ngse-oando/oando-shares

21. Section 56 Company and Allied Matters Act 2011

22. See the actual Decree; https://gazettes.africa/archive/ng/1972/ng-government -gazette-supplement-dated-1972-02-23-no-10-part-a.pdf

23. For a detailed South Korea vs Nigeria economic breakdown see; https://country economy.com/countries/compare/south-korea/nigeria

rians in the field of enterprise is, nonetheless, boundless as it has been generally acknowledged.

Since the end of the oil boom in late 1970s, Nigeria has been trying to unleash this creative energy through an amalgam of legislative interventions: Nigerian Enterprises Promotion Decree 34, 1987, was aimed at reviving foreign interest in the economy by allowing listed companies to issue controlling but non-voting shares to foreigners, similarly the Nigerian Investment Promotion Commission Act, 1995, Investment and Securities Act, 1999, Foreign Exchange Monitoring and Miscellaneous Provision Act, Immigration, Industrial Inspectorate Acts etc. All of these are designed to make investing in Nigeria very easy. The right of aliens to own and operate business in Nigeria is guaranteed in law.[24] Foreigners can, in addition, come to Nigeria to execute projects without incorporating companies. Companies can be registered a lot quicker than it used to be in the past. It is even now possible to register a company in this country; same day express service, at the One Stop Investment Centre (OSIC), Abuja (assuming the computer is not down, which invariably it often is). The country offers numerous (too numerous to enumerate here) tax incentives to those who choose to invest.

Well, what all this is saying is simply that the dearth of foreign investment in the Nigerian economy in sufficient quantity is not for want of the enabling laws to make that happen; foreign investors want to see us pulling our own weight first, especially in terms of creating a more conducive environment to do business. Diversion of public funds is another big issue that is endemic in our country; so too is our penchant for foreign (consumer) goods, which obliterates our own indigenous efforts. What matters above all, for capital flows across the globe, is not ultimately the laws in a particular country (important as they are), but the experience of doing business there.

1.05 Can Nigeria Ever Stop Importing Rice?

16 May 2017

If there is one area of public policy that the Jonathan administration got right, it is the attention focused on rice as a major economic issue during the last year of the administration. Although the outcome of the pervasive

---

24. Ss. 20 (4) and 54 (1) Companies and Allied Matters Act, 2011.

14 · 1 · ECONOMY

initiative did not result in a cascade of rice production across the mills, it nevertheless resulted in a release of new energy, motivation and drive of farmers and would-be farmers across the country to partake in the upcoming bonanza. The public education (propaganda if you like) on the issue was a masterclass; thanks largely to the flamboyant if somewhat eccentric Minister for Agriculture, Dr Akinwumi Adesina, now President of the African Development Bank. Endowed with fertile land, boundless energy and technical knowhow of its people at least in the key area of agriculture, Nigeria "has no business importing rice" proclaimed the former minister. Rice is consumed in enough quantity in this country that any producer is apparently guaranteed sufficient market for every grain. So, it is really a no brainer for investors desirous of a healthy return on their capital. Why is that not happening though? Why is there not a mad rush by rice farmers in this country given its lucrative nature?

It is not happening simply because, first, there is a dearth of locally produced rice. Second, there is an avalanche of rice streaming through the borders of Nigeria from all over the world, especially, Europe, America, Asia and Brazil. In case anyone is wondering, this is not a new phenomenon; it has been going on for as long as anyone can remember, certainly, since the 1980s when importation of anything and everything into the country virtually became government policy. The cost of importing rice; the cost in foreign exchange, has been going up and it currently stands at USD26 billion annually.[25] Now, imagine this amount of money going into the pockets of local farmers in this country instead of bolstering farmers in other countries? The more imported rice we entertain, the more the capacity of Nigerian farmers is diminished because it is more expensive to produce rice locally than it is to import. Now, also think of the cost in unemployment on top of the lost earnings. In addition, think of the loss in innovation and technical advancement in the area of agriculture due to indolence, and abandoned machinery in the farming sector.

Before we get too gloomy about this, however, let us not forget the fact that rice importation has indeed produced mega millionaires and billionaires in this country, who now have a vested interest in the status quo and would go to any length to protect that. Furthermore, Nigeria is paying money; loads of money to import rice because there is demand for it. It is called market forces

---

25. Based on figures from the Central Bank of Nigeria https://www.cbn.gov.ng /rates/exchratebycurrency.asp

1 · ECONOMY

in which many countries in the developing world are trapped. So, how do we get out of the logjam?

What the Jonathan administration decided upon was the adoption of the tried and tested Import Substitution Industrialisation (ISI).[26] It is also being carried over by the current administration through the ebullient if somewhat lugubrious Minister of Agriculture, Mr Audu Ogbe, who asserts that Nigeria should be "self-sufficient" in rice production by the end of this year. This assertion, not backed by evidence, in my view, is a statement of hope rather than expectation. Remember President Muhammadu Buhari claiming, in the same vein, that Boko Haram had been "technically defeated" almost two years ago, and how forlorn that hope has since become? May be Mr Audu Ogbe knows something the rest of Nigerians do not yet know though. He is, after all, a farmer himself. His own pigs can fly I am sure. Anyway, that aside. The policy of substituting imports is not new. It is an economic concept that has been around since the 1970s and much favoured by development economists around the world. Put simply, it is a policy that places priority on locally produced (manufactured) goods instead of importing them. It is, on the surface, apple pie and motherhood stuff; who can disagree?

The problem with ISI is that it leads, in no small measure, to government intervention in the running of the economy. Tariffs, very high tariffs, have to be imposed in order to 'protect' the local production from foreign imports. What this effectively does is to subside a whole load of local (inefficient) industries by protecting them from competition. High tariffs would also incur countermeasures on the part of countries whose products are being 'unfairly' targeted from the Nigerian market. Furthermore, unless domestic production capacity is quickly increased, high tariffs may introduce artificial scarcity into the local market, thereby increasing prices in the short to medium term. For the sake of argument though, let us assume there is a total ban on rice importation. As a member of the World Trade Organisation (WTO), Nigeria will not be able to get away with this without contravening the provisions of the organisation which frowns on anything that impedes "free trade".

Let us assume, then, that high tariffs and a ban on importation by land did the trick of encouraging local rice production in Nigeria and we became indeed "self-sufficient", that would still not be the end of the story, I am afraid. Let us assume, finally, that the typical rice producer, Mr Bassey Okoh, has a family of four. The family furnish their house with foreign items, buy foreign generators

---

26. This is where local manufacturers of certain goods receive government subsidy in order to discourage identical imports.

for use on their farm and at home, buy foreign cars, send their children to foreign schools, and watch foreign programmes on their foreign plasma TV screens. Mr Bassey Okoh would then have inadvertently used state subsidies on his farming business to import inflation into the country via the other sectors of the economy. Whatever gains he would have made as a bourgeoning farmer would have been eroded by the high cost of other consumer items the economy would have forced on him. ISI as a policy, willy-nilly, becomes a circular idea.[27]

The trouble with ISI is that once you target one particular industry for protection, one inevitably has to target every other sector in the economy in order to achieve an even balance; an implausible as well as impossible feat to achieve in the golden age of free trade. Apart from that, Nigeria will never stop importing rice because self-sufficiency per se is not a panacea against importation, neither should it be. America, for instance, is self-sufficient in car production, yet, it is one of the biggest net importers of cars in the world, especially from Japan. The American car industry succeeds because it is a good brand and there is general belief in its reliability. Rice importation is a symptom, not the cause of our inability to produce and consume what we eat.

1.06 Diversifying or Decentralising Nigerian Economy?

13 June 2017

Having spent so much money in a bid for re-election, the President Goodluck Jonathan's administration created a financial bubble that was bound to burst one way or another.[28] Public expenditure was on the upward trajectory certainly in the last two years preceding the general election. As it turned out though, billions of dollars meant for procurement of arms were diverted and frittered away with reckless abandon.[29] Similarly, oil revenues were corruptly splattered around like confetti by a very powerful, but morally bankrupt min-

---

27. For a conceptual understanding see; "understanding Import Substitution Industrialisation" https://corporatefinanceinstitute.com/resources/knowledge/economics/import -substitution-industrialization-isi

28. It is usually known in Western media parlance as "pre-election give aways"

29. See; "Ex-Nigerian official accused of siphoning billions" https://www .voanews.com/a/ex-nigerian-officials-accused-siphoning-billions/3063476.html And "$31 billion stolen under President Jonathan of Nigeria" amongst others http://sahara reporters.com/2012/11/24/31-billion-stolen-under-president-jonathan-nigeria-%E2%80 %93punch

ister for petroleum resources, Mrs Diezani Alison-Madueke.[30] The former governor of the Central Bank of Nigeria, Professor Charles Soludo was therefore merely stating the obvious in his recent comment on Nigeria's financial predicament, that the spending habit of the last administration created the building blocks for the current recession.[31] This sentiment has also been echoed repeatedly by the administration of President Muhammadu Buhari in a frantic effort to dissuade Nigerians from entertaining the bad and insatiable appetite for spending on importation of (mainly Western) consumer goods. "We are not a petrol economy", the Minister of Finance, Mrs Kemi Adeosun asserted recently. With respect to the minister, this is incorrect. We are, in fact, a de facto petrol economy. What I suspect she and the administration want to do is to re-engineer the economy away from petrol to production of goods, hence, the current trendy buzzword, diversification.

The word 'diversification' drips from the lips of every government minister, and expert commentator in such a robotic reflex, and with such an arresting regularity that the general public too, appear to have caught the bug. Like the "change" mantra of the All Progressives Congress, diversification, it appears, has become the one word panacea to our socio-economic malaise. It is so clear and clean-cut that its object is now beyond disputation. Or, is it? For a start, if it's the answer to everything, then, it is concomitantly the answer to nothing. If it is a mere propaganda by the current administration to drum up support for its economic policy, then, it is doing pretty well indeed. If, however, it is meant as a serious debate to a serious economic problem, then, it is one that is largely being conducted in a vacuum at the moment.

To prevent the public from being blindsided about this, it is important to cast our minds back to how Nigeria became the de facto petro economy that it is today. In real petrol economies like Saudi Arabia, Qatar, Kuwait, etc. oil accounts for one hundred percent of their foreign exchange earnings, ours is close to ninety per cent. Petrol economies nurse no qualms about foreign imports since there is abundance of petrol dollars to pay. Everyone would agree, this is where Nigeria differs from the real petrol economies. Furthermore, Lagos and Kano combined are bigger than the populations of the three petrol

---

30. It will be recalled that the former minister of petroleum resources fled to the UK, where she was arrested by Scotland Yard detectives, then, released on bail. She has been formally indicted by the Nigerian government and is currently going through extradition proceedings.

31. See; "Jonathan government's bad spending habit caused recession, says ex-CBN boss Soludo" https://thenationonlineng.net/jonathan-govts-bad-spending-habit-caused -recession-says-ex-cbn-boss-soludo/amp

18   1 · ECONOMY

economies mentioned here, and in the case of Saudi Arabia, its population is actually declining, while its income from oil is steadily climbing up.[32] On the contrary, we have a burgeoning population that is set to hit the significant landmark of 200 million in a few years' time. Consequently, the revenues from oil for Nigeria, is only a drop in the ocean vis-à-vis that of the real petrol economies. That, nonetheless, has not stopped our leaders from running this country as if it too, were a real petrol economy. The Minister for Mines and Steel Development, Dr Kayode Fayemi, on assumption of office proclaimed the mission of his ministry as one committed to helping ensure the diversification of the economy from overreliance on petrol. While the intention of the honourable minister is laudable, it is, nonetheless, an unattainable mission. The economy is an organic structure that feeds on one another. Try as they might, the burden of diversifying the Nigerian economy is not one that can be borne by the Ministry of Mines and Steel Development alone.

Bearing that in mind, let us consider the critical elements of Nigeria's economic activity and see who controls them. Top of the list are: petroleum and the petrol chemical industries, mines and steel, hydro-electricity power plants, major road infrastructure, the railways, agro-industrial sector, banking and finance, land holding (the state, by law, is the owner of all land in Nigeria), water supply, to name but a few. These are the mainstay of our economy, and they are all controlled from the centre, by the Federal Government. Nothing moves within any of these without the say-so of the Federal Government. They have been expropriated on behalf of "all Nigerians" as they have been declared as belonging to the "critical sectors" of the country's economic wellbeing. Remember, banking and finance are being controlled by the Central Bank of Nigeria and Securities and Exchange Commission, both of which are federal agencies. You see, when our leaders boast to foreigners about how much our economy has been "liberalised" for the purpose of attracting direct foreign investors, I chuckle a bit. I know, and I am sure they too know that we do not run a free market economy in Nigeria; what we have is state capitalism at best, and a command economy at worst.

State capitalism is used here advisedly; there is nothing inherently wrong about the concept. This, after all, is what China and Russia are doing. It is what gave rise to the so-called Asian Tiger economies of Singapore, Hong Kong, South Korea and Taiwan, who now thrive in the technological fast lane of the world's advanced economies. The problem with state capitalism, in the case

---

32. See; "population decline an imminent, unexpected global problem" https://www.arabnews.com/node/1713841

of Nigeria, is that the state, itself operates as a captive object for powerful vested interests, who would stop at nothing to preserve their position of privilege and overarching influence. State capitalism is good if, like the Asian Tiger economies, it is run for the benefit of everybody, but it is debilitating if it is run to secure gains for a select, obdurate and myopic few. Diversifying a state capitalist economy like ours is like putting lipstick on a pig; it remains a pig. Consequently, the solution for revamping our economy ought to be decentralisation; it is the clarion call to action of our time. Besides, it is a more accurate way of portraying the way forward than "restructuring", which is rather bland, loaded and is given to all kinds of mischievous interpretation. Diversification without decentralisation is tantamount to a fool's errand, it is whistling in the dark.

1.07 AMCON's Dubious Economic Function

27 June 2017

Asset Management Corporation of Nigeria (AMCON) is a government agency established by an Act of the National Assembly in 2010, "for the purpose of efficiently resolving the non-performing loan assets of banks in Nigeria; and for related matters".[33] The consolidation (or shrinking) of the banks in Nigeria from over one hundred to just 25 in 2005[34] revealed not only the level of the insolvency of some of them, but also the extent to which the whole financial system was nearly dragged into the abyss due to the amount of reckless debts they had hitherto stockpiled. A humongous amount of money; 800 billion naira was taken from the public coffers to bail out the banks on the orders of the then Governor of the Central Bank of Nigeria, Mallam Lamido Sanusi II. Since it was said to be an emergency, there was no Parliamentary input into the requisition of the cash by the CBN. It was needed to secure the solvency of the Nigerian banking industry, full stop. AMCON thus became the vehicle through which the assets of the beneficiaries of the CBN largesse could be "managed" and redistributed in a fashion that secured and protected the creditors of those banks. Once this had been done, the banks were offloaded back into private hands and business, as it were, continued as usual. Lest we forget, the money from the CBN does not belong to the Governor, neither does it belong to the President

---

33. AMCON's enabling legislation; https://amcon.com.ng/amcon-act.php

34. For the consolidation documents of 89 banks to 25, see; https://www.cbn.gov.ng/documents/consolidation.asp

20   1 · ECONOMY

of the Federal Republic of Nigeria; the money belongs to the tax-paying public. That said, there is a context to AMCON's raison d'être, which helps put things in perspective.

Since 1999 when the then President Olusegun Obasanjo was sworn in on the 29th of May, Nigeria has maintained a fledgling but sustained period of democratic governance. Before then, the country had been under a prolonged spell of military dictatorship which, in fact, had become the norm throughout the continent of Africa. The 1980s saw the rise in agitation for democracy and wider participation on the continent. It was also a period tied to crippling public debt and growing unsustainability of the state in Africa. For fear of Africa being engulfed by a succession of failed states, the West, spearheaded by the International Monetary Fund, made transition to multi-party democracy a major conditionality for foreign aid across the continent. Freedom of political association became intertwined with "free market" and liberal economic policy as a panacea to poverty and social malaise spreading across the states in Africa. In short, the state was conceived of as an impediment to prosperity by international financial institutions. Economic policy should be 'liberalised' as far as possible and private enterprises be allowed to thrive, rise or fall on their own ability and capability.

The sudden collapse of the Soviet bloc in 1989 accentuated the apparent supremacy of "market forces" over state diktat as a tool for economic policy. It was also around this same period that a bright government functionary in the United States of America, named Francis Fukuyama, wrote his seminal paper: "The end of History and the Last Man" in 1992,[35] in which he argued that the ideological rivalry between capitalist (the West) and socialist (Eastern bloc) economic doctrines had ended with the triumph of capitalism, which he predicted would spread around the world like bushfire. The debate over how "free" free enterprises ought to be in a democracy is still raging until today. There are those who see limits to the free market dogma, and there are those who, barring acts of criminality, see no limits to free market at all. It matters not that the market is a dog-eat-dog jungle, harbouring only the survival of the fittest. Companies and enterprises ought to be allowed to prosper, fail, and bounce back at will. Government should have no business in business other than as an "enabler" of entrepreneurial activity. This line of thinking became the convention throughout the 1980s and 1990s, until the Wall Street crash of 2008[36] prompted

---

35. The book can be accessed via; https://www.pdfdrive.com/the-end-of-history-and-the-last-man-e55209109.html

36. The Wall Street Crash was a financial meltdown which started in the US housing market, culminating in cascading events affecting the markets worldwide. For an interesting

1 · ECONOMY

governments and analysts in the West to ponder the merits of untrammelled free enterprises. To regulate or not to regulate once again became a hot topic of debate across the globe. It was thought that some industries are simply "too big to fail", thereby posing a systemic risk that threatens the whole of the economy if left to implode. The USA embarked upon far-reaching reforms of its financial system and introduced legislation; the "Dodd-Frank Wall Street Reform and Consumer Protection Act 2010",[37] which places certain limits on free enterprises operating in the critical sectors of the US economy. It was hailed at the time as a welcome piece of legislation whose time had come, but the Act is being considered for repeal by the current US Administration of President Donald Trump for having gone too far in "restricting" free enterprises.

It is within the above discourse that our own AMCON was borne in Nigeria, but questions remain: Should free market not also mean freedom to experiment and fail in business? Is that not how progress is made? Or should government always remain in the shadows to offer bail out to failing companies? If so, what is the rationale for picking winners? Given the finite resources at the disposal of the state, what is the basis/logic for selecting which enterprise to bail out, and which to abandon? In their abiding wisdom, the drafters of the AMCON Bill had targeted the banking industry and "related matters". This has allowed the body not only to focus on rescuing the banking industry alone, but to henceforth fish around for 'related matters', which could mean, well, whatever. Since the Act has left the door so widely open to accommodate any enterprise that suits the fancy of officials, AMCON has, ipso-facto, expanded its focus to what it considers the "critical sectors" of the economy. For heaven's sake, I am yet to understand exactly which sector of our economy can be brushed aside as not being 'critical' at this point in time.

Arik Air[38] is the latest example of a private enterprise in distress, of which AMCON has mounted a hostile takeover, because, they say, it is such a "critical sector" of the economy. It will soon be "streamlined", rendered solvent and handed back into private hands. The question simply is this, should AMCON be at liberty to use infinitesimal amount of public funds to save private enterprises from their own failures, make them solvent, then, hand them back to fat cat directors backed by greedy shareholders in the name of "free market"?

---

chronicle see; "The 2008 crash; what happened to all that money?" https://www.history.com/news/2008-financial-crisis-causes

37. See; "Dodd-Frank Wall Street Reform and Consumer Protection Act" 2009 https://www.govinfo.gov/content/pkg/PLAW-111publ203/pdf/PLAW-111publ203.pdf

38. The airline cancelled all its domestic operations in 2012 following a raid on its premises by government officials

Is it fair to rob Paul to pay Peter in this way? Someone please tell me if I am missing something.

1.08 DMO and the Paradox of 'Debt Management'

4 July 201

Last week, this column cast the spotlight on Debt Management Office[39] (DMO)'s sister agency; Asset Management Corporation of Nigeria. It only makes sense that we juxtapose the function of both to draw a useful parallel and overlap between them. The agencies, particularly DMO, by their very nature, have made the issue of debt a non-issue in public discourse. Banks are in debt, no worries, just call in AMCON and it is all solved. Similarly, states are in debt, and are on the verge of bankruptcy, ah, well, DMO will take care of things. These agencies are accountable to their Boards (whose membership are subject to the patronage of the President of the Federal Republic of Nigeria), their heads are appointed for a fixed (renewable) term of five years, and do not have to worry about ministerial oversight. Therefore, since debt in Nigeria has been depoliticised in this way, concomitantly, public discussion of it has waned over time. This is an alarming trend in Nigeria's public finance. To all intent and purposes, we have agencies in this country given untrammelled powers to accumulate ('manage' if you like) debt by stealth. Public discussion of the work and remit of these agencies is, more often than not, guided by bankers and other financial stakeholders, and democratic accountability; man-on-the-street angle is conspicuous by its absence.

The Act establishing the DMO was signed into law in 2003,[40] at the height of Nigeria's external debt crisis, when the former Managing Director of the World Bank, Dr Ngozi Okonjo-Iweala was rushed into the then hot seat of the Ministry of Finance to apply her accrued experience in the field to harness the generosity of external lenders to cancel Nigeria's debt. Being a hard core technocrat, the Minister of Finance wanted to rid the ministry of its debilitating political/party hacks impeding both the transparency and functionality of the ministry by creating an arms-length body that would be 'above politics' as it

---

39. For the composition and breakdown of its functions visit; https://www.dmo.gov.ng

40. For a detailed (line-by-line) scrutiny of the Act, see the pdf version; https://www.dmo.gov.ng/publications/other-publications/dmo-establishment-act/1289 -dmo-act-1/file

were. And, it has to be said, the structure put in place and the assiduousness with which it was implemented earned the wily minister domestic and international plaudits. The policy did, indeed, create an era of prudential management of the country's finances but, arguably, it has become victim of its own initial success. Levels of public debt and its management are at the core of finance in any advanced economy; elections are won and lost sometimes on account of that alone. To remove that from the arena of public debate as we have done in Nigeria is both commendable and lamentable almost in equal measure.

The administration of the former President Obasanjo at whose behest Dr Iweala served, deserves credit for rebalancing our economy at a time of severe financial crisis, which ultimately culminated in a massive debt forgiveness for Nigeria from international lenders.[41] It should also be noted that the honourable minister was systematically eased out of her post to become the Minister of Foreign Affairs, as her strident technocratic view of financial matters irked the President and his political acolytes, who wanted a free hand in disbursing largesse and patronage as they saw fit. Dr Iweala's unceremonious redeployment to a new, revenue-neutral, ministry of foreign affairs drew condemnation from several quarters in and outside the country, and quite rightly so, in my view. However, with or without Dr Iweala, DMO has become embedded in our financial architecture hence, the need to ask searching questions about its remit and functionality. For a start, AMCON and DMO are both capable of acquiring humongous amounts of public debts, disposing of such at will, and issuing various kinds of debt instruments. Why then is one called "asset" management, while the other is called "debt" management? Debt is a form of asset for DMO if it augments its acquisition, and it can be repackaged and resold. Asset is a form of debt for AMCON if it becomes toxic and in large volumes. We are trying to maintain a distinction between these two bodies, but as the reader can surmise, it is a bit of a stretch to do so convincingly. Unless someone tells me otherwise, it is a distinction without a difference I am afraid. Asset and debt are not mutually exclusive concepts in capital markets dealings. To set up two government agencies alluding to such exclusivity is patently wrong. There is nothing the DMO does that cannot be incorporated into the remit of AMCON and vice-versa.

In order to justify its position and add lustre to its profile as an apolitical body, DMO has embarked upon a public relations exercise of some sort of

---

41. For the full package of Nigeria's external debts written off by the 'Paris Club', see the pdf file; https://www.dmo.gov.ng/publications/other-publications/nigeria-debt -relief/570-nigeria-s-debt-relief-deal-with-the-paris-club/file

late. First, it issued the "FGN Savings Bond", loftily described as "a retail savings product accessible to all income groups". Minimum subscription is as low as five thousand naira, up to a maximum of 50 million naira. There is a return of five per cent fixed interest and it bears no risk as it is a sovereign bond. See; "Of bonds, capital markets and casino capitalism" (1–3), PUNCH February 14th 2017, where the rudiments of bonds as financial instruments are dissected for public consumption. Throwing bonds at 'Joe public' this way perpetuates the myth of "financial inclusiveness" of the All Progressives Congress and the Presidency, no doubt. It also serves to engineer the false consciousness of workers-cum-Capitalists mind-set that the ruling elite in this country would like to promote. By the way, how many plumbers, bricklayers, market women and other artisans have taken up the bond issue anyway? Likewise the recently introduced and oversubscribed "Diaspora Bonds" on America's stock exchange. While this may have been aimed at Nigerians resident abroad, in the USA in particular, the ultimate subscribers to the bond issue will largely be non-Nigerians desirous of making a quick buck. Bonds, by nature, have no nationality, no sentimentality, and certainly, no permanent abode. The Americans allowed it on their exchange because their citizens (not necessarily Nigerians in the diaspora) stand to gain from it, pure and simple.

Finally, the DMO is issuing the "Sukuk" this week, which is a form of Islamic bond. This topic has also been explored in this column in the recent past: "Islamic finance and the prosaic ethics of capital", PUNCH April 25th 2017. Islamic ethics forbid the reaping of gratuitous interest on any type of financial instrument. In an ordinary bond issuance, you get your bond certificate and collect your annual interest and principal on maturity without further ado. Islamic finance basically frowns at this type of money-making out of money as a position in capital markets. With the Sukuk, consequently, your money is tied to an asset; a tangible asset, out of which the subscriber gets a share of the proceeds. These then are some of DMO's attempt at enhancing "inclusiveness" in the economy. It is, by so doing, also blunting the sharp edge of capitalism by gobbling up debt by a select few of corporations and state bodies. It is the antithesis of free market. To cite just one example, DMO recently acted to arrange a bailout for a number of hard up states, but it is arguable that, although allowing the insolvent states of the Federation to go under would have been dire for the residents of the states concerned, but it would have forced the debate about the viability of the existing states and the need for regionalism to the fore, but DMO blunted this possible scenario and the opportunity was lost. We gained nothing from the crisis except accumulation of more debts. DMO may be the proverbial necessary evil, but is it really also desirable?

1.09 The Elusive Quest for Tax Revenue

8 August 2017

"In this world, wrote Benjamin Franklin (1706–1790), nothing can be said to be certain, except death and taxes". Franklin, a renowned polymath, was one of the founding fathers of the United States of America. The sardonic phrase attached to his name has endured and been reaffirmed through the centuries. The idea that nothing is certain in life, but death and taxes, clearly rings true, generally, in most Western (liberal) societies, but it rings rather hollow in many others. For instance, death is certain in this country for sure, but taxes? Well, your guess is as good as mine. Even in the Western societies where tax-paying is a civic obligation taken seriously, even religiously, by majority of citizens, it is amazing to see the length some of them would go to avoid it. Ask Donald J Trump, the billionaire current President of the United States, who devised all sorts of schemes to avoid paying taxes on his myriad of businesses. When challenged by his opponents during the Presidential campaign of 2016 on this fact, he gave a rather nonchalant repost: "well, paying low taxes makes me clever". Against US Presidential convention, and in contrast to his main challenger, Hillary Clinton, he pointedly refused to make his tax returns public. Needless to say, the brash and bombastic candidate, Trump, went on to win the election to become the 45th President of the United States.

The more inevitable any government tries to make tax paying to become, the more inevitable it is that people would find ways of avoiding it. It is commonplace to see multimillionaires in the West relocating to the "tax havens" of Monaco, Cayman Island, Barbados, Virgin Island, Gibraltar, etc. just in order to avoid paying income tax in their own countries. Companies move production from their parent homes to overseas bases, to take advantage of lower (even zero) taxes and cheap labour. Across the ages, the struggle to augment government revenue through taxes is juxtaposed by the need to attract investment through lower taxes. It is the cardinal aim of every government to make taxes low, and collect high revenue at the same time. It is a difficult balance to achieve at the best of times. It is also an open ended argument between economists throughout the world. People love the welfare provision funded by taxes, but no one really loves paying for them. By the way, of itself, tax avoidance is not an offence, but tax evasion is. Many engage in the former and not the latter. That too, however, is a fine line. Drawing that line is what keeps accountants and lawyers busy — and, I might add, for ever happy.

At a stakeholders' forum in Abuja, last week, the National Tax Policy review committee made a not too startling, but nonetheless, worrying revelation that only "10 million" Nigerians actually pay tax. According to the Minister of Finance, only 20% out of the 70 million workforce in Nigeria pay tax.[42] There is a slight discrepancy in these two figures, but that is beside the point. The broad, underlying consensus is that there is something approaching a chasm between citizens' earnings and government tax intake in this country. This is buttressed by the recent revelation by the Vice President, Professor Yemi Osinbajo, that: "only 214 people pay between N10 million and N20 million tax every year in Nigeria and most of them reside in Lagos". As I said earlier, tax avoidance is by no means unique to this country, but the level of our compliance is abysmally low, certainly, compared to what goes on in Western countries. Why is this?

Why, for instance, do we have our Western-educated elites comply with their tax obligations whilst living and earning a living in the West, but fail to do the same the moment they are on home soil? And, why do the teaming number of artisans and craftsmen, who ply their trade in the "informal sector" in this country, feel less inclined to submit their earnings to the scrutiny of the Federal Inland Revenue? These income earners operate in the shadows as it were, below the radar of the tax authorities. Again, I ask, why is there no broad compliance on payment of tax by citizens in this country? The answer can be gleaned from this simple illustration.

Madam Alice is a patriotic Nigerian citizen, who has just returned from a prolonged stay and work in London. She is a no-nonsense career woman and an upright citizen of this country. One day she was assaulted and robbed of her possession, in broad daylight, in some part of Lagos mainland. She instinctively rushed to the nearest police station to report the horrific incidence and urged the police to accompany her to the spot to apprehend the assailants, who were still brazenly milling around and robbing other people. "What did you say they took from you, Madam?" the duty officer asked brusquely. "My passport, travellers' cheques, bank cards, everything!" screamed Madam Alice, wearing an understandably anguished look on her face. The officer behind the desk cleared his throat, muttered a low, inaudible, utterance before retorting: "Madam, you no thank God"? Perplexed but unbowed, Madam Alice would have none of that indolent attitude from a supposedly law enforcement officer

---

42. See; Taiwo Oyedele, "Guess how many Nigerians pay tax and how our government spends the money" https://www.pwc.com/ng/en/assets/pdf/tax-watch-june-2016.pdf. The then Minister of Finance, Kemi Adeosun had said in 2017, "we have just 40 million active tax payers out of an estimated 69.9 million https://www.premiumtimesng.com/news/top-news/234327-214-people-nigeria-pay-taxes-n20-million-adeosun.html

1 · ECONOMY

funded, after all, by the tax payer. She insisted on the immediate apprehension of the robbers, who she thought were a menace to society. At this point, the Inspector of Police who was listening to the conversation from his office flung his door open, slowly walked up to Madam Alice and said. "Ok, Madam, you know where the robbers are?" But, before Madam Alice could respond, the officer followed his question with a deadpan: "Alright, Madam, go bring them; we will charge them immediately".

To cap it all, Madam Alice has had little or no reliance on the state for anything hitherto; she feels no presence of the state in her life whatsoever. She lives in a gated community with her family, provides her own electricity, security, pipe borne water, healthcare, education for her children, etc. She subsequently decides to withhold payment of taxes to the state permanently. Is she right? Wait. Before answering yes to this question, imagine if all the Alices in this country permanently withheld their taxes in a similar way. Government would grind to a screeching halt. What then do we do when the state has reneged on fulfilling its part of the bargain to provide basic amenities, protect life and property of the citizen, and election after election has made no difference? Since it is unrealistic to expect Madam Alice to carry on paying her taxes rather dutifully, and regardless, is her withdrawal from the tax system an appropriate and justifiable response? If it is, then, who takes responsibility for the ensuing collapse of the state?

The level of tax compliance will not increase unless and until the state ensures security and welfare of its citizens (at home and abroad), but the state cannot fully do this unless and until it has enough tax revenue to meet its obligations. This is a classic chicken and egg situation for Madam Alice and millions of her compatriots in this country. Which one do YOU think comes first, the chicken or the egg?

1.10 Crippling Cost of Borrowing; Who Cares?

24 October 2017

The chronically high cost of borrowing, otherwise known as interest rate, has represented a tightening noose around the necks of businesses in Nigeria for the last thirty years, at least. It shows no signs of abating, and certainly no visible end in sight. Interest rate is best understood as the cost of borrowing money from the bank, but it encompasses other aspects: mortgage, cars, hire-purchase, and a host of back street moneylenders, also known as "loan sharks".

We live in an economy where borrowing from the bank routinely incurs interest repayment of between 15 and 35% at the best of times.[43] No economy anywhere in the world has ever developed at this level of rate. For good or ill, no advanced economy in the world imposes this type of burden on its citizen either. On the contrary, interest rate in developed economies rarely, if ever, hits double digits. In Western European economies, for instance, it is generally below 5% and in the United States of America[44] and United Kingdom it is hovering at around 1%.[45] It has remained decidedly low for almost 10 years in these countries. This column has highlighted this problem severally during the course of this year. The topic has also come up for discussion in different economic and business fora on and off the television screens. I am, therefore, not going to re-run any of the arguments here and now, except to offer one compelling reason for the huge disparity between the level of interest rate in advanced economies and a "developing" one such as Nigeria's.

When we quibble about economic numbers, it tends to fly over people's heads because the so-called experts often couch the debate in esoteric language inaccessible to the vast majority of us living in the real world. You will know the effect of a high level of interest rate if you have ever tried to build or buy a house, or a car, which you have to finance from borrowing. On the other hand, high interest rate is also speaking to you on a different level; it is encouraging you to save because you can reap gratuitous rewards from sitting back and doing nothing. If, however, you de-personalise the issue, you will see how interest rate impacts the overall economy in terms of business and investment decisions. You look around you and see a deserted warehouse, or trade centre; it is very likely to be the result of a crippling interest rate, which then impedes the creation of jobs, and a steep growth in the teaming number of school leavers without a job ensues.

Furthermore, an investor would respond to a high interest rate by moving his money away from companies (who need the investment) into banks (who then lends to you at a high cost). Meanwhile, the stock market is where most big corporations go to raise cash in order to buy new plants, machinery, and employ people. It is the most closely watched financial market in every economy. It follows, therefore, that the higher the price of a company's stock, the better it will be in a position to grow and expand its activity. If Nigerian banks, which

---

43. Trend in Nigeria's cost of borrowing; https://data.worldbank.org/indicator /FR.INR.LEND?locations=NG

44. USA interest rates up to 2022; https://www.federalreserve.gov/releases/h15

45. UK interest rates up to 2022; https://www.reuters.com/world/uk/boe-raise-rates -again-march-inflation-peak-soon-after-2022-02-14

often claim they want to partner the government in fostering economic growth continue to lure investors away from the financial market through a high interest rate strategy, what about the government itself? Governments around the world rely on, first, "monetary policy", meaning control over the rate of interest and inflation. This responsibility is often delegated to an 'independent' central bank. Politicians, however, never fail to set the right targets for the head of their central bank. The question is what realistic target can the Nigerian government set for interest rate, when our government is the biggest customer for our banks?[46] Large scale deposits are made to Nigerian banks by a variety of government departments, yielding healthy returns, which are then diverted to somebody's personal benefit. Before it was streamlined to the "Treasury Single Account" (TSA),[47] government departments, and agencies routinely maintained dozens of accounts with Nigerian banks, from which interest accrued and disappeared into thin air. Admittedly, the TSA has put a check on that for now, but it is only a matter of time before we are back to business as usual. Now, if the banks can rake in deposits from government agencies and lend back to the same government at exorbitant rates of 15, 20, 30% or more, why bother considering struggling manufacturers in our industrial wastelands for loan advance?

Government functions, also, through the instrumentality of its "fiscal policy", that is, to say, setting the amount it takes in taxes and spending. A budget deficit is the excess of government expenditures over and above tax receipts in a financial year. Deficit is a normal and regular occurrence, except in a rare situation of stupendous wealth, such as it is in the Kingdom of Qatar, where the country often dispenses with income tax from citizens and residents because it has enough revenue from oil. Government deficit in Nigeria is offset by borrowing (apart from external sources) heavily from Nigerian banks. The same vested interest that owns and controls the banking industry is the same vested interest that holds the reins of power in government bureaucracy. They, in turn, set the regulatory parameter for the Legislature to consider in passing laws for the financial sector. Slashing the high rate of interest is like asking turkeys to vote for Christmas in that regard. The question for the curious mind, however, is that, though powerful

---

46. "Nigeria local debt stands at 21 trillion"; https://www.vanguardngr.com/2021/09 /nigeria-owing-n35-5trn-local-debt-stands-at-n21-trillion/ For a salient report on this by Mohammed Abubakar see; "Sustainable Debt and Fiscal management—The Nigerian Experience" 2015 https://olc.worldbank.org/sites/default/files/Mohammed%20Abubakar_1.pdf

47. TSA is a new innovative scheme to guard against fraud by shrinking the hitherto federal government's multiple bank accounts to just one payment platform supervised by the central bank https://www.cbn.gov.ng/out/2016/bpsd/guidelines%20for%20the%20 operations%20of%20tsa%20by%20state%20governments%20in%20nigeria.pdf

vested interest also governs the American and UK economies, how come they, nevertheless, respond to consumer demands in the way we do not see in our own economy? The answer, quite simply, is citizenship; a loaded concept we are yet to grapple with in our country and elsewhere in Africa.

As a way of fostering economic growth, developed economies rely on active participation of their citizens in productive activity. They extend credit to them across the income and demographic divide irrespective of class or ethnicity. The credit economy is so pervasive that the plasma television screen you watch with your family, the music centre in the corner of your living room, the chair you and your guests sit on, not to talk of the house you all crowd in, are, more often than not, tied to credit of one sort or another. What this means is that questions of interest rates and inflation are no longer abstract concepts; they have become the concerns of everybody, not just a select few of horizontal economists and financial pundits talking above the heads of citizens as we have in this country. The necessary symbiotic relationship between government and the governed is missing in our economy, as elections have become a mere ritual without consequences. Without prejudice to the current administration of President Muhammadu Buhari, imagine what would happen to a government that presided over a 20% interest rate in a Western economy, then, has the brass neck to seek re-election to a second term. My friends, it is not enough to wring your hands in despair; get involved and have a say in who governs!

1.11 First Law of Development

7 November 2017

The word 'development' is an elusive term everybody knows something about, but it means different things to different people. How then, can there be a prescriptive "law" for such an indeterminate object? Well, there is, and it will become crystal clear by the end of this piece. For now, let us break the term down to small, every day, digestible portions. We recognise development in good roads, hospitals, solid dwellings, good transport network, uninterrupted power supply, modern educational institutions, clean water, stable and transparent judicial system, high per capita income, etc. Every country we recognise as 'developed' anywhere in the world has elements of all the above in sufficient numbers. That being the case, what role do we ask of the government we elect to perform in bringing about development to our country? I mean, what does it really boil down to for the everyday person? Loads of factories with smoking chimneys bellowing into the atmosphere? Low inflation? Higher or lower taxes? Government spending? Borrowing? Reflation? Prayer and fasting? What?

Generally speaking, many people on both sides of the Atlantic give credence to only one thing as the key to development; trade. Governments around the world go out of their way to lend support for their home industries to expand their overseas trade. The whole world is dotted with numerous alliances and trade blocs for mutual benefits; European Union, Asian and Pacific trade pacts, North Atlantic trade pact, down to the East African trade pact and our own West African trade pact, also known as ECOWAS. Twenty-three (mainly) Western leaders created the General Agreement on Tariffs and Trade in 1947, which took effect the following year. It was aimed at reducing tariffs and assorted trade barriers amongst the signatories. Soon after, other countries began to apply to join the club and the process of negotiating the entrance of new membership continued incrementally, through the "Uruguay round of agreements" until 1994. Some 123 countries having come on board the gravy train of free trade, it was re-christened the World Trade Organisation, the commencement of which kicked in right at the beginning of 1995. It created a set of complex rules to help police the free flow of trade between the signatories. It also ensured that those initial foundation members did not and could not have given up their competitive advantage over the new comers across Africa and Asia. There lies the trouble.

Big multinational corporations became a lot more empowered to expand and exploit trade opportunities across the globe as Western governments preached the gospel of free trade and rolling back the frontiers of the state. It follows, logically, that a conglomerate of companies moved fast to dominate and set the rules on the international stage, making "profit maximisation" their watchword. The new wave of "free trade" and "globalisation", however, increased the income gulf between states rather than narrowing it. The countries with developed technologies and long histories of trade, saw wages and incomes rise in their homelands, while the less developed countries remain in the periphery. Put it this way, free trade is a beautiful concept if you already have something to trade with, but not so for those who still have their feet glued to the starting blocks. As an illustration, let us say 12 people come to an imaginary Garden of Eden for some expected bonanza. Two of them appear with their heavy duty trucks and ten come with wheelbarrows. Free entrance and free harvest are then proclaimed as the rules of engagement inside the Garden. It is only a matter of time before the two participants with the trucks outrun the ten with wheelbarrows. This is exactly what globalisation has done to world trade. The countries in the "G7" or "G8" in the world, that is, the countries that bind themselves together in any of this group of seven, or eight, dominate and exploit all the others outside. They call the shots; they run world trade primarily for their own benefits, drawing economic resources from the poorer nations back to the already richer nations, and who can blame them? After all, everyone has already signed up for "free trade".

What the rest of the world outside the magic circles of the rich and powerful is left with is often an almighty scramble for the crumbs. This is euphemistically referred to as: "Foreign Direct Investment", the equivalent of the begging bowl in international capital. The bulk of such investment we attract in this country is in the oil, gas and other extractive industries. That is obviously where they can make more money for repatriation to their country. Just as the gulf between rich and poor nations has widened with globalisation, so too, is the gulf in income between citizens in different countries. The rich are getting richer, while the poor are steadily getting poorer. In America, for example, the richest one per cent earns as much as the poorest eighty percent of Americans.[48] And in Nigeria, half a dozen individuals own more than ninety per cent of the wealth in the country. That said, this is the logic of capitalism. It is an economic model the world has accepted as "inevitable". The election of President Donald Trump in America was meant to be a repudiation of the capitalist logic the country itself has exploited so successfully for decades. It is also what is propelling the opposition leader, Jeremy Corbyn, towards power in the United Kingdom, if opinion polls there are anything to go by.[49]

Exploitation of the poor by the rich is not a new phenomenon though. As long as you maintain a free market for entrepreneurs, business leaders and foreign investors to thrive, the wealth will trickle down to the rest of society soon enough. We are told it is the only way that guarantees prosperity; that ensures everyone has some bread on the table — eventually. Please do not rush to put the blame on Adam Smith, Milton Friedman, and Frederick Hayek, including "wicked moneybags", venture capitalists, hedge-fund managers and the likes. From time immemorial, it is a logic that finds justification in the Holy Book itself. It is the first law of development: "For whosoever hath to himself shall be given, and he shall have more abundance: but whosoever hath not, from him shall be taken away even that he hath" (Matthew 13:12).

---

48. See a report by Christopher Ingraham; "The richest 1 percent now owns more of the country's wealth than at any time in the past 50 years", 'Washington Post', December 6, 2017 https://www.washingtonpost.com/news/wonk/wp/2017/12/06/the-richest-1-percent-now-owns-more-of-the-countrys-wealth-than-at-any-time-in-the-past-50-years
49. Corbyn actually lost the election to a massive conservative landslide in 2019.

1.12 9Mobile: How (Not) to Resurrect Business Failure

23 January 2018

If there is one overriding government economic objective that resonates with the public above all else, it is that the economy needs a massive in-flow of foreign direct investment not only in the critical sectors alone, but also, generally, in all sectors of the economy. Foreign Direct Investment (or FDI as they are called), is important in boosting domestic production through enhanced capacity. It is also important in bridging the technological gap between developed and developing economies. Above all, where appropriately targeted, the FDI helps generate prosperity through creation of jobs, thereby easing social tension in and among communities. That being the case, therefore, it should be a matter of consternation that Etisalat, the progenitor of 9Mobile, which brought a chunk of foreign capital into the Nigerian telecommunications industry in 2008, has decided to pull out of the industry and moved its investment onto greener pastures elsewhere. Asked whether they plan to return to Nigeria anytime soon, the Chief Executive Officer of Etisalat International, Hatem Dowidar, said: "There is a new Board and we are not part of that company ... the train has left the station on that one ..." This is a stunning development for a provider with over 20 million subscribers, 14% market share, and the fourth largest after MTN (47%), Globacom (20%), and Airtel (19%).[50]

The Nigerian telecommunications industry is reputed to be one of the most lucrative in Africa, given the burgeoning population fast approaching the 200 million mark,[51] and given the penchant for Nigerians to stay on the phone for prolonged periods of time, rabbiting on with family and friends at home and abroad literally around the clock. Millions of us do just that on a daily basis. In fact, it would not be too far-fetched to describe the industry as a cash cow; a money spinner, for the wily investor. Consequently, for anyone to be walking away from it willy-nilly is not only counterintuitive, it is surely a bad omen for prospective foreign investors with an eye on Nigeria. The case is still evolving in court; so, one is by necessity constrained on the extent of one's commentary for now. That said, there are a couple of general aspects to the matter, in public domain, which portend troubling auguries for all concerned.

---

50. For wireless subscriber market share in Nigeria by carrier from 2015–2021, visit; https://www.statista.com/statistics/671676/mobile-subscription-share-in-nigeria-by-operator

51. The Nigerian population is one of the most intractable data for analysis. It has been estimated variously to be between 170 to 220 million as of February 2022.

First of all, Etisalat was so much in a hurry to dissociate itself from Nigeria that it gave the successor company to its brand, 9mobile, only three weeks (as opposed to the usual three months minimum) to cease using its name. This only adds to the mystery of what the foreign investors could have really gone through doing business in this country. Several market analysts have since identified economic downturn, currency devaluation, dollar shortages, etc. as the factors most likely responsible for forcing Etisalat out of its operations in Nigeria. Yes, these factors are the usual suspects, and yes, they are indeed poignant, but there are also risk allocation strategies the company could have put in place, which they did not. For instance, they did not need to have waited until their boat had capsized, when in fact they could have jumped off and swam their way to safety in good time to rebuild. There is the market way of running business, and there is the Nigerian, or should I say, African-specific tactical nous that provides the ballast for steadying a ship in choppy waters.

Moreover, when the regulators banded together with the Central Bank of Nigeria to organise a "rescue mission" for the ailing company, they opted to assemble a new team of managers to take charge of 9mobile going forward. This prompt action is to be commended as it reflects the severity of the problem at hand. However, no matter how well-intentioned this might have been at the time, it has the appearance of institution "insiders" putting their friends and chums into high rewarding positions in the market — not minding the fact that the individuals put forward for the board of 9mobile are outstanding people of stellar quality. This does not remove the suspicion. This is particularly in view of the stinging rebuke from Justice Ibrahim Buba of the Federal High Court in which he described the original ex-parte application obtained in July 2017, by the regulators, to establish the new board for 9mobile as, basically, fraudulent. The ex-parte judgement that gave them the power to constitute the board was obtained "by misrepresentation of facts", said the judge. They have now been ordered to revert to the status quo ante, meaning the appointment of the individuals to the board of 9mobile has been nullified. For the personnel of major Nigerian financial institutions to be lambasted by a Federal High Court Judge in this way speaks volumes, irrespective of the outcome of their appeal.

Perhaps, what people find most mind-boggling is the fact that the regulators did not opt for the option of a receivership. A receivership would surely have been more suited to this type of corporate insolvency than a quick handover to a handpicked management board. They (the regulators) have the power to appoint a receiver, or they could even have applied to the court for one. A "receiver" is a court appointed trustee, who "receives" and assumes rights over associated business assets and properties of a company in distress. This generally allows for an opportunity to restructure and remodel the business, following which a new board subsequently takes over, having settled the creditors. A receiver can, in certain circumstances, attempt to revive, but with Etisalat not willing to budge on its position, this would be impossible. The other option is for the receiver to liquidate, but, the regulators have made it clear this would not be in the public interest. We are thus left with the option of the receiver running the company on his own, pending a suitable buyer showing up. The regulators say they have not opted for this route because they did not wish to "alarm" the market. Receivership is a well-known business strategy that needs not alarm anyone with a professional take on this, any more than a hurriedly assembled crack team of managers would.

As the court deliberates on the appeal by the regulators, they will have the interest of the shareholders and creditors at the front of their concerns. They will also (as they should) have the interest of the subscribing public hovering over their deliberations. In this wise, they will come down on one side or the other, but it cannot be a situation of winner-takes-all. They will be guided by the twin principles of corrective and distributive justice. The former is concerned with reversal of wrongs and the undoing of transactions entered into prior to the business failure. The latter is concerned with achieving a fair disbursement of common advantages and common burden for the greater good. 9mobile is a private company with a substantial public interest angle at its base.

Finally, and lest we forget, Virgin Atlantic invested heavily in the country's aviation industry by giving birth to Virgin Nigeria in 2005, which ran a successful operation until Richard Branson and his Virgin Group were forced to relinquish their interest in Virgin Nigeria in 2008. A new home-grown crack team of local experts were quickly assembled to run the company. The airline, by then a sinking ship, morphed into Air Nigeria in 2010, under the Chairmanship of Jimoh Ibrahim, but finally collapsed in 2012. Those who fail to learn from the lesson of history are doomed to repeat it.

1.13 Parallel Universe of the IMF and Nigerian Government

13 March 2018

Report of the 2018 "Article IV"[52] mission to Nigeria conducted by the International Monetary Fund (IMF) in December 2017 came to light a couple

---

52. This report can be accessed via this link; https://www.imf.org/en/Countries/NGA

of weeks ago, and it makes grim reading for the government almost on all fronts. It pours scorn on the government's claim that the economy has finally turned the corner; that the green shoots of recovery are now upon us. Not so quickly, says the IMF. It says that although the country may have tiptoed its way out of recession, the economy remains "vulnerable", and it will only "muddle through" in the medium term. Growth in non-oil; non-agriculture sector constitutes 65% of the overall economy and it actually shrank in 2017 relative to the same period in 2016. They, however, "welcome" actions to improve power sector and business environment under the Economic Recovery and Growth Plan (ERGP). This is an on-going initiative of the current administration to map out a medium-term plan for economic growth for 2017–2020. Unlike previous such initiatives, it has a "delivery unit at the Presidency" to drive implementation of its key priorities. It also aims, among other things, to "ramp up" oil production to 2.5mbpd by 2020. Let us be totally honest, such a plan would have been run through the key personnel attached to Nigeria inside the IMF. It is not even worth debating the handiwork of the organisation on the plan. It is simply what happens; nothing happens to economic planning in this country without the blessing of the IMF.[53] Their recommendation of certain policy measures (fiscal and monetary for example) carries so much weight that no serious planning or finance minister would dare go against. Given this, how come, then, that their prognosis for Nigeria's economic outlook seems so at variance with that of the government?[54] What explains the basis for this parallel universe?

First of all, let us clear up a couple of assumptions about the nature of IMF and government. The former is a lending institution, while the latter pre-occupies itself, most times, with spending. Their worldview is bound to differ somewhat. While one tends to be conservative, austere and amoral, the other tends to be expansive, lavish in parts and all-embracing in whole. Furthermore, while one is accountable to the global finance of the West that created it, the other is (or ought to be) accountable to the teaming masses of the people that gives it power. Although the IMF lends money to a struggling government, it does not enjoy doing so. In fact, it does not wish to do so if it could be avoided. It sees itself as a lender of last resort, which means, when all a country has left to go on is looking up to the heavens for a miracle. That being so, the

---

53. This is a fair assumption since any such planning would impact the external debt status of the country in which the organisation is a major stakeholder.

54. The government is adamant that the economy is on the upward trajectory according to the Minister for Budget and National Planning; https://guardian.ng/news/nigerias -economic-outlook-for-2018-positive-udoma

institution has grown since it was set up as part of the post-World War II international economic order led by the USA. By the way, even the USA runs a budget deficit. A budget deficit occurs in any economy when the amount it takes in from taxation is less than its expenditure. Solution? Borrow, of course. Like all other developing nations, Nigeria scampers around looking for someone to borrow from all the time. How about borrowing from Messrs Aliko Dangote or Mike Adenuga[55] and their ilk, for instance? They have billions of unused dollars in assets after all. They could lend to the government and reap high interest dividends and become even richer, you might think? No, not a chance. Individuals do not lend to government because the risk is simply too great. In that case, is it not possible for a government to approach commercial banks? Yes, they often do, but bank interest rates can be killing for anyone, not least a government with scant resources. Why not simply impose higher income and corporation taxes? Well, that is not as easy as it sounds either. Higher taxes discourage investment; it puts people off coming into a high taxing country in preference for a low taxing one. Country after country are busy chasing private investors and wooing them with juicy tax rates and concessions that it would be economic suicide to wantonly raise taxes and hope for the best.

The above is precisely what drives governments towards the IMF. Nowadays though, the institution does a lot more than throwing money around; it basically takes over the running of the finance ministry of the borrower with their crack team of financial experts from Washington, USA, where it has its headquarters. What is the IMF assessment of the Nigerian economy overall? It is that growth is expected to pick up slightly in 2018 to 2.1%, but it will "stay flat in the medium term". This is rather grim indeed, given that we need growth to be 5% and above over a sustained period of time to have any realistic hope of stemming the tide of unemployment and mass starvation in this country. Consequently, following the precepts of the IMF, "fiscal consolidation should be accompanied by a monetary policy stance that remains tight to further reduce inflation and anchor inflation expectations …" Now, what does this gobbledegook mean in a lay man's language? "Staying flat" means we remain in a recession-like economic environment for the foreseeable future. The IMF's prescription for that is "fiscal consolidation". It simply means the government should cut back on its expenditure, hitting the poorest even harder, since it cannot impose higher taxes to meet its growing expenditure on essential serv-

---

55. Aliko Dangote is the richest person in Africa, while Mike Adenuga is tiptoeing not too far behind him.

ices. This is happening at the same time as we have an urgent need for a massive investment in our road network and transportation. A "monetary policy stance that remains tight"? Oh yes, this explains the high interest rate policy of the CBN. But how can the manufacturing sector thrive under a high interest rate policy of the IMF? Their main priority is curbing inflation; not boosting employment.

Lest we forget, there was a reference to the USA itself having a massive budget deficit. It runs close to $2.3 trillion dollars in fact.[56] It is the highest of such deficits in the history of the modern world.[57] It makes the country the largest debtor on earth, in fact.[58] What is IMF going to do about that, you might be wondering? Answer is, nothing; nada! IMF does not and cannot lend to the USA, or any Western economy for that matter. It could, in theory, lend to a Western economy in dire straits, but the organisation is not structured for that purpose. Instead, the USA and other Western capitalist nations borrow largely from private investors operating in capital markets and other financial outlets. Why? Because they have financial "credibility" to do so, and we in Africa do not. This state of affairs gives the IMF an inordinate power over our economic destiny. When they give 'advice', (diktat, if you prefer), they do so in double breath often. They want us to promote an "inclusive growth strategy" that focuses on employing labour and increasing social welfare for citizens. At the same time, they advise against government spending, and advocates tight monetary control and tax incentives for the rich as the only route towards prosperity. We dance to their tune at will; they say jump, we say how high. They ask us to run a mile towards them, and as soon as we get there, they immediately insist we prove we can walk on water too. This is euphemistically referred to as IMF "conditionalities".

Well then, readers, I say that we are in an economic straightjacket largely of our own making by our continuing inability to take our destiny into our own hands. President Trump in the USA has just done that last Thursday, by imposing higher tariffs on importation of steel into America to "protect American jobs". It is a "national security issue" for America, he insists. Imagine this coming from the motherland of capitalism and free trade? The same people preaching the virtue of deregulation to us. What an irony! So, instead of fixing,

---

56. $2.3 trillion up to 2021 https://www.cbo.gov/topics/budget

57. Although this is projected to fall to $1.2 trillion in 2021–2031 https://www.cbo.gov/publication/57339

58. See; "US Congress approves boosting debt limit to $31.4 trillion" (Reuters, December 2021) https://www.reuters.com/markets/rates-bonds/us-congress-vote-debt-limit-hike-averting-default-risk-2021-12-14

tilting and indeed stealing the vote in 2019, let the next election be a choice between alternative visions for the liberation of our economy from the palsied grip of international capital.

1.14 NNPC/Multinational Oil Contracts: Grand Bargain or Grand Larceny?

10 July 2018

Towards the tail end of the Jonathan administration, the then Governor of the Central Bank of Nigeria, Lamido Sanusi, accused the Nigerian National Petroleum Corporation (NNPC), of failure to remit at least $25bn dollars into the Federation Account.[59] There was a lot of jumping around over the revelation, but nothing happened. Last year, the Minister of State for Petroleum Resources, Dr Ibe Kachikwu accused the same corporation of awarding multibillion naira contracts to outside agents "without due process". There followed the usual kerfuffle; a lot of jostling and arm-wrestling between officials, but in the end nothing happened. This year, NNPC currently stands accused of failure to remit billions of naira into the Federation Account, run by the Federation Account Allocation Committee (FAAC). Minister of Finance, Mrs Kemi Adeosun, last week, "felt the figures the NNPC was proposing for FAAC were unacceptable".[60] The corporation, she maintains, is operated "as a business", the Federal Government representing the interest of the shareholder, while the corporation also represents, wait for it, the interest of the same shareholder. This schizophrenic imbalance is part of the problem. The personnel of the corporation are constantly being encouraged to adopt the posture of a private business in their modus operandi; to operate in the market environment where 'greed is usually good', while at the same time being required to be mindful of their role as a public entity, where the focus is on the noble cause of service to country. These are two conflicting and conflictual ends. For all we know, the "standoff" between the NNPC and the Minister of Finance may soon melt into the early morning fog—as they do.

What is even more egregious in all of this is the way in which the corporation is being used, or is allowing itself to be used as a tool for foreign

---

59. See; "So where did the money go?" https://www.africa-confidential.com/article-preview/id/3868/So_where_did_the_money_go

60. See; "NNPC's 'Unacceptable figures' caused deadlock of FAAC meeting—Adeosun". https://businessandmaritimewestafrica.com/nnpcs-unacceptable-figures-caused-deadlock-of-faac-meeting-adeosun/ Also see; "Nigerian lawmakers to investigate state oil firm over remittances. https://www.reuters.com/article/us-nigeria-revenue-idUSKBN1K02DS

exploitation of Nigeria's natural resources in the guise of "direct foreign investment", which the Nigerian economy cannot do without. What is exasperating to a lot of well-meaning Nigerians is essentially the award of licenses to certain multinational companies to dig for oil, and how this is costing the country billions of dollars in lost revenue. How does that happen?

Well, it is a classic situation of owners of natural resources meeting with owners of capital and technology, to do business. They both desperately need each other, but which do you imagine has the upper hand? In an ideal world, they should both exhibit an equal bargaining strength, but they do not. Owners of natural resources are weaker; much weaker than owners of capital and technology. Why? Because owners of capital operate within a 'unionised' framework. They enjoy 'union' protection from the World Bank, World Trade Organisation, International Monetary Funds, International Financial Centres, etc. To all intent and purposes, these are de facto trade unions for the rich, and the very rich. These international financial institutions exist to protect the interest of capital, what else? They set the rules that protect the interest of capital across the globe, and anyone found transgressing the rules is severely and severally sanctioned. Now, who is it that sets the rules that protect owners of natural resources across the globe, you might ask? You guessed it; nobody! Owners of natural resources are few, but are permanently in disarray, while owners of capital and technology are many and well organised. They are the ones who should indeed be chasing owners of natural resources in a cut-throat competition with one another, because demand for natural resources is greater than their supply, but the organisational strength and resilience of capital gives them the upper hand to exert concessions in trade negotiations. So, this is precisely why it so happens, that it is ironically the owners of natural resources who are always crying out for owners of capital and technology for investments. And, the latter know how to strike a really good bargain. Consequently, when the NNPC wanted investment in the exploration and lifting of oil in Nigeria, it flung its doors wide open to all takers. But has the corporation gone too far in selling the family silver?

Since there is no point sitting on an abundance of crude oil without having the means to put it to economic use, the NNPC decided to enter into Joint Operations Agreement with a series of multinational companies decades ago. This merely involves NNPC selling rights to oilfields (acreages) to other people in exchange for royalty. This remained the position from the inception of the corporation in 1977. Then, in 1993, NNPC's need for capital caused it to negotiate and issue the first batch of Production Sharing Contracts (PSC) to multinationals, where a formula for sharing the wealth coming up from beneath Nigerian soil was done. The multinationals having seen the rewards flowing from dealing in oil in this country over a sustained period of time decided to come with an even bigger force than hitherto. They lobbied for, and helped push through the "Deep Offshore and Inland Basins Production Sharing Contract Decree 1999",[61] shortly before the military left the stage. For an area 201–500 meters depth NNPC takes 12%, in an area 501–800 meters depth it is 8%, in an area 801–1000 meters depth it is 4%, and finally, in an area 1000 meters+ depth it is 0%. Section 16 of the Act provides for a review of the Agreement after fifteen years, and for the adjustment of the PSC terms once the oil prices rose above $20 dollars (this happened in 2000). As usual with these things, no such review has taken place, and no such adjustment has been implemented with the attendant loss of billions of dollars to the Federation account. How come?

This issue was in fact the subject of Femi Falana's ire in his characteristically caustic letter to the Minister of Petroleum Resources, Dr Ibe Kachikwu, back in 2015, in which the (still) restless Senior Advocate of Nigeria demanded the repeal of section 5 of the Act, which allows for 0% royalty on waters deeper than 1000 meters. He wants the National Assembly to repudiate that particular section of the Agreement if not the whole Act in its entirety. I am sure the learned silk also knows too well that there are vested interests inside the hallowed chamber who would have been co-opted into the multinational deal ab initio. Consequently, the forces within are the proverbial turkeys who dare not vote for Christmas. They will prevaricate, obfuscate, complicate and confuse the issues to an impasse. Pressure, therefore, has to be mounted from outside the comfort zones of the National Assembly. Every candidate standing for election in 2019 must be made to pay an electoral price unless they publicly commit to the repeal of the obnoxious section. This should include the President himself. That is the immediate task at hand, but it goes deeper than that.

The multinationals who hoodwinked the National Assembly and NNPC to commit the country to 0% royalty on waters deeper than 1000 meters had the wherewithal to strike a grand bargain with their sound assumption of the huge bounty from mineral oil deposits located 1000 meters below the ground of our shores in this country. Such is their financial muscle and our penchant for foreign capital that they would most probably have walked away from a deal without the clause (a sweetener in financial jargon), in the Agreement. But as it turned out, the clause is a trap door in which we, collectively, have fallen through. This would not have been revealed to the NNPC contract negotiating

---

61. For the pdf copy of the Act see; https://taxaide.com.ng/files/Deep-Offshore-and
-Inland-Basin-Production-Sharing-Contracts-Decree%201999.pdf

42 1 · ECONOMY

team at the time, of course. As far as they knew, the multinational engineers were going on a "frolic of their own" in the shallow waters and in the creeks hence, their willingness to sign up to 0% royalty for fifteen years. We are talking of billions of dollars, which analysts have put within the range of $60–100bn US dollars loss to the Federation Account thus far. On the other hand, it could very well be that far from being a bunch of ignoramuses, the NNPC negotiating team may themselves have been part of this lamentable 'deal of the century'. Multinationals are not to blame for this state of affairs, however, the elites who made themselves willing tools in this grand larceny are the real culprits. Foreign investors are never on a charity mission to any country outside their home turf; they are and always will be on a mission to exploit even if it means watching their host country bleed to death from excessive profit. That is what their shareholders demand. It is up to the electorate in this country to make demands on their own leaders and push for a higher level of accountability. In the final analysis, the poor and powerless in this country can only be kept at bay for so long. The backlash is not long coming.

1.15 NNPC, FAAC, Minister of Finance, and the Missing Billions

24 July 2018

Barely two weeks ago, this column attempted to disentangle the case of NNPC and the unremitted funds to the Federal Allocation Account Committee (FAAC) from oil contracts, see; "NNPC/Multinational oil contracts: Grand bargain or grand larceny? PUNCH, 10th July 2018". The very next day, the House of Representatives launched a probe into the affairs which was splashed across the media as: "Reps probe N100b under remittance by NNPC". The Minister of Finance, Mrs Kemi Adeosun, had locked horns (like the diligent Minister that she is), with the all-powerful, majestic NNPC Board, declaring their account to the FAAC, chaired by the Minister, "unacceptable" and urging them to render the full account of the missing billions before any funds were released to the federating units. In a more vibrant democracy, this alone would have choked up the headlines for days if not weeks on end until it was resolved, and someone made to account. But, here in Nigeria, there was a palpable air of indifference and a sense of déjà vu about the shenanigans from the top level government functionaries. I myself had written in the 10th of July piece that the "standoff" between the Minister and NNPC would "likely melt away in the early morning fog—as they do". What happened?

1 · ECONOMY   43

Last week, it was widely reported that the subsequent meeting of the FAAC ended in a "deadlock" and had been suspended indefinitely. There really was no "deadlock"; in fact, the meeting could not go ahead due to a lack of quorum. Just imagine this, a serious issue of non-remittance of funds was reported to the committee by the Minister of Finance one week, and there was a lack of quorum for the FAAC to do its due diligence the very next week? Either we have an utterly supine Minister of Finance, or "characters in the shadows"; the "deep state" had gone to work on the 'intransigent' Minister. Then, what happened just a couple of days ago? Members of the FAAC rushed back to the Committee and voted to work within the ambit of the "unacceptable" account hitherto presented by the NNPC. The Minister of Finance was asked to find a way of clearing up her reservations about the NNPC submission with the corporation later. Questions about the unremitted billions have been set aside; kicked into the long grass. This is a very Nigerian (Third World) approach to public finance that the London-trained Minister of Finance might see as a culture shock, and a rude awakening of some sort. She had tried valiantly to do the right thing, acting to safeguard tax payers' and Federal Government's interests in rejecting an incomplete, perhaps, fraudulent account from NNPC; the goose that lays the golden egg for us all. Tried as she might, it looks as if the "deep state" clipped the Minister's wings, she took a bow, and life goes on.

What about the House of Representatives' probe of the unremitted funds announced two weeks earlier? NNPC had remitted N127 billion instead of 147 in (monthly) royalties and Petrol Profit Tax (PPT). A total of N668.898 billion was released by the FAAC across the three tiers of government made up of statutory distributable N575.475 billion, and N93.423 billion from VAT.[62] Besides, oil producing states collected their 13% derivatives, while revenue generating agencies collected some N15 billion. I have put up all these figures to highlight what was at stake in the "standoff" between NNPC and FAAC and how the former had held the latter pretty much to ransom, forcing the Honourable Minister of Finance to blink first. In her earlier show of defiance, the Minister of Finance was seen batting for Nigerians; the silent majority in the stake. She escalated and elevated the issue of public finance and accountability to the right and appropriate level, where it should have resulted in someone falling on their sword. But things do not work like that in our country, just yet. State governors gave their backing to the stance taken by the Minister, ordering

---

62. See; "FAAC gives in to pressure, disburses N668bn from federation account" https://www.thecapital.ng/faac-gives-in-to-pressure-disburses-n668bn-from-federation -account

their commissioners of finance to stand their ground. The same governors then went back to Aso Rock, behind the back of the Minister to lobby the President to prevail on the Minister to back off and let the funds flow. Why? Because they, the governors, started taking flak from civil servants in their states for the delay in paying their salaries. Meanwhile, the 'big boys' at the NNPC were having belly laughs at the expense of the Minister of Finance and wondering how much longer she could hold out. Lo and behold, it did not take very long. The next meeting of the FAAC called by Adeosun to review the situation was more or less boycotted, leaving the Minister a lonely figure inside the FAAC, at which point she threw in the towel; calling off the boxing match, NNPC having thrown the knockout punch on FAAC and its Chair, Mrs Kemi Adeosun. The very next day, the announcement came that the bounty from NNPC would be shared as presented after all. This is "to cushion the hardship being experienced by civil servants in many states of the country", according to the statement released by the Federal Government. "Efforts are being made to address the unsatisfactory remittances", the statement concluded.

If the Honourable Minister of Finance and her team find my dig at them in this write up slightly unfair, it is not without justification. Former Governor of Central Bank of Nigeria tried in vain to 'expose' the leakage and diversion of funds in the NNPC, what happened to him? He was vilified and derided for not getting his sums right. Current Minister of State for Petroleum Resources, Dr Ibe Kachikwu, took it upon himself to 'cleanse' the corporation of waste and leakages, what happened to him? He was removed from his position as Group General Manager, and placed in a ceremonial role of Minister of State in the department. The Minister of Finance is thus in good company although, she is unlikely to return as Minister of Finance in the next round of ministerial appointments.[63] We are suffering in this country from the classic effect of the "Third World Syndrome", where individual characters in a lopsided government bureaucracy routinely find themselves drowned out, or worse, thrown under the bus the moment they raise their heads above the parapet. The Minister of Finance was left to fight a lone battle against the attitude of "business as usual" inside the NNPC, she lost. While she will not be remembered for being the one who finally lanced the boil in the continuing wastage and pilfering of the federation account in this country, she will be remembered for

---

63. The Minister of Finance was indeed forced out of government a few months after her showdown with the FAAC over an allegation that the certificate which purportedly gave her an exemption from the mandatory National Youth Service Corps programme upon graduation from university was 'forged'. See; "Kemi Adeosun: Minister resigns over forged certificate" https://www.bbc.com/news/world-africa-45535075

1 · ECONOMY

at least trying. That is already more than can be said of the majority of her fellow ministers in the current Federal Executive Council.

1.16 High Inflation as a By-Product of High-Level Corruption

21 August 2018

Figures released by the National Bureau of Statistics (NBS) last week show inflation at 11.14% in Africa's largest economy.[64] The inflation rate represents both a drop and an increase, depending on how one looks at it. Taken from the Consumer Price Index (we will come to that later), year-on-year, it is an increase for July 2018 because it is 0.09% less than the rate received in June 2018 (11.23%). However, looking at it across the last eighteen consecutive months, it represents a drop in "headline inflation" year-on-year. "Headline inflation" represents raw inflation figures supplied to the NBS on a number of goods and services every month, reflecting everyday reality of citizens. With throngs of people in huge markets at Obalende (Lagos), Oshodi (Lagos), Mushin (Lagos), Aba (Delta), Onitsha (Imo), Port Harcourt (Rivers), and most state capitals up and down the country, how does the NBS collate inflation figures from these venues? Surely, not by word of mouth. How many "mystery shoppers" do they deploy to the markets for their findings? Inflation figures must be, and are indeed rooted in real life experience of citizens to make it meaningful.

Well, NBS recruits thousands of "informants" on a regular basis, covering every nook and cranny of the Nigerian economic activity, hand them a basket each, and send them out shopping, quite literally. These foot soldiers then provide the organisation with real price data for computation. For a good measure, the "informants" are given a list of the items within which to do their shopping (by the way, with the juicy and pricey perks on offer, would you not wish to be one?). The list of the assorted items currently runs into more than seven hundred on the market. It is the aggregation of figures from these that gives the NBS the Consumer Price Index, or CPI, as it is commonly referred to. So much then for "headline inflation". It is one that grabs the headlines, so to speak; the one that encapsulates everything. It is to be distinguished from "core

---

64. After hedging upward and downward in the last couple of years, inflation rate is now 15.60% according to the federal bureau of statistics as of, February 2022 https://www.nigerianstat.gov.ng

inflation". This is derived from the same figures minus the prices of food and energy (oil and gas), as these are thought to be too volatile to be reliable. They are too prone to sudden reversals and the odd jitters. Let us not join issues with economists down the ages, who argue over which set of figures really reflect the true cost of living at any given period. These figures are analysed from the premise of economic theories, sampling techniques and other statistical assumptions to arrive at differing conclusions and prognosis. That is not the purpose of this piece.

Our purpose is to take the debate away from economists and market analysts for a moment, and do a reality check. We want to see how far the debate about inflation figures and their consequences in this country mask a larger truth about the hidden self-interest of the rich and powerful. For instance, the highest increases, according to the NBS, were reported in the prices of medical services, household furniture, vehicle spare parts, domestic services, pharmaceutical products, paramedical services, hairdressing saloons and personal grooming, motor cars, etc. These are all elite-driven consumer items; imported inflation from foreign lands. Their penchant for foreign consumer products helps maintain the country's inflationary figures at a ridiculously high level for the rest of society. Furthermore, when, as expected, inflation begins to creep up again in the run up to the 2019 elections, the economists and pundits will still be arguing over numbers, while we know that politicians and their business backers would have pumped a lot of money into the economy for the sole purpose of buying votes in order to either get into power or for its retention. In addition, if you are a home owner with landed properties all over the place (the exclusive preserve of the urban metropolitan elites), your interest is in keeping inflation up, not down, because it adds to the value of those properties. The paradox is that inflation erodes the value of money in the pockets of ordinary citizens. They need more money to buy fewer goods, and with no corresponding rise in wages, and paltry (or non-existent pension) payments for the retirees, a whole load of people become trapped inside poverty and looking up to God for a miracle.

If you have ever wondered why our level of inflation remains stubbornly high in this country, the above are some (not all) of the reasons. Why would inflation be kept at 2.9% in the USA, 2.7% in the UK, and 2.6% in France, and we rejoice at inflation recording almost 12% in Nigeria? Ok, those are figures from the advanced economies of the West, you might say. What about Brazil 2.76%, India 4.2%, and Malaysia 3.8%? These are the economies with which we like to be compared after all. And how about continental Africa? In Ghana, current inflation stands at 9.6%, South Africa 4.4%, Morocco 2.5%, and Tunisia 3.7%, all in single digits. Let me say, at this juncture, that a little inflation in any economy is not a bad thing. You need to encourage people to do some spending in order to stimulate growth and create employment. The opposite of inflation is deflation, which is just as bad as having a high rate of inflation. In a situation of deflation, people are reluctant to buy at today's prices, in the hope that current prices will go down further tomorrow, and the day after. Supply of goods and services gradually outstrips demand, leading eventually to stagnation and recession. It is a more difficult logjam to disentangle an economy from, as experienced by Japan in the 1980s.

To control inflation governments have to impose taxes, but not too much as to discourage investment. They also need to push up their interest rates to curb the level of money in circulation. The tragedy for us in Nigeria is that our government is taking both of these highly necessary measures. At the same time, both of these measures equally need to go precisely in the opposite direction to enhance an inclusive economic policy. The question, as always, is knowing where to draw the line; getting the balance right. At the moment, the Central Bank of Nigeria is intensely focused on curbing imported-driven, elite-backed, inflationary pressures underlined by their taste and lifestyle, by maintaining a high interest rate—to curb the amount of money in circulation. The high interest rate policy, by consequence, bites hard on the poor, propertyless citizens denied access to credit as a result. Anytime you hear the CBN banging on about issuance of treasury bills, floating of bonds etc. to attract investors, it attracts high interest rates as well. The same government then borrows from banks at high rates of interest, which then has a domino effect on every petty trader and local industry up and down the country. An economy run only for the interest of capital and kept in tow by corrupt influences, cannot endure.

1.17 Nigerian Workers Deserve Living (Not Minimum) Wage

13 November 2018

With Labour's agitation for an increase in the minimum wage well and truly thrust unto the top end of political discourse in this country for the umpteenth time, coming on the heels of the threat of a nation-wide strike on the issue, it is only appropriate, therefore, that this column finds space for an informed opinion on the hottest political issue of the day, especially as it is set to be embroiled in Presidential politics in the election cycle. It has probably been timed by union leaders to fall into such, as it is a rare opportunity to catch the Buhari administration on the back foot, and to hold their feet to the fire. Outside the

48   1 · ECONOMY

election cycle, it might not command as much attention as it currently does. More so, potential negative consequences of an unresolved labour dispute could spell trouble for the ruling party, hence, the heightened desire on the employer (government) to settle. Figures (20–65 thousand naira) have been bandied about on the right level for the national minimum wage, which is described as a wage below which no one should fall: "a price floor below which workers may not yield their labour" if section 34 of the 1999 Nigerian constitution is anything to go by. This was recently emphasised by Labour Minister, Chris Ngige, thus: "The intendment of the minimum wage therefore is not about uniformity to hold back rich states or members of the private sector who have resources to pay higher from doing so ..." This column would strongly argue that the ideal of a minimum wage for workers has never been founded on economics, since it is the anti-thesis of the free market, yet every industrial nation on earth has enacted legislation to incorporate one. What makes it so compelling?

The answer is wrapped in a combination of history and society's primordial need for self-preservation. It is the one drag on "free market" economics enthusiastically embraced even by the most vociferous proponent of the philosophy anywhere. Minimum wage, as it happens, is too important to be left to market forces and the corrective "invisible hand" of the market. You find people debating its level, here and there, and everywhere, but no serious analyst or public servant questions its basis, its ideal or raison d'être, anywhere. The reason for this, above all else, is history. Karl Marx (1818–1883), the greatest revolutionary theorist of the 19th century, in his observation of the conditions of wage labourers, artisans and the skilled working class in European factories, and England in particular, concluded that the world economy is divided between the owners of capital and those offering their labour. Furthermore, that the wages being offered by owners of capital bear no reflection to the true value of labour. Owners of capital are fixated on exploiting the surplus value of workers to accumulate capital for re-investment. The more workers put in for their employers, the less benefit they derive in fact from the attendant growth, but they have no choice, but to continue toiling since they, themselves, do not have access to capital ownership or its control. According to Marx, history tells us though, that this exploitative relationship cannot last for ever before there is a violent revolution between capital and labour, of which labour will be triumphant. This has been divinely (historically) ordained. It is a matter of when, not if, it happens.

The above would have been dismissed as another Ivory Tower conjecture from a busy-body middle-class intellectual propounding and joggling unrealistic theories of society in the air, but for the fact that a mode of

1 · ECONOMY

reasoning; Marxism, emerged from it and was the basis of the "Peasant" (Bolshevik) revolution in Russia in 1917, and subsequent copycat workers' revolution around the developing world (Cuba's Castrol 1959–2016), Provisionary Revolutionary Government of the Republic of South Vietnam 1969–1976), People's Revolutionary Government, Grenada (1979–1983), Ethiopia and the "Marxist-Leninist Derg" (1974–1991) Samora Machel in Mozambique (1975–1986), to name but a few. Fearing the worst, Western capitalist nations responded after World War II by embracing workers' rights and incorporating union leaders into the apparatus of government in their respective domains. That has remained the consensus ever since; evolution, yes please. Revolution? No, thank you, not in our own backyard. All sorts of employment rights and protection in the workplace became the norm rather than the exception. The Marxist's dream of a worker's revolt across the world has since been blunted and reduced to negotiation over wage demands, welfare provision and strike action seen as the last resort. That is the genesis of the perennial minimum wage debate we often witness here and elsewhere.

Minimum wage, of itself, is a highly misleading concept. It creates the impression that minimum standard of living is being taken account of. Nothing could be further from the truth. A minimum wage that is applied across the board regardless of location is at best arbitrary, and at worst, punitive. If, for instance, a minimum wage is set at 30,000 to be applied nationally, how does that reflect the cost of living of a worker living in, say, Lagos, compared to one living in, say, Ohafia, Abia State? Or, Damaturu, Yobe State? How far would a 30,000 naira minimum wage take you in Lagos for one month when the cost of transportation alone will almost gobble up all you have? Minimum wage does not offer a means for addressing the real living wage crisis in this country, when the state has neglected responsibility in providing basic amenities such as public transport, health, schooling, road infrastructure, personal security, all of which have a bearing on the take home pay. Minimum wage becomes a con and a trick on our collective conscience. Union leaders make rabble-rousing speeches in an election cycle; they threaten fire and brimstone on the ruling party, then, get their long-awaited invites to government circles for 'talks'. They soon emerge from a protracted negotiation to claim 'victory' for having secured an increase to the minimum wage. You see, these union leaders are part of the ruling clique themselves for, living wage, not minimum wage is where the real battle line should be drawn, and they know it.

A minimum wage that is left dangling on its own, without being contingent upon anything else is nothing but a chimera. If union leaders are lacking in courage to fight for a living wage, let them at least peg whatever minimum wage they agree with the government on the consumer price index for example, so they both rise in tandem. Otherwise, we will be back again to resume this 'fight' in a couple of years' time. As far as the Federal Government is concerned, they have done a good job of outmanoeuvring the union leaders. Any government doling out fifteen million naira net, (monthly take home pay) for its legislators, and managed to pin down union leaders to thirty thousand naira net, (monthly take home pay) for workers in this country has struck the bargain of the century. It will take ten years for an average worker to earn what a Senator of the Federal Republic of Nigeria takes home in one month without breaking sweat. It is no wonder President Muhammadu Buhari cannot wait to sign the accord into law even before the dust settles.

1.18 When a Country's Debt Becomes a 'Crisis'

30 April 2019

At the meeting of the "Bretton Woods" (IMF and the World Bank) Institutions' group meeting in Washington DC last week, it was revealed that Nigeria's fiscal deficit (the Federal Government funding gap) now stands at a staggering 4.62 trillion naira, or $USD 12 billion.[65] I say staggering because it was not too long ago, during the last year of President Olusegun Obasanjo, in 2007, that Nigeria was running a mere 0.5 trillion naira deficit, representing 2.9% of the GDP (Gross Domestic Product). Now, as of today, the Federal Government deficit at 4.2 trillion represents close to 20% of the country's GDP. But, wait a minute, the Honourable Minister of Finance, Mrs Zainab Ahmed, hurriedly issued a statement saying: "Nigeria not in debt crisis" — yet, one would suppose. Yes, going by the immutable laws of financial economics, we still have little room for manoeuvre in fact. We can still push our deficit spending up to 25% of the GDP before the Bretton Woods institutions start panicking. Ever wondered why these foreign (mainly Western) bodies seem more concerned about our debts than we are?

Just think about this. If a bank lends a roadside vendor one thousand naira and he is unable to pay it back at the agreed time, he will be in trouble, because he risks having the whole of his merchandise confiscated by the bank to cover the debt. Now, if the same bank lends the same customer 1million naira in exactly the same condition, and is unable to pay, who do you imagine would be in trouble? If you get that logic, then, you understand why the IMF, World

---

65. See; https://www.businessamlive.com/fg-recorded-n4-62tn-fiscal-deficit-in-2019-cbn

1 · ECONOMY

Bank and other international financial houses break out in cold sweat at the news of Nigeria's high debt profile. You will also understand why IMF is keen on Nigeria to withdraw petrol subsidy as it provides avenue for a perpetual drain on Federal Government resources, thereby increasing our propensity to borrow even more. 'Pile up debts for the generations yet unborn, if you like, but, do not go so far as to put at risk the money we have put into your crappy economy' appears to be what they are really trying to tell us, is it not? Makes sense if you buy into the logic. So many other things around the debt issue, however, make much less sense.

The average annual salary of a newly qualified professional (lawyer, accountant, lecturer, etc.) in this country is around 1million naira a year. Compare that to the Nigerian Senator's monthly take home pay of 15 million naira,[66] many of whose highest educational attainment is a secondary school leaving certificate or even less. To fully appreciate the meaning of "Nigeria not in debt crisis", imagine that our average professional in this country is having to spend 200,000 naira more than his annual take home pay of 1million, (20% of his annual disposable income), just to make ends meet. He does this by borrowing, with no prospect of augmenting his take home pay through any other means. He is then advised to borrow even more, to a higher level, say, 250,000 naira, (25% of his annual disposable income). It would be tempting fate to imagine that this particular professional would refrain from stealing from the public purse if given a chance. And, in a situation like this, would YOU take an easy bribe if that came your way? Just wondering. The professional's predicament is analogous to the situation we find ourselves in as a country in respect to the deficit. The Federal Government's funding gap has become chronic. How much is too much? When is a budget 'crisis' not a crisis?

Imagine further that the hapless professional still finds it harder to lead a regular life with his family and is advised to borrow 500,000 (representing 50% of his annual take home pay) or, even higher borrowing of 1million naira, extending to 100% of his annual take home pay. What happens to him and his household? He, at this point, would have fallen into a trap; the debt trap as it is called in the world of finance. Well, as bizarre as the picture we are painting here looks, many countries around the world are actually doing just that. China's funding gap, for instance, is equivalent to 50% of its GDP, South Africa 57%, India 70%, UK 87% Brazil 88%, and USA 106%. It gets worse; Italy's funding gap runs currently at 131% of its GDP, Portugal 124%, and Greece

---

66. See "Nigerian Senator Salary Calculator: How do you compare"? BBC April 1 2018 https://www.bbc.com/news/world-africa-43516825

52   1 · ECONOMY

176%.[67] Based on this, you might say Nigeria is in good company, right? Why can't we just take more loans from whomsoever is willing to lend us? Economists and disciples of Keynesian economics call it "deficit finance". The problem is more foreign borrowing means less ability to control our own economic destiny, as the terms for servicing the debt are fixed by the lenders. Making a switch to domestic borrowing would not make that any easier as it would lead to high interest rates. Interest rates for domestic manufacturers are already crippling enough. Print more money? Well, in theory yes, but in practice, it leads to a loss of value of the currency. There are many other measures such as compelling banks to increase their reserve for the benefit of CBN, but none of those offer any easy fix.

How do countries like Portugal, Italy and Greece get away with running such high deficits without pronouncing a 'crisis' in those countries? The simple answer is that they are part of the Euro-Zone of the European Union with substantial access to trade and investment. Moreover, the European Central Bank is committed to their survival. It has to. This is not to mention the political "project" of the European Union which envisages "an ever closer union" of the member states. What about China, South Africa, India, Brazil, UK, etc. running high deficits without pronouncing a 'crisis'? These are essentially industrialised countries with products to build and sell to the outside world. As long as they have regular orders on their books, and the cash flow situation looks healthy, bingo! In other words, it is not the amount a country owes that constitutes a crisis; it is the ability to service the debt that is key. Your funding gap can be as low as 5% in an economic cycle and you find yourself in 'crisis', while another country can run a deficit of up to 100% of their GDP and still finds itself bankable. Consequently, for our finance minister to simply look at the relatively low funding gap and concludes as some economists do, that we can still borrow even more, is foolhardy to say the least. South Africa's funding gap at 57% is cushioned by its reliance on its strong industrial and manufacturing base. It is the most advanced economy in Africa. Same goes for India, Brazil etc.

Nigeria's main earning from export is oil (86%),[68] the price of which it has no control over, 75% of the country's national budget goes on revenue.[69] Borrowing for investment is one thing, but borrowing for revenue is quite another.

---

67. See; Funding gap, country ranking; https://www.oecd-ilibrary.org/sites/6ea613f4 -en/index.html?itemId=/content/component/6ea613f4-en

68. See; "Oil accounts for 10% of GDP, 86% of export earning", 'The Guardian', August 9 2021 https://guardian.ng/news/oil-accounts-for-10-gdp-86-export-earnings-sylva

69. See; "Nigeria's 2022 budget highlights", PWC publications, 2022 https://www.pwc.com /ng/en/publications/budget.html

The projection for the future is one of more external borrowing through issuing of bonds, money from the World Bank, China and African Development Bank. It is not a free lunch. We have an insatiable appetite for borrowing which can only be quenched by producing and consuming what we need locally rather than incessant imports. Nigeria's funding gap has reached a crisis point. It is only a matter of time before the IMF makes that official. The operative word, for now, is that it is "unsustainable". Nonetheless, the crisis is staring us all in the face, except for our Minister of Finance.

1.19 Why Companies Go Public (I)

19 November 2019

This column initially started as a weekly commentary on financial and economic law, but has since taken liberty to digress unto other areas to take issue with diverse public policy discourse as it arises. Last week's write-up, for instance, took up the "sex for marks" controversy in higher institutions by asking whether academics ought to be moral agents in any circumstances. We shall continue to lend this space to air pressing issues of national significance, but from time to time, return to the theme of finance, economy and the law as it happens.

So, this week and next week's topics are an attempt to bring a dry area of economic law into common parlance. That is the issue of why a hitherto private limited company (LTD), would choose to transform itself into a 'public' company, known as "Public Limited Company" (PLC). Why would a thriving family-owned company designed for passing on to the next generation suddenly opt for a structure which kicks its doors open for Joe public to come and acquire a portion of it, and effectively become its part owner?

Part ownership of large corporations is as simple as buying a portion of their shares in the market. In fact, you can even find yourself sitting on the board of such corporations from nowhere if the percentage of your purchase is significant enough. You do not have to know anything about business, or the intricate details of financial markets either. All you need to have is money, or "capital" as it is called and the company would happily sell a portion of itself to you, and give you regular updates on its performance and future activities, plus a yearly return on the company's profit (also known as dividend) for as long as you maintain your shares; money begets money. You are in effect, a risk taker. The "City" loves and wants more of you. They would pay you handsomely for doing nothing because when it rains, a substantial portion of your money is turned into an umbrella for them. Both parties hope for long-lasting sunny days, however.[70]

The process of going public is called floating or "Initial Public Offering" (IPO). A company would go to the Nigerian Stock Exchange, for example, to seek advice and find someone who will help place their shares in the hands of investors. In other words, you, and many other 'loaded' individuals inside or outside the country. These shares are known as "securities", not to be confused for the word security. The biggest of such IPOs is about to happen with the most profitable company in the world: Saudi Arabia's Aramco. More about that is in part two of this essay.

The stock exchange exists to channel money into businesses, which in turn, is used to generate profits for companies, who will then re-invest in other companies and ventures. It is the machine for allocating capital. It is where floating takes place, but it can also be on a similar exchange in other countries like South Africa, the United States (New York), the United Kingdom (London), Hong Kong, Japan etc. Companies' listing on the stock exchange area is a mix of different nationalities and origins. You need a nominated adviser (or nomad) and your success will depend on the prospect of your company. A company valuation is not a function of how much assets it actually owns; it is a function of how much the public thinks it is worth. If, for instance, you created a company in which you only have N1m worth of assets and the investing public thinks it is worth N1bn, then, that is what it is when you float. On the other hand, a company would not float if the owners think it is worth several billions of naira, and the public only thinks it is worth only a fraction of that. It is better for a company to be a little undervalued, than to be seriously overvalued prior to going public. That is the state of the market; it is outside the company's control. It is the job of the NSE to attract (not force) companies to list on the exchange in order to attract investors to buy shares in them. The exchange thrives by having multiple buyers and sellers doing the rounds in order to enhance its own reputation. There is no guarantee any company on its books will do well, as it is not within its competence. The buying public makes that decision.

The crucial thing for the NSE, in conjunction with the Securities and Exchange Commission, is to ensure up-to-date information in the form of a prospectus (particulars) of the company desirous of going public. It is also important to ensure a level playing field by stamping on any attempt to use "inside information" (not available to the public) for the advantage of an individual investor. It is not

---

70. See the popular and highly influential, easy-to-read, jargon-free book; "All you need to know about the City" by Christopher Stoakes, Longtail, 2012. First published in 2005, it is still in print.

1 · ECONOMY

too long ago when several Nigerian banks collapsed and their managements accused of insider dealing: Intercontinental and Union Banks were two prominent examples. The top managements of these banks were accused of, and indeed found guilty of trading in their own shares for the sole purpose of manipulating the market into believing that they were more profitable than they actually were. This led to an overvaluation of their share prices on the exchange, leading to the eventual collapse of those shares when the truth came out. Meanwhile, individuals within those banks had made a "quick killing" in the markets before the rest of the worthless shares were dumped on the unsuspecting public. The cases are still being tried in court over a decade later.

Transparency and a level playing field are two key demands of the NSE and SEC. There is absolutely no compromise on these. That is the main essence of the two financial regulators. "Insider" knowledge comes either in the form of information, which enables the person to gain an advantage or to avoid a loss. For instance, let us assume a board member of a medium-sized oil company in Warri whose engineers had just reported the discovery of massive crude deposits deep inside the forest in Zambezi, quickly passed on the information to his associate who then bought a huge amount of the company's shares at the current price. The company later published its engineers' report in its annual submission to the authorities, creating an instantaneous positive reaction from the market. The company's shares then, quadrupled on the back of the announcement, making the board member a fortune. That is a crime.

On the other hand, say, a top government functionary working inside the Presidency overheard an important information at the meeting of the Federal Executive Council where a decision had been made to ban the importation of all foreign-made motorbikes. He then passed that information to a friend of his with a substantial investment in foreign-made motorbikes. The friend then quickly sold off his shares before the government announced the ban as envisaged by the insider. The industry's share price then took a tumble resulting in an almost total wipe out. The one who got out in time, of course, saved his own bacon. Others go home licking their wound. That too, is a crime.

1.20 Why Companies Go Public (II)

26 November 2019

As pointed out last week, there are several reasons why a company might want to 'go public'. First and most obvious is to raise capital for investment. Second, a company might go on the list to expand its operations. Third, a company might go on the list for prestige and added visibility. Fourth, going public might be an effective exit route for the company's initial investor: the venture capital providers. Lastly, listed shares have an immediate value, an immediate price at which they can be sold, for instance, in a Mergers and Acquisition scenario. Ideally, before floatation takes place, the company finds a "sponsor" or "sponsors" who propose it to the exchange. Then, the services of a broker are engaged to put together a prospectus, which contains detailed financial information of the company, and it is periodically updated every three months. The corporate broker acts as the interface between the company and the shareholders. Then, the additional team of "receiving bankers", reporting accountants and lawyers complement the squad. Any offer to the public, IPO, requires a prospectus.

Aramco is currently the world's most profitable company and is scheduled to go public next month. It will list on the Riyadh Stock Exchange as the world's biggest IPO ever. It has hired 25 'bookrunners', banks with specialist knowledge of markets. The banks will arrange and take orders for the issue of shares. Between two and three banks normally do that. The global record for bookrunners for an IPO is currently held by the Postal Savings Bank of China, which listed in 2016 with twenty-six banks. Banks that get involved in these things not only earn millions of dollars in fees, but they also get a big boost to their standing.

Aramco is Saudi Arabia's equivalent of the Nigerian National Petroleum Company. It is currently worth an estimated $1.2tn. It is half of the whole of Africa's GDP combined. It gives us the scale of the capital involved here. Some (internal) estimates even value the company a lot higher, like $2tn. Like the NNPC, the company is state-owned, and owes its origins to the groundwork of Chevron back in the 1930s. A deal was struck in 1933 between Saudi Arabia and Standard Oil Company of California, now commonly known as Chevron, to survey and drill for oil. A new firm (Aramco) was created to push the proceeds onto the market. As the Arab-Israeli conflict got under way in 1973, production and supply of oil became precarious and of strategic importance to governments around the world, so, Saudi Arabia decided to buy up the entire company. The country, as many would know, has the biggest oil reserves after Venezuela. It is the second largest producer of oil after the US. So, Aramco is super big, super rich. It is the world's largest unquoted (i.e. unlisted) company. Who would not want to own a piece of this company, I wonder? It generated $46.9bn net profit in the first half of 2019 alone. Almost all was paid out in dividends to its shareholder, the Saudi state. By contrast, Apple, the world's largest company by value, posted a net profit of a 'mere' $21.6bn. And, Exxon Mobil, the largest listed oil company, posted a 'meagre' $5.5bn.

1 · ECONOMY

At the moment, the company has no plans for foreign shares listing. "For the international listing part, we will let you know in due course", said Aramco Chair, Yasir al-Rumayyan, last week. The proposed listing has been hailed as "historic" for the world's "most reliable" oil company. This is hugely important to us in Nigeria because of the country's long and enduring ties with Saudi Arabia and because of the investment potential the oil industry here can attract from Aramco. Nigeria is Africa's largest producer of crude oil, but despite having dozens of highly qualified petroleum engineers and other technical know-how in the field, it still relies on importation of refined oil for domestic consumption. Nigeria can produce, but lacks almost any capacity to refine. This is surely not for want of expertise, but for misplaced priority. Anyway, that is another debate for another time.

Suffice it to say that what happens to Aramco interests us in Nigeria, as we desperately need someone to invest in the industry if only to help generate local capacity, and 'indigenise' oil production. But, the immediate question on many people's minds is why Aramco is interested in going public. It is not struggling for capital, surely? It is equally hard to imagine the company going public for prestige and visibility since it continues to sit on its own special pot of gold in the sandy oil fields of Saudi Arabia. My guess is that this is the first IPO done for political/strategic calculations, as opposed to pure economic logic.

Saudi Arabia is currently being run by a restless and fiercely ambitious Crown Prince Mohammed bin Salman, a man in his mid-30s, anxious to re-cast the image of the Kingdom as fuddy-duddy, archaic, Islamised and repressed, to one full of vibrancy and optimism. The dastardly murder of a major critic of the Kingdom, the Saudi journalist, Jamal Khashoggi, last year by Saudi secret agents in Turkey,[71] represents a huge blow to the Crown Prince's ambitions. The country has since embarked upon a continuous damage limitation exercise with a whole range of initiatives to deflect attention away from the heinous crime, which (except for Nigeria) has been universally condemned.

Furthermore, unlike Nigeria, Saudi Arabia can see a long term decline in demand for fossil fuel and a steady rise in alternative (renewable) energy sources. So, it makes sense to begin the process of diversification from crude oil while it can afford to do so. Any major diversification from fossil fuel will

---

71. On October 2 2018, Jamal Khashoggi, a US-based journalist and critic of Saudi Arabia's government, walked into the Saudi consulate in Istanbul, Turkey, where he was murdered. For details see; https://www.bbc.com/news/world-europe-45812399#:~:text=On%202 %20October%202018%2C%20Jamal,remains%2C%20and%20who%20was%20responsible.

58   1 · ECONOMY

hasten the demise of the oil cartel, OPEC, of which Saudi Arabia plays a pivotal role. Saudi Arabia also wants to generate increase in tourism from around three per cent currently to about 10% of GDP by 2030.

Despite all this, the trouble with the IPO is still that Saudi Arabia is in the middle of, perhaps, the most visible trouble spot in the world. Only last month, in September, the oil fields of Abqaiq and Khurais, both owned by Aramco, were hit by a drone attack, blamed on Iran. Oil prices remain vulnerable and susceptible to spontaneous armed confrontations, capable of crippling supplies and creating uncertainty in the industry. This has to be a major concern for investors, but I do not think it is strong enough to deter them from buying up the shares for now at least. The Islamic State terror group in the region is in retreat, and Arab rebellion appears to be at its weakest in a decade. This is in addition to the fact that Saudi Arabia's oil is one of the cheapest to extract, as it is pretty close to the surface. So, the much heralded IPO will soon come to pass, but let us wonder and imagine in Africa, a situation where a single extractive company is empowered under the sovereign authority of a 'United States of Africa', to negotiate an IPO even for a fraction of the continent's mineral resources on behalf of all Africans. Imagine how much money that would bring into the coffers for our collective welfare. Mass poverty vanquished overnight. Imagine, that it could be the day Africa emphatically took charge of her own economic destiny; finally able to determine the prices for her resources. The world would eat at the feet of the continent when the day arrives. Let us keep dreaming of such a day.

1.21 Why Companies Go Bust

3 December 2019

In the last couple of weeks, we have explored the reasons why large corporations choose to go public rather than remaining as a private entity. We highlighted the on-going floating of the most profitable (unlisted) company in the world; Saudi Arabia's Aramco, with an estimated market value of close to $2tn[72] (almost two thirds of Africa's GDP combined).[73] Now, it would interest you to know that these large corporations also go bust, sometimes without

---

72. See; "Saudi Aramco's IPO is set to value the oil giant at up to 1.7 trillion" CNBC Nov 2019 https://www.cnbc.com/2019/11/17/saudi-aramco-ipo-set-to-value-company-up -to-1point7-trillion.html

73. Combined GDP for Africa is said to be $2.6 trillion. For a country-by-country breakdown of GDP in Africa, see; https://www.statista.com/statistics/1120999/gdp-of-african -countries-by-country

1 · ECONOMY

warning, irrespective of their profitability or market share. At the other end of the business spectrum, eight out of ten new businesses fail within eighteen months of operation according to Bloomberg.[74] That is a whopping 80% of businesses going bust long before they are able to properly set up their stalls. Although there is no such thing as 'too small to fail', there has been talk of some businesses being "too big to fail". This illogical economic rationale came to prominence in the wake of the 2008 financial meltdown, which started with the housing bubble in the US. Faced with the imminent catastrophic collapse of Lehman Brothers (Merchant bankers)[75] and AIG (Insurance giant),[76] the US Federal Reserve was presented with an impossible choice. Which of these two entities to rescue with taxpayer's dollars? Their response gave us the definition of "too big to fail" that others inside and outside the USA are still grappling with today.

The thought of government providing a safety net to a failing business is anathema to free market, and free enterprises. Tampering with the "invisible hand" of the market is asking for trouble at best, and at worst, it is anti-competition and a restraint on free trade. That being said, no market anywhere in the world is entirely free of government interference, indeed, direct intervention. It is not entirely wrong. Japanese economy would not have grown as dominant as it became in 'high tech' without government intervention; likewise Singapore, Malaysia, and the rest of the 'Asian Tiger economies'. More importantly, China rose from the ashes of Communism to become the second largest economy in the world, quite literally through government active participation in its 'command' economy. In Nigeria, as elsewhere in Africa, the free market dogma is one that has been foisted on the continent by the Washington-based International Monetary Fund but, it is one, I have to say, that has since been enthusiastically embraced by all. It is hard to see any in-coming government anywhere in Africa advocating anything other than privatisation, tax cut and deregulation. It is the new normal for the African; the new economic orthodoxy, whatever political party or ideological view they hold.

---

74. See; "bottom line of start-up failures". Bloomberg, 2002 https://www.bloomberg.com/news/articles/2002-03-03/the-bottom-line-on-startup-failures

75. See; "history credits Lehman Brothers' collapse for the 2008 financial crisis", Brookings, Sept. 2018 https://www.brookings.edu/research/history-credits-lehman-brothers-collapse-for-the-2008-financial-crisis-heres-why-that-narrative-is-wrong

76. For an illuminating take on both AIG and Lehman Brothers, see; Michael Grunwald, "the real truth about the wall street bailouts". 'Time' Sept 2014. https://time.com/3450110/aig-lehman

60 1 · ECONOMY

In this respect, the position of Nigeria's Asset Management Corporation of Nigeria (AMCON)[77] is a very curious one indeed. It exists to absorb and protect the assets of commercial institutions on the verge of collapse. Remember the "too big to fail" concept talked about earlier? In a lopsided, fragile economy such as Nigeria's, virtually any major corporation is too big to fail. It has left the country in an odious position of rescuing "distressed" banks and other industries with public (taxpayer) money, and putting them back into private hands once they become stress free. It is a special type of capitalism that welcomes public money at times of stress, and insists on privatisation at times of profits; socialising debt, while privatising wealth. This is exactly what the government denied to Lehman Brothers, the fourth largest investment bank in the US, when it was forced to apply for bankruptcy in 2008 after 158 years of operation. That, of course, led to the exodus of its clients and the contagion effect of that quickly spread to other corporations, who saw their shares plummet in quick succession. When it came to 'AIG', the insurance giant, the US government baulked at letting go, and decided it was indeed too big to fail. Congress appropriated $700bn dollars[78] to help shore up the company and a handful of others. Prior to this, in the UK, in 1995, a commodity trader on the Singaporean SIMEX platform built up an untenable 'position'[79] in respect of the future performance of the Japanese Nikkei 225. Things went horribly wrong for him, and he was forced to liquidate, leading to the collapse of Barings, the world's second oldest investment bank in operation since 1792.[80]

More recently, a couple of months ago, Thomas Cook, the world's largest travel agent founded in 1841 with billions of dollars' worth of assets, with an annual sale of $12bn, and almost 20 million customers worldwide, was forced to file for bankruptcy as it was unable to raise a mere $300 million dollars to stay afloat. It closed down 178 years after it started trading.[81] I am sure some

---

77. Supposedly created to: "be a key stabilising and revitalising tool established to revive the financial system by efficiently resolving the non-performing loan assets of the banks in the Nigerian economy". See; https://amcon.com.ng

78. See; "Congress approves $700 billion Wall Street bailout" 'The New York Times', Oct 2008 https://www.nytimcs.com/2008/10/03/business/worldbusiness/03iht-bailout .4.16679355.html

79. A "derivatives" strategy, but essentially gambling in common parlance.

80. See, Elliot Smith: "The Barings collapse 25 years on: What the industry learned after one man broke a bank", CNBC, Feb 2020 https://www.cnbc.com/2020/02/26/barings -collapse-25-years-on-what-the-industry-learned-after-one-man-broke-a-bank.html

81. For a fuller background account see; https://www.business-standard.com/article /international/178-yr-old-company-thomas-cook-files-for-bankruptcy-as-bailout-talks-fail -119092300156_1.html

1 · ECONOMY

readers are wondering why a company of that size and of that fame, looking to raise $300 million dollars could not find lenders. Pity it did not fall within the ambit of AMCON. The British did not wish to embrace the "too big to fail" concept even though the immediate consequences had to be catastrophic for any economy. The message it sent to other businesses is crystal clear; adapt or die. There is wisdom in that, surely. But, what the reader should know is this. There are only two types of money available to businesses: debt (loan from banks and other lenders), and equity (from the share-buying public). A business can be profitable with huge assets, and still go bust. Conversely, a business can be making losses and still stay in business. So, what went wrong for Thomas Cook, you may wonder?

In general, profit depends on whether your cost of production is less than the unit price on the market. How quickly do you have to meet those costs? Answer is, it does not really matter. It explains why a business may look rosy on paper, but finds itself running out of cash. For businesses, it is more important to have a robust cash flow than it is to make a profit. A business can remain unprofitable for years as long as it has a steady cash flow, who cares? Banks prefer lending to businesses with strong cash flow and marginal profitability than profitable businesses with lousy cash flow. Investors invest in future prospects more than considerations of today's visible problems. This is why businesses rely heavily on borrowing all the time. Borrowing is also good for another reason; it is tax deductible. Capital markets bridge the borrowing gaps for large corporations. Nigerian businesses, however, are in a twin dilemma. The capital market is not deep enough, not as strong as it might be, and bank interest rates are prohibitive (20, 30, 35% in many cases), because the banking industry in this country is effectively a monopoly run by the CBN. Interest rates in other countries are in single digits. Yes, we are not witnessing daily collapse of big businesses as a result of the government intervention, but the country's capacity is not getting stronger either. Economists describe Nigeria as an 'emerging' economy. It depends on what the country is emerging from. How long does it take to emerge from a straitjacket? And how many businesses need to go bust until then? It is a structural dilemma needing political leadership from the bottom up. Enough said for now though.

1.22 Nigeria's Unabated Stagflation: Why it Matters

9 February 2021

The latest figure on the rate of inflation released by the National Bureau of Statistics last month is a biting 15.75%,[82] the sixteenth straight rise in as many months. (Ghana 13.9%, South Africa 5.7%, Kenya 5.39%, Rwanda 1.3%).[83] Put simply, inflation is a rising cost of living measured by "Consumer Price Index", that is to say, a certain number of groceries taken from a stall in the market, and their prices checked to see how far up they have risen since the last exercise. More sophisticated measures are also used: headline inflation, underlying inflation and core inflation. No point delving into those. On the whole, inflation can either be one of three types: demand-pull, cost-push, or built-in. Nigeria suffers from all three, but mostly from the third. Conversely, Nigeria's economic growth forecast was 2.1% before the pandemic, but it has now fallen to 1.5% in 2021 and 2.9% in 2022.[84] That means very little or no money to fund government. Government revenues are expected to fall from 8% of GDP to 5% by the next financial year. Nigeria is neither producing nor selling goods. Eighty per cent of the country's exports come from oil,[85] the price of which is determined by "market forces". The chunks of the rest of exports are "Nollywood" and related products. When you have a combination of slow, (sluggish or zero) growth and high inflation, the result is stagnation plus inflation (better known as stagflation). Nigeria Plc is effectively bankrupt. This is what makes jostling for the Presidency in 2023 between APC and PDP largely an irrelevant sideshow. This stark economic reality will not only remain, it will endure. This needs not be, though. It is only so because of the choices we make; a long story, but not as complicated as you might think.

---

82. Based on Central Bank of Nigeria figures https://www.cbn.gov.ng/rates/inflrates.asp

83. For the exact figures on inflation rates in every African state up until December 2021 see; https://tradingeconomics.com/country-list/inflation%20rate?continent=africa

84. Growth projection for Nigeria by the African Development Bank for 2021 was 1.5% and 2.9% in 2022 https://www.afdb.org/en/countries-west-africa-nigeria/nigeria-economic-outlook. Compare this to the analysis done by Chukwuka Onyekwena and Mma Amara Ekeruche "Understanding the impact of the covid-19 outbreak on the Nigerian economy". Brookings, April, 2020 https://www.brookings.edu/blog/africa-in-focus/2020/04/08/understanding-the-impact-of-the-covid-19-outbreak-on-the-nigerian-economy

85. Oil and gas account for more than 91% of total exports according to reliable data https://www.afdb.org/en/countries-west-africa-nigeria/nigeria-economic-outlook

1 · ECONOMY

First, rising inflation might be a thoroughly bad thing for some, it is actually good news for many others. Most importantly, it is good news for homeowners, whose properties appreciate as a result. People in rented accommodation (majority of Nigerians) groan under any steep rise in rent and consumer goods; but landlords and property speculators smile all the way to the bank. Manufacturers also see a rise in cost of production, which is duly passed onto the buyer in terms of increased prices. However, since Nigeria does not generally produce what its citizens consume, it is the foreign manufacturers who benefit from any increase in prices. In other words, inflation is being imported into the country through the front door, literally. We import oil, (since we lack the capacity to refine crude oil) spare parts, electrical as well as electronic goods, generators, building materials, cosmetics, clothes, supermarket stocks, including toothpicks, even the national staple; "Indomie" is a foreign (Indonesia) import in case anyone was ever in doubt. Inflation is "structural" or "built-in" in that regard. In the post-World War II "Keynesian" economic consensus, government used to take it upon itself to "reflate" the economy, then, introduce "price control" to prevent steep rises. That worked superficially, and intermittently, but it created distortions in the operation of the market. The consensus was finally broken by the neo-conservative free-market Thatcher/Reagan "revolution" of the late 1970s/1980s. It is now (almost) universally accepted that you cannot 'buck' the market, even if you were an authoritarian regime capable of coercing citizens to push down prices. It will not work, and if it does, it is unsustainable.

This is where the story becomes rather interesting. How does government exercise 'control' over inflation given that the rates are, invariably, determined by the market? Well, that is done by applying the "monetary" tool of interest rate. Governments (through Central Banks) increase or decrease the cost of borrowing depending on their economic agenda and priorities. The dilemma for ordinary citizens in Nigeria is this. Cost of borrowing needs to be (almost) permanently kept high in order to avoid a run-away inflation. Rising cost of borrowing then becomes crippling for the small-scale business enterprise the country relies on to boost domestic capacity, hence the heavy reliance on oil exports. Who benefits? Of course, the multi-billionaire moneybags stashing away cash in high-interest-yielding bank accounts, which the banks invariably lend to government. Capital then moves significantly away from company equities into savings. Austerity (deep cuts in government spending) follows on the prodding of the IMF. This translates into a squeeze on the poor, and suppression of dissent. This is the vicious cycle of panic and paralysis that has remained the hallmark of the Nigerian economy for the last thirty years. But, why?

As will become clearer, Africa's largest economy (Nigeria) is being run, managed, and kept for the benefit of international capital. It is the classic anti-people economy, which works for the favoured few at the expense of the wretched many. Have you ever wondered why economic policy makers in this country are drawn exclusively from the ranks of bankers, accountants and economists? Finance Ministers and their economic teams, are usually "experts" from those sectors. This is not simply a reflection of our penchant for paper qualifications; it is what the IMF and other international finance houses insist and demand of us as a condition for continued "aid". Remember, Dr Okonjo-Iweala, a "technocrat" economist, was headhunted (begged, in plain language) to become Finance Minister under former Presidents Obasanjo and Jonathan. Juxtapose that with the current President of the European Central Bank, Madame Christine Lagarde, a lawyer, with no specific training in either finance or economics. She had also previously served as Managing Director of IMF (2011–2019). Current UK Minister of Finance, Rishi Sunak, graduated in politics, philosophy and economics (PPE), as a single honour degree. He would not be appointed even a deputy Finance Minister in Nigeria. His two predecessors in the same office from the previous administrations are history graduates, who would be nowhere near the treasury in Nigeria. Current US Deputy Treasury Secretary, Wale Adeyemo, is a lawyer. Former World Bank President, Paul Wolfowitz (2005–2007) is an American political scientist. I can go on, but you got the drift. There is a very important reason for this anomaly.

Questions of bread and butter, consumer items, imports, exports, salaries, employment and unemployment, etc. are not simply matters for economists and bankers crunching numbers and battling with monetary and fiscal policies; they are issues bordering on political power, and electoral mandate. Nonetheless, our Western financiers insist that those critical issues be kept away from the purview of politics. They insist that those we put in charge of the economy must be apolitical "technocrats" who would do nothing but run the economy at the behest of international capital. In their own terrain, however, the calculation is different. For them, the economy is too important to be left to economists. The top of economic and finance teams in their own yard are people with particular "leadership" skills not exclusively drawn from the ranks of economists alone. In this regard, people making economic policy must have a broad understanding of the economy, yes, but a special ability to make (politically sensitive), people-centred economic decisions. Economic policy must reflect political choices propagated and cemented at the polls. Technical details of policy and number crunching can, and is usually thrashed out by the highly paid, and highly educated civil servants below them.

Alas, Nigeria does not have the benefit of a highly trained, highly efficient, and corruption-free government bureaucracy through which economic policy could be filtered. Neither do we have credible elections; the ultimate weapon for democratic accountability. That, in a nutshell, explains the insistence on direct involvement of, and preference for "technocrats" in policy making in our country and continent. It is also why our economy continues to be run for, and on behalf of international capital. Long live stagflation!

Chapter Two

Finance/Capital Markets[86]

2.01 Sovereign Wealth Fund: Cui bono?

29 November 2013[87]

For those not familiar with it, "Cui bono" is the Latin equivalent for: Who stands to benefit? I use it in the title for precision; it also alludes to something that might be underhand or slightly dodgy beneath the surface. That said, in the next week or so, the House of Representatives' Committee on Finance, is set to "probe" the appointment of Goldman Sachs and UBS as managers of the country's Sovereign Wealth Fund, which currently stands at $1bn. The Nigeria Sovereign Investment Authority Bill became law in 2012. Thereafter, the Co-ordinating Minister for the economy and Minister of Finance, Dr Okonjo-Iweala, set up the management board of the newly established Nigerian Sovereign Investment Authority. Uche Orji was head-hunted from America to be its first Chief Executive Officer. He declared the fund a "major milestone" for Nigeria. The fund itself is sub-divided into: Future Generations Fund, Nigerian Infrastructure Fund and Stabilisation Fund. It is not clear whether they now permanently replace the Excess Crude Account into which excess revenues from oil are kept. This all sounds rather neat and savvy; so, what is

---

86. Writing about finance and capital markets in a jargon-free, yet technical language, is an art. Christopher Stoakes' masterpiece; "All you need to know about the City" Longtail, 2012, is one of its kind in this field. First published in 2005, the book has continued to prove its worth. His irreverent take on the 'City' has done much to unmask the masquerades behind the financial headlines and their modus operandi. This chapter owes much to the author both in style and substance.

87. Although the bulk of the essays selected for this book fall within the years 2016 and 2021, this particular one has been selected for inclusion due to the continued reference to it in media and academia.

there for the House of Representatives to "probe" so early in the day? And, why are several state governors grumbling about it? Clearly, the funds have been put beyond their reach, thereby strengthening the Executive by creating yet another power of financial patronage in the Presidency or, is there something potentially even more sinister in the air?

The SWF as a concept is as much a question of morality as it is of economics. The ideal of saving for the rainy day, "future generations" etc. is incontestable; more like apple pie and motherhood: who can possibly be against that? Although, it has been around for over 50 years, the SWF only recently became a cause célèbre amongst some resource-rich countries. The credit crunch of the last few years has heightened the awareness of it as well. The Pacific Island of Kiribati, for instance, established its funds some 50 years ago out of its guano exports. It has now amassed more than $400m. Norway's is about $400bn, Kuwait's SWF is close to $1tn. China, and Russia are also building up huge surpluses in their SWF. Australia and Canada are among a few developed economies involved in the scheme. The common thread that unites all of these SWF countries, however, is that they have genuine surpluses. Can we say the same of Nigeria? Are revenues from excess crude genuine surpluses or the quacks of fluctuations in the oil market? Besides, where is the morality in saving for a future generation when, for instance, teachers and university lecturers (responsible for training tomorrow's leaders) are poorly paid, and are often forced to undertake prolonged industrial actions for redress? University libraries and laboratories have become shells of their old selves across the country. Too many of our graduates come out of these institutions barely able to read and write; many of them remain unemployed and quite frankly, unemployable. In addition, with rampant poverty in the country at large, and life expectancy in Nigeria still only hovering around 50 years, where is the morality in sacrificing the future of today's (lost) generation in order to provide for the ones yet unborn?

Apart from the allure of saving for the "rainy day", other reasons why some nations build up surpluses in their SWF are political and strategic. The SWF is, in effect, a concealed state capitalism. It enables a sovereign state to build up surpluses to cherry-pick investment opportunities in strategic industries in other countries. This is precisely what China has done by holding more than $1tn of America's debts.[88] It explains why you often see American business leaders kow-towing to Chinese exigencies in the field of commerce. That is why, despite Western criticisms on "human rights", they appear to be falling over themselves to get into the Chinese market. America's debt problem largely orig-

---

88. See; "Major foreign holders of US Treasury securities as of January 2022" https://www.statista.com/statistics/246420/major-foreign-holders-of-us-treasury-debt

2 · FINANCE/CAPITAL MARKETS

inates from 'spending explosion' rather than inability to produce.[89] Where Africa trembles from negative comments from Washington, China is unruffled. Now, is Nigeria's SWF being built with a latent political edge to it? Are we looking around anywhere in Africa to invest the funds in strategic industries in, say, Congo DR, Angola, South Africa amongst others? It appears not. Yes, it is a good idea for Nigeria to join the ranks of SWF countries,[90] but really, so what?

Another important consideration is the choice of the fund managers; UBS and Goldman Sachs, both of which are household names in the world of international finance and investment, but is that, of itself, a sufficient criterion for their appointment? What is the rationale for this export of capital? The irony is that, these two financial powerhouses are no longer the paragon of financial virtue they once were. Goldman Sachs had to be bailed out to the tune of $10bn by the US government in 2008, an amount which was later returned.[91] The bank subsequently admitted to misleading investors and had to pay $550m in fine. Similarly, in 2008, UBS had to accept a Swiss government bailout; having suffered one of the heaviest losses from the US sub-prime crisis. As recently as two years ago, the bank also lost over $2bn from a shady deal by one of its employees.[92] Nigeria, and Africa in general, ought to stop fawning over these multinational financial houses for no reason other than their dominant presence. Is there no Nigerian, or African finance powerhouse worthy of such a lucrative contract? Are we such self-certified nonentities in the field of international finance, to be distrusted even by our own? Or, is there a deeper interest at play in the award of the contract in the first place? Has there been a full declaration of interest on the part of the entire staff of the NSIA, including the minister herself? Besides, in order to avoid the spectre of personnel feathering their own nest — either by omission or design — no member of the NSIA should be allowed to pursue employment, consultancy or other interests (directly or by proxy), with any of the fund managers now, and for at least three years after severing their engagement with the NSIA. This potential revolving door for palm-greasing at our expense should be clamped now.

Finally, a sovereign wealth fund contains one fundamental assumption; that the sovereign shall endure. What if, (God forbid), Nigeria fragments into sep-

---

89. See; James A. Dorn. "The Role of China in the US Debt Crisis", 'Cato Journal, Vol 33 No 1 (Winter 2013)' https://ciaotest.cc.columbia.edu/journals/cato/v33i1/f_0027418_26658.pdf

90. SWF countries by total assets: https://www.swfinstitute.org/fund-rankings/sovereign-wealth-fund

91. https://abcnews.go.com/Business/story?id=7341888&page=1

92. See; "How did UBS lose $2bn" https://www.bankinfosecurity.com/how-did-ubs-lose-2-billion-a-4064

arate regional entities tomorrow? In that unlikely, yet probable scenario, who takes custody of the fund? Is there a trust instrument attached to the fund that takes account of that? These questions are not simply the ramblings of a pesky policy analyst; they are questions that should be of interest to everyone, not least the peoples' elected representatives. The question, "Cui bono", should be ringing non-stop in their ears as they mull over the issue in the coming months.

2.02 FRCN, Corporate Governance and Regulatory Overreach (I)

10 January 2017

The Financial Reporting Council of Nigeria (FRCN) recently published its long-awaited National Code of Corporate Governance (NCCG)[93] applicable to both private and public businesses and corporations in Nigeria. Commencement date was October 2016, but its full implementation is still a subject of a legal tussle between the Council and Eko Hotels Limited ("Eko Hotels"), whose objection to the Council's remit is currently before the Court of Appeals. The company had successfully argued before a Federal High Court in Lagos, in 2014, that under section 77 of the FRCN Act, 2011, Eko Hotels is neither a publicly quoted nor a public interest company. In other words, FRCN has no right to subject "private companies that routinely file returns only with the Corporate Affairs Commission (CAC) and the Federal Inland Revenue Services" to the new NCCG. The Federal High Court agreed, and the appeal by the Council is now before the Court of Appeals. If successful, the NCCG will be mandatory for all private companies in Nigeria.[94] As for charitable and not-for-profit organisations, it will be "comply or justify", but it will not be mandatory for the public sector immediately until an executive directive is secured from the Federal Government. Basically, there is nothing novel about having codes of corporate governance. In fact most, if not all, regulatory industries in Nigeria already have their own bespoke corporate governance codes. What is new, however, is that this is the first time an integrated (mega) code

---

93. See; "Nigerian Code of Corporate Governance 2018 (NCCG 2018): Guidance and Template for Reporting Compliance". Financial Reporting Council of Nigeria, Federal Ministry of Industry, Trade and Investment. https://www.financialreportingcouncil.gov.ng /nigerian-code-of-corporate-governance-2018-nccg-2018-guidance-and-template-for -reporting-compliance

94. The NCCG has since become mandatory for both private and public companies in Nigeria.

2 · FINANCE/CAPITAL MARKETS

is being proposed that will supersede the existing local codes. The stakes, therefore, are rather high, and the attention devoted to that in this column in three instalments, serves to underline the fact.

First, what is this thing called "corporate governance"? Can the governmental structure (Executive, Legislature and Judiciary) be transposed unto corporations, with the Executive representing management, the Legislature representing shareholders, and the Judiciary representing the market? Can a set of codes be weaved together from these to create corporate governance? Before delving into this rather quirky thought any further, the reader's mind ought to be disabused of any notion that government or corporation can ever adequately mirror the other. Imagine, for example, Nigeria being one big corporation, and President Muhammadu Buhari serves as its Chief Executive Officer, then, imagine him having a Board (Senate and House of Representatives) pursuing interests that are diametrically opposed to that of the Chief Executive Officer; blocking his appointments to key positions in the company, issuing statements contradicting his executive directives, raising panels of enquiry to investigate important business deals, withholding credit facilities for mergers and acquisition, etc. How would such a company make progress, let alone profit? Now, imagine a corporation trying to mirror the governing structure of a representative government. Imagine asking the shareholders to debate a proposal to expand, or to retrench staff in a bid to remain solvent, the Chief Executive Officer seeking to elongate his term in office, shareholders routinely going to the press to denounce their own company on critical business issues, etc. There is a world-wide interest in corporate governance because of the recognition of the divergence between private companies and democratic governance. Second, it is also the recognition that business cannot continue as usual especially in the wake of the 2008 financial meltdown which saw scores of business closures and a real threat of a global depression. So how has the corporate governance debate manifested itself in this country and elsewhere?

The business of running a business has, for centuries, been intertwined with the idea of freedom and right to property in Western economies. It is an idea championed most succinctly by Adam Smith (1723–1790), the High Priest of laissez-faire economics, in his treatise; "The Wealth of Nations"[95] first published in 1776, after spending nearly a decade working on it. The wealth of nations, he asserts; 'depends on the individual exercising their God-given

---

95. See; R.H. Campbell, A.S. Skinner, W.B. Todd (Eds) ADAM SMITH. An Enquiry into the Nature and Causes of the Wealth of Nations. Liberty Classics/Oxford University Press, 1976. http://files.libertyfund.org/files/220/0141-02_Bk.pdf

72   2 · FINANCE/CAPITAL MARKETS

freedom to accumulate wealth, and companies and entities are the most potent vehicle for achieving this end'. Since people could establish and dissolve businesses at will, the guiding philosophical trend in the market place has been "mind your own business", and even more important, *caveat emptor* (known in general parlance as buyers beware). Government, essentially, needs to "hands off" and allow the ingenuity and entrepreneurial skills of the individual to thrive with minimal interference. This is thus the rock upon which businesses were founded in the industrialised West for centuries. The world has since gone through prosperity, recessions, and depressions at various intervals leading to searching questions being asked as to the raison d'être of business and the running of companies in particular. There was thought to be a need to make businesses more accountable for the way they conduct themselves, while at the same time maintaining the orthodoxy of neo-liberal economics in Western societies. This debate rumbled on, in the case of the United Kingdom, through the "Thatcher revolution" in 1979,[96] until a series of scandals engulfed a number of businesses and financial institutions in the late 1980s. Most notable of these were the collapse of the Bank of Credit and Commerce International (BCCI) in 1991, and the unseemly dealings of the late tycoon, Robert Maxwell,[97] in the management of a chain of companies 'owned' by him.

There have been several measures taken in individual jurisdictions aimed at imposing discipline on organs of corporations. These have been done through the mechanism of various company laws and other domestic legislation. Nigeria's Companies and Allied Matters Act 1990 (CAMA)[98] has introduced several measures along this line, building on other previous measures dating back to the Ordinance of 1912, 1917, 1922, to the Decree of 1968. In Britain, the first bold attempt at capturing these measures in a code of corporate governance happened with the "Corporate Governance Committee" set up in May 1991 by the UK's Financial Reporting Council, the Stock Exchange and the accountancy profession. The committee was chaired by Sir Adrian Cadbury, who headed the publication of the "Cadbury report" in 1992.[99] The report has since metamorphosed into the Organisation for Eco-

---

96. Mrs Margaret Thatcher was Prime Minister of the United Kingdom from 1979 to 1990.

97. Robert Maxwell was a prominent Labour Party Member of the UK Parliament, and a businessman.

98. See the full text of the Act via; http://www.placng.org/lawsofnigeria/laws/C20.pdf

99. For the original, full text of the report, see; Adrian Cadbury. Report of the Committee on the Financial Aspects of Corporate Governance, December, 1 1992 (The Committee on the Financial Aspects of Corporate Governance) Gee — A division of Professional Publishing Ltd, 1992. https://www.frc.org.uk/getattachment/9c19ea6f-bcc7-434c-b481-f2e29c1c271a/The-Financial-Aspects-of-Corporate-Governance-(the-Cadbury-Code).pdf

nomic Cooperation and Development (OECD)[100] code of corporate governance across Europe. It also provides the benchmark upon which Nigeria's own efforts are based.

2.03 FRCN, Corporate Governance and Regulatory Overreach (II)

17 January 2017

The Cadbury report makes it clear for the first time that issues pertaining to financial irregularities in companies, as well as misdemeanours of individuals at various layers of a company structure reach far beyond management; they touch on 'governance' in essence. But why was it necessary to develop the novel concept of governance in respect of companies, which are, in law, distinct and separate personalities? Legally speaking, a company is a person, separate and distinct from its subscribers (founders) and its shareholders: [Salomon v Salomon & Co Ltd (1897) AC 22].[101] People are familiar with stories of how Mr X owns company A, B, C, etc. This is only true in a generic sense; no one really owns an incorporated entity. It has a life of its own; it can sue and be sued, buy and sell properties, even be prosecuted in a criminal court. This, of course, is a legal fiction, but that is how it functions in corporate affairs. It underlines the genesis of a company's ability to roam free in the market place and within an economy, but that created its own snags: top personnel in a company could, literally, get away with murder since the offending act would have been committed by the faceless 'company'. Similarly, negligent actions of key personnel could be easily smoothed over even where that led to the company going bankrupt. After all, according to this legal fiction, everything could be done and hidden behind the 'distinct personality' of the company. This was the situation in global trade until the House of Lords (now the Supreme Court), decided in subsequent cases that the "veil of incorporation" just like the masquerade mask, could be lifted to see the face of the person behind it, especially in cases of fraud. The masquerade, in African folklore, is of the ancestral; revered and

---

100. See; F. Jesover and G. Kirkpatrick. The revised OECD Principles of Corporate Governance, 2005. https://www.oecd.org/corporate/ca/corporategovernanceprinciples /33977036.pdf

101. It is a landmark UK judgement which firmly upheld the doctrine of corporate personality as a separate legal entity and thus the shareholder cannot be personally liable for the insolvency of the company.

74   2 · FINANCE/CAPITAL MARKETS

fearless. Alas, there are situations where some of these heavenly creatures over-step their bounds and the public pounce to unmask them and bring them back to planet earth in extreme cases. It happens (albeit) rarely.

Having said the above, it may not be enough to simply unmask the errant masquerade, sometimes, the more you look, the less you see; the masquerade remaining incognito even as one stares it in the face. Consequently, it may be necessary to set new rules in order to prevent a reoccurrence. Community leaders and the High Chiefs are consulted and members of the public invited to make submissions, lessons learnt, new lines drawn and the show goes on. The codes of corporate governance developed by the Cadbury report follows this logic. The committee's original remit was to review those aspects of corporate governance specifically related to financial reporting and accountability, but was quickly widened to include all aspects of corporate governance in its entirety.[102] The thrust of the finding in the report was that listed companies needed to strengthen both their control over their businesses and their public accountability. As pointed out in part one of this essay, last week, the Committee on Corporate Governance was prompted by the collapse of the Bank of Credit and Commerce International (BCCI),[103] and the rampant be-haviours of top executives of major private companies in the UK. Nigeria has had its fair share of boardroom shenanigans: the rescued banks and insider dealings, collusion between different organs of companies, payment of eye-watering bonuses to Chief Executive Officers (CEOs), whilst not declaring div-idends, "round tripping", i.e. making bogus sales of company assets, "book cooking", i.e. manipulation of accounting statements, self-perpetuation, i.e. one CEO sitting tight for years, if not decades.[104]

When one looks at all the various organs in a company and their relationship to one another, combined with the imperative of transparency and accountability, one understands that this goes beyond the simple conscripts of company law principles; it strikes at governing as a fundamental principle. This has necessitated a number of theoretical models to help pull the thread together. A cursory look at some of these would suffice. First, the 'agency' model postulates that organs of governance in a company are mere agents. The real principals are shareholders. Second is the 'shareholder' model which

---

102. Ibid. Cadbury Report.

103. The Bank of Credit and Commerce International was an international bank established in 1972 by a Pakistani financier, Agha Hasan Abedi. It had offices in London, Karachi and several other cities in the middle-east and beyond

104. As an example see; 'Guardian' editorial: "SEC, NSE and infractions in capital market", April 8 2019 https://guardian.ng/pinion/sec-nse-and-infractions-in-capital-market

asserts that the most important elements in a company are those who have invested in it. Everything else should therefore revolve around their interest. This sounds laudable until one realises that many shareholders know next to nothing about running a business. Moreover, certain investment portfolios are so complex that they require expert knowledge to manage. Third, is the 'stakeholders' model, which calls for the aggregation of all the vested interests in a company, i.e. the investors, shareholders, government, directors, employees, contractor, society etc. for common good.

As pointed out before, the OECD has come up with a standardised version of the codes presented in the Cadbury report and they have, to a varying degree, been incorporated in a number of regulatory agencies in this country: Securities and Exchange Commission, the Nigerian Stock Exchange, the Central Bank of Nigeria, to name but three. Even the Corporate Affairs Commission[105] through the Companies and Allied Matters Act (CAMA) has tried to reflect the OECD codes in various forms, but has missed out on some crucial issues, especially in relation to the need to separate the offices of Chairman and Chief Executive Officer from being held by a single individual. Under CAMA, the Board of Directors can appoint one of its own as either Managing Director or Chairman whereas, this is specifically forbidden under the OECD codes. Even the provision to prevent self-perpetuation, which led to the restructuring of some banks in terms of the tenure of their CEOs, is not being adequately adhered to as many of the compulsorily retired CEOs have found ways of operating in the shadows; still able to direct the affairs of the banks without being physically present. These are some of the challenges taken on board by the FRCN. But has the new National Code of Corporate Governance (NCCG) it proposes gone too far? Or not far enough?

2.04 FRCN, Corporate Governance and Regulatory Overreach (III)

24 January 2017

The first major codes of corporate governance were put together by the Securities and Exchange Commission (SEC) and Corporate Affairs Commission (CAC), in 2003, for the regulation of public companies in Nigeria. This was reviewed in 2007, and 2009. Other regulatory agencies have since followed

---

105. Corporate Affairs Commission is the regulatory agency for private companies in Nigeria.

suit: Central Bank of Nigeria (CBN), Nigeria Stock Exchange (NSE), Federal Deposit Insurance Corporation (FDIC), etc. However, codes of corporate governance are not to be confused with Corporate Social Responsibility (CSR) of which many household name businesses are wont to be associated. According to a detailed research and campaign by World Business Council for Sustainable Development,[106] fairness requires businesses, especially big multinational businesses, to take an active interest in the environment in which they operate to make it better for their host communities. This is not just for charity; it makes good business sense to protect the planet from environmental degradation. It is even being suggested by many that these giant corporations set aside a percentage of their annual profits to cater for the unwitting hazards created from business exploration. This is particularly poignant in Less Developed Countries, where these giant conglomerates occasionally paint pavements, erect signposts, design street names, clear space for communal gardens etc. and claim, by that, to have discharged their CSR.

What prompted this three-part essay was the case of Eko Hotels Limited v FRCN,[107] currently before the Court of Appeals. Being a private company, Eko Hotels had argued in the Federal High Court in Lagos, in 2014, that the proposed National Code of Corporate Governance put forward by the FRCN mandating all companies to register with it and be bound by a unified code of corporate governance is inapplicable to private companies as the FRCN's jurisdiction only extends to public companies. The Federal High Court agreed, saying that the express mention of the parties to be covered by the Act implies that those not mentioned should be excluded. Under the "Objects" of the FRCN Act 2011,[108] section 11 (b), the Council is to give guidance on issues relating to financial reporting and corporate governance to bodies listed in 2 (2) (b), (c) and (d) of the Act, which indeed, backs up the Federal High Court's ruling in favour of Eko Hotels. That notwithstanding, section 11 (c) of the same Act implores the Council to "ensure good corporate governance practices in public and private sectors of the Nigerian economy". To buttress this, section 7 (2) (a) of the Act empowers the Council to "enforce and approve enforcement of compliance with accounting, auditing, corporate governance and financial reporting standards in Nigeria". On the face of it, this sounds clear enough that the law is on the side of the FRCN? Well, if only it was that clear cut.

---

106. WBCSD

107. See; 'Nigeria Regulatory Newsletter', May 19 2014 https://pwcnigeria.typepad.com /files/frcn-restricted-from-regulating-private-companies.pdf

108. The Act can be accessed via the Federal Government of Nigeria Official Gazette: https://gazettes.africa/archive/ng/2011/ng-government-gazette-dated-2011-06-07-no-54.pdf

2 · FINANCE/CAPITAL MARKETS

To complicate matters for the Appeal Court justices, section 8 (1) (a) of the Act states one of the functions of the FRCN as being to " … develop and publish accounting and financial reporting standards to be observed in the preparation of financial statement of *public interest entities*" (my emphasis). For the avoidance of doubt, "public interest entities" is interpreted in section 77 to mean: "governments, government organisations, quoted and unquoted companies and all other organisations which are required by law to file returns with regulatory authorities and this excludes private companies that routinely file returns only with the Corporate Affairs Commission and the Federal Inland Revenue Services". The opening statement of the Act is also significant, as it gives the FRCN responsibility for: "developing and publishing accounting and financial reporting standards to be observed in the preparation of financial statement of public entities in Nigeria; And for related matters". On the face of it therefore, that puts the ball back in Eko Hotels' court one might say? Well, not so fast.

The Act has produced a classic ambiguity which will ultimately get some 'settlement' at the Supreme Court. Whenever there is a propensity for multiple and conflicting interpretations for any Act, the task before the courts is to ascertain the 'intention' of Parliament when the Act was passed. The justices will need to weigh a number of the "Canons of Interpretations" at their disposal. If they take an expansive (social policy) view of the Act, they may side with the FRCN, but if they adopt a liberal, business efficacy view, they will side with Eko Hotels Limited. My own view, for whatever it is worth, is that their Lordships should adopt the latter on the ground that Parliament could not have intended that FRCN becomes an overarching; overbearing bureaucracy that would create bottlenecks and red tapes for business even as laudable as the ideal of corporate governance appears to be. Moreover, since all the other regulatory agencies already have, and do enforce codes of corporate governance mirroring that of the Organisation for Economic Cooperation and Development (OECD) in many cases, what is left for the FRCN is simply to act as an 'umbrella organisation' for the regulatory agencies in the area of financial reporting and corporate governance. In other words, businesses should be supervised by their respective regulatory agencies and not be made liable to the diktats of another layer of regulatory super agency such as the FRCN seeks to constitute itself into. If, however, this is what Parliament intends, then, the FRCN Act will need to go back to the National Assembly for amendments, which will make that crystal clear. For now, though, FRCN can only coordinate; not usurp the powers of existing regulatory agencies.[109]

---

109. The matter is yet to come before the Supreme Court for a final and definitive ruling.

2.05 We've Had Pro-Democracy Activists, Why not Activist Investors?

7 March 2017

The current democratic dispensation has been frail, fledgling, floating, even failing in parts, but it has limped on and it is edging towards the twenty-year mark. By the time of the next Presidential contest in 2019, we will already have a cohort of voters in Nigeria who have never known anything other than a democratic order. They will not know what it is to live under a dictatorship; jailing of journalists, killing of opposition figures at random, no debate of public policy, no Senate confirmation hearings, no budget presented to the National Assembly, no elections, no ballots; no campaign slogans on rolling city-centre billboards, no flamboyant posters and no razzmatazz; only obnoxious decrees and the military jackboot. Such was the life.

Yet, the political freedom that they (the spring chickens) now enjoy; indeed take for granted, was hard-fought; even so hard fought that several prominent and not so prominent individuals paid the ultimate price for it. When the civilian government of President Shehu Shagari fell to a military dictatorship of the then General Muhammadu Buhari in 1983, the regime of which was itself toppled in 1985 by General Ibrahim Badamasi Babangida, Nigeria began a crusade for the emancipation of the populace from oppression that took until May 1999, when Olusegun Obasanjo (himself a military dictator from 1976–79) took office as a civilian President of Nigeria. Those who spearheaded the campaign for freedom and a return to civilian rule at home and abroad during those heady days were dubbed "pro-democracy activists"; a lot of them rather relished being so dubbed, as it was rightly seen as a badge of honour.

What fascinates many people though, is why was it such a life and death issue to fight for political freedom and apparently not so critical to fight for economic freedom? What made several gallant male and female, young and old citizens to defy the odds to come out swinging at dictatorship and not a sight of them taking up the fight with the same zeal and commitment for economic pluralism? Why is there a dearth of "pro-development" or "pro-investment" activists trying to spread the wealth as it were? Or is political freedom an end in itself? Put another way, does economic emancipation willy-nilly follow political freedom, as right-wing political ideologues assert? Why is it not good enough to leave the political space in the hands of a select few, and it is alright to leave the economic space to a few (self-serving) business moguls? Is the economic space simply to be reified as "laissez-faire"; the arena for the

2 · FINANCE/CAPITAL MARKETS

survival of the smartest? Or should we simply align with the ideological purist on the left of politics in assuming the "imminent collapse" of capitalism under the weight of its own contradictions without further ado? But even if that is destined to happen, who pays the bill until it does?

That said, here are examples of how an activist investor might operate in the real world of capital markets. Like pro-democracy activists, the activist investor is a socially (dare I say progressively) conscious entrepreneur who researches and targets individual companies. He decides on acquiring interest in, say, "growth stock". That is, a fast-growing (fairly new) company, which does not pay much by way of dividends but pays huge rewards in increased share price. By contrast, another such investor may choose "income stocks", which pays relatively high dividends (albeit) with a much restricted potential for growth. Without mentioning names, these types of companies are usually household names known for their stability and strength. The rider though, is that the sheer demand for this type of investment may end up driving up their share value anyway. Another outlet for an activist investor is to embark upon "value investing", that is to say, unearthing companies that are under-valued on their fundamentals: good product or service, good management, good brand, good market etc. none of which is reflected in their current share price. The textile industry comes readily to mind here. The investor holds on to the share for a long time before reaping handsome rewards. United States' Warren Buffett (a multi-billionaire), is a good example of a value investor, who during eight years of Obama administration, fought for a progressive tax code that would have resulted in the fabulously rich paying a lot more on their incomes. He has reportedly given away nearly all the billions he amassed in his lifetime to good causes instead of using them to entrench his offspring in a life of luxury.[110]

If pro-democracy activism is about expanding the democratic space without constraints, investment activism is about maximising return in the home country, while minimising risk. In the pro-investment 'campaign office', the future is inherently unknown, whichever computational methods is used to measure the risk. While the voter is spurred on by the elusive ideals of freedom and the promise of a better tomorrow by the pro-democracy activist, markets are also

---

110. Upon signing to give up most, if not all, of his wealth to charity in his lifetime, in an innovative "giving pledge", like a number of billionaires of his ilk have also done, Buffet stated: "Were we to use more than 1% of my claim checks (Berkshire Hathaway Stock Certificates) on ourselves, neither our happiness nor our well-being would be enhanced. In contrast, that remaining 99% can have a huge effect on the health and welfare of others". https://givingpledge.org/pledger?pledgerId=177

driven, paradoxically, less by what is obvious, but more by what everyone thinks might happen. If everyone thinks Nigerian billionaires and high-level government functionaries, for instance, will put their money in the country's local hospitals instead of travelling overseas for expensive treatments, then, the market in both Nigerian pharmaceutical industry and hospitals' share prices will rise, thereby becoming a self-fulfilling prophesy. This is what creates market momentum. Momentum in the political space is created by events, momentum investors in the markets are those able to spot the mood of the market and jump on board before it becomes overloaded. They also know exactly when to jump off before it changes in the opposite direction. There are also the "contrarian" activists, who do exactly the opposite of what they believe everyone else is doing. Markets react to expectations of what might happen in the future and the activist as well as other market participants "discounts" this in today's prices.

In the final analysis though, what matters is not whether this or that company or product is good or bad for investment, but whether one can get enough people to buy it from the investor in future at a higher price than he paid for it. It is also often said in capital markets, that how much investment one puts on a product or a set of products depends on whether one wishes to 'eat well or sleep easy'. Ever tried going to bed on a full stomach? It is an extraordinarily difficult contradiction to resolve at the best of times. By consequence, we should welcome the activist investor who breaks out in each direction, that is to say, eating well and sleeping easy. If you think the battle for democracy was hard enough, well, the battle for economic democracy is (short of a revolution) eternal. Unlike democracy, capitalism offers no free lunches.

2.06 SEC's Tepid Response to Market Infractions

14 March 2017

The Securities and Exchange Commission (SEC) is the main body charged with the duty to regulate the financial industry in Nigeria, more specifically, the capital markets, under the Investment and Securities Act 2007.[111] The Commission carries out this duty by issuing a range of directives aimed at the ef-

---

111. For the actual text of the Act, see; file:///C:/Users/Mr%20Tok%C3%A8/Downloads/THE-INVESTMENTS-AND-SECURITIES-ACT-2007_NIGERIA%20(1).pdf

fective management of the capital markets' operations on the one hand, and the behaviours of the market participants on the other. This is done against the assumption, indeed, necessity for the freest movement of capital in and out of the economy. The philosophical argument over the optimal regulatory approach is as varied as the participants in the markets. Relax regulation too much and you risk giving succour to fraudsters. On the other hand, embark upon a more prescriptive regulatory regime, and you risk stifling competition and drying up liquidity[112] from the market. The balance between "draconian" and "proportionate" is often a difficult one for officials of the SEC to draw when faced with the need to impose sanctions.[113] Other SECs around the world fare no better with these things, in fact.

The Obama administration in the USA, for instance, took strong regulatory measures to guard against the kind of abuse which nearly resulted in the collapse of the American banking industry in 2008.[114] The Dodd-Frank Act, 2010,[115] aimed at "protecting Wall Street and the consumer", was thought to have introduced the most sweeping changes to America's finance industry in a generation. Those measures are now being ripped apart by the new US administration under President Donald Trump, who sees the answer to the same problem in less, not more, regulation.

If the American finance industry is vulnerable to market abuse, needing legislation for protection, perhaps one should not be too surprised to find that Nigeria too, has its fair share of abuse from unscrupulous institutions and individuals. It is thus within this context that the SEC's "Capital Market Master Plan" (CMMP 2015–2025)[116] can be better appreciated. The plan contains a number of measures to boost investor confidence in the Nigerian market. The Commission has also been busy finding and punishing offenders, but it appears the punitive measures taken thus far against abusers in the Nigerian market are not far-reaching enough. Although the SEC does not have criminal enforcement

---

112. Refers to how quickly an investment can be sold without negatively impacting its price. https://corporatefinanceinstitute.com/resources/knowledge/finance/liquidity

113. For a fuller explanation of the SEC's sanctions regime see the publication on their website; https://sec.gov.ng/sanctions-on-quoted-companies

114. See; Kevin Drawbaugh. "Long, bumpy road ahead for Obama financial reforms". 'Reuters Business News', March 2009 https://www.reuters.com/article/us-financial-regulation-systemic-sb-idUSTRE52P7QK20090326. In addition, see; 'Obama Whitehouse Archives' on the economy. https://obamawhitehouse.archives.gov/the-record/economy

115. Ibid. The Act was dubbed "the most far reaching Wall Street Reform in history" by the Obama administration.

116. See; Capital Markets Master Plan 2015–2025 file:///C:/Users/Mr%20Tok%C3%A8/Downloads/PRESENTATION-IN-LONDON-Mounir-Gwarzo-June-2015.pdf

82   2 · FINANCE/CAPITAL MARKETS

powers, it does not need to; the civil enforcement powers opened to it are wide enough and could even be expanded to make it more effective. The civil enforcement powers are both administrative and injunctive.[117] The Commission may institute various administrative proceedings either as an alternative to, or in addition to, a civil action. An injunction is by its nature preventative in the sense that it is aimed at prohibiting individuals and corporate bodies from embarking upon further violations, but it is handy for the Commission because, unlike private litigants seeking injunctive relief, the SEC generally need not demonstrate either irreparable injury or an inadequate remedy at law.

Furthermore, although an injunction may appear fairly innocuous to the layman, it could turn out to be 'drastic' depending on the person or body involved because of its collateral effects. The publicity that usually follows such a measure by the SEC can be pretty devastating particularly since participants in the finance industry pride themselves on their ability to maintain confidentiality with clients. Administrative orders may have less overbearing collateral impact, but may, nonetheless, have negative repercussions for business or the careers of the individual under sanction. The SEC has taken several hundred entities to court for market abuse within the last ten years. These entities include: banks, individuals and assorted capital market operators for a varying range of offences including: price-fixing, share price manipulation, insider trading and outright fraud. The latest of these entities involved Partnership Investment Company Limited (PICL), and Partnership Securities Limited (PSL).[118] In a similar vein, Marian Moses Ventures Limited, an illegal operator, was convicted by the Federal High Court Kaduna Division only last month for soliciting and collecting deposits from members of the public without a licence from either the SEC or CBN. It was ordered that the company be wound up and its funds used to compensate its clients.[119]

All of the above being good, but the SEC needs to go further by insisting on a disgorgement of all "ill-gotten gains" following from any violation. The primary purpose of disgorgement is not to compensate investors (although this is not precluded); rather, disgorgement is designed to purge a violator of the amount he was unjustly enriched with, including any incidental increases in value. In this wise, a disgorgement order compels a market abuser to account

---

117. See; SEC Law and Enforcement https://sec.gov.ng/directorates/legal-enforcement-2

118. See; SEC Administrative proceedings report on this matter https://sec.gov.ng /sec-administrative-proceedings-committee-decision-in-respect-of-partnership-investment -company-plc

119. For the record of proceedings in court see; https://ndic.gov.ng/wp-content/uploads/2020/08/RE_FRN-VS-MOSES-SAMANJA-AUDU-MIRIAM-MOSES.pdf

for all profits reaped through securities law violations regardless of actual damages to their victims. The SEC would be free to determine the extent and scope of the "ill-gotten gains", although the order will only apply to gains that are causally connected to the securities violation and not funds legitimately earned. In any case, SEC will not need to prove violation of securities regulations in order to disgorge ill-gotten gains in respect of third parties. Consequently, in a court action, the Commission can join third parties as "relief defendants" or entities in receipt of unlawful transfers with no legitimate claim to the funds or assets. In disgorgement proceedings,[120] the SEC will only be required to demonstrate a reasonable proximity of the ill-gotten gain to the securities violation. Then, the burden shifts unto the defendant to demonstrate that the SEC has been unreasonable in its calculations.

With these additional tools in SEC's armoury, the stake could not be higher for people engaged or trying to engage in market manipulation of one kind or another. The unequivocal warning to them is that, they may not only have to cough up the ill-gotten gains from their accounts in-to-to, they may also have to supplement the account to their last dollar. The costlier the consequences for market manipulation, the less incentive there is to commit one, and conversely, the higher the level of public confidence in the nation's capital markets.

2.07 Forex: CBN Governor's Parallel Universe

11 April 2017

It is coming up to almost one month since the Central Bank of Nigeria's strong intervention in the foreign exchange (forex) market to meet "genuine" demands from the public. Genuine users of forex are to be interpreted as covering all transactions for invisible trade (i.e. excluding exchange of material goods). So, the CBN thinks it can single out 'genuine' users of forex, then, flood the market with tons of greenbacks (US dollars), through commercial banks and other outlets, and send out a brigade of "mystery shoppers" to catch out errant financial institutions who, if caught, would be subject to sanctions. Then overtime, the "unpatriotic" and "selfish" speculators in the

---

120. For a quick overview, see UK House of Lords judgement in AG v Blake and Another https://publications.parliament.uk/pa/ld199900/ldjudgmt/jd000727/blake-3.htm There is also a scholarly text by the London School of Economics on the principle http://eprints.lse.ac.uk/63664/1/__lse.ac.uk_storage_LIBRARY_Secondary_libfile_shared_rep ository_Content_Sage,%20N_Sage_Disgorgement%20from%20property_2016.pdf

84   2 · FINANCE/CAPITAL MARKETS

shadows (parallel market) will soon be out of a job, as the naira slowly gathers strength against the dollar and other hard currencies. Based on the halt in the naira's slide against the dollar (from 500 naira to one dollar last month, to something like 360 naira to one dollar now), it seems the CBN Governor, Godwin Emefiele, has performed, and is performing wonders; rumbling the maladroit speculators and giving them a bad run for their money. In the short term, yes, this can work and is working, but it is unsustainable in the long term. Here is why.

Commercial banks are the vehicle for conveying financial errands for consumers and suppliers of money in an economy. They have a pivotal role in the amalgam of financial/capital markets and the wider macro-economic outlook of a country. So, take the interest rate conundrum for instance. It is hovering, officially, at about eighteen per cent, but in the real economy it is between twenty to thirty per cent, even more in some extreme cases. If the banks can charge up to thirty per cent interest on borrowers, why would they risk putting money in capital markets to boost companies' shares? Why also, would they lend to small and medium-sized enterprises at say, ten per cent or less in order to boost that critical sector to the economy? There is simply no incentive for them to do so. In Nigeria's cash and carry economy, they make borrowing available only to those who will fetch them instantaneous returns like government and parastatals, contractors and money bag politicians throwing their weight around in election circles. Manufacturing and small-scale enterprises can go hang. Government, on the other hand, can spend money to boost demand, but the money to do that will have to come from either cutting essential services or borrowing. The Nigerian public has not shown any appetite for either of these options in recent times. CBN can make a drastic cut in the interbank interest rate to, say, five per cent or less from the current sixteen per cent.[121] Unfortunately, though, any gain from this is likely to be directed at imports because that is where the commercial banks will target for instant returns. In the main, Nigerian banks are not investment-minded; they are traders.

Now, let us take a look at forex. The biggest users are indeed the banks themselves. They use it for domestic and international transactions. CBN hands out about eighty million US dollars per week to 20 banks for onward lending to end users, and a paltry twenty million US dollars per week to some three thousand bureaux de change across the country.[122] CBN then sent out a circular say-

---

121. See; Central Bank of Nigeria https://www.cbn.gov.ng/rates/interbankrates.asp

122. For an overview of the forex market in Nigeria, see; the CBN analysis https://www.cbn.gov.ng/intops/fxmarket.asp

ing: "Any bank that fails to comply with the rules of this and other extant forex guidelines shall be sanctioned, which will affect the executive and other officers of the bank". This is like putting the Dracula in charge of the blood bank. The CBN Governor, as a consummate commercial banker, knows this. The governor ought to initiate policy for the economy as it is, and not the Nigerian economy of his imagination. As with the persistent dilemma of power distribution in this country, the generator importers; the mega-millionaires and pipeline saboteurs who profit from keeping others in the dark will do their utmost to ensure the status quo of power failures prevails even with a mega minister, "technocrat" (Governor) Babatunde Fashola in charge. He too is only just finding out. The banks, in the battle field of finance, are the fifth column in this country. They gave birth to the so-called parallel market in forex because it suits them. Creating artificial scarcity in dollars in circulation generates money for them. They will cooperate with the diktat of the CBN governor only by upholding the line of least resistance to his goal. Quite frankly, it is crass of the CBN to create a dedicated line for customers not attended to within twenty-four hours for their Basic Travel Allowance to call, or send an email to the apex bank. Consumers of financial products cannot become vigilantes for the cause of the CBN. They just want service, and if it is not forthcoming, they move on.

Furthermore, the CBN's show of force in the forex trade is unsustainable because the dollars being expended are not earned; they are proceeds from oil receipts. Oil products are denominated in dollars; they do not form part of what we generate and price in local currency, which are then traded for dollars. Oil receipts in exchange for forex is a fire brigade approach to public policy; it is voodoo economics. The current bubble of a rise in the value of the naira will, ipso-facto, burst in the short to medium term. We have a deep-seated structural problem in our economy, which will make it difficult to bridge the divide between the official and parallel markets for forex. A carefully crafted policy would not aim at eliminating this divide entirely, but at bringing it to a level where it becomes inconsequential. This is in addition to the vested interest in the commercial and financial industry that prefers the status quo. How about asking bank executives to declare their interest; any financial interest in parallel market operations? The vested interests are studying the current policy of flooding the market with dollars by the CBN and are busy plotting their next move. It is a matter of when, not if, they strike. The vultures are circling.[123]

---

123. The Governor of Central Bank, Godwin Emefiele has recently announced the scrapping of selling forex to commercial banks by the end of the year 2022. All the elements of the column's analysis have proved almost literally correct. https://www.pulse.ng/business

86   2 · FINANCE/CAPITAL MARKETS

2.08 Forex: Nigerian Banks in the Dock

18 April 2017

Ask anyone in a random survey which profession they find most trustworthy, the answer would most probably be: "bankers, of course". They are ranked only behind people in the medical profession in some surveys. Journalists, estate agents, mechanics, insurance brokers, politicians and the like are generally despised, if not loathed, by the general public, some for understandable reasons. By practice, people walk into the bank, leave their hard earned cash in its custody and simply walk back out. We get statements of our monthly or quarterly transactions from the banks, and without even bothering to peruse, we file or throw them away, believing in their intrinsic truth. Now, the same revered institution is being accused of a grand larceny by the Nigerian Senate.

Last Thursday, a Senate committee was said to have "discovered N30tn forex fraud in ten years by banks".[124] It is to be recalled that this column was devoted to banking malpractice in the forex saga last week. CBN policy of handling the banks millions of US dollars for onward distribution to end users was castigated in the column as being akin to putting the Dracula in charge of the blood bank. The swift Senate reaction, whether galvanised by the column or just a mere coincidence, is gratifying anyhow. Their action will be most appreciated by the public at large. That said, the Senate's interest in this matter needs to go deeper than is currently contemplated. The banks have been directed to respond to the Senate's "queries" within the next three weeks. The regulatory authorities; CBN, Ministry of Finance, and that of Budget/National Planning have also been summoned to appear before the Senate Committee next month alongside the Chief Executive Officers of the commercial banks.

For a start, the multiple layers of supervisory/regulatory functions over the issue of forex is an anomaly that needs to be rectified. Right now, there are too many overlaps in the functions of the CBN Governor, Minister of Finance and that of the Budget/National Planning. All three are effectively acting out the role of Minister of Finance, which should not be the case. The ambiguity was, most probably, not intended when the Presidency created the Ministry for

---

/cbn-to-stop-sale-of-forex-to-banks/v3mjyzr See also the announcement by the CBN itself https://www.cbn.gov.ng/Out/2021/CCD/CBN%20Update%202021%20(July)%20.pdf

124. The Senate findings made news headlines across the world https://www.reuters.com/article/ozabs-us-nigeria-cenbank-arrests-idAFKBN0OH2M920150601

2 · FINANCE/CAPITAL MARKETS

Budget/National Planning with a substantive minister in charge. It was created for political expediency, but it has robbed the Ministry of Finance of a key responsibility in the management of the country's finances. The forex issue is as much a political as it is an economic matter. Mrs Adeosun should be the person taking the lead on it; not the Governor of CBN, who, though eminently qualified, ought to be confined to the CBN premises.

The forex issue is not a new phenomenon in the Nigerian economy; it has long been accepted as part of its inevitable decline, only the accelerated rate of this decline in the recent months has highlighted the urgency of the problem. The other side of the forex saga is the chronic interest rate that is stifling the manufacturing sector, especially as it affects the small and medium-sized enterprises. Why would any bank commit any money into the capital markets to help boost company shares if they can find other people to lend to at the prime rates of 20, 30, and 35%? At a time when other countries keep their interest rates as low as five per cent and even much further down, Nigerian banks are touting their loans to small and medium-sized companies at the exorbitant rates of 20–30% or more. The bulk of these small and medium-sized enterprises are then forced to operate in the shadows; using loan sharks for their borrowing requirements and using the parallel market for their foreign exchange needs. What is needed, therefore, is not some Senate hearings that will be subsumed by politics. It is not too difficult to imagine how many of the country's representatives are directly or indirectly funded by bankers, and how many of them have substantive financial interest in the banking industry themselves. Furthermore, the Senate Committee proclaimed that as much as N30tn forex fraud has been committed by the banks in the last ten years. This amount is staggering if not incredulous.

The point is simply that, taken at face value, the Senate's charge of N30tn fraud would mean that the entire forex transaction in the country's economy in the last ten years has been fraudulent! It is an astonishing, if not outlandish claim. Nonetheless, the banks stand accused for this and other reasons enunciated in last week's column and today's. This should be beyond politics for the sake of everyone. Consequently, only an independent commission of experts and other stakeholders can do a thorough job of unravelling these sinister issues of forex and crippling interest rate in the economy. It is a job not to be left with the experts per se. Economic matters are far too important to be left with economists alone.[125]

---

125. The brouhaha stirred up by the Senators quietened down, and soon became a non-event.

2.09 Budget 2017 Through the Lens of Capital Markets

30 May 2017

It is that time of the year again for the chattering classes and financial anoraks to get into prolonged squabbles over the budget, I mean, its presentation, the number crunching elements and implementation. At over seven trillion naira, we are told the budget is the highest ever laid before the National Assembly.[126] In the past week, the airwaves have been filled with pundits and experts inside and outside the corridors of power telling us who gains and who loses, and several column inches have been devoted to general and specific issues in the papers around the budget as well. The online coverage is no less engrossing. The Department for Budget and Planning, for instance, has published details of the budget running to one thousand and five hundred pages long, in addition to that of series of other online experts. Despite the pervasive hoo-ha, I am not entirely convinced that the majority of citizens in this country feel connected to, or engaged with the budget talk at all. What, after all, is the point of budgets amidst daily power failure, dilapidated road network, crumbling school buildings, hospitals with little or no equipment, and of course, rising unemployment? The question makes many people wonder: What is the budget aimed at if not for the continued financing of wages and salaries of government employees and politicians?

First and foremost, let us put the big numbers in a bit of a perspective. Seven trillion naira seems a huge sum indeed, but it is not that much considering the extent of the country's needs. Nigeria has a borrowing gap of at least fourteen trillion naira just to fulfil basic needs.[127] We consume what we do not produce and produce what we do not consume, so the total sum of the budget is still a drop in the ocean regardless. The main reason why people are indifferent to the budget talk is perhaps the fact that there is a déjà vu feel to it all. Budgets come and budgets go with little or no apparent changes to the people's daily life. I know a lot of people who have wondered in private conversations why

---

126. See full details from the Budget Office https://budgetoffice.gov.ng/nbi/app/index.php/2017-budget

127. See a report by Reuters; "Nigeria will keep borrowing to fund the gap in the 2017 budget — Ministry of Finance" https://www.reuters.com/article/nigeria-economy-idUSL8N1K44EJ And 'Budget Info' Frequently Asked Questions on the deficit funding by the Budget Office https://www.budgetoffice.gov.ng/nbi/app/index.php/frequently-asked-questions

we should not simply have just two items: power and road infrastructure for the entire national budget and declare an economic emergency to bring these to fruition if need be. Any political party that succeeds at those two alone will be re-elected in perpetuity in this country. Well, putting aside these initial observations, let us see how the budget relates to Nigeria's capital market. Given that there is such a huge funding gap in it, conventional wisdom tells us that the void should be filled by either borrowing (opposed to by the majority), or taxation (a major disincentive to investment).

Companies and private individuals constitute the bulk of the wealth creators in any economy, not government. To start or strengthen an existing business, an entrepreneur needs capital, and where does that come from? It comes from personal savings, inheritance, or gratuitous donations from friends and family. Failing that, the option for most people is to raise debt through bank loans, which is paid back over a period of time. For over seventy per cent of businesses in this country, these are the two main sources of financing opened to them. That situation, of itself, is unsustainable for the largest companies; the power houses of industrial production in this country. Consequently, the large companies, whose turn over runs into billions and trillions annually, go to capital markets to raise funds by selling their shares in return for dividends. People who put money into capital markets are not just shareholders; a large proportion comprises of institutional investors like pension funds and insurance houses. So, what entices them to invest? The short answer is, of course, a healthy return on their investment. What then is their main focus on the budget talk?

Investors look out for growth and the potential for growth as a way of maximising profits. They take a long hard look at the macro-economic environment in which they have invested or are about to invest. They want to see a commitment to lower taxation, deregulation, and lower (or manageable) inflation. In the 1980s, this view of the market became prominently known as "supply side" economics.[128] It is unabashed in its advocacy of business interest. Lay-offs, downsizing, and the like are by-products of this view of economic activity and it is all in the name of efficiency and productivity. That view of the economy has now become the orthodox, that is, mainstream in international capital markets. When one hears of market operators in this country pledging to "partner" with the government in achieving growth, it sends a shudder down the spine. After all, the Nigerian economy, everyone

---

128. For a simplified explanation see; James D Gwartney. "Supply Side Economics" https://www.econlib.org/library/Enc/SupplySideEconomics.html

90 2 · FINANCE/CAPITAL MARKETS

agrees, needs "reflating", that is to say money to pump into the economy to create jobs, boost demand and education; a heavy dose of the old Keynesian economics.[129] It is diametrically opposed to the view of capital and the markets. Politicians therefore need to strike a careful balance between social and capital imperatives. Policy makers cannot move too far in one direction without jeopardising the other.

Nigeria is not alone in facing down this dilemma though. Political leaders around the world have to wrestle with similar problems all the time. The election of Donald Trump in the USA was largely premised on the perception of his "pro-business" manifesto, which his administration is trying to pursue despite the difficulties it is having in other areas. So too is the election of President Emmanuel Macron of France, last week, who has vowed to reform the French economy along the lines of supply-side economics. In this country, however, it is not entirely clear what manifesto the country voted for other than the "change" mantra of the All Progressives Congress of the current administration. The ballot in this country is often offered on a platter to anyone strong enough to get rid of an incumbent loathed by the public. A party's economic agenda ought to be clear and unambiguous prior to voting. Blank cheques to politicians must cease. Vote first; ask questions later mentality must end on our shores for the long term benefit of all of us.

2.10 Rise and Fall of Nigeria's Banking Services

6 June 2017

Once upon a time, you had a transaction to make, you walked into the local branch of your bank, you were attended to with courtesy; you did what you had to do, and walked back out. In the same vein, you had a somewhat hazy business idea, which you broached with the cashier; he referred you to their business manager, who then sat with you to examine the pros and cons of the idea. With some tweaks here and there, he thought it was a good idea on which the bank could lend you money. He made a further appointment with you to come back for a review, after which the loan for your business was granted,

---

129. For an interesting contrast see; Sarwat Jahan, Ahmed Saber Mahmud, and Chris Papageorgiou. "What is Keynesian Economics?" 'Back to Basics'. IMF (Finance and Development) September 2014, Vol 51 No 3 https://www.imf.org/external/pubs/ft/fandd/2014/09/basics.htm

2 · FINANCE/CAPITAL MARKETS

and the bank stayed with you for the next couple of years to nurture the business. That was a snippet of the post-independence banking service in this country. The customer base of the banking industry was, of course, much smaller than it is now, but so too were the resources available to look after them. Crucially, however, the banks saw themselves as partners in the national development effort of the country at large.

Then, came the blessing (or curse, depending on your sensitivity) of oil and expansion of trade at the dawn of the 1970s, coupled with the Arab-Israeli War of 1973, which led to the quadrupling of oil prices.[130] Nigeria became awash with redundant cash right through to the 1980s, to the point where one government minister under President Shehu Shagari's administration (1979–1983), bemoaned a unique Nigeria dilemma as being not where to obtain money, but how to spend it.[131] The gates thus opened up to all comers for banks, and they sprang up in their dozens.

New banks sprang up then as we have political parties rushing to INEC for registration in contemporary Nigeria. As with the so-called "mushroom parties" often talked about, so too "mushroom banks" sprang up alongside established and well-funded ones. Before the consolidation of the banks was concluded in December 2005, it was commonplace to have a family house type of bank structure, where the husband was Chairman, the wife, Chief Executive Officer, and the son, General Manager. The International Monetary Fund's induced liberalisation policy in the 1980s, across the developing world, made it easy for any journeyman operator to obtain a licence to start a bank. Banking thus became less customer-focused, and more centred around shareholder and founders' interest. The golden age of banking as service to community and customer was gone. The liberalisation idea did not last long though, but it lasted long enough to inflict a lot of collateral damage on Nigeria's financial architecture as a whole. Instead of being partners in development, the banks became white elephants and even parasitic to the country's economic wellbeing. The restructuring that followed in 2004, under the then Governor of Central

---

130. The Organisation for the Petroleum Exporting Countries (OPEC), twelve countries in all, placed an oil embargo on the United States (for its support of Israel in the war) in October 1973. This led to the quadrupling of oil prices almost overnight. For an American historical perspective see; "Oil Shock of 1973–74", Federal Reserve Archives. https://www.federalreservehistory.org/essays/oil-shock-of-1973-74

131. The statement was originally credited to the former Nigerian Military Head of State, General Yakubu Gowon (1966–1975), at the height of the oil bonanza to Nigeria. See further; https://www.thecable.ng/how-to-spend-it

92 2 · FINANCE/CAPITAL MARKETS

Bank of Nigeria (CBN), Professor Charles Soludo, was as timely, as it was within the rubrics of the international standards set by the "Basle Committee" of bankers based in Switzerland.[132]

The restructuring, or "consolidation" as it was then known, significantly brought down the number of banks in Nigeria from almost one hundred to the current twenty-five adjudged to have met the new twenty-five billion recapitalisation requirement.[133] The weeding out of the "mushroom banks", though highly essential, has produced its own snag: there are now too many customers chasing too few banks. This is illogical, as it is an inversion of capitalism. It is very difficult to come out of the premises of the average bank in this country today with a good customer experience for the day and time spent. Queues for the simplest transaction are usually long, the hallways and customer 'service' desks are crowded like it is in the marketplace at times, and the Automated Teller Machines (ATMs) are beset by "network problems" of all sorts leading to unseemly scrambles and jockeying for position in queues. Simple current account openings take over six months to complete in some banks, as befuddled bank officials shuffle customers from one help desk to another. The CBN, under Governor Lamido Sanusi II, hurriedly introduced the "cashless policy"[134] initiative as a panacea to the bank overcrowding. It is typical of such initiatives to be introduced in complete oblivion of the reality of life on the ground. A society which has more than eighty percent of its population living in darkness through power shortage suddenly wants to shove a cashless policy idea down the peoples' throats? What are the computers going to run on? What are the small businesses going to run on? Are policy makers aware of the phenomenon of people in this country literally scrambling to find somewhere to charge their handsets upon entering an office or a room with electricity because the power in their phone has dried out sometimes for several days? Consequently, the solution to the de-

---

132. The Basel Committee—initially named the Committee on Banking Regulations and Supervisory Practices—was established by the central bank governors of the Group of Ten Countries at the end of 1974 in the aftermath of serious disturbances in international currency and banking markets. For more on this visit the bank of international settlement website; https://www.bis.org/bcbs/history.htm

133. See; Prof. Charles C. Soludo. Governor, Central Bank of Nigeria. "Consolidating the Nigerian Banking Industry to Meet the Development challenges of the 21st Century". CBN Headquarters, Abuja, July 2004. https://www.cbn.gov.ng/OUT/SPEECHES /2004/GOVADD-6JUL.PDF

134. See; "Sanusi Charts Way Forward for Cashless Policy at Conference". 'Business Day' June 2013 https://businessday.ng/banking/article/sanusi-charts-way-forward-for -cashless-policy-at-conference

cline in banking services in this country is not to coral customers into the cashless Eldorado that does not and cannot exist in the absence of the requisite infrastructure, but to make the existing banks more competitive by ushering in more participants into the sector. In my view, the number of banks in this country per population has become abysmally low.

Just think of it, at twenty-five banks, and a population of one hundred and seventy million,[135] Nigeria has one bank per seven million people. Clearly, the country needs at least three times the number of banks it currently has. London alone has more banks inside it than the whole of West African countries combined. What about America? The State of California alone has close to three hundred local banks, and hundreds more of foreign banks, almost totalling the number of licenced banks in Sub-Saharan Africa combined. Well, those are advanced industrialised nations; you might be forgiven for thinking. Okay, what about Ghana then? With a population of a little over twenty seven million, and twenty-seven banks, Ghana has roughly one bank per one million people. Similar comparison applies in the case of South Africa, Kenya, and even more so, Egypt. This is buttressed by the fact that Nigeria runs the largest economy in Africa! We need more, not less participants in the banking industry to mobilise capital, encourage local industries especially in the agriculture sector, boost consumer activities, generate employment through loans for self-development etc. The pendulum has swung too far away from ordinary bank customers in this country since the banking consolidation.

In the final analysis, our existing banks are no longer risk takers; they are too ensconced in quick money, government loan deals, treasury bills, executive bonuses etc. to care. They behave like the Biblical Pharisees who know the price of everything but the value of nothing. The fewer the participants in the banking industry, the less competitive they have become. We need the number of solid and solvent (not "mushroom") banks commensurate with the country's growing population and economic needs. The added competition that comes with that will bring the banks back to basics, in addition to driving up their optimal level of efficiency.

---

135. Nigerian population is estimated at around 200 million now, in 2022. No official figures exist to buttress this conclusively.

2.11 Nigeria's Financial 'Intelligence' at the Crossroads

25 July 2017

Nigeria's Financial Intelligence Unit (NFIU)[136] is an arm of the Economic and Financial Crimes Commission (EFCC), which is charged with collating and analysing highly sensitive financial data (intelligence) on individuals, corporations, parastatals, government departments, businesses, etc. The data so collated are not readily available on documents or normal transactions; it is the whole gamut of metadata, which lends a telescopic view on the heartbeat of the subject under consideration. The NFIU collates data that make all other data meaningful; it often provides the last jigsaw in the puzzle beyond all contestation. The NFIU, by definition, is the most important financial information unit in the country. It liaises with other financial information units in other parts of the world, with the view to harmonising information on crucial areas of national interest and the macro-economy. This is underlined by an important preamble.

Increased volume of trade and global interaction between states in the 1990s, coupled with the threats of terrorism and money laundering across borders, meant that some type of international coordination of financial units of similar kind was needed. As is usual in these situations, a group of Western financial information bodies got together at Egmont, Belgium, in 1995 and agreed to set up an "informal" umbrella body to oversee their activities, hence, the "Egmont Group",[137] which has since expanded to some one hundred and sixty-seven countries around the world, including Nigeria. The group provides "a platform for the secure exchange of expertise and financial intelligence to combat money laundering and terrorist financing". Although, not stated, its remit also includes issues of counter-industrial espionage to some degree. At this juncture, I do not think the reader needs convincing about the significance of this group, from which Nigeria has now been suspended. The country has been suspended having ignored several warnings from the group to stop "political interference" in the work of the NFIU, as well as other kinds of 'abuse' of the

---

136. Located in Abuja, Federal Capital Territory https://www.nfiu.gov.ng

137. A body of 167 Financial Intelligence Units (FIUs) spread across the world, pool resources on information-sharing mechanisms among its members to combat money laundering, terrorist financing, and associated predicate crimes. It is located in Toronto, Canada. https://egmontgroup.org

group's platform.[138] This sounds familiar in the field of international sports as well, where Nigeria's membership of the Federation of International Football Associations (FIFA) has had to be suspended several times for precisely the same reasons.

Thankfully, though, the country has been given until December this year to clear things up or face expulsion from the group. Let us be clear about this, Nigeria was on the blacklist of international financial institutions until it gained membership of the group in 2007. It follows, therefore, that any expulsion from the group would usher in a new form of sanctions and re-blacklisting of the country's financial institutions. Suspension, of itself, is not only an embarrassment; it is already costing the country a huge loss of credibility. Credibility is everything in international finance. Access to the group's secure web, ESW, is already under suspension, preventing the authorities from benefiting from exchange of information with other members of the group on crucial domestic and international matters. The group has no legal standing, structure or hierarchy, and it has no power to compel any errant member to toe the line as it were. Paradoxically, however, and for a non-governmental organisation, it is one of the most feared financial authorities in the world. There is thus the rude awakening of an expulsion from this august body staring us in the face, which would effectively cast the country as a leper in international financial boardrooms across the world. Plus, it will take several years of painful negotiations to be readmitted. How then did we conspire to tilt ourselves to the edge of this financial precipice?

Let us cast our minds to how the Nigerian Football Association (NFA), often finds itself enmeshed in petty squabbles with government officials over funding and personnel, and with everything being the subject of barter between the organisation and the political elite in the country; the chairman, nationality/ethnicity of the coach, the players (whether home-grown or foreign-based), international friendlies between which countries, team selection, remuneration, training, the lot. All of these, too often, and to the chagrin of FIFA, tend to become embroiled in government bureaucracy and political machination of one type or the other. So too, is the position of the NFIU, as it is currently. For a start, it is not a detective agency yet, curiously, it sits within the EFCC which, amongst other things, is a detective agency. NFIU is not and should not take an interest in whether or not any individual is prosecuted, or whether market abusers are punished or not, or whether domestic terrorists are apprehended or

---

138. The suspension, which has since been lifted provoked alarming headlines in the media, forcing the authorities to put in place measures to placate the Group without further ado.

not. Its role is to provide concise and unadulterated information to all the relevant bodies, including the EFCC. It follows logically, therefore, that the EFCC cannot put itself in the position of the puppeteer vis-à-vis the NFIU as it has sought to do from inception. The two bodies must be decoupled without further ado.

As the Nigerian Senate is hurriedly trying to craft a new legislation to free up the NFIU, there has been a lot of jockeying for position on the part of several other government agencies: Securities and Exchange Commission, Central Bank of Nigeria, Ministry of the Interior, Office of the Attorney General of the Federation etc. desirous of bringing the NFIU within its orbit. It is a measure of how pivotal the role of the organisation is. It is a repository of an enormous amount of vital information which, when carefully analysed and dissected, can be of immense benefit to the recipient. In fact, so vital are some of the data gathered that it can literally be the difference between life and death for an entity. Information, it is said, is power. It is no surprise, therefore, that the EFCC has fought so hard to retain control of it. Information is the lifeblood of the EFCC itself, but its object is radically different from that of its adopted child; the NFIU.

To be successful, therefore, and based on international best practices, the NFIU needs to be revamped, and yes, restructured as an autonomous and apolitical body. It should not owe its survival to the whims and caprices of any other body in the country, not even the Presidency. To this end, its funding should not come from a single source. The Federal Government having made the initial capital outlay for the foundation of the revamped NFIU should then literally back off. Its revenue should thereafter come from the existing stakeholders, pari-passu. To take a cue from President Muhammadu Buhari himself, the new NFIU should belong to everybody, and at the same time belong to nobody.[139]

2.12 Stock Exchange and the Mechanics of Markets

4 September 2017

Last week, the European Union blocked the proposed £22bn merger between the London Stock Exchange and its German rival, Deutsche Börse. The deal, if approved, would have resulted in the strongest exchange in Europe with a near monopoly presence across European markets.[140] The European Commission

---

139. The NFIU is now domiciled within the Central Bank of Nigeria.

140. For a multifaceted perspective, see; Dirk Schiereck (2017) "Why the merger between Deutsche Börse and the London Stock Exchange will strengthen Frankfurt as a financial centre".

2 · FINANCE/CAPITAL MARKETS

blocked the deal as it has the potential for stifling competition.[141] Negotiations had been on-going for over a year, and it is the third time the merger had come to the table; the two previous occasions being 2000 and 2005. With "Brexit" now a reality, it is unlikely the merger will be resurrected in the foreseeable future if ever. What will probably fascinate people in this part of the world is the thought of one established stock exchange buying up another equally well established one. What, for instance, would be the reaction of the public in this country, were the Ghanaian or Kenyan Stock Exchange to come up with a proposal to buy up the Nigerian Stock Exchange? Are stock exchanges not owned by governments? Are they not part of sovereign assets? How does that work?

Ever since the Lagos Stock Exchange opened for business in 1960 with a total capitalisation of eighty thousand pounds sterling, it has metamorphosed into the Nigerian Stock Exchange with thirteen additional branches across the country and approximately nine trillion (a significant dip from the high of over twelve trillion a few years back) naira market capitalisation.[142] It is a place to go, basically, to buy and sell (exchange if you like) money. It is the nerve centre of the capitalist money-go-round of the economy; a place to make plenty of money and also, incidentally, to lose tons of it. In a free and open economy, the stock exchange is actually a club; a private club for members only. It provides its own regulations for its members to ensure adherence to its listing rules, providing clearing and settlement rules and guarding against insider dealings by any of its members. With the volume of trades in world economy, stock exchanges have become businesses in their own right, with an exchange often quoting itself on its own list. Almost all exchanges are now incorporated with shareholders wanting healthy returns on their investment.

In less open and competitive market environment though, or what is euphemistically called the "emerging markets", like Nigeria, stock exchanges are more likely to (still) be government-owned or government-run as an external agency. This is essentially for security reasons as they tend to be more

---

Technische Universität, Darmstadt, Corporate Finance Department, Germany. https://www.deutsche-boerse.com/resource/blob/136034/c2590bda5150d5d2862dae7327291649/data/schiereck_study_en.pdf

141. The proposal was blocked by the European Commission under its EU Merger Regulation https://ec.europa.eu/commission/presscorner/detail/es/IP_17_789

142. Market capitalisation of a company is the product of its current market price multiplied by its number of outstanding shares. For example, if a company has N1m ordinary shares as its number of outstanding shares and a market price of 20k today, the market capitalisation of the company becomes; N1m ordinary shares x 20k = N20m https://sec.gov.ng/understanding-market-capitalisation

98   2 · FINANCE/CAPITAL MARKETS

vulnerable to shocks than is the case with more sophisticated market systems in the West. Speculative trading is the hallmark of exchanges all over the world, but the price of openness and laissez-faire can be painful at times. In 1992, George Soros conducted the "trade of the century" by holding the monetary system of Great Britain to ransom,[143] by betting against the country's currency. In the process, he and his team of hedge-fund managers made billions of dollars at the expense of the British tax payers. Several years down the line, in 1997, speculators attempted a similar trick on Malaysia; a buoyant emerging market in Asia. The then Prime Minister of the country, Dr Mahathir Mohamad, was swift in his reaction to the possibility of a raid similar to that inflicted on the UK being done to his country by announcing the introduction of the **death penalty** to anyone caught doing that to the country's economy.[144] The UK could lose billions of dollars on its exchange and look the other way, but Malaysia? Or Nigeria for that matter? Perhaps not.

The above explains why Nigeria still cannot afford to have a "floating" rate of exchange for the Naira, nor a completely privatised exchange either. Capital markets are not for the uninitiated; they accommodate vultures and vampires in droves. This, in turn, is why exchanges have brokers, whom one approaches to deal and negotiate with investors. They are required to execute deals on behalf of their clients as agents. They are not allowed to buy and sell shares in their own accounts, meaning, they are not supposed to be engaged in the business of accumulating deals for themselves for fear of compromising the integrity of the transactions they conduct on behalf of their clients. This is for a good reason, as a broker who is also amassing shares for himself from different companies on the exchange could advise his client to buy shares in the same companies in order to drive up the price. Similarly, the broker, tired of holding particular shares, could simply dump those shares on his unsuspecting client. This is why there was a separation of roles between dealers and brokers, the former was the market makers with all the information on particular companies, while the latter was the one who went round looking for the lowest price (if the client wants to buy) and the highest price (if the broker's client wants to sell).

---

143. The 'bet' turned Soros into a celebrity trader with global influence overnight. For glimpse of the worldwide reports on the incident, see; "How George Soros broke the Bank of England", 1992. https://www.thebalance.com/black-wednesday-george-soros-bet-against-britain-1978944

144. See; Edward A. Gargan. "Premier of Malaysia Spars With Currency Dealer". September, 1997 among several other media highlights on the hot button issue. https://www.nytimes.com/1997/09/22/world/premier-of-malaysia-spars-with-currency-dealer.html

Nowadays though, this distinction has all but disappeared as most exchanges are now electronic and it is commonplace to have dealer-brokers (albeit) with tighter regulation. Members have to notify the exchange as soon as a deal is concluded, with specific details including volume and price, which is immediately circulated to all via a dedicated screen. No excuses for computer being "down" or anything like what you tend to see in government bureaucracy. These transactions involve billions and trillions of naira as it happens, so, no room for errors and omissions. Readers would have seen reports of fines in billions of naira on companies caught up in market infractions in the recent past. Confidence in the market is paramount and any act aimed at undermining that, either deliberate or inadvertent, is dealt with as a matter of urgency.

Maintaining a liquid market is the bread and butter of the Nigerian Stock Exchange and all others. It is what they are all competing for. The stock exchange is sensitive to buy and sell orders as these are capable of either driving up or depressing prices. The asymmetry between foreign portfolio investors and local (i.e. Nigerian) investors on the NSE is, to say the least, lamentable. By the way, "liquidity" is the market jargon for easy flowing of transactions. The larger and more liquid a market, the less impact individual orders will have on it because if you have, say, only two (foreign) billionaires in a market of one hundred traders, any action taken by one of the billionaires is likely to have a swift and immediate impact on prices across the board. On the other hand, if you have twenty-five (local) billionaires in the same market, the action of one foreign billionaire is unlikely to have the same ripple effect. Consequently, the larger and deeper the market, the more liquid it becomes.

2.13 US Dollar: The Power and the Glory (I)

19 September 2017

Before delving into the substantive issue this week and the next two weeks, let me first of all let you, the reader, into one of the columnist's closest guarded secrets. It is that much of the ideas and inspiration generated for this weekly column derive from casual conversations with people one runs into at random. The most fertile venues for pinching ideas are inside taxis, airport lounges and drink joints. Others are social gatherings with friends, relatives and colleagues. Sure as daylight, I have picked up an idea from such a gathering, from a fifteen year old, to generate a topic on financial law for this column in the recent past. Thus, it is from a similar gathering that the inspiration for this three-part essay came into being. Writers do not generally

100 2 · FINANCE/CAPITAL MARKETS

acknowledge the sources of these ideas because it is unnecessary. And in case you are wondering, it is not plagiarism either. Ideas are free. The way and manner (including the context) in which an idea is used, however, is usually peculiar to the author/writer and, as such, should not be copied without due acknowledgment. Anyway, that aside.

At a cosy gathering of friends in a neighbour's yard a couple of days ago, a bright, tall and lanky teenage school boy was handed a one hundred dollar bill by his uncle as a gift for passing his exams. I listened attentively as the overjoyed boy was bouncing around, soliciting for a good naira rate from the relaxed evening guests. He plans to go to university next year to study law and was boasting about his desire to charge his fees in dollars, in future, like Aare Afe Babalola (SAN) does. Babalola, of course, is an advocate per excellence, who rose from nothing to the pinnacle of the legal practice in Nigeria. The boy had read a passage in his memoire: "Impossibility made possible",[145] where he talked about charging in dollars. Aare Babalola also cited in the book an incidence that happened at his former client's, President Olusegun Obasanjo's private residence. He had gone to see him for instructions on a pending case, and as he and the coterie of SANs[146] Aare Babalola had assembled in Obasanjo's defence were trouping in one after the other to take their seats, the former President exclaimed in awe of the battle-hardened wigs: "Ah, Chief, no wonder you charge in dollars!" This passage made quite an impression on the young man, whose uncontrolled enthusiasm in turn, spurred me to write this three-part essay.

Since Aare Babalola and his ilk appear to have turned charging in dollars into a *cause célèbre;* the surest indication that one has 'arrived' at the dizzy height of stupendous wealth, it was completely lost on the little boy, indeed a young man, that the one hundred dollar bill dangling in his hand, not that long ago, used to be the exact equivalent of one hundred naira note used for buying a pack of "pure water"[147] today. Yes, one dollar used to exchange for one naira; even for less than that at times, in this same country of ours, and in so many people's life time.[148] At the material time though, simply being a

---

145. Afe Babalola. Impossibility Made Possible. Afe Babalola University Press, 2011.

146. Senior Advocate of Nigeria is the British equivalent of QC or Queens Counsel

147. Common name for sachet water sold to and bought by people in the street. Much of it is derived from unfiltered water from the local well, so, it is really a misnomer to label it pure water.

148. For more on this, see; US Dollar (USD) to Nigerian Naira (NGN) exchange rate history https://www.exchangerates.org.uk/USD-NGN-exchange-rate-history.html And, Nigeria Exchange Rate against USD, 1957–2022 https://www.ceicdata.com /en/indicator/nigeria/exchange-rate-against-usd

2 · FINANCE/CAPITAL MARKETS

Nigerian carried with it a lot of pride. Nigeria became a self-proclaimed "giant of Africa". That sounds pretty outlandish now, of course, but it did not quite fall out of place at the time. Judging by how much of our wealth has since been squandered, and is still being squandered, it would be hard to quibble about being dubbed the sleeping giant of Africa now.

How is it, then that one dollar is now exchanged for three hundred and eighty naira in today's market? How come, then that the Ministry of Finance in this country offers the incentive of remuneration in dollars for investors instead of the naira; a de facto "dollarization" of the country's economy (albeit by the back door)?[149] It has even become cool amongst the flamboyant and the well-heeled, to 'spray'[150] in dollars at high-society parties instead of the naira. How come then that the dollar has become such a rarefied commodity, almost as important as the air we breathe in, in this country? Fixated by the daily bulletin on the Central Bank of Nigeria's latest moves to pomp more dollar into the market, most people under the age of thirty in this country see the ubiquitous presence of the dollar in our everyday life as a given; a *fait accompli*. That is, it is just what it is, but my contention is that it is what it is not because it was inevitable, but because of the choices we have made as a country. It is not by accident that the dollar has come to be seen by Nigerian citizens as a better store of value than the naira. That state of affairs did not happen overnight, our erstwhile leaders created the foundation for it over a period of time.

It is thus vitally important for the young man aspiring to earn his legal fees in dollars (no blame), and the vast majority of Nigerian youths to understand the trajectory of the dollar as the dominant force that it has become in our economy, and for that matter, in the overall global trade. As we chart the debate henceforth, I would urge the reader to contemplate how, if ever, we are likely to witness a return to the dollar-naira parity again in our country, or, whether that is even desirable any longer. More alarmingly, could the steady growth of the dollar transactions (aided and abetted by the Ministry of Finance) in this country see the eventual death of the naira as a legal tender in favour of the dollar? Would Nigeria become, in effect, a mere appendage of the United States' global economy for all practical purposes? It happened most recently

---

149. See; David O. Olayungbo and Kehinde T. Ajuwon. "Dollarisation, Inflation and Interest Rate in Nigeria" CBN Journal of Applied Statistics. Vol 6 No 1 (b) (June, 2015) https://www.cbn.gov.ng/out/2015/sd/dollarization%20inflation%20and%20interest%20rate %20in%20nigeria.pdf

150. It is the vulgar (yet socially tolerated) act of throwing money like confetti on the revellers on the dance floor at social functions.

102   2 · FINANCE/CAPITAL MARKETS

in Zimbabwe, under the "Marxist revolutionary", "President-for-life", Robert Mugabe.[151] How can we avoid the slippery slope in this country?

2.14 US Dollar: The Power and the Glory (II)

26 September 2017

The dollar is a common name for more than twenty currencies around the world, including; USA, Canada, Australia, Hong-Kong, Singapore, New-Zealand, etc. The US dollar is the focus of this topic because of its pervasive influence and use. It is being used as the official currency of over forty countries and territories, and is unofficially being used in several others such as: Afghanistan, Bolivia, Cambodia, Guatemala, Lebanon, East Timor etc. Besides, many economies such as Nigeria, peg their currencies to the value of the dollar, making them the junior partner to the US dollar, and concomitantly subject to the whims and caprices of its Central Bank, the US Federal Reserve. As a matter of fact, majority of US dollar banknotes are held by people and institutions outside the territory of the USA.[152] Based on our earlier discussion in part one, last week, the ambitious young man whose enthusiasm for the dollar sparked this three-part essay is only one of several millions of individuals around the globe enthusiastically holding on to their hundred dollar bills. Interestingly, more than seventy per cent of US one hundred dollar bills are held outside the USA.[153] This puts the USA in either a precarious or indeed powerful position, depending on whichever angle one chooses to look at it. The world has not always been this beholden to the US dollar to this extent though. What happened?

At the turn of the industrial revolution in the eighteenth century, Britannia (UK), "ruled the waves" as it is said. As the greatest sea power of the time, it led the way in steam and locomotive engines used to move goods across countries and continents.[154] The Sterling provided the financial stability that aided

---

151. See; Joseph Noko. "Dollarisation: The Case of Zimbabwe". 'Cato Journal'. Vol 31 No 2 (Spring/Summer 2011) https://www.cato.org/sites/cato.org/files/serials/files/cato-journal/2011/5/cj31n2-9.pdf

152. Richard D. Porter, and Ruth A. Judson. "The Location of US Currency: How Much is Abroad?". US Federal Reserve Bulletin, Monetary Affairs Division, October, 1996. https://www.federalreserve.gov/pubs/bulletin/1996/1096lead.pdf

153. Porter and Judson, ibid.

154. Stoake, ibid.

2 · FINANCE/CAPITAL MARKETS 103

international trade until World War1 exerted a great toll on Britain's ability to finance its military and the expansion of its economy.[155] Thereafter, the USA stepped in to guarantee a stable international exchange. Part of what led to the war was the "Mercantilist"[156] doctrine of the great powers in the economic sphere, which basically encouraged a beggar-my-neighbour approach to economic development. Countries were busy trying to exploit loopholes in the international financial system such as it was, by engaging in competitive devaluation strategies, limiting imports and expanding exports. It was a recipe for disaster, which partly accounted for the two World Wars.[157]

It was against this background that forty four "Allied nations" (direct participants in the Wars), gathered together for the United Nations Monetary and Financial Conference inside Mount Washington Hotel, Bretton Woods, New Hampshire, USA, in 1944, to jaw-jaw about conflict and financial instability in the world. The meeting culminated in an agreement; the "Bretton Woods Agreement",[158] to set up what we know today as the International Monetary Fund, commonly known as the IMF. The Agreement also included the setting up of an International Bank for Reconstruction and Development, which is better known today as the World Bank. These two institutions were set up primarily for the reconstruction of Europe, and the United States, not having been affected too much by the ravages of the Wars (much of Europe laid in ruins), understandably stepped up to the plate by taking the leading role in reshaping international trade and finance. It was '*Pax Americana*'[159] of some kind. Thereafter, the dollar took a preeminent role in guaranteeing international exchange backed by the powers of the newly formed "Bretton Woods Institutions" i.e. the IMF and World Bank.

In a nutshell, therefore, the dollar became the number one reserve currency of the world throughout the twentieth century, the American century as it has been dubbed. This has allowed the US to pursue an expansionary economic and foreign policy anchored on the "military-industrial complex", giving itself the latitude to borrow at will, while apparently taking punitive financial

---

155. Stoake, ibid.

156. Lars Herlitz (1964) The Concept of Mercantilism. Scandinavian Economic History Review, 12:2, 101–120. Published online by Routledge, 2011.

157. Barry R. Weingast. War, Trade, and Mercantilism: Reconciling Adam Smith's Three Theories of the British Empire. Stanford University, 2013

158. Bretton Woods Agreement Act, 79th US Congress, July 1945 https://www.govinfo.gov/content/pkg/COMPS-10334/pdf/COMPS-10334.pdf

159. Refers to a period of relative peace and stability that extended throughout the area of American influence beginning with the end of World War II

measures to deter others from doing the same thing. Europe soon recovered, but the rest of the world needed to catch up, and take advantage of the new global economic order. The Bretton Woods Institutions now shifted their attention to the countries left behind by the original Agreement; the so-called "developing" and "third world" countries. These countries came on board a system already rigged against them; where the rules of the game had already been set in favour of the "foundation members". Whereas the USA and other Western European nations can use monetary policy to increase government borrowing, other nations have to go through the IMF to do the same thing often at much greater cost to their economies. Rich countries, especially the USA, became net importers of capital from developing countries, most notably China.[160] The USA, through an aggressive policy of low interest rate, uses Treasury bills to attract money from other countries. The Chinese, on the other hand, have been pursuing their own aggressive growth strategy, which has seen their economy grown by an average of 8% in the last couple of decades. The excess cash generated by that is then used to buy American Treasury bills in huge quantity.[161]

Based on this, the USA has seen a steady rise in the level of its public debt, which now stands close to twenty-one trillion dollars and rising. Just imagine; Nigeria was struggling to issue Treasury bills to offset a meagre three billion US dollar debt last month! Yes, the USA has a twenty-one trillion dollar public debt profile, but who cares? It is roughly equivalent to its annual GDP. Any company that maintains such a huge black hole in its books would have long been declared bankrupt. Moreover, any developing country that tries anything close to the Americans would have the IMF crack team of technocrats parachuted in from Washington to give advice on "urgent reforms" of its financial institutions. Anyone that attempts such a 'reckless' economic policy; anyone but the USA, would have its fingers badly burnt, and quite rightly so in many people's view. The question though is, why has this not affected the dollar as the number one reserve currency in the world? Why has the dollar's dominance not been affected even at the time of severe global economic crisis of 2008, which saw many US banks going bankrupt, the housing sector in a meltdown, and several manufacturing industries laying off workers?

---

160. Office of the US Trade Representative https://ustr.gov/countries-regions/china-mongolia-taiwan/peoples-republic-china

161. Latest reports suggest China and US lead rise in global debt to a record high of $US305 trillion — IIF https://www.reuters.com

2.15 US Dollar: The Power and the Glory (III)

3 October 2017

Despite the financial crisis emanating from the US housing sector that spread onto the banking and other financial institutions globally in 2008, it has not significantly affected foreign holdings of American financial assets, which runs into trillions of dollars.[162] There is a sizable US dollar holding in the Euro-zone as well as thousands of business transactions being conducted in dollars on a daily basis. At the same time, though, there is a funding gap in US public spending, especially on infrastructure, and there is not much money available to embark upon that. Rather than borrowing more money, why cannot the US simply print money for their own use at home? If the chunk of US dollars is already out there, in foreign hands, it makes sense to mint some new (additional) notes and coins to meet pressing needs, does it not? Ah well, it is not that simple. Printing more money would lead to inflation, meaning an increase in the cost of goods and services, also meaning that the value of the dollar will plummet. That means, in effect, that the real value of the debt to other countries, institutions and individuals holding the US Treasury bills will reduce. That, of course, would be seen as the US reneging on its obligations to those foreign investors.

Moreover, any dramatic fall in the value of the dollar would have domestic ramifications as holders of US debt include pensioners, insurance and other financial institutions inside the US. It would certainly have political consequences in the electoral cycle. Pensioners and retirees in the West constitute a much more potent electoral force than they do here in Nigeria and elsewhere. Governments are often careful not to mess with that group of voters. Given how unpalatable that option appears to be, the US could decide to default on its debt obligations. It has happened at various times to big nations in history. Much of the developing world was up in arms about crippling debt in the 1980s/90s and were threatening to withhold servicing those debts en mass, forcing the international financial institutions like the "Paris Club" to reschedule the debts and cancel a great deal of it. Nigeria was one of the beneficiaries of the debt cancellation programme. On the face of it, the US appears to be in a uniquely advantageous position of defaulting on its debt obligations since the debts are held in dollars. This unique position, however, is a double-

---

162. US Department of the Treasury — Preliminary Report on Foreign Holdings of US Securities at end of June 2021. https://home.treasury.gov/news/press-releases/jy0613

edged sword. You swing it one way, and it reverts back the other way. Any default on American debt obligations would send the whole capitalist system into a death spiral.

Consequently, for the middle income countries, the so-called "emerging economies", holding US financial assets is a luxury many of them cannot afford, but cannot cease to want. Where else do they pack their excess cash reserve? Their own currencies are unable to compete with the dollar as a reserve currency. Nigeria may not have excess cash reserve in its Sovereign Wealth Fund, but ninety per cent of its foreign earnings come from oil, traded in dollars. Much of the international financial transactions are wholly dependent on acquisition of US assets because of its strength and depth. The US dollar used to account for eighty percent of the world's foreign exchange, until the 1980s.[163] It still accounts for two-thirds of global foreign exchange. So, despite the skyrocketing US public debt profile, their Treasury bills are still seen and accepted as the gold standard of capital investment around the world. The largest proportion of banks around the world not only trade in US dollars, but they have accumulated so much of American financial assets that, it is now in their mutual interest to prevent the value of the dollar from crashing. In US military parlance, this is called the doctrine of "Mutual Assured Destruction", MAD for short. It is what Professor Eswar Prasad, of Cornell University, in New York, generously describes as the "dollar trap".[164] Let us call it the dollar morass.

Having said all of that, the resentment or even envy, which some countries naturally feel towards the position of the US in world finance is only tempered by the fact that it is a country of long, stable democratic governance. It has strong institutions like few others in the world; it also has a trusted legal superstructure to keep the show on an even keel. This is quite apart from its unrivalled military might, which it uses to project itself as the world's policeman on occasions. Despite the "gridlock" exemplified by the two dominant political parties in Congress, the system does function for the Americans. The markets have a way of discounting political shenanigans of the Washington elite from time to time. It also has a way of managing a rampaging and unconventional

---

163. See; "US Dollar Share of Global Foreign Exchange Reserves Drops to 25-Year Low". IMF Blog. Insights and Analysis on Economics and Finance, May 2021. https://blogs.imf.org/2021/05/05/us-dollar-share-of-global-foreign-exchange-reserves-drops-to-25-year-low

164. See; Eswar Prasad. "The Dollar Trap: How the US Dollar Tightened its Grip on Global Finance". Dyson School of Applied Economics and Management, Cornell University, April 2015. https://www.cornell.edu/video/eswar-prasad-dollar-trap-global-finance

President it sometimes elects, such as the current President Donald Trump.[165] Going back to where this discussion all started, what then is our last message to the young man with the hundred dollar bill, who desires to charge his fees in dollars instead of naira at his future law practice in this country?

It is that in basic economics, money indeed has three functions: a medium of exchange, a unit of account, and a store of value. As a medium of exchange, the naira still fulfils its function — reasonably well. As a unit of account, well, given that the aspiring young lawyer will be buying mostly foreign goods, the naira will be of less use. As a store of value? With the proliferation of foreign domiciliary accounts on offer by Nigerian banks, and with the Ministry of Finance busy offering dollar incentive to investors, the naira's long-term use as a store of value is on a shaky ground to say the least. So, like it or lump it, barring a radical departure from where we are heading, dollar takeover looms in this country. To a lot of people, this may amount to no more than a statement of the obvious, but it is no less heart-rending.

2.16 Why Banks Fail

10 October 2017

Despite numerous bank failures in the recent past around the world, and the grubby, shady deals regularly entered into by bankers, it is, by and large, a pretty respectable profession. It is one that many young people still aspire to, and it is an industry no economy can do without. The odious aspect to the profession owes its origins to history. Bankers started out as a bunch of self-serving money changers. The biblical reference to the role of money changers is unedifying, as they once incurred the wrath of Jesus Christ himself, who angrily chased them out of the Temple. "Banco" is the Italian word for bench. In ancient times, money changers would sit on it whilst displaying their wares to customers. Their initial institutional customers were the old merchants, who needed deposit facilities to store their precious metals, especially gold. The money changers soon realised that these deposits could be recycled and put into other commercial and industrial activities. However, the problem then, as now, is what to do if the depositors start retrieving their gold and precious metals simultaneously? Short answer is they go bust. Whenever that happened to the money changer-cum banker, in the past, the bench, i.e. "Banco" on which he sat was symbolically broken in the open for people to see. This was

---

165. Current President is Joe Biden since 2020

known as "Bancarotta", or a broken bench, otherwise called bankruptcy in today's parlance.

The process whereby people withdraw their deposits simultaneously is called a bank "run".[166] Bank runs are generally understood to be a terrible occurrence, but the process also, paradoxically, provides the means to eliminate inefficiency and bad (toxic) investment or asset from the system. Closure is the result of irreconcilable problems in a bank's fundamentals. More often than not, financial authorities tend to step in to save a bank under stress because of the risk of contagion, that is, the possibility of a closure spreading like bush fire onto other banks, creating a systemic risk for the whole sector and beyond. Nowadays, though, ordinary customers enjoy a degree of protection from bank runs. Their deposits are often guaranteed by the banking regulator up to a certain amount. Institutional investors in the banks, however, are more exposed to all types of speculative runs. It is the game they understand and indeed, enjoy playing. They look and model the action of other players in the game on their computer software, and try to anticipate what the other may be up to at a given period. At times, they join in the stampede of mass withdrawal and other times they ignore such.

A good example of this was provided by the Hungarian hedge fund manager and philanthropist, George Soros, in September 1992.[167] By the way, hedge fund management simply means a private investment house, where people with gargantuan amounts of excess cash deposit their money to be used to make even more money, by playing high-risk and highly rewarding bets on the exchanges. The amount involved is usually so large that placing it in the run-of-the-mill commercial bank for a pre-determined interest rate makes no sense. When the calculus comes right for a hedge fund manager, it comes really big, and when it goes wrong, well, billions of dollars could go up in flames in minutes. Soros, whose family brought him to London, fleeing Communism in his home country of Hungary in the 1960s, graduated from the London School of Economics, and thereafter set out to play the capitalist game of making money.[168] He soon made enough to set himself up for life in the UK, but he wanted to apply his canny knowledge to something bigger and even more exciting. So, he left for New York, in the United States, whereupon he coaxed enough wealthy indi-

---

166. Martin Brown, Stefan T.Trautmann, and Razvan Vlahu. Understanding Bank-Run Contagion. European Central Bank. Working Paper Series, No 1711/August 2014 https://www.ecb.europa.eu/pub/pdf/scpwps/ecbwp1711.pdf

167. Kuepper, ibid.

168. Soros is Founder/Chair, Open Society Foundations. https://www.opensocietyfoundations.org/george-soros

2 · FINANCE/CAPITAL MARKETS

viduals into entrusting their money to him to 'manage' (or gamble with), depending on your taste and financial sense.[169] His big break came when, in 1992, he put all the billions of dollars at his disposal into betting against the UK staying in the Exchange Rate Mechanism (ERM) of the European Union. This prompted a run on British banks, and the government intervened multiple times with a hike in interest rate to put a brake on the outflow of capital from the UK economy. Undeterred, Soros threw even more billions of dollars at it, steadfast in his hunch that the UK would be forced out, then, others joined in the stampede which, true to prediction, eventually forced the UK out of the ERM. Soros and his clients became multi-billionaires instantly.

Interestingly, when Malaysia was going through a similar financial turmoil and became aware of a rumoured plan of Soros's imminent trade on their exchange, the Malaysian Parliament hurriedly passed legislation to impose the death penalty on anyone caught speculating on their hard-won effort at stabilising their currency. Soros, then in his late seventies, understandably opted not to take a chance, and has since returned to Hungary a hero with his 'loot'.

In a situation like we have just discussed, it is always open to the country's central bank to step in as the bank of "last resort"; a view enunciated by none other than the English economist, Walter Bagehot (1826–1877), who advised central banks to, amongst other things, announce in advance their readiness to lend to banks without limits to make them stay solvent. This doctrine was first put into practice by the Bank of England in the "Barings crisis" of 1890.[170] Others around the world have since followed the logic to this day. The Central Bank of Nigeria (CBN) has carried this responsibility furthest. It has moved from simply being a regulator to supervisor of banks in Nigeria. It imposes term limits on Chief Executive Officers of banks, suspends and dismisses management of banks at will, countermand major investment decisions made by banks, etc. In addition to this, the CBN has the additional support of the country's Assets Management Corporation of Nigeria (AMCON), whose primary function is to "manage" (take over if you like) the assets of any entity critical to the economy, found to be in distress. Nothing could be more cast-iron for the solvency of Nigerian banks than this, you might think.

---

169. See Soros compelling biography via the Open Society Foundations, ibid.

170. Ramaa Vasudevan. "Quantitative easing through the prism of the Barings crisis in 1890: Central banks and the international money market". 'Journal of Post-Keynesian Economics'. Vol 37, 2014, Issue 1 https://www.tandfonline.com/doi/abs/10.2753 /PKE0160-3477370107

110   2 · FINANCE/CAPITAL MARKETS

Well, risk-taking is part of the raison d'être of commercial banks, it is written in their DNA. This, however, is more apparent than real in the case of Nigerian banks. The CBN ought not to overegg their supervisory remit too much lest it stifles thrift and innovation. Moreover, try as the CBN might, Nigerian banks cannot be protected from the headwinds of globalisation and the constant clarion call for deregulation in international finance. Moreover, increasing penetration of financial services by non-banks, providing high-quality banking services will eventually force the banks out of the CBN's protective (comfort) zone. By any acceptable yardstick of international banking services, Nigerian banks live a much sheltered life at the moment for a good reason; they have run amok once before, costing the Federal Government a whopping one trillion naira to bail them out.[171] That said, the current philosophy of the CBN to the effect that any bank in Nigeria is always worth more alive than dead is untenable in the long run.

2.17 SEC's New "Derivatives" Platform

14 November 2017

The Nigerian Stock Exchange under the auspices of the Securities and Exchange Commission (SEC) in their attempt at deepening the Nigerian capital markets recently introduced a new layer of financial trading known in larger exchanges around the world as "derivatives". It is a form of trading usually seen in more advanced economies because of its complex nature; not one for a small market like ours. As a matter of fact, our Stock Exchange is so lopsided that one individual; the Dangote group owns about 43% of the total.[172] For that reason, Mr Dangote might as well be recognised as the 'controlling shareholder' of the exchange in this country. For so many obvious reasons, derivatives is for the grown up, but there is nothing wrong with our exchange trying to punch above its weight. It is entirely possible for us to grow into it over time, with persistence and all other things being equal. But first, what exactly is this thing called "derivatives" anyway?

Conceptually, derivatives are products whose value is derived from other assets. Ah, What? What does that really mean? Not very much to anyone, except to the experts inside the SEC and other financial junkies outside. As-

---

171. See Reuters report amongst others. https://www.reuters.com/article/nigeria-banks-idUKLH48480820090817

172. See; African Markets Publications https://www.african-markets.com/en/stock-markets/ngse/dangote-group-controls-43-of-nigerian-stock-market

2 · FINANCE/CAPITAL MARKETS

suming Mr Smart, a man with serious money in his bank account, goes shopping for his family at his local supermarket and sees truck-loads of bananas being delivered there and shoppers ceaselessly yanking them off the shelves in their bundles. Clever Mr Smart thinks there is money to be made from this particular commodity; bananas, and is convinced that the price will soon go up for him to make a quick killing. So, what does he do? Mr Smart is a man of considerable means; he has billions of naira to his credit waiting to be recycled into his favourite sport; capital markets. Well, Mr Smart could start a farming business in bananas, but he doesn't want that, because that will take too much time and effort. So, why not rent a warehouse, stack hundreds of millions of bananas in it, and sell to supermarkets across the nation? Good idea, but he is not interested in having any physical structure under his control. His only, and main asset is capital, and he wants to find a way of recycling it to make more money here and now; money begets money.

So, Mr Smart, living up to his name, comes up with an idea. Why not call his broker-friend, who specialises in this type of commodity and strike a deal? He subsequently commandeered one million tranches of bananas at a cost of ten million naira. From his contact with the producers of bananas, the broker arranges for a 'delivery' of the commodity for Mr Smart, and this is where it gets interesting. Mr Smart is not at all interested in the delivery of a single tranche of bananas to himself. The broker, therefore, marked up the requested quantity in his stock, and simply enters it against Mr Smart as 'sold'. No physical exchange has taken place. Mr Smart gleefully rubs his hands together, a tinge of contentment on his face, and waits. True to his prediction, the price of bananas indeed skyrocketed and doubled in three months. Thereafter, Mr Smart called up his broker-friend and instructed him to 'sell' the one million bananas he has been keeping for him. The bananas are promptly 'sold' back into the market at twenty million naira. Mr Smart's original outlay of ten million naira has become twenty million in just three months. That value added for him is said to be 'derived' from the value of the bananas inside warehouses, and on supermarket shelves owned by faceless and nameless others around the country. Applied to multiple products being traded at the same time, in like manner, such a market is called "derivative(s)".

In case you are wondering how Mr Smart could get away with 'buying' and 'selling' items he does not take actual possession of, well, welcome to capital markets. Meanwhile, all the actions he took via his broker-friend would have appeared in flickers on the computer screens of all the participants and stakeholders in the market, including that of the regulators. Market moves are never isolated incidents; in every action, there is a reaction.

112   2 · FINANCE/CAPITAL MARKETS

Even if things remained unmoved following a particular action, that in itself is a reaction. As this would have affected the real life of buying and selling of the commodity, could Mr Smart have been compelled to take possession of the goods? In theory, yes, but in practice, that does not happen. Does he go home with the twenty million naira windfall in full? Of course, not. The broker gets paid a percentage, and the Stock Exchange takes a cut in "processing fees". He pays his own staff, and everyone goes home singing kum bah yah!

I know, you are probably thinking, what happens if Mr Smart had got it completely wrong and the price of bananas had fallen instead of rising? Oh, yes, that too happens. But remember, like many people of his ilk, Mr Smart is a risk taker, he would probably have taken a separate order with the view to the market going in the opposite direction, so, he would have been covered in any event. I know this is an oversimplification, but it makes you appreciate its complexity a lot better. There are other structural aspects, including the regulatory framework that I have not discussed in this piece.

The new platform appears to be no more than aspirational; an expression of hope rather than an expectation of an immediate impact on the market. The regulators understand the lack of public education on the issue. In this regard, the SEC has embarked upon teaching little kids the basics of the market, to "catch them young" as it were. It's a good idea only in so far as education on any subject is good per se. My own take, however, is that teaching the basics of the market to kids is not really the answer when the level of education in other subjects is even more troubling across the board. No point giving little kids an early knowledge of the markets if their knowledge of other equally relevant subjects: maths, English language, economics, statistics, etc. remains as generally shallow as it currently is. Our tertiary institutions are so woeful, that a lot of them are merely graduating illiterates, year-on-year.

Besides, no one is really teaching kids the mechanics of the market even in advanced countries. They provide their children with a rounded education in the main, and allow their minds to roam free towards the market and other outlets. No one gave Mark Zuckerberg internet lessons as a kid; he was playing around with it in his college dormitory and came up with the idea of Facebook from there. No one taught the late Steve Jobs computing as a kid, he picked it up himself and came up with 'Apple' along the way. Bill Gates, the billionaire founder of Microsoft was studying computing before dropping out to start his own business. All of these people are exceptional individuals, I know, but they also live in a society that provides basic educational infrastructure in good libraries, books, internet, light, classrooms, teachers, etc. Capital markets cannot be taught, and understood in a vacuum. I say give

2 · FINANCE/CAPITAL MARKETS

our children good basic (early) education and some will take the markets by storm soon enough.

2.18 SEC's Litany of Corporate Governance Lapses

5 December 2017

The suspension of the Director-General of the Securities and Exchange Commission, Mr Mounir H. Gwarzo, announced by the Minister of Finance, Mrs Kemi Adeosun, last week, might have been considered a routine exercise if not for the fact that the SEC is the ultimate regulator of Nigeria's financial industry. In other words, it is the regulator's regulator, hovering above the likes of the Nigerian Stock Exchange, Nigerian Deposit Insurance Corporation, even the Central Bank of Nigeria in these matters. It registers and regulates security exchanges, all offers of securities by public companies, registers, and regulates individual and corporate capital markets operators, facilitates a nationwide system for securities trading, registers and regulates the workings of venture capital funds and collective investment schemes, facilitates the linking of all markets in securities with information and communication technology facilities, keeps and maintains a register of foreign portfolio investments, protects the integrity of the securities market against all forms of abuses including insider dealing, etc.[173] You got the gist. Who then regulates the regulator's regulator when the person sitting at the very top of this strategically important organisation stands accused of the kind of market abuse and insider dealing it is empowered to detect, deter, and prevent? The allegations against Gwarzo (hailed by the SEC as a man of "uncommon leadership") are lengthy, and are not exactly new. They have been allowed to fester for several months. It is the first indication of a lamentable failure of corporate governance at the SEC.[174]

The Director General is alleged to have awarded himself a "severance payment" in excess of one hundred million naira following his appointment to his position, having moved from being a commissioner to the position of DG. The glaring question is; how does a mere changing of roles within the same

---

173. See; The Investment and Securities Act 2007 file:///C:/Users/Mr%20Tok%C3%A8/Downloads/20090915470014THE%20INVESTMENTS%20AND%20SECURITIES%20Act%202007%20(2).pdf

174. Gwarzo was subsequently acquitted of the corruption charges against him in 2021, https://thenationonlineng.net/court-acquits-gwarzo-former-sec-dg-of-corruption

entity amount to "severance"? The package was passed through the Board; wait for it, on the recommendation of the newly promoted DG, Gwarzo himself! This is another indication of a deplorable failure of corporate governance at the SEC. Furthermore, the DG is alleged to have traded on his inside information to benefit six companies which he owns or have a substantial interest in. How the DG did not make clear his conflict of interests to the Commission when awarding the alleged contracts, is something that baffles outside observers. It is a further indication of a dreadful failure of corporate governance at the SEC. In addition to these, the Ministry of Finance had been aware of some, or all of these transgressions by the DG for several months and had commenced its own internal investigation into the affair. Why would such a highly sensitive matter affecting the integrity of the entire financial sector take several months, more than ten months, we are told, to result in the suspension of the DG? This is the clearest indication yet of a woeful failure of corporate governance at the SEC, for which the Ministry of Finance also has questions to answer. Is it any coincidence that the DG's suspension kicked in just as it started its own investigation of the oil company, Oando, for a number of market infractions? Could the DG's suspension be a pre-emptive strike by the powers that be to scupper any investigation of the oil company?[175]

Legally speaking, the DG of the SEC is a semi-detached government apparatchik. In this case, he does not report directly to the Minister of Finance, but to the President of the Federal Republic of Nigeria, who alone has the power to appoint and remove him from office subject, of course, to the Senate's approval. Mrs Kemi Adeosun was acting on delegated authority in the suspension of the DG. No one is quibbling about that, but what worries people is her department's capacity to investigate the DG in this kind of situation. The Ministry of Finance is a member of the SEC Board, which ought to have overseen the various infractions committed by the DG or anyone else on the Board. An outside independent panel of enquiry should be constituted to conduct an in-depth examination of the whole affair and report within weeks, not months. The integrity of Nigeria's capital markets and the finance industry is in jeopardy for as long as this lingers. The DG Chairs the Africa Middle East Regional Committee of the International Organisation of Securities Commissions. The stakes could not be higher in an industry where credibility is everything. If the Ministry of Finance is unable to do this, then, the burden falls on the Senate to institute its own hearing/investigation into this as swiftly as possible. One

---

175. The Minister of Finance refuted claims of any link between the two https://www.reuters.com/article/nigeria-oando-probe-idAFL8N1O833C

fears, though, that political intrigue may get in the way as it usually does with such a high-profile enquiry.

The greater issue to tackle is the inadequacy of the SEC corporate governance procedure within the body itself. After all, this is the body that set limits of corporate governance measures for others in the financial sector. The SEC Board as presently constituted, which includes a representative of the Ministry of Finance on it, is demonstrably flawed. First, how did the Board exercise its oversight function when confronted with the remuneration package pushed through by the DG, authorising the payment of over one hundred million to himself? As a member of the Board and its Accounting Officer; Investment and Securities Act 2007 (3) (1) (b), the DG is the same person who recommends approval of his own remuneration to the Board. Where does this rank in any measure of corporate governance? And on the question of the SEC and its dealings with several companies in which the DG has direct pecuniary interests, section (11) (1) of the ISA Act is pretty clear on this. "A member of the Board of the Commission who is directly or indirectly interested in (a) the affairs of any company or enterprise being deliberated upon by the Board of the Commission; or (b) any contract made or proposed to be made by the Board of the Commission shall, as soon as possible after relevant facts have come to his knowledge, disclose the nature of his interest to the Commission at the meeting of the Board of the Commission.[176] We must presume at this point that the DG made all the relevant disclosures as it concerned the six companies with which the SEC is alleged to have contracted.

If after making the disclosures, the DG was, thereafter, not supposed to 'participate or continue to participate in any deliberation or decision of the Board of the Commission with regard to the subject-matter in respect of which his interest is so-disclosed', section (11) (2) (a). At this point, we must also assume that the DG duly complied with this provision of the law, and did not participate. If the Board, of its own volition made the decision to award contracts to companies properly declared by the DG, then, it would have acted against international best practice to not only avoid actual bias in its deliberations, but also, crucially, to avoid giving the appearance of bias in the discharge of its duties. The Ministry of Finance that has now suspended the DG would have been an active participant in the Board's deliberations on the award of the contracts in issue here. Has the Ministry come to equity with clean hands in this case? These are issues of great public interest, the resolution of which cannot come soon enough.

---

176. The Investments and Securities Act 2007, ibid.

2.19 Painful Lesson for 9Mobile Shareholders

24 April 2018

We return to the column's regular theme of capital markets law this week with the news that Justice Binta Nyako of the Federal High Court, Abuja, has blocked the proposed sale of 9Mobile, (formerly Etisalat) to Smile.com and Glo Network on the 17th of April, ordering the parties to maintain the status quo until everyone has been put on notice. The application for an interim injunction to halt the sale had hitherto been brought "ex-parte", meaning without the knowledge of the defendants in the suit, which include; Karlington Telecommunications Ltd, Premium Holdings, First Bank of Nigeria PLC, Central Bank of Nigeria, Etisalat International Nigeria Ltd, and Nigerian Communications Commission.[177] Consequently, the matter has been adjourned until the 14th of May for "mention" meaning, for further direction of the court, when all the parties should have had time to serve all the court processes on each other. The case may then proceed to trial, and it may not, depending on Justice Nyako's latest assessment. The Plaintiffs in this case are major shareholders in 9Mobile, principally; Afdin Ventures US Ltd and Dirbia Nigeria Ltd. There are numerous others, but these are the ones said to be most aggrieved by the proposed sale, meaning, that they have most to lose from it. By their own estimates, they stand to lose all of their investment estimated to be $USM43, 330, 950.[178] They claim that the problem with Etisalat (the forerunner of 9Mobile), resulted from "mismanagement of funds", which means no dividends have been paid since 2009.

In addition, they also claim that the defendants took several loans from 13 Nigerian banks, with the view to expanding and boosting their telecom business, but the money was not "properly utilized" leading to heavy indebtedness for Etisalat, and by extension, 9Mobile. It is further alleged by the Plaintiffs, that the defendants had reached an agreement to sell to Smile.com and Glo Network "without the knowledge of the Plaintiffs", and "without paying the Plaintiffs the money with which they bought their shares". They are opposed to what they view as a "clandestine" sale of the company to the detriment of the

---

177. The case attracted wide media publicity throughout its duration. See, for example; https://marketingedge.com.ng/legal-firework-looms-over-etisalat-sale

178. On the figures see also; https://globalfinancialdigest.com/court-set-aside-sales-of-9mobile-to

2 · FINANCE/CAPITAL MARKETS

Plaintiffs. In addition to having their investment repaid in full, they are seeking one billion naira in general damages. Let me say, first of all, that, from the Plaintiff's original point of view, Etisalat was a highly valuable, highly profitable, growing company, which was the main reason why they put their hard-earned cash into it in the first place. They say they bought shares in the company through a "private placement" in 2009. That is really meant to say that the shares were not sold to them through the official exchange. It does not matter.

In capital markets parlance, there are two types of money: equity and debt. Yes, 'debt' is a type of money, it falls into two types: loans and bonds. Equity is the term used for shares issued by companies either through private placement or on an exchange. When an investor puts up money to buy shares in a company, it makes him a part-owner of the company. Shareholders are indeed part-owners of companies, flowing with both the smooth and the rough. It is akin to a kind of "for-better-for-worse" commitment to a spouse, except that the company has no moral boundary; it is usually open to a marriage of convenience with anyone for the right price. As the company makes profits, it pays its shareholders dividends out of those profits. At the best of times, shareholders get an income stream from annual dividends, and a profit (capital return) on the sale of their shareholding, when they choose to dispose of the shares for whatever reason.

Thus, a shareholder can either remain in a profit-making company, sipping champagne while his investment grows and produces dividends year-on-year or he can jump off the train while the going is still good, and try his luck elsewhere. Exactly what point to do either of the above is the unknown and unknowable trade secret guided by the capitalist's most enduring savoir faire: market forces. It is often asked of a voracious investor of capital: do you want to eat well or sleep easy? It is difficult to achieve both at the same time. Eating well means risking more and more of your money, but with the potential for a huge windfall in the end. Sleeping easy means putting little money into much less risky ventures, with the potential for only modest, but steady returns. It is not an easy balance to strike, but it is the stuff market analysts and financial lawyers everywhere are paid huge sums to undertake for investors. If it was that easy, the world would be full of multimillionaires and billionaires all over the place. One thing is for sure though, in terms of shares, what goes up does not stay up for ever and a day; it must come down. It is an immutable, unyielding, cast-iron law of gravity.

Judging by what is available in the public domain, it feels as if this salutary lesson was lost on the Plaintiffs in this case. They appear to be inviting the court to criminalise investment decisions taken in the course of usual business dealings. First is their demand of a refund of their investment. As I understand it, it was not given as a loan; it was given to acquire shares in what the share-

118   2 · FINANCE/CAPITAL MARKETS

holders and their agents thought was a lucrative business ab initio. Remember, shareholding makes you a part-owner of the business. You take the highs and the lows. Think about this, if a company gave you an extraordinarily high return at a time you thought they were not performing that well, would you refuse the dividends? What allegations would you then level at the company in court? Furthermore, the Plaintiffs claim the crisis in the company stems from "mismanagement of funds". 'Mismanagement' is a loaded word; it is either linked to fraud or sheer incompetence. One is actionable, the other is not. So, which? It is also alleged that the company has not paid dividends since 2009. Of itself, this is neither a crime, nor a breach of contractual obligations. Dividend is a privilege, not a right. Dividends are only to be declared "on the recommendation of the directors" (Companies and Allied Matters Act (1990), Part A, XIII).[179] Paying dividends is subject to the company being able to pay its debts as they fall due. As a matter of fact, it is unlawful for a company to pay dividends "if there are reasonable grounds for believing that the company is or would be, after the payment, unable to pay its liabilities as they become due" (Companies and Allied Matters Act (1990) Part XIII (381).[180]

A note of caution: nothing that I have written in this piece should be construed as nullifying the Plaintiffs' case against the proposed sale of 9Mobile. It is simply that they need to identify more tenable lines of attack against the defendants, of which there are plenty. It is not my job to enumerate them in an open space like this. The main object of today's piece as usual, was to use the 9Mobile saga as a teachable moment on the topsy-turvy of shareholding and the legitimate expectation of dividends that it brings when the times are right, and the heartache it generates when time runs out on it.

2.20 Nigeria's $2.5bn Currency 'Swap' with China

15 May 2018

Reports of Nigeria and China's deal a couple of weeks ago, to do a currency 'swap' equivalent to $US2.5bn[181] while not being exactly earth-shaking in the scheme of things, inside capital markets, it is, nonetheless, a major development

---

179. For ease of reference, see; CAMA, http://www.placng.org/lawsofnigeria/laws/C20.pdf
180. ibid.
181. See the 'Bloomberg' financial report; https://www.bloomberg.com/news/articles/2018 -05-03/nigeria-china-sign-2-4-billion-currency-swap-to-boost-trade?utm

2 · FINANCE/CAPITAL MARKETS

in Nigeria's drive to expand international trade beyond oil and gas. The deal, we are told, took over two years to negotiate. For something that appears to so many as a win-win situation, whatever took the negotiators so long to put pen to paper? What does the 'swap' entail in fact? It is a type of financial instrument understood by experts and participants in the market, but it also has huge public policy implications, discussion of which has, thus far, been closed to the ordinary citizen not versed in financial matters. On the other hand, the enthusiasm surrounding the deal makes you wonder if there can possibly be anything bad about it at all; yet, there are plenty of critical angles to explore while embracing the deal simultaneously.

First, a 'swap' is a type of financial instrument associated with the "derivatives" trade. Derivatives are values derived (gained) from trading on items owned by other people in the marketplace.[182] A good example is a country's currency. It is a form of gambling, only that when sanctioned by the stock exchange, it is no longer gambling; it is playing the financial field. Let me leave detailed discussion of this for another time. In business transactions, a currency trade can exist for delivery for a future date. For instance, if, as a businessman, you want to protect your business from a future rise or fall of a particular currency from which you derive income, you buy such currency, pegged at today's price, for delivery at a future date. This is also used for speculative trading, of course. The most common type of swaps in capital markets are interest rate and currency swaps. Again, let me leave detailed discussion of interest rate swap for another time. Suffice it to say that it involves looking for a more convenient interest rate than the one you negotiated with your bank when you took out a chunk of loan. Your bank has tied you to an agreement you cannot get out of without paying a humungous amount in penalty. There is a whole market full of people just like you, and all you do is find someone in the crowd who likes the rate you currently have (say, fixed rate), and you prefer to have theirs (say, flexible rate) instead. You then swap, meaning exchange. You take on his repayment obligations and he takes on yours with neither of the lending banks knowing anything about it. Classic capital markets.

In terms of currency swap, it enables a company to raise funds in domestic market, where the cost is likely to be lower. A business raises (borrows if you like) funds which it drops at an agreed (local) bank for the convenience of another business, in another jurisdiction, where it wants to do future trade. The business in the other jurisdiction conversely replicates the exact position in reverse. It involves an initial agreement between, say, company A and B to

---

182. This was explained in the earlier piece on the subject above

exchange currencies at current (spot) rate. The money is physically deposited in each person's yard. Any fluctuations in the value of the currencies are neutralised through the bank acting in a counterparty (an intermediary) capacity. Company A and B can now pay for goods and services in each other's territory with the money deposited or swapped with each other. At the end of the deal, the principal reverts (swapped) back to the owners. For a more graphic illustration, let us say, Dangote Group[183] wants to set up a cement factory in Detroit, USA. Conversely, General Motors wants to set up a car factory in Kogi State, Nigeria, and both want to avoid the risk of currency fluctuations. Dangote Group deposits one billion naira at an agreed bank in Nigeria, and General Motors deposits one billion dollars at an agreed bank in the USA, assuming dollar-naira parity. They settle up their obligations towards each other periodically. Thereafter, Dangote Group has no problem accessing dollars in the USA for their business transactions to the tune of $1bn, while General Motors has no problem accessing naira for its operations in Nigeria to the tune of N1bn. At the end of the agreed period (could be two, three, four years or more), they swap the original money back. That, in a nutshell, is the nature of the current deal involving Nigeria and China. What then is the problem?

First, instead of private companies doing the deal as in other market economies, it is the state getting directly involved in business activity here. While the Chinese are adept at micro-managing the market in their own economy, we are just climbing through the wobbly ladder of state capitalism in this country. Wobbly, because we have a history of state intervention in this country as elsewhere in Africa that is distinctly odious. There is not a single shiny example of a successful state-run, or state-backed enterprise to speak of anywhere on the continent. China has hundreds of such. Besides, the state actively participating in the wheeling and dealing world of finance (a space generally reserved for private entrepreneurs) creates a fundamental distortion as the mechanics of markets become vulnerable to the might of the state in places. How can capital markets deepen in an environment where the major participant; the major stakeholder is the state itself? Moreover, the actual money swapped between China and Nigeria; RMB 16 billion or 720bn naira is only a fraction of the almost two trillion naira worth of trade between the two countries each year.[184] Question is, will the Nigerian manufacturing sector

---

183. The Dangote Group is the largest conglomerate in West Africa, with presence in seventeen countries across Africa. https://www.dangote.com

184. For a full breakdown of the figures, see the National Bureau of Statistics report; 'Foreign Trade in Statistics' (Q4 2019). file:///C:/Users/Mr%20Tok%C3%A8/Downloads/FOREIGN_TRADE_STATISTICS_Q4_2019.pdf

benefit from increased exports out of this deal? The answer is emphatically no. Nigeria imports Chinese manufactured goods these days, while they focus on importing oil and gas from us. In fact, out of every one item sent to China, they send nine in return. There is a huge trade imbalance in favour of the Chinese. Consequently, this particular deal will enhance, not reduce it in the short term at best.

The most galling irony in all of this is that our policy makers cannot seem to get it. On the one hand is the desire for a "closer tie" between Nigeria and China, when the latter sees Nigeria as no more than a consumer market for their goods. We turn to Chinese technology to boost our manufacturing capacity, but then, cannot satisfy our insatiable appetite for Chinese imports and, mark my word, China is not about to set us up here to rival their domestic manufacturing industries either. Minister of Finance, Kemi Adeosun, has been touting the idea of creating a "Panda bond"[185] aimed specifically at attracting Chinese investment into the Nigerian manufacturing sector. Let me say this simply, that it will not happen; whatever funds generated from such bond would most likely be used to service cost of imports from China. How nice it would be to hold the minister's feet to the fire on this; although, I know she means well for the country's struggling manufacturers. But, the road to hell, they say, is paved with good intentions.

Finally, there is also a whiff of irony in the largest economy in Africa, and a self-avowed regional "leader", not actively seeking out partners in its own backyard. As a matter of fact, Nigeria has refused to sign the new "Africa Continental Free Trade Area" (AfCFTA) agreement already signed by 44 out of 53 countries in Africa to promote intra-Africa trade and development.[186] African leaders have never placed much premium on expanding trade with each other, but are full of complaints about trade imbalances with the industrial West and others. So, I say by all means, Nigeria please get the Chinese money, and collaborate with them on boosting local industries. But also please sleep with only one eye closed as the Chinese have done with American companies setting up stalls in mainland China for the past twenty-five years. That is, appropriate, not beg for, their technical know-how, particularly their intellectual property. By any means necessary.

---

185. See; "Nigeria eyes China's Panda bond market to help plug $11bn deficit". Financial Times, April 2019 https://www.ft.com/content/fd59fb30-fe50-11e5-99cb-83242733f755

186. See; "Nigeria's refusal to sign the AfCFTA". Businessday report, March 2018 https://businessday.ng/editorial/article/nigerias-refusal-sign-afcfta

2.21 Combating Corporate Greed Through Corporate Governance

5 November 2019

The idea that corporations should be 'governed' as opposed to just being 'managed' is a recent phenomenon that has caught on pretty fast in the wake of the 2008 world financial crisis. Mary Uduk, Director General of Nigeria's Securities and Exchange Commission, at a conference last week, pointed out the Commission's directive ("codes of corporate governance")[187] issued for the benefit of companies and how the poor response to it is eroding confidence in the capital markets. She then re-affirmed the Commission's on-going efforts to "ensure effective regulation of firms". The question that boggles people's minds is why firms need to be regulated at all in a free market economy. The immediate answer lies in history. In the days of Adam Smith (1723–1790), the guru of free market private enterprises, companies operated as small holdings plying their trade in a fairly disjointed and scattered economy all over the world. There has since been a shift in ownership from individual to the large, publicly financed corporation, coupled with the separation of ownership from control. Corporations themselves are now recognised as 'individual beings' in the eyes of the law, with specific rights, responsibilities and protection even from their owners, hence, the need for corporate governance. But, what was the mischief that led up to all this in the first place? What is 'governance' to do with anyway?

Corporate governance has an important economic history which sheds light on the questions raised above. At the end of World War II (1939–1945), European economy was in ruins and the once thriving private enterprises led by the UK were in the doldrums. Government (under the auspices of the US "Marshal Plan")[188] took it upon itself to rebuild the economy not only by injecting much needed cash, but more poignantly, by building and owning corporations in tandem with the private sector. This was the post-war consensus known as the "mixed economy"[189] formula, on the back of which much of the

---

187. See; code of corporate governance for private companies file:///C:/Users/Mr%20Tok%C3%A8/Downloads/CODE%20OF%20CORPORATE%20GOVERNANCE%20FOR%20PUBLIC%20COMPANIES.pdf

188. US Office of the Historian, https://history.state.gov/milestones/1945-1952/marshall-plan

189. See: "What is mixed economy" https://corporatefinanceinstitute.com/resources/knowledge/economics/mixed-economic-system

2 · FINANCE/CAPITAL MARKETS

Western "welfare state"[190] was built. This proved largely successful as society became prosperous, but at a rising cost on the state and its now badly run and inefficient public enterprises. So, the political clamour for a change of direction, and a new philosophy had reached a crescendo when Mrs Margaret Thatcher took over power as Prime Minister in the UK (1979–1990), and Ronald Reagan became President of the US (1981–1989). They were both seen as 'right wing' political ideologues, committed to "rolling back the frontiers of the state". Consequently, a wave of former publicly owned enterprises was sold off into private hands, who were encouraged to re-affirm the centrality of private business: profit maximisation.

So, it was in the 1980s feverish Thatcher/Reagan free market dogma, private enterprises and untrammelled profit across the Atlantic, that 'greed' suddenly became good. What mattered most was money, fast buck, consumerism and ever rising company equities. It really was free-for-all business environment, which saw a phenomenal growth in Western economies, low interest rate and the new philosophy of 'me' and 'now' underlining business ethos. That, of course, led to corporations running amok and using companies as vehicles to amass private wealth with no accountability either to the workforce, the population, or to government. This was unsustainable in the long run, and so, European leaders, alarmed at the increase in corporate misdemeanours, adopted the first report into the modality for a corporate governance to avert the risk of contagion and bring corporate greed into check. "The Financial Aspects of Corporate Governance" under the Chairmanship of the British financier and entrepreneur, Sir Adrian Cadbury, submitted its report in 1992,[191] later incorporated by Europe's Organisation for Economic Cooperation and Development. Where was Nigeria, and the rest of Africa at this time?

Africa was in the palsied grip of a debilitating public debt crisis precipitated in part by the activity of banks and finance houses in Western Europe, which had encouraged African governments to borrow money for investment when the economic expansion of the 1980s Thatcher/Reagan 'revolution' took off. So, while it created a culture of boardroom greed and corporate management laxity for Western economies, it created a bloated public and unpayable debt for the economies in Africa. The heads of states of African countries in

---

190. Assar Lindbeck. The Welfare State — Background, Achievements, Problems. Research Institute of Industrial Economics. Working Paper No 662, 2006 https://www.ifn.se/Wfiles/wp/wp662.pdf

191. See the watershed document; The Cadbury Report https://www.frc.org.uk/getattachment/9c19ea6f-bcc7-434c-b481-f2e29c1c271a/The-Financial-Aspects-of-Corporate-Governance-(the-Cadbury-Code).pdf

124 2 · FINANCE/CAPITAL MARKETS

alliance with international non-governmental organisations thereafter, embarked upon a sustained campaign to cancel the debt burden on the continent under the auspices of the "Jubilee 2000" debt forgiveness umbrella.[192] Western finance houses did, in fact, give in to the demand of the campaign, but only on the condition that recipients of any debt forgiveness dismantle and disengage the state from economic and business affairs. In other words, aid and other financial help from the West, including the IMF, were made conditional on the implementation of a wholesale privatisation of state assets across the board.[193] They also wanted African states to "roll back the frontiers of the state" as they had done in their own yard a decade earlier. It was following the privatisation programme of the 1990/2000s in Nigeria and Africa that corporate governance became an issue in line with a similar framework in the West.

Corporate governance prescription contained in the first Cadbury Report highlighted the crucial distinction between day-to-day management of a company and its governing norms. This is succinctly summed up in the opening sentence: "The effectiveness with which executive boards discharge their responsibilities determines Britain's competitive position. They must be free to drive their companies forward, but exercise that freedom within a framework of effective accountability. This is the essence of any system of good corporate governance". The latter report; "Committee on Corporate Governance Final Report", was released in 1998.[194] It gave detailed proposals on the principles of corporate governance, role of directors, their remuneration, audit, shareholders, etc. This is more or less the template from which Nigeria and other 'emerging' and developing countries have established their own. In many cases, they have simply copied from the original, lock stock and barrel. And, that is where the muddle begins for the African market regulators. First, corporate governance has been diluted (to the public at least) to mean "Corporate Social Responsibility". It is not the same thing. The latter has to do with the social responsibility of companies to their host communities; nothing to do with reorganisation or accountability of executive boards.

---

192. Chris Jochnick and Fraser A Preston. Sovereign Debt at the Crossroads: Challenges and Proposals for Resolving the Third World Debt Crisis. Oxford Scholarship Online, 2006 https://oxford.universitypressscholarship.com/view/10.1093/0195168003.001.0001/acprof -9780195168006-chapter-15

193. Patrick Imam. Effect of IMF Structural Adjustment Programmes on Expectations: The Case of Transition Economies. IMF Working Paper WP/07/261, 2007 https://www.imf.org/external/pubs/ft/wp/2007/wp07261.pdf

194. Committee on Corporate Governance. Final Report file:///C:/Users/Mr%20Tok %C3%A8/Downloads/hampel.pdf

Second, any conception of corporate governance in Africa needs to take account of the oligopolistic nature of the market on the continent. Dangote alone, for instance, controls more than 40% of the Nigerian stock exchange.[195] Is corporate governance the real issue for us, or is it corporate control? Do we want to champion profit maximisation or should profit optimisation become the objective? Should corporate governance be statute-driven or should it be voluntary? Certainly, law alone cannot bring about good corporate governance anywhere in the world. Should the Security and Exchange Commission's much vaunted "effective regulation of firms" be aimed at correcting or compensating for the absence of good corporate governance within commercial entities? My view is that Africa's approach to corporate governance ought to be pragmatic rather than doctrinal. Yes, we too now sing from the same hymn book with Western countries on corporate governance, but have we taken the time to trim its sails to our own business weather conditions?

2.22 China: Generous Lender or Loan Shark?

25 August 2020

So much has been said and written about sovereignty and loan in reference to China in the last week that the public will have found a little bewildering. That Nigerian loan negotiators, willingly signed away the country's sovereignty at the behest of China; that the negotiators did not even know or bother to find out the terms of the agreement; that they simply signed what amounts to a blank cheque in favour of the Chinese. The National Assembly has been aghast at the turn of events and has been delving into the details.[196] The person fronting the loan request, the Minister for Transportation, Chibuike Rotimi Amaechi, has given evidence to a House of Representatives Committee, where he warned the members not to meddle too much into the agreement for fear of offending the Chinese, which could then scupper the deal and the country's rail project. There are two narratives on offer to the public from this. One, that China is an enormously generous and kind lender, with the sole intention of helping the infrastructural development of Nigeria through its "Belt and Road Initiative" that extends throughout Africa. China, it is thought, gives loans without any ulterior motive; without the slightest intention of seeking "hege-

---

195. See the earlier comment on this above.

196. This was widely covered by domestic and international media. For example see; https://businesstraffic.com.ng/nigerian-parliament-sets-up-inquiry-into-chinese-loans-to -nigeria

mony" over an inch of the territory of Africa, unlike the old colonial masters of yesteryears. The other narrative is one which alarms everyone including China itself. It is that the country is a predatory lender, who does not care very much about how the money lent is spent as long as it can get its hands on the precious resources of the borrowing nation in an anticipated default. These are powerful, and highly seductive lines. But, neither gives the correct interpretation of reality.[197]

International movement of capital and commerce is one that is totally devoid of sentiments and injured feelings, of the kind enveloping the debate over the Chinese loan. Loan deals, unlike other commercial transactions, are rarely, if ever, susceptible to parity and asymmetry of negotiating strengths. On the contrary, a loan deal is usually a David and Goliath situation. And, guess who usually comes tops? The day the beggar dictates his own terms is the day he ceases to be a beggar. The Nigerian National Assembly can huff and puff about loss of sovereignty all day long, until the cows come home, it will not make a blind bit of difference to the country's inherently inferior negotiating position vis-à-vis China or any other lender for that matter. You need my money, here are my terms. That is the bottom line the Nigerian law makers appear to find stomach-chilling at the moment, but they will get over it. China under Xi Jinping's leadership has moved into the space long vacated by Western economic interest in developing nations across the world. China has invested more than $b700 dollars in 112 countries across the developing world to date.[198] China is the single largest creditor to Africa, holding almost a quarter of the continent's total debt.[199] Chinese investment presence has been felt more in Djibouti, Ethiopia, Kenya, Niger, Angola, etc. Angola is a particular case in point. It has one of the highest per capita incomes in Africa with loads of revenue from oil. It is, nonetheless, exposed to Chinese loans to the tune of $b25 dollars.[200] Those who wish to play down the Chinese loan to Nigeria are quick to point out that Nigeria's exposure to Chinese loan, at just over $b3 dollars, or 3.94% of the total debt burden of $b80 dollars is really small beer. Or is it?

---

197. For factual information of Chinese loans to Nigeria, it is best to review the figures provided by the country's Debt Management Office, the statutory body empowered to provide such information https://www.dmo.gov.ng/facts-about-chinese-loans-to-nigeria

198. See; "How China Is Reshaping International Development". Carnegie Endowment for International Peace, 2020 https://carnegieendowment.org/2020/01/08/how-china-is-reshaping-international-development-pub-80703

199. World Bank Review https://www.worldbank.org/en/country/china/overview

200. See; DMO report, ibid.

2 · FINANCE/CAPITAL MARKETS

It is difficult to play down Nigeria's level of indebtedness to China considering the mountain of debts the politicians continue to build up elsewhere. Since the APC assumed the reins of power, the country's debt profile has taken an upward trajectory; from 12 trillion naira in 2015, to over 30 trillion naira till date, and counting.[201] Nigeria is not only borrowing from China, it is also busy accumulating debts from the IMF ($b3.4 dollars), World Bank ($M750 dollars), "Sukuk" (Islamic) bond ($b1.5 dollars), and (162 billion naira direct borrowing). This is not to count several layers of state borrowings all over the place. Talk of mortgaging the future of the unborn in this country? Look no further. This is what puts the 'miniscule' Chinese loan in a proper context. What the law makers and many commentators find disconcerting about the loan is the 'offending clause' in the agreement which reads: "Borrower hereby irrevocably waives any immunity on the grounds of sovereign or otherwise for itself or its property in connection with any arbitration proceeding pursuant to Article 8 (5).... except for the military assets and diplomatic assets". Many experts and influential commentators have given their words of reassurance that this is pretty normal, anodyne stuff. In other words, it is a standard form agreement. While this position is generally correct, it is missing the point. It is that such loan undertakings are quasi Treaties, and should always be subject to ratification by the National Assembly. In this case, it has not, simply because the Debt Management Office has been empowered by the Debt Management Office Act 2003 and Fiscal Responsibility Act 2007, to comb through such deals on behalf of the Executive branch. Consequently, the National Assembly can shine a light on it once it has been signed and, (if that is the intention), sow the seeds of confusion and cynicism around it as a show of their disgust, but that is all they can do.

Anyway, why would China wish to continue lending to Nigeria, and Africa, despite the growing public outcry over a possible new wave of Chinese "debt entrapment" sweeping through the continent? After all, it was not too long ago that the continent was engrossed in a moral crusade demanding debt forgiveness from Western lenders. Much of the unpaid and unpayable debts were indeed forgiven, and written off,[202] leaving room for new and fresh lenders to throw the dosh at the continent. China has stepped into the vacuum not necessarily as a Good Samaritan, but principally for self-interest. First, China has built up trillions of dollars in foreign reserves over the last thirty years of

---

201. ibid

202. See; "Industrial Countries Write Off Africa's Debt". United Nations Newsletter, October, 2005 https://www.un.org/africarenewal/magazine/october-2005/industrial-countries-write-africas-debt.

economic growth and expansion.[203] She has invested a lot of it buying the US Treasury bonds in their trillions, but has come to realise how 'risky' this strategy has become in view of the new 'Cold War' between China and America. China is set to overtake the US as the leading economy in the world by 2030, if not earlier. America's attitude towards the growing Chinese economic influence has become decidedly hostile across the aisles in US Congress. China must, therefore, find other outlets for the surplus cash in its coffers hence, the pivot towards Africa and other less developed nations. Second, the loan deals serve China's need for raw materials as well as her long term geopolitical interest.

As for the "loss" of sovereignty in respect of Chinese loans to Africa, this is simply poppycock, I am afraid. How much sovereignty could Africa have already lost to the IMF and its draconian and infamous "Structural Adjustment Programme" over the last three decades? IMF regularly, and practically fills the finance ministries of many states on the continent with personnel directly from Washington, 'advising' them of reform mechanism, and setting their macro-economic priorities for them. On the face of it, therefore, Nigerian officials seem happy to hobnob with their Washington-based, Western finance 'mentors' because sovereignty is assumed to have been conceded anyway, but when China asks them to put pen to paper on a small aspect of that, they suddenly throw up their hands in horror? Honourable Members of the House of Representatives, please give us a break!

2.23 Rise of Non-Interest (Islamic) Banking

6 October 2020

Let me say from the outset, that this week's write-up is from the rubrics of financial law. This is all the more so for the technical nature of the subject matter, and the need for wider public education about it. In a novel capital market move last week, 29/09/20, Jaiz Bank's floating of N13b "private placement"[204] barely made the headlines except for a cursory mention in a couple of dailies. This is probably because it has become run-of-the-mill, or that the public just does not give a hoot. Neither of these is true in essence, although it is fair to

---

203. See a Reuters Report; "China's July Forex Reserves Rise to $3.236 trillion" https://www.reuters.com/article/china-economy-forex-reserves-idUSAZN01H2L9

204. "Jaiz Bank Plans N13b Private Placement". Nigerian Investment Promotion Commission, October, 2020. https://www.nipc.gov.ng/2020/10/05/jaiz-bank-plans-n13b-private-placement

2 · FINANCE/CAPITAL MARKETS

say that Jaiz Bank is no longer associated with the more common label; 'Islamic bank' even if that is what it actually is. It is also rational to eschew the label given that a host of other banks in the high street are being fronted by people of the Christian faith, but none of them is tagged 'Christian bank'. Islamic banking has only really gained currency in mainstream finance fairly recently, starting with the opening of the first of such banks in Dubai in 1975. Its presence now (in over 70 countries), is a reflection of the growing confidence and financial power of majority of Muslim states around the world, but most notably in Asia and the Middle-East.

Nigeria, majority Muslim, but ethnically diverse, is avowedly a "secular" state by design. Bizarrely though, it is a member of the Organisation of Islamic Cooperation (OIC). Fifty-three of its fifty-seven members are majority-Muslim states. Those who pushed for Nigeria's membership of the OIC despite its secular constitution, point to the country's membership of the Commonwealth countries and their Anglophone worldview, and the need to counterbalance that with the OIC with its Islamic worldview. The former fervently believes in interest (riba) as an equitable reward, the latter does not.

The first thing that should strike the reader at this juncture is how come people are not rushing down to Jaiz Bank in a stampede for their allocation of interest-free loans? After all, mainstream commercial banks in this country are notorious for the exorbitant interests they charge on loans (22% on average, though CBN guideline is considerably lower).[205] How come any bank dares throw money at people with no obligation to pay interest? Why, ipso-facto, is Jaiz Bank not found on every corner of the major towns and cities in Nigeria, dishing out well-needed cash to businesses struggling with crippling interest rates? Well, Jaiz Bank or not, Islamic finance or not, it is still the power of market forces, is it not? And, you guessed it, there is no such thing as a free lunch in capitalism. That begs the curious question as to how non-interest banking survives and even thrives in the dog-eat-dog world of finance and capital accumulation. Let us remember, 21% of the world's population is of the Islamic faith,[206] and less than 5% of global securities (in the capital markets) are Sharia-compliant.[207] Total Sharia-compliant products in the world

---

205. See; Central Bank of Nigeria 'Money Market Indicators' https://www.cbn.gov.ng/rates/mnymktind.asp

206. World Religions Statistics and Pie Charts: https://www.age-of-the-sage.org /mysticism/world_religions_populations.html

207. Islamic Capital Market — Fact Finding Report. International Organisation of Securities Commissioners. July, 2004 https://www.iosco.org/library/pubdocs/pdf /IOSCOPD170.pdf

130   2 · FINANCE/CAPITAL MARKETS

are under $2 trillion[208] so there is a considerable scope for growth in that sector. Still, how does a bank that charges no interest recoup its investment? One thing for sure is, unlike teachers, Islamic banks are certainly not hoping for their rewards in heaven.

First, let us examine the content of the Jaiz Bank's "private placement". What exactly does that entail? The answer is, it is simply another way of saying offer of shares. Public offer involves the issuance of fresh shares not to the 'public' at large (contrary to what the layman might assume), but to a wide group of institutional investors. "Private placement" is simply a different type of offer made to a smaller group of institutional investors say, a dozen or thereabouts. And it is called a 'placing' where only a handful of institutional investors between them will take up the whole issue either to keep or sell-on. Jaiz Bank says they are doing this in order to generate capital that they plan to invest in small and medium size enterprises. They are also doing that, I would add, because it is cheaper and cost-effective. The businesses so benefited will, of course, turn in tangible profits for the bank. Jaiz Bank wants to be the "leading non-interest financial institution in sub-Saharan Africa" according to its Managing Director, Hassan Usman. Judging by the bank's recent profit forecast of N600million after tax,[209] it is on track to fulfil that goal. So far, so good it seems. Why then is the bank not expanding more rapidly, scooping up new customers along the way? It is because Islamic finance has strict limits to the type of business they extend funding to. Speculative markets (gharar), brewing, gambling industries, entertainment and a host of others are excluded.[210] Furthermore, all investment packages have to be vetted and approved by an Islamic board of scholars. And, these scholars do not always subscribe to the same doctrinal interpretation of Sharia law. It goes with the territory; lawyers, by nature, often draw different inferences from similar facts in front of them. The lack of uniformity is a hindrance to the development and growth of Islamic finance as Muslims in different regions do not always accept products sanctioned under a different interpretation of Sharia.

In respect of making money, Islamic banking is more in tune with asset finance. Rather than make loans like the typical high street bank does, they fund the assets for customers by buying them, then, selling (either simultaneously or later) back to the customer for payment at an agreed date with a "mark-up" (murabaha),[211] generating a healthy return for the bank. Islamic banking is

---

208. Ibid.
209. The bank posted N4.37bn profit in 2021, https://jaizbankplc.com/jaiz-bank-posts-n4-37bn-profit-in-2021
210. Islamic Capital Market ibid.
211. Ibid.

somehow insulated from the credit crunch afflicting the market in bad times, but it needs a much larger pull of customers to sustain growth. So, is there an attempt to 'Islamise' the country where Islamic banking operates? The answer is of course not. That is even an absurd suggestion by any objective assessment. Does it promote Muslim 'brotherhood' and potentially augment tolerance of the Islamic faith? Of course, it does. And why not? Christians too have or used to have) a phobia for moneylending. Jesus Christ threw out the moneylenders from the Temple remember? Besides, interest free banking is only 'Islamic' in a limited way. Interest-free finance of consumer goods has been a major way of boosting sales in high street malls for half a century in Western economies. Even the Sharia idea of prohibition on investment in 'non-Islamic' products is not exclusive to the Muslim faith either.

'Ethical' investors in Western economies also create their own list of contraband items. Apartheid South Africa suffered from international boycott of its manufacture exports for decades. Iran currently suffers from a wholesale boycott of its international trade initiated by the Trump administration in America, with third party consequences. What Islamic banking struggles with more than anything, is image, underlined by the irrational fear that any wealth accumulated in its name might be diverted to further the cause of religious fundamentalism at some unfathomable point in the future. Or in the case of Nigeria, to 'Islamize' the country. No such thing is ever possible while Nigeria remains. Money, it is said, is the root of all evil. That too is a shared belief across all religions. It has taken a while before Islamic banking became rooted on Nigerian soil. It is actively encouraged across Western markets where there is no immediate fear of Islamization, and frankly, where non-interest banking is less beneficial to the populace. It is treated with apprehension here in Nigeria, ironically, where there is a greater need for such, and apprehension because Islam remains a political, and not a religious philosophy.

2.24 Bureaux de Change, Banks, and Economic Saboteurs

3 August 2021

Mention "bureau de change" (BDC) to anyone in the street, and the person is likely to be totally bemused and nonchalant. You would be adding insult to injury if you were to press on with the mention of; "forex" or "foreign exchange" or "dollars". BDCs are not your ordinary business serving ordinary people; they exist for the pleasure of the middle class and the super rich. They are the biblical moneychangers who once attracted the wrath of Jesus, (Isa in the Quran). He was said to have chased them out of 'his father's house' with vengeance. Governor of Central Bank of Nigeria, Godwin Emefiele, has just performed the modern day equivalent of the act. He has banished BDCs from the lucrative trade of buying and selling CBN-issued US dollars, vowing never to let them back into the 'chop n chop' magic circle again. CBN is the main repository of the US dollars in this country. It "allocates" (sell if you like) same to a select few for onward distribution (sale) to the public. The immediate consequence of the dramatic shift in policy is that many hitherto thriving BDCs up and down the country face closure and imminent redundancies in their ranks. And, what concerns the ordinary man about that you might ask? Well, Nigeria is a net importer of consumer goods including; spring water, rice, clothes, shoes, motorbikes, toothpaste, Brazilian and India hairs, etc. Practically everything the ordinary man uses and relies on for survival. All of these items and hundreds more must be paid for in dollars at source.

It follows logically that prices of consumer items depend on the strength and ready availability of the dollar by comparison to the naira. The rate of exchange between the two currencies is the most closely watched in commerce and industry in this country. Any movement up or down has profound impact on the daily lives of every citizen. BDCs are structured in such a way that they stand to make money whichever way the exchange rate goes. Any negative variation is usually absorbed by the customer. Right now, they stand accused of "graft" and grand larceny. According to Emefiele; "They have turned themselves away from their objectives. They are now agents that facilitate graft and corruption in the country. We shall henceforth channel all forex allocation through the commercial banks". He stated this on the 27th of July 2021, Tuesday, last week precisely.[212] The immediate question that pops up in people's mind is this. Who gave the errant BDCs license to operate in the first place? And who is the regulatory agency that should have devised the mechanism for monitoring, and evaluating them? CBN, of course! Did the Governor tender any apologies to Nigerians for his dereliction of duty on that score? Of course not. In the 1990s, through to the early 2000s, licensed BDCs in the country counted less than 100. The CBN had since been busy issuing licenses like confetti to new entrants, running to over 5,000 as of last week, with additional 5,000+ applications pending.[213] What is the reason for the proliferation of BDCs?

---

212. As reported by the financial news outlet, 'The Cable' and several others. https://www.thecable.ng/breaking-cbn-stops-sale-of-fx-to-bdcs

213. For the evolution of BDCs in Nigeria, see; "Foreign Exchange Market in Nigeria". Central Bank of Nigeria Publications. https://www.cbn.gov.ng/intops/fxmarket.asp

2 · FINANCE/CAPITAL MARKETS

Where big companies engage in cross-border transactions, which they must settle in dollars or some other hard currencies, that does not usually create problems, and where it does, the companies have their own means of resolving them through various financial instruments, currency "derivative" being one. The banks play a major role in mediating foreign exchange transactions between large companies. The difficulty is located at the lower end of forex, where most people are. This also includes small and medium-sized businesses, which do not run on huge budgets. These are the categories one often run into inside the banks, spending hours trying to do foreign transactions. The reader may recall Emiefele's "strong intervention" in the foreign exchange market to meet "genuine" demands from the public back in March 2017. Since being appointed Governor of the Central Bank in 2014, Emefiele has been struggling to sort out the persistent 'official' versus 'parallel' markets quagmire. It is a situation where the CBN set a rate of exchange; the official rate, and those working in the 'black (parallel) market', set their own. The public face of the parallel marketers are those commonly referred to as 'Mallams' in flowing baggy robes rushing after nice-looking cars in busy streets, with their calculators in hand, touting for business. Emefiele had vowed, in 2017, to rumble the parallel market by "flooding" it with tons of dollars to halt the fall in naira. Consequently, CBN allocated $80m dollars per week to 20 banks, and $20m dollars per week to some 3,000 BDCs, who steered the middle way between the official and parallel markets.[214] The Governor's bravura worked momentarily, with the naira gaining considerable strength against the dollar. That was then.

What subsequently happened was that the gap between the official and parallel market created room for currency arbitrage, which the BDCs were only too happy to milk dry. This column commented at the time: "The CBN's show of force in the forex trade is unsustainable. The current bubble of a rise in the value of the naira will burst in the short to medium term. A carefully crafted policy would not aim at eliminating the divide between official and parallel market entirely, but would bring it to a level where it became inconsequential" (See; "Forex: CBN governor's parallel universe", the PUNCH 11 April 2017 and "Forex: Nigerian banks in the dock", the PUNCH 18 April 2017). Based on monetary principles, a 'floating' exchange rate is the ideal, but that is a pipe dream in the context of Nigeria. Nonetheless, the Governor responded by com-

---

214. All banks are henceforth to receive amounts commensurate with their demand per week, which would be sold to customers who meet usual basic documentary requirements, according to the CBN https://www.cbn.gov.ng/out/2017/ccd/press%20release -new%20fx%20market%20rules.pdf

134 2 · FINANCE/CAPITAL MARKETS

ing up with the idea of licensing hundreds of BDCs with the view to making forex as accessible as garri[215] is in the market. BDCs were to freely disburse up to $5,000 to individuals conducting all transactions in 'invincible trade', such as school fees, travel allowance and the like. CBN now found cause to allocate $20,000 to over 5,000 BDCs, amounting to a staggering sum of $100m dollars per week. The BDCs were now to be found on every corner, but the dollar scarcity and the slide in the naira against it continued unabated. Why? Because CBN had simply created the gravy train for currency speculators and charlatans sponsored by willing partners from within the banking sector itself. CBN had issued licenses without the requisite monitoring and oversight mechanism to check abuse.

Right now, CBN has done a policy summersault and announced that the banks are to be the main vehicle for disbursing dollars after all. "Regulators will deal ruthlessly with banks that allow illegal forex dealers to use their platform". But a lot of people (including the Nigerian Senate) believe the bankers themselves are the 'illegals'. Since the CBN really wants to be 'ruthless', this time around, how about tying some of them up against the pole on the bar-beach in Lagos?[216] CBN has also set up a 'hotline' through which it hopes to harvest information on their fellow travellers' bad conduct. We must treat the whole of Emefiele's pronouncement last week with a pinch of salt. Remember this alarming headline: "Senate committee discovered N30tn forex fraud in 10 years by banks". That was the news back in April 2017.[217] The discovery jolted everyone; Ministry of Finance, Budget and Planning and others. They were to report back to the Senate within "three weeks", but nothing concrete came out of it. The banks, which stood accused of committing the most egregious forex fraud on Nigerians for a decade leading up to 2017, are now to be entrusted with the responsibility of managing forex going forward. Is this not putting Dracula in charge of the blood bank, again?

---

215. Cheapest of the staple food in the market.

216. Bar-beach is the infamous venue for carrying out the death sentences of convicts, often by the Federal Government's 'firing squad' in the 1970s

217. See the coverage by the National Assembly news outlet https://orderpaper.ng/senate-implicates-banks-n30tn-forex-scam-summons-ministers-cbn-gov

Chapter Three

Economic and Financial Crime

3.01 EFCC, Courts, Stolen Funds, and Legal Technicality

11 June 2019

The former Chief of Training and Operations Officer, Air Vice Marshal Olutayo Oguntoyinbo, had been standing trial for receiving a "gift" of N166m from a contractor under his management, but was sensationally acquitted of the charge of "corruptly accepting the gift", last week, at the High Court in Abuja. The alleged "gift" had been transferred by the contracting company; "Societe D'Equipments Internationaux Nigeria Ltd", into the account of a company run by the Nigerian Air force Chief in the course of the contract implementation. Justice Olukayode Adeniyi pronounced the verdict of not guilty of the charge proffered by the EFCC under the Corrupt Practices and Other Related Offences Act, 2000. The "gift", which had hitherto been forfeited to the Office of National Security Adviser Recovery Account, was now said to have been "erroneously recovered" according to the court's ruling, and is to be returned to the Air Chief forthwith. "The defendant is hereby discharged and acquitted of the one count preferred against him by the prosecution", the judge ruled. The judge also agreed with the defence counsel that the prosecution had failed to prove the "gift" was more than just a gift; that it was an inducement in fact. In other words, the contractor in question had not accompanied the deposit of the "gift" with an incriminating note saying; 'here is the bribe as agreed'. Phew! This is either justice at its best or at its worst depending on your sense of outrage about corruption and legal technicality.

To stretch credulity to breaking point even further, the contract was agreed with (ONSA) Office of the National Security Adviser, it then went through the

136   3 · ECONOMIC AND FINANCIAL CRIME

Chief of Air Staff at the NAF, then, down to Air Vice Marshal Oguntoyinbo for final disposal. It was argued, and the judge accepted that the chain of command in this case removes Oguntoyinbo from direct influence on the award and implementation of the contract. The judge was not persuaded; "that he was in any significant position of influence over the contracts ..." The only inference we can draw from the judge's summation is that the gift was made purely out of the goodness of the contractor's heart, nothing to do with the award of the contract itself. Is that so? Perhaps the biggest hole in the prosecution's case was the inexplicable absence of the contractor's agent, Mr Hima Aboubakar, who paid the money into Air Vice Marshal Oguntoyinbo's company account. So, it was wrong for the prosecution to have sequestered the "gift" "having not shown that the defendant corruptly received the money ..." concludes the judgement. This judgement cannot and should not stand, it is perverse, and EFCC should seek to overturn it at the earliest possible opportunity, with Mr Aboubakar being compelled to testify.

Bribery is a universal scourge with which countries all over the world have been trying to come to grips, particularly more so, in the years since the fall of the "Berlin Wall" in 1989. Bribery involving corrupt officials has been more of a problem in Africa and other developing countries than it has been in Western democracies. To this effect, legislations have been effected in prominent Western countries aimed at helping to stem the tide of official corruption across boundaries. America's Foreign Corrupt Practices Act 1977, Kleptocracy Asset Recovery Initiative (2010), UK's Proceeds of Crime Act 2002, Bribery Act 2010 are two cases in point. Nigeria has been urged to tighten the law in this area as well. Over time, effort has been made to consolidate the effectiveness of various anti-corruption agencies such as; The NDLA, ICPC, EFCC and NAPTIP Acts into one biting element. Section 6 of the EFCC Act, 2004 was specifically amended for this purpose. The Proceeds of Crime Act 2014 (s.3) amended S.6 of the EFCC Act thus: "To enable the rapid tracing and freezing of stolen assets and multiple avenues for asset recovery, including confiscation without a conviction, and private (civil remedy) actions". The judgment in Oguntoyinbo's case has driven a coach and horses through this amendment.

The problem we have in Nigeria, as elsewhere in Africa, is our over-reliance on criminal jurisdiction to prosecute bribery and corruption cases. It does not work. Bribery and corruption are notorious crimes with peculiar attributes that make them nigh impossible to prove "beyond a reasonable doubt" as happened in the Oguntoyinbo's case. This is more so because cases of this nature are decided by a single judge sitting alone. We do not have a jury system here as they do in Western jurisdictions, where the 'story' can be put to a panel of

3 · ECONOMIC AND FINANCIAL CRIME

137

jurors sitting alongside the judge in court. The jury applies the law as directed by the judge, and also applies the standard of probity expected of the accused by society. There is little doubt that a jury hearing the evidence before the court in the Oguntoyinbo case would have returned a verdict of guilty. That works well in those jurisdictions. Here in Nigeria, we run a different system of single judge sitting alone and rendering judgement. Bribery and corruption cases should be taken out of criminal proceedings in the main. We need a paradigm shift from incessant focus on criminal process to one that makes people accountable as fiduciaries. Civil servants and government functionaries are trustees of the public purse. Any money they come about without an account is clawed back with interest. In Oguntoyinbo's case, therefore, he would simply have been required to account for the N166m in his account as a person in a position of trust vis-à-vis public funds.

To deploy the civil jurisdiction route, there needs to be a change in the law designed to place a burden on public service employees holding bribes and public funds. A bribe, in that case, becomes a part of public funds, which once given is taken to have been given to the state. It follows the maxim; equity regards as done that which ought to have been done. A bribe once given, ought to be handed back to the state and will be disgorged from the resources of the bribe taker, as he is deemed to be accountable for such monies he receives in a position of trust. That being said, all the anti-graft agency needs to do to kick off the process is to open a case against a Politically Exposed Person suspected to be in possession of state funds, and he is made to account for the funds so identified. The beauty of this is that he does not have to be guilty of any offence; he only has to have behaved in breach of his fiduciary obligations. Furthermore, the ill-gotten funds can be traced to personal accounts worldwide, and if nothing is left, they can also be traced to property, including the shirt on his back.

Let us remember, Africans fear the loss of property far more than they do the loss of liberty. We would take a chance on going to jail than risk losing property we plan on passing on to family members. The looter's conscience does not extend beyond breaking the chain of poverty within his own clan only. The rest can go hang. Spending time in jail has long lost its potency in continental Africa; it has become an anodyne prickle. Jail time does not carry the same opprobrium on the accused in Africa, as it does on the accused in Western jurisdiction. Detailed legal reasoning on this can be accessed via google: Money Laundering Prosecution and the African PEP: Case for tougher civil remedy options/ Tayo Oke/Journal of Money Laundering Control Volume 19 (1) 2016.

3.02 EFCC, Transparency International, and the Game of Numbers

28 January 2020

Transparency International (TI), in case anyone is still in doubt, is the organisation dedicated to shining a light on corrupt practices in countries around the world. The organisation compiles annual records of what it terms "corruption perception index" and ranks countries based on a carefully worked out criteria which, by and large, have been accepted as reasonable and fair. It has no power to sanction anybody or any nation. Its real power lies in moral suasion, and, as they say, information. Information, after all, is power. Why do many governments around the world fret over its reports? Well, for the obvious reason that they help shape international opinion of the countries so-ranked. The naming and shaming effect may be the intention of the organisation's hierarchy, but their reports could also have damning consequences for foreign investment decisions of business leaders and financiers desirous of spreading their wealth around. These days, countries compete keenly for foreign investments hence, the attention, reaction, and airtime given to any negative (or, for that matter, positive) reports emanating from TI. The latest report placing Nigeria high on the list of "most corrupt countries" in the world rankles for that reason.[218]

The Economic and Financial Crimes Commission has reacted rather furiously to TI's lack of acknowledgement of the high numbers of arrests and convictions it has secured in the last couple of years alone.[219] Indeed, the "acting" Chairman of EFCC, Ibrahim Magu, has every reason to be proud of his achievements as the leading figure in the organisation. High (and low) profile figures have indeed been caught and successfully prosecuted in the last year, many more are in the pipeline. Under Magu, the hitherto missing 'fear factor' has truly come back to the operation of the EFCC. That said, the organisation has displayed a profound lack of understanding of the essence of corruption in its reaction. Corruption as it is, is not the same as corruption as 'perceived'. EFCC's angry reaction was premised on corruption as given on their own turf, but not on corruption as perceived in the wider society, which is even more economically damaging than the former.

---

218. See; Transparency International country rankings. https://www.transparency.org/en /countries/nigeria

219. See this column quoted in the review of the press; the "pressreader". https://www.pressreader.com/nigeria/the-punch/20200128/282346861782766

3 · ECONOMIC AND FINANCIAL CRIME

Moreover, high record of arrests and convictions, of themselves are great, but they are not conclusive evidence of increase or decrease in corruption. In the first place, if, as is often alleged, the arrests and convictions of high profile figures are influenced by partisan politics, then, the gain from the increased rate of convictions is 'tainted' in a way. You cannot fight corruption with corrupt motive, on the basis that the end justifies the means. For the avoidance of doubt, the column is not pointing an accusing finger at EFCC in this regard, but merely providing background analysis. Conversely, therefore, low record of arrests and convictions is no conclusive indication of the presence or absence of corruption either. It could actually be that people are being deterred from corruption based on the fear of EFCC. So, the organisation could end up being the victim of its own success in such a scenario. Furthermore, and for practical purposes, not all corrupt practices are arrestable, or prosecutable. If they were, then, 80% of the Nigerian uniformed officers would be in jail. So, a low record of arrests and convictions does not indicate an absence of corruption in that particular domain. Core corruption is notoriously difficult to reduce to the number of arrests and convictions, for it is embedded in the system. It revolves around the inability of citizens to go about their daily lives unencumbered, and without the need to induce anyone. It is a daily experience; a debilitating way of life in this part of the world.

On its part, and for all the good work it does, TI's methodology for measuring corruption is also fundamentally flawed as far as Africa is concerned. The good reputation TI has built around its annual reports over the years, I am afraid, is based on a lack of deeper understanding of the political economy of corruption on the continent. The "index" it supplies, and relied on by policy makers around the world does not, and has never fully taken account of the peculiarity of the African continent. Let me explain. More than 70% of economic activities in Africa is connected to the state.[220] The African state is "civil service" in nature, but there is absolutely nothing 'civil' about its comportment and interaction with citizens. The modern African state remains essentially contested amidst unresolved crises of legitimacy. By consequence, commitment to the protection of its commonwealth is not universal. The lack of commitment (or withdrawal of support from citizens) can sometimes be for perverse reasons (i.e. my turn to 'eat'), and other times, it can be for perfectly understandable reasons, hinging on whether the state

---

220. See; "Reaping the Potential Benefits of the African Continental Free Trade Area for Inclusive Growth". United Nations Conference on Trade and Development (UNCTAD). Economic Development in Africa Report, 2021. https://unctad.org/system /files/official-document/aldcafrica2021_en.pdf

is viewed as one founded on fairness and equity or not. Using Western matrix of good governance, and probity, it would be easy to see corruption everywhere in Africa without a clear understanding of its immutable roots. The other aspect is the one dimensional way in which the yardstick for measuring corruption is construed.

Western interpretation of moral rectitude in business affairs vastly diverges from the African socio-cultural milieu. For instance, in Africa, it is regarded as ethically sound to present an elaborate gift to a person about to discharge an onerous (albeit legitimate) duty in one's favour. It is understood to be an advance show of gratitude to the official, in traditional Africa. According to TI's matrix, though, that would constitute bribery, but in Western business practice, it would count as "business expense". If you pay someone millions of dollars to just 'go away' after running down a significant part of a large, profitable corporation, it is seen as "golden parachute" in Western financial parlance, and high bribery if looked at in the African environment. And if you pay an exceptionally gifted individual millions of dollars to quit their job in a government department in order to take up a post in a thriving financial outfit, it is seen as "incentive" in the West, but would be castigated as corruption in an African setting. Lest anyone misconstrue the argument here, there IS corruption on a grand scale in Africa as already explained above, the issue is the methodology deployed for measuring it. This is important because it carries financial consequences either way. My guess is that TI sometimes tilts a negative rating onto a country not necessarily because of increasing level of corruption, but in order to nudge the country's leadership to do more.

This is very much like the Nobel Peace Prize Committee conferring the honour onto a leader in the middle of peace-making in order to achieve the overall goal of the committee going forward. In other words, it does that to use the prize as a ballast around a leader in the thick of a battle. It is to urge such a leader not to waver. A good example would be Ethiopia's Abiy Ahmed, still in the middle of a struggle to build peace in his beloved, but troubled country in the Horn of Africa. He was, nonetheless, awarded the honour last year. Does it make sense for TI to find heavily against Nigeria this time round in order to encourage President Muhammadu Buhari, seen as an anti-corruption "crusader", to do more? A finding of less corruption would induce complacency. It sounds rather counterintuitive, but it is conceivable nonetheless. Or could it just be that there is a new form of corruption that bears no relationship to numbers? Purely perception? But perception itself is based on a set of underlying assumptions. It is those assumptions which call for re-evaluation in order to guide against bias and distortion in future TI reports.

3.03 EFCC's Persistent Failure at Criminal Assets Forfeiture

16 July 2020

For those interested in financial crime proceedings in this country, and I guess many of you are, it is such a relief when one sees news headlines highlighting how much properties the EFCC has compelled convicted criminals, as well as suspects, to forfeit to the Federal Government. We hear of "properties in Dubai, houses in Abuja, plots of land in Calabar, luxury apartments in Lagos, recovery of N980b in five years", etc. All supposedly confiscated and forfeited to the FG. You doff your hat to the gallant EFCC top management batting for Nigeria. Then comes the stinker: "Court refuses to forfeit Saraki's properties to FG", and "Court discharges forfeiture order on assets linked to Stella Oduah" in last week's news headlines. These two are just the very latest examples of the constant EFCC setbacks in these matters. Same happened in the case of Cecilia Ibru, Mrs Patience Jonathan, former governors Peter Ayodele Fayose (Ekiti), and Rochas Okorocha (Imo), to mention but a few. There is not a single high profile property forfeiture by EFCC that has not been subsequently reversed or in the process of being reversed, or watered down to the miniscule by the courts. The definition of madness, according to Albert Einstein, is doing the same thing over and over, and expecting a different result. It has been argued here before, and it is worth restating: EFCC's current approach to financial crime prosecution and property forfeiture is no longer fit for purpose. And for the umpteenth time, here is why.

Let me be as simple as it can be made to the wider readership. EFCC methodology is honed on an aggressive criminal prosecution of financial crime as the best way of stemming the tide of official corruption, money laundering and financial crime in general. In other words, arrest, put on parade, prosecute, secure conviction and forfeit assets in that order. Followed to its logical conclusion, the process is cumbersome, and often becomes mired in a cobweb of legalism. It takes an average of five years to bring a criminal proceeding to a conclusion.[221] In some notorious cases, this could easily take ten years or more, during which government would have changed, and the priorities of a new

---

221. See; "Corruption on Trial?" The Record of Nigeria's Economic and Financial Crimes Commission, Human Rights Watch, August 2011. https://www.hrw.org/report/2011 /08/25/corruption-trial/record-nigerias-economic-and-financial-crimes-commission

142   3 · ECONOMIC AND FINANCIAL CRIME

administration may have changed with it as well. Indeed, Nigeria is the best place to stand trial for high profile financial crimes, because the lawyers, especially the Senior Advocates of Nigeria they rely on to get them off, not only have knowledge of the law, but have useful contacts in the judiciary as well. They enter into 'battle' with the prosecuting authorities, (as they must), and fight them to a standstill, (as they do).

To make matters worse, the prosecution in Nigeria is in the bad habit of proffering several dozen counts against an accused. James Ibori, for instance, had over one hundred counts, and the EFCC lost them all.[222] He was later arrested and prosecuted in London on a simpler twelve counts, and was convicted and sent to prison in 2012.[223] In fact, faced with the incontrovertible and meticulously assembled array of evidence against him in open court, he chose to plead guilty as the presiding judge, Anthony Pitts, had warned that he could expect to be sent down for twenty-six years if he contested the charges and lost. He got a reduced thirteen years for not wasting the court's time contesting the charges. Even where a conviction is secured against the accused in Nigeria, the Supreme Court almost invariably throws the spanner in the works for the prosecuting authorities. And, where assets were up for forfeiture and announced with fanfare in the press, it is only a matter of time before that runs into a judicial cul-de-sac.

To crown it all, high profile sentencing in Nigeria is often one of the lightest there can be. Remember the Chief Executive of a bank, found guilty of brazen theft of shareholders' funds running into billions of naira, and only got a few months sentence, much of it served recuperating in a hospital? With all the money and pain it took to secure a conviction for former Governor Orji Uzor Kalu, he only got 11 years sentence, which has now been set aside. They love you, EFFCC, they really do. It gives me no pleasure saying this, but listen to what the Deputy Speaker of the House of Representatives, Hon Ahmed Wase, said only last week on Senator Kalu's prison sentence: "My leader, late Chief Solomon Lar, told me not to fear as a politician to go to prison. He told me that going to prison is a badge of honour".[224] This, coming from a Principal Officer of the Nigerian Legislature, is nothing short of

---

222. See; "Nigeria court quashes graft case against ex-governor" Reuters, December 17, 2009 https://www.reuters.com/article/ozatp-nigeria-corruption-20091217-idAFJOE5BG0K 120091217

223. See; "Corrupt Nigerian governor gets 13-year UK jail term". Reuters, April 17, 2012 https://www.reuters.com/article/britain-nigeria-ibori-idUSL6E8FH3J820120417

224. See; "Nigeria: Prison Experience a Badge of Honour for Politicians". 'This Day', in All Africa.com, June 9, 2020 https://allafrica.com/stories/202006090648.html

breath-taking. Here is a senior law maker in this country openly lampooning, thumping up his nose at the criminal process as it concerns the ruling elite. It lays bare the futility of criminal prosecution this column has been highlighting again and again. Also, that, EFCC's chosen methodology, is well and truly redundant. (See; "Why Kalu's prison sentence falls short" the PUNCH December 10 2019).

Now, you have heard it from the horse's mouth; criminal conviction and prison sentence have no deterrence value on public officials in this country. Time spent in prison is a "badge of honour" for them. It is not only in Nigeria though, it is an African phenomenon (See; "Why we celebrate (not jail) corrupt leaders in Africa" the PUNCH May 1 2018, and May 8 2018). The reason why serving time in prison has little effect on politicians in Africa is historical and has been well covered in two parts on the dates cited above. The African elite fear the loss of their property far more than they fear the loss of their liberty. Criminal conviction for theft of public property has no resonance in the wider community either. "Oh yes, is he the only one"? "But, they are all doing it". "His political enemies are fomenting trouble for him". "So and so from such and such ethnicity committed the same offence and nothing happened; why our own man"? You get these side yawns often from bewildered constituents in the towns and villages whose values have been debased through many decades of public pilfering by politicians.

So, to reiterate the alternative remedy this column has been advancing for years. Instead of putting Distinguished Senator Kalu through the criminal jurisdiction again, take him to court as a TRUSTEE of public property and let him ACCOUNT for everything, the billions of properties in his name, including the shirt on his back. To be declared a trustee of public property is an extremely onerous position for anyone to be in. The courts will have to be persuaded with a mightily strong argument. But once a trust relationship has been found to exist, the state does not have to show any wrongdoing on the trustee's part, only that he has acted in breach of his "fiduciary" (sacred) obligations. This particular route is novel. It has never been tried anywhere in Africa before. It does not require proof of any kind, it does not allow for any appeal through the criminal courts. As a trustee of public property, the burden of proof is reversed; the onus is on the person in a position of trust to account. Any subsequent seizure and forfeiture of assets cannot be appealed. Plus, it does not mean the accused is shielded from criminal prosecution, but it means the properties they have spent a lifetime acquiring and building up are traced and disgorged, including all incidental values attached. Make Kalu the test case, please, EFCC. We are rooting for you!

3.04 Kleptocracy Assets Recovery Initiative: Dog that Bites!

1 August 2017

Kleptocracy Assets Recovery Initiative (KARI) is an American extra-territorial legislation aimed primarily at treasury looters in Africa. By contrast, and in a twist of irony, the latest (home-grown) Parliamentary initiative against the same crime emanating from Nigeria is one offering "amnesty" for looters; a kind of 'Looter's Charter', which has been roundly condemned by many prominent figures in the country. That being so, though, the biggest amnesty being offered to treasury looters in this country, at the moment, is arguably a paralysed and ineffectual Economic and Financial Crimes Commission (EFCC). The organisation's operations are being stymied by the continuing row over its Chairman, and the cobweb of legalism in the justice system. Despite tons of recovered loots in the last couple of years involving public figures: army generals, former ministers, senior civil servants, top-rank party managers etc.), not a single 'big fish' has been convicted and sentenced. People have been paraded, yes. The cameras have filmed the EFCC operatives in action severally, yes, but where are the convictions and sentences in a court of law flowing from all of that? And crucially, where are the recovered loots?

Asset-stripping of the state for personal gain in Africa has been with us since the "Berlin Conference" of 1885, which formalised the partition and subsequent balkanisation of Africa into the several bits that it is today. Then, the colonial powers focused on digging up and repatriating Africa's natural resources to accelerate the development of the 'Motherland' of European countries. Then, upon independence, African leaders carried on this trend by laundering the proceeds of loots from the newly-established states and repatriating same to the Motherland by buying properties and stashing money away there, protected by the doctrine of privity of contract. That means, in effect, that whatever transpires between an individual and the bank in which they stash their stolen wealth is entirely a matter for them.

This cosy arrangement was what made it possible for African wealth to be funnelled into European and American banks and real estate for decades. This, to put it simply, is what is meant by "kleptocracy". To remove all ambiguities, however, it also means, according to the Cambridge English Dictionary, "a society whose leaders make themselves rich and powerful by stealing from the rest of the people".

The consciousness of European leaders was suddenly awakened to this phenomenon in the 1980s, as a result of numerous 'bad deals' entered into by their

3 · ECONOMIC AND FINANCIAL CRIME

banks with African leaders, and also owing to the growing economic migration into Europe by people fleeing poverty and mismanagement from Africa and the developing world. Several anti-money laundering legislations were enacted and foreign aids were tied to "economic reform" and "democratisation". These exerted a great deal of pressure on a lot of obdurate and sit-tight African dictators to loosen their grip on power, but it was never enough. Internal agitation from civil society groups across Africa also gave rise to a new awakening and push for more transparency and accountability of political leaders. It was thus against this backdrop that, the United States of America elected its first African-American President, Barack Obama, who then appointed America's first African-American Attorney General, Eric Holder in 2008.

It was a momentous period in America and world history. The in-coming administration carried a wave of expectation and hope that was far above anything the constraint of the office could ever allow to materialise. That expectation included the faint hope that maybe, just maybe, the power of the American Presidency could be used to alter political events on the African continent. President Obama gave speeches in Cairo, Egypt, in June 2009, and Accra, Ghana, the following month in July 2009. The Ghana speech was particularly noted for its symbolism and substance. The main thrust of the speech is best paraphrased thus: 'If a President stays in office because he fears no one else can hold the country together without him — that in itself, is an acknowledgment of failure; a failure to build long-lasting institutions'. The stage was thus set for Eric Holder's big moment at the African Union Summit precisely a year later in July 2010, in Kampala, Uganda. He spoke with eloquence, wit, and passion. He drove home his message in the spirit of brotherhood and a rare evangelical zeal. "I am proud to bring greetings from President Barack Obama and the American people" he said to a thunderous applaud. "I am proud to be counted among the African Diaspora — this continent is my ancestral home, I am of this place. Your work is of special and emotional importance to me".[225]

With those soothing words, Eric Holder surreptitiously landed the spine-crushing blow; the introduction of KARI. Henceforth, any type of property identified in America as being even tangentially connected to corruption in Africa will be impounded and confiscated. The main targets of the move were, of course, the numerous heads of states and governments in the audience, glumly staring the combative Attorney General in the face as he declared an auspicious end to a safe haven for Africa's stolen wealth found in America. It

---

225. See; "Attorney General Holder at the African Union Summit". United States Department of Justice, July 25 2010, https://www.justice.gov/opa/speech/attorney-general-holder-african-union-summit

146   3 · ECONOMIC AND FINANCIAL CRIME

has since been used to devastating effects against various individuals and bodies across the continent. The latest of this is the wire-taped conversation between Mr Kola Aluko and Mrs Diezani Alison-Madueke, in which the former Minister for Petroleum Resources in Nigeria warned Aluko against buying a 200-foot yacht costing close to ninety million dollars. "You can lease instead of sinking funds into a yacht.....Nigerian oil and gas industry is under all kinds of watch".[226] She is alleged to have warned the beneficiary of her ministry's largesse, Mr Aluko. How he must now wish he had heeded that onerous and ultimately prophetic warning.

Anyway, US prosecutors are now confiscating those assets running into several hundred million dollars as "the fruits of an international bribery scheme". In time, the individual persons will also be made to face justice in a court of law for laundering proceeds of crime. EFCC have moved quickly to cooperate with both the US and UK authorities in these cases, as they regularly send personnel to give evidence in court, where conviction and sentencing are bound to follow. KARI is a relatively new (2010) initiative, but has quickly shown that it can bite. EFCC has a relatively longer pedigree in this battle. The organisation, established in 2004, has demonstrated its ability to bark from time to time, but has yet to prove of late that it can bite.

3.05 Between White Collar Crime and Business Efficacy

17 October 2017

If you ever wondered what sort of people get involved in criminal activities your mind would have instantly been fixated on the usual criminal gangs on our streets, the armed robbers invading peoples' homes at night or even in broad daylight these days, the kidnappers, marauding herdsmen, "area boys", pickpockets, etc. All of these conjure up a sardonic hold on our psyche; terrifying, rough and menacing. What if you were then told that the people who commit the most egregious financial crimes in this country do so from the comfort of their offices? They generally look like, and indeed, are respectable citizens, occupying positions of responsibility, making investment and business decisions affecting the lives of millions of citizens on a daily basis. These people

---

226. This was widely covered in the press, as is usual in these cases. See, for example; "Diezani warned Aluko against buying $80m yacht". 'thecapital.ng', July 16, 2017, https://www.thecapital.ng/diezani-warned-aluko-against-buying-80m-yacht

3 · ECONOMIC AND FINANCIAL CRIME

do not generally appear rough or menacing, on the contrary, they are usually well turned out in French and Italian suits, suave, articulate and approachable. They run businesses; they are corporate leaders, high-level civil service functionaries and community leaders. More often than not, they donate to charity and religious bodies; they are feted and hero-worshiped at high-society functions. Because they are not the archetypal violent criminals, they are referred to as "white collar" criminals. They wear clean shirts and blouses, and sit in air-conditioned offices whilst they engage in their nefarious, 'victimless' crime. Victimless in the sense that, they do not have to aim the gun at or kill anyone themselves, in the process.

White collar crime is the most dangerous, most intractable and most corrosive crime that exists in our society. Most dangerous because it is perpetrated by people who coat the crime with the veneer of respectability and authority, which indeed they exercise over thousands, if not millions of lives in society. Imagine a business executive who raided his company's pension funds for his or her own private use would be directly responsible for the subsequent misery that would befall the old and the frail senior citizens who may die in penury as a result. Or a top government functionary who diverts money earmarked for ammunition to combat the Boko Haram terrorists, who then went on the rampage, killing scores of innocent citizens in towns and villages around the country because there were no sufficient arms to repel them. Is the government functionary concerned not worse than the terrorists? The only difference being that one sits in a fully air-conditioned office, in suit and tie, or flowing mufti, while the others take cover in the bushes and in the ravines.

Let us focus on the business world for the rest of the discussion here, first, because it attracts even less attention and less scrutiny by the public. Second, in order to highlight how one country, the United States of America has enacted legislation that extends to Nigeria and other countries to combat the menace of white collar crime, and why more than forty years after the legislation was enacted, white collar crime appears to be on the rise, perhaps more than ever before.

In substance, 'white collar crime' is somewhat of a catch-all phrase. Its parameters extend to: fraud, misrepresentation, customs, computer/wire fraud, securities, commodities, intellectual property, taxation and the like. The USA enacted the "Foreign Corrupt Practices Act" (FCPA), in 1977,[227] which penalises American citizens who get involved in the crime whilst on business

---

227. See; "Spotlight on Foreign Corrupt Practices Act". US Securities and Exchange Commission https://www.sec.gov/spotlight/foreign-corrupt-practices-act.shtml

148   3 · ECONOMIC AND FINANCIAL CRIME

anywhere in the world. This also includes companies; any American-based company and entities that are subject to American law. What this means in practice is that even foreigners who bribe American citizens and companies can expect to face the wrath of the law upon entering into the United States if ever. Tough? Yes, until you consider the elements of the offence: First, to be guilty, one needs to make payment, offer, or promise of anything "of value" to any foreign official with corrupt intent for the purpose of inducing such foreign official to use his influence with a foreign government or company to do any act in violation of the lawful duty of such official ...

"Lawful duty" is the elephant trap in all this. It is an affirmative defence if the offer made to bend the potentially corrupt official was lawful under the "written laws" and regulations of the host country. It is equally a defence if the 'payment' 'gift' 'offer' or 'promise' of anything "of value" that was made was a reasonable bona fide expenditure such as travel and lodging expenses incurred by or on behalf of a foreign official. Here then is the rider. It is highly unlikely that any country's written law would be so permissive as to sanction the act of bribing anyone. The legislation was carefully crafted to discount and disavow a whole load of cultural practices Americans deem anathema to business efficacy. For instance, handing the good old kola or a bottle of gin to someone who is about to render another one a huge service is culturally acceptable in Africa. It is an advance appreciation of the anticipated service one is about to receive. It is embedded in African culture like the "Thanks Giving" is in America. American authorities, nonetheless, frown at this, as they think it constitutes the gateway to bribery for us. But how is this different from an executive "package" often involving eye-watering sums used to secure the services of an individual in American companies long before the individual has done a day's work? They call that "incentive".

In Africa, if you pay somebody a lot of money to leave their job to make way for another person, it is called bribery. In America, it is called "ex-gratia" payments or a "golden parachute" for an executive whose contract the company found difficult to terminate at will. And if a top government functionary enters into a scheme which diverts an investment commitment from a multinational company to his village with a whole load of tax benefits to the company concerned, what is this called in Africa? "Corruption", or "nepotism"? In America it is called a "gentleman's agreement" or a "sweetheart deal". You see, the "corrupt practices" the Americans decry so much in our economy, and are openly flogging us for, have their origins in the USA itself. As a matter of fact, there is more corruption in the "land of the free; home of the brave" (USA), than it is in Nigeria; the difference being the level of sophistication involved on both sides. To employ a crude analogy with technology, one is digital, and the other still runs on the old analogue system. That said, this piece is in no way, tacitly or impliedly, an endorsement of corrupt practices of any kind in this country. It is merely designed to put the discussion in a different perspective and to stimulate a more critical examination of the menace in our society.

3.06 EFCC and PEPs: Caught in a Cobweb of Legalism

21 March 2017

Economic and Financial Crimes Commission (EFCC), and Politically Exposed Persons (PEPs), are hogging the limelight again for very familiar reasons. The former has been busy trying to make some serious charges stick on the latter, especially, notable former government ministers under the Jonathan Administration. Mrs Diezani Alison-Madueke, the former Minister for Petroleum Resources, stands accused as the Queen of financial criminals; the pretty face of official corruption and abuse of office in this country. She is yet to be proven guilty though, so, we should reserve any final judgement until there is a verdict in a court of law. Nonetheless, if true, what Mrs Alison-Madueke has been accused of, and is being investigated for, both in this country and in the United Kingdom, would be the most brazen raid on the public purse this country has ever known. It dwarfs anything James Ibori could have stolen while he was Governor of Delta State. In fact, it makes it look like kindergarten stuff by comparison. It shows corruption, indeed, is a beast of no gender.

Consequently, (and maybe) to the disappointment of some readers of this column, this piece is not going to focus on the on-going confirmation hearing of the acting EFCC Chief, Ibrahim Magu. Although it is tempting to join in the hoopla of the Senate's cat and mouse game with the President on that issue, but I am afraid, it is largely a red herring. Instead, the focus is on the raison-d'être of the institution itself, and its ability to fulfil its mandate in stemming the tide of financial crime in this country.

Based on the very latest revelations, Mrs Alison-Madueke was alleged to have arranged the transfer of N450million to Dele Belgore and Professor Abubakar Sulaiman respectively, from several hundred million dollars stashed away in a Nigerian bank.[228] The two recipients of this money have

---

228. Widely covered in the media. See, for example see; 'today.ng' https://www.today.ng/news/nigeria/dele-belgore-abubakar-suleiman-admitted-collecting -n450m-diezani-alison-madueke-rig-2015-elections-efcc-witness

now being arraigned by the EFCC as co-defendants in the case against Alison-Madueke. When the former Governor of Central Bank, Sanusi Lamido cried out over unremitted billions of dollars from the petroleum ministry a couple of years ago, some were aghast at the seemingly "alarmist" claim by the Governor and he was put under intense pressure to either put up or shut up. PricewaterhouseCoopers, a management consultant firm from London was hurriedly engaged to conduct a 'forensic examinations' of the petroleum ministry's books. It gave the books a clean bill of health, with an important caveat: the consultants can only go by the data in front of them, supplied by the ministry. In other words, they are management consultants; not police detectives. No one gave evidence under oath. Now, then, that people are giving evidence under oath, we are seeing a completely different picture of the gargantuan amount of money siphoned out of the treasury, including money from the office of the National Security Adviser meant for the procurement of arms, but ended up in the private accounts of individuals close to the Jonathan Administration.

The corruption probe (not the recession) has come to define the Buhari administration's engagement with the public since inception, and is likely to remain so until the next election in a couple of years from now. The financial crime issue is intimately interwoven with the recession, dilapidated infrastructure, unemployment, budget deficit etc. from which the country is reeling. We have been treated to a parade of witnesses and defendants, all of them PEPs, caught with their fingers in the cookie jar as it were. Some have made confessional statements, while others are busy contesting the allegations against them in court — as it is their right so to do. A lot of money has been seized in both local, and hard currencies, some hidden in real estates, commercial banks, underneath mattresses and even in rabbit holes in remote villages in the country. Nigeria urgently needs a bank; a dedicated bank for looted funds for the sake of transparency and accountability. The bank can also serve as a collecting point for culprits desirous of settling out of court. Its account could be published online quarterly for all to see. More specifically, though, EFCC's ability to function is hampered by the "dual mandate" nature of its operations. First, it is charged with the obligation to prove its case against a defendant "beyond a reasonable doubt" in a court of law. Second, it is also charged with the responsibility to nip corruption in the bud through pro-active preventative measures. These are two diametrically opposed philosophical foundations. It is this palpable weakness in its foundation that its opponents are exploiting to stymie its operations.

Already there is a deluge of cases on the EFCC's books awaiting prosecution in court, while a dozen others are pending investigation. Sooner or later the organisation will run into charges, counter-charges, amendments of charges, dropping of charges, plea-bargaining, motions and jurisdictional matters to resolve, you name it. Over time, the heat and the spotlight on the accused will fade as they are slowly reabsorbed into society. To be successful, the EFCC and the country at large need a paradigm shift away from criminal to tougher civil remedy options in going after the horde of PEPs bent on asset-stripping the state for personal gain in this country. The EFCC Act will have to be amended to accommodate a more expansive focus on civil remedy options, and its leadership has to be opened to civilian heads; people with strong moral authority and a proven anti-corruption pedigree. Being a commissioned officer in the Nigerian police is an asset, but it should not be the deciding factor for selecting the head of this august body. We have such eminent civilian leaders in abundance in this country capable of leading the organisation. For now, though, there is only so much that can be shoved into my allotted space here, this week. A detailed discussion of the tougher civil remedy options by me was published in the Journal of Money Laundering Control (JMLC), 19 (1), January 2016. It can be googled via: JMLC/Tayo Oke.

Chapter Four

Education

4.01 Why Nigerian Universities are Graduating Illiterates

26 March 2019

The Academic Staff Union of Universities (ASUU) called off their strike over pay and conditions a few days to the 16th of February 2019 general elections. The strike commenced on the 4th of November 2018, and had threatened to run through the elections, creating an own goal for the All Progressives Congress and the re-election of President Muhammadu Buhari into a second term in office. The terms of the "memorandum of action" agreed to between ASUU and the Federal Government was not exactly clear to the public. It was thus not easy to say with certainty whether it would turn out to be another stop-gap measure designed to buy off a dangerous adversary at a sensitive time in the middle of elections, or whether at last, a lasting solution had been found to this intractable problem of strikes, and disruptions in Nigeria's university education system.[229] The main victims of the strike; the hapless students, will now have to put up with a forced elongation of their duration in school as is the case when such strikes happen. In Nigeria, it is commonplace for a student on a four year degree programme to find himself still enrolled on the same course two or three additional years later than scheduled, due to enforced disruptions of the kind just witnessed. The problem we are talking about affects only public (taxpayer-funded) institutions, of course. Private institutions are not affected since ASUU

---

229. As of June 2022, the universities have gone on strike again, for the past six months, also in the run up to the 2023 general elections, although frantic efforts are being made to come to an agreement before then. Time will tell if the intended agreement turns out to be another stop-gap measure.

has no licence to operate in them. This column's best guess is that incessant ASUU strikes in public universities is a major disincentive to enrolling in them, and an incentive to opt for private universities instead, where one's commencement and graduation days are almost set in stone.

There is no gainsaying that public universities in this country used to rank alongside any standard university anywhere in the world. There was massive investment in them, coupled with the dedication and commitment of the academics working in them. Condition of service and studying used to be so congenial that once recruited, an academic would chart a career path for himself until retirement without thinking too much about taking on other odd jobs to supplement his income. We are talking of the giddy heights of public investments in education in the 1960s, 1970s, and early 1980s. During this period, you could walk into any of the first generation campuses and see the array of academics and researchers from across the world, milling around and pursuing their varied interests in science, medicine, social science and humanities. Such were the glory days. Nowadays, though, those same institutions are now shells of their former selves. No one takes pride in them anymore, not least, the political class, some of whom have gone on to build rival private universities to deplete interest and erode confidence in the public ones even further. Those who can afford it amongst them send their children to schools in Western countries, namely; UK, USA, Canada, Australia, etc. Others opt for private universities in the country. As a result, public universities in Nigeria have become production factories for half-baked graduates and illiterates unable to justify the qualifications bestowed on them.

You would be forgiven for thinking that it is a little bit unpatriotic to be saying these things out loud this way. It is washing one's dirty linen in public as it were, except that it is to point out that this is an open secret. Education establishments around the world, who once had huge respect for certificates from Nigeria's universities, now look down on them. We would even argue that not airing this problem in a public forum like this is both unpatriotic and a dereliction of duty. On that note, we do not need to scratch our heads too much to understand the puzzle in the title of this piece. In its robust defence of the strike action, ASUU went on social media and other outlets to alert people to the plight of university employees and institutions in this country. It set out a litany of calamities that have befallen the public institutions in this country over many years, due to official neglect. Brief excerpts from their dossier underline, indeed, affirm the choice of title for this week's column.

According to ASUU's detailed research into the state of public universities in this country, justifying why ASUU went on strike; "internet services are

4 · EDUCATION

non-existent, or epileptic and slow in 99% of Nigerian universities", "Nigerian universities library resources are outdated and manually operated. Book shelves are homes to rats/cockroaches", "76% of Nigerian universities use well as source of water, 45% use pit latrine, 67% of students use bush as toilet", "77% of Nigerian universities can be classified as glorified primary schools. Laboratories are non-existent", "80% of Nigerian universities are grossly under-staffed", "78% of Nigerian universities rely heavily on part-time and visiting lecturers", "88% of Nigerian universities have under-qualified academics", "90% of Nigerian universities are bottom-heavy, with junior lecturers forming large chunk of the workforce?", "only 2% of Nigerian universities attract expatriate lecturers, over 80% of Ghanaian universities attract same", "89% of Nigerian universities employ their own (local ethnic) staff", "Nigerian university medical students train in the most dangerous environment, some only see medical tools in books", "80% of published journals by Nigerian academics have no visibility in the international knowledge community", "laundries and common rooms in many universities have been converted into rooms where students live in open prison style", "over 1000 students being packed in lecture halls designed for less than 150 students".[230]

The above highlights are by no means exhaustive. The tale of woes documented by ASUU is much longer; it is stupefying in essence. If you add the nonchalant attitude of the students to their study environment; fiddling attendance, falsifying records and assignments, open and blatant plagiarism, paying for lecturer's notes (and marks in many cases), indulgence in illicit affairs with lecturers in exchange for marks, one can see how worthless the certificates handed to many of the students at the end of their endeavours have become. Many graduates from the universities are embarrassing for their ignorance of the most elementary stuff like: who is the current President of Nigeria? Or how many states comprise the Nigerian federation? Some have been known to confuse Tafawa Balewa (the first Prime Minister of Nigeria) for a folk singer from the north, and Awolowo (the first Premier of the old Western Nigeria) for a traditional ruler from some ancient village in the Western part of Nigeria. Yes, these are products of Nigerian universities!

What is even more embarrassing is that these illiterate products of the universities go on to find very good, high-paying government jobs on a fast track to senior management positions. Many also find similarly high rewarding jobs in the private sector as well. In no time, many even find themselves in political

---

230. See; "why ASSU strike is justified" https://www.nairaland.com/6170104/why-asuu -strike-justified#94764201

office, wielding power and influence. One only has to pay a little attention to the utterances of some of the elected representatives in State and National Assemblies to make one think and wonder in bewilderment. There is apparently no penalty for failure in school under our system, as who you know counts more in life than what you actually know. The title of your college degree matters more than its substance. Your ability to drop names to gain access is more important than your ability to read and write. Under the circumstances, where is the incentive for hard work? More importantly, where is the incentive to acquire knowledge? None, it seems. It may be time to privatise all Nigerian universities. What do you think?

4.02 Should Academics Be Moral Agents?

12 November 2019

This topic touches on a very sensitive, delicate issue of discipline in universities, and other institutions of higher learning in this country. It is about the right boundary between a lecturer and his student and whether, aside from imparting knowledge, a lecturer also stands, or ought to stand in locus parentis (in place of parents) vis-à-vis his student. Put simply, should lecturers be involved in teaching morality to students, or should that fall squarely on the shoulders of parents? Should campuses in higher institutions engage the services of moral police to put open display of affection in check? More crucially, should all forms of sexual contact between and amongst students be forbidden? We have seen a couple of 'exposes' on university lecturers allegedly engaging in "sex for marks" and how those caught have faced the wrath of the institution's disciplinary brigade, and quite rightly so in many people's view. That still begs the question: Should there be a blanket ban on any form of sexual contact between a lecturer and a student, even where that is freely given and is between two consenting adults? This is a vexed question that has not been properly debated amidst the furore and moral outrage provoked by the news headlines on the "sex for marks" scandals of recent months.

While stories of sordid relationships and illicit affairs on campuses abound, the flip side is also that a lot of lasting marriages are known to have been consummated on college campuses as between students, lecturers, or lecturer and student. Should there be room for (excuse the phrase) 'sex for love' between a lecturer and a student? I ask this because it reminds me of my days as a student in the UK. One of my heads of department waited until he had officially disengaged lecturing with a female colleague of ours, before starting a discreet relationship with her, which eventually culminated in a marriage to the young

4 · EDUCATION 157

lady, whom he then mentored along the academic path until she became a lecturer herself in the same department of the same university. No one raised an eyebrow, and everyone embraced them as if it meant nothing to anyone other than the couple themselves. The critical point there is that such incidence was never seen through the lens of morality, but only as a matter of policy. The intimacy between my then head of department and the student was not about sex at all, since it took place between two consenting adults. It was seen entirely as a matter of power and influence, which no longer existed at the start of their relationship.

Having said that, even 'sex for love' is fraught with all kinds of risks so much that it is right for it to be forbidden with a student over whom a lecturer continues to exercise power and influence. Nothing to do with morality, but policy. That said, "sex for marks", or for any other material gain is crude and it is in a completely different category. It is way outside the remit of the discussion in this piece. It is outright corruption, breach of trust, abuse of power, and is universally and roundly condemned. Now, going back to the question, should college campuses be free for open display of affection towards the opposite sex amongst the student population? Or is it the job of academics and college authorities to turn their students into hyper moral beings, willy-nilly? That is to say, no touching, hugging, petting or kissing with the opposite sex, pronto! Picture a scenario where students simply walk alongside each other ashen-faced, and in a zombie-like fashion. How unusual and incredibly disconcerting that would be? If, however, we choose to go down that path, is that not a slippery slope towards "Talibanisation" of campus life? Because, in the final analysis, whose morality ought to prevail anyway? Muslim? Christian? Hindu? Confucian? Jewish? Animist? Traditionalist? 18th century? Which? And if it is not the job of college authorities to get involved in championing a moral cause, is there not also the potential for another slippery slope towards a free-for-all, anything-goes, nihilism?

Should college authorities simply focus on collecting fees, and imparting knowledge in a moral vacuum? More like the old Philistines, who knew the price of everything but the value of nothing? This just goes to show clearly that the question of on-campus moral rectitude is not given to the black and white narrative that the media portrays sometimes. It is never an open and shut case for any institution of higher learning. It would be easy for these institutions if parents had done their homework on their own children, instilled moral values in them before packing them off to higher institutions. As an illustration, if a student with a penchant for recreational drugs enrolled in an institution that preaches zero tolerance to such, or one that preaches abstinence on campus, how does it enforce the established rules without being vilified as turning the institution into a "glorified secondary school"? Is there not the caveat; to be forewarned, is to be forearmed?

There is a strong strand of opinion in academia which denies moral agency of any kind of their lecturers. This was once strictly enforced in this country during the bad years of military dictatorship in the 1980s, when academics were routinely hounded out of their jobs for "teaching what they are not paid to teach". Apparently, academics were not paid to delve into the morality of military presence in civilian life and the value of free speech. That was the reactionary elements in the military against academic freedom as it represented an existential challenge to them. But that is what harping on moral policing of any kind does; it stifles liberty, and flies in the face of rational thinking. This is why many academics around the world do not conceive for themselves any role beyond imparting knowledge to students. Many do not even see themselves as "teachers" in the conventional sense, but merely 'lecturers', in to make a good delivery, and out once that is done. Whatever the student takes from that is entirely his own business. That position is also reaching another extreme, of course, and it is untenable in the modern age. Students cannot and should not be treated as empty vessels waiting to be filled up and closed up at the behest of 'lecturers'. There are a lot of extraneous matters in campus life that diverge from strict impartation of knowledge. No lecturer can bury his head in the sand like an ostrich and let things fly over. The ostrich may end up being consumed by fire lit by a bunch of rudderless students in whom it has failed to instil discipline. You get my drift? For higher institutions, it is a case of damned if they do and damned if they do not.

4.03 Why "VC" Position Is Keenly Contested in Nigeria

19 January 2021

By convention, Vice Chancellors (or President in America) manage the affairs of their institutions efficiently, diligently and above all, quietly, without attracting attention. They simply get on with the job as it were. They generally hope and expect that if, and when, there is a light shown on their activity, it will be on the institution itself, its progress, achievements and future endeavours, rather than on the personality of the VC. Any undue attention on such a peripheral issue is seen as evidence of failure and decline in the institution's standing. VCs are supposedly smooth operators; serious-minded, cerebral and powerful yet, rarely seen and rarely heard. It is not unusual for a student or even an academic staff to go through an entire period in university

4 · EDUCATION

without having a single encounter with the VC. That, in a nutshell, is the universal norm that has been turned on its head here in Nigeria. A VC in Nigeria is (for want of a better word) HE, who must be obeyed; an emperor with a sharp dagger in his hand. When a VC sneezes in a Nigerian university, everybody catches the flu. Beneath the veneer of resume and selection process, a VC assumes his throne through main plots, sub-plots, intrigues, and chicanery wrapped in a load of skulduggery. In Nigeria, a VC rules rather than administers. Such is the polarising position of the VC nowadays, that at the end of his term, there is clamour for his reign to end or be elongated almost in equal measure. What really is the apple of discord?

Let us wade through this mind-boggling quiz by extrapolating anecdotal evidence from various institutions across the country without mentioning names. This is important in order to avoid distraction from the issue at hand. All the scenarios painted here will have been experienced by many universities to varying degrees. First, the main attraction in the position of VC in this country is the power of patronage it bestows. Universities are categorised into: federal, state and private, based on funding; the federal government, state government, and private individuals in that order. For the federal and state universities, the VC's position is akin to that of a senior civil servant. The President of the Federal Republic of Nigeria and State Governors double as "visitors" (i.e. proprietors) of federal and state universities respectively. They have the ultimate power to hire and fire. The VCs of private institutions, by definition, are answerable to their private owner(s). In other words, a VC's appointment in a public university is 'political' and has become rather more so these days. Such appointments sadly mirror the 'isms' and 'schisms' in the wider society. Long gone are the days when it was based solely on merit. The process is now bedevilled by nepotism, ethnicity, favouritism, and clannishness. In some instances, it has become a bazaar.

A VC's appointment in Nigeria is made on a certain understanding and an expectation of a payoff from the victor. The "visitor" will casually hand the new appointee his 'list' of persons for preferment in the employment and deployment of personnel. This is not to mention the award of sundry contracts. A VC would usually feel compelled to weed out 'redundant' personnel from a past administration, then, quickly finds himself in a vicious circle of 'regularisation' and 'de-regularisation' of appointments. The VC does not only have to contend with the 'list' from the august visitor; he also needs to satisfy other similar 'lists' emanating from various powerful corners, who were perhaps, instrumental in his appointment. Simply put, it is open racketeering. That said, the most important qualification for a VC in Nigeria, today, is the ethnic, even village origin, or clan affiliation of the candidate. Perish the thought of such

160 4 · EDUCATION

ephemeral considerations not mattering to anyone. It is highly unlikely these days for a non-Yoruba person to be VC in Yorubaland; or an Igbo or Hausa to emerge VC in each other's yard without a fuss. Not only is the state of origin taken into account; the flimsiest geographical affiliation and bloodline are also reified as pivotal. Consequently, once appointed, the VC invariably spends almost his entire time massaging various egos and benefactors; his eyes completely taken off academia and diligent administration.

The rare occasions where academic qualifications come into play in the appointment of a VC appear to be when vested interests remain aggrieved, or someone has an axe to grind. Then, there is an intense search for 'gaps' in the candidates' resumes. Recently, a candidate for VC, a professor of many years standing, on a shortlist of three, was suddenly accused of not having a PhD, and therefore would not be able to preside over the award of PhDs in the university. It is being argued that the candidate's name should be expunged from the shortlist for that reason. How crass? How mendacious! Do they know how many successful football coaches around the world never played the game on a professional level? Or, how many successful tennis coaches never played tennis at any level before? Think of the Williams sisters, who dominated the tennis world for almost two decades. They were coached by their father who only studied the game by watching videos and reading coaching manuals. Do they know how many successful hospital administrators never studied medicine? You got the drift. Having a PhD for a senior academic position is useful, but its importance is highly overrated in this country.

For starters, a PhD title is not a mark of genius; it is an attestation of ability to conduct research at an advanced level. Such ability can be acquired by means other than a structured PhD training. To argue against the appointment of a professor for VC, for not having a PhD, is grasping at straws really. It is specious reasoning at best, and a lazy poppycock at worst. Universities in the West are awash with outstanding non-PhD scholars and professors who are excellent and proven researchers in their field with a lot to pass on to others coming through the system. Are those hallowed institutions any less productive than Nigeria's own dilapidated, empty shells of institutions that they currently are? Can we stop splitting hairs over PhD or no PhD please?

A position of VC in a private university does not suffer from the same melodrama constantly witnessed in public universities, because they are not beholden to political overlords and entrenched vested interests. Also, ethnic coloration of staff is yet to become an issue in those institutions. Demand for expertise is still higher than its supply, so too is the rate of staff turnover. That said, a VC in a private university requires a different skills-set than their counterparts in public institutions. They have the triple burden of being academically sound, a good administrator, and business savvy. The university's financial health and balance sheet weigh heavily on their minds in a way unfathomable in public universities. They are more consumer-oriented, because they have no choice. Above all, there is no government rescue package for an insolvent private university; only pity. By that logic, some of them sometimes go too far, bending the rules, sacrificing academic excellence on the altar of consumerism in a garbage-in-garbage-out sort of fashion. Who becomes VC in a private university thus also acquires special significance, for entirely different reasons, although no less troubling. I very much hope that this piece is not taken as casting unwarranted aspersions on the academia in this country, as it contains some painful truths we must face up to, if the institutions are to come out of the doldrums they are currently in.

4.04 NUC: Assessing the Assessors

2 February 2021

The National Universities Commission (NUC) is a body first set up in 1962 inside the Cabinet Office as an advisory agency which, over the years, metamorphosed into a corporate body enacted by statute in 1974,[231] under its first Executive Secretary, Professor Jibril Aminu.[232] It is now one of the most active and commonly recognised regulatory agencies firmly embedded in the Federal Ministry of Education. Its mission statement states: "To be a dynamic regulatory agency acting as a catalyst for positive change and innovation for the delivery of quality university education in Nigeria".[233] On any rational examination of the agency, it is anything but "dynamic". On the contrary, it has remained static and highly bureaucratic, with a jaundiced view of higher education incompatible with the needs of today's diversified and fast-moving knowledge acquisition from multiple sources. Its remit and raison d'être has not been reviewed for sixty years. Its service delivery has remained in-ward looking, dreary and notoriously predictable. A centralised education system is the anti-thesis of "dynamism", "positive change", and "innovation". Its rigid

---

231. National Universities Commission Act 1974, https://www.nuc.edu.ng/wp-content/uploads/2019/06/NUC-Act0001.pdf

232. For an interesting profile of this peripatetic civil servant, see; http://africandynasty.blogspot.com/2013/09/professor-jubril-aminu-profile.html

233. National Universities Commission, https://www.nuc.edu.ng

162   4 · EDUCATION

hold on the education system in a multi-ethnic, multi-nation, federal state is backward-looking, especially when there is pressure on countries to "roll back" the frontiers of the state in all other aspects of public life. Let us dig deeper.

Part of the mandates of the NUC is to: grant approval for all academic programmes run in Nigerian universities; establish all higher educational institutions; maintain quality assurance of all academic programmes; channel external support to Nigerian universities, among others.[234] To achieve this, its administrative structure consists of a Governing Council, and a Secretariat with twelve Directorates: Academic planning, inspection and monitoring, management and support, students' support, establishment of private universities, research, innovations and information technology, etc.[235] It is clear the NUC is a behemoth, breathing down the necks of every university in Nigeria. This cannot possibly be right. That no audible objection is being raised about this all too pervasive and intrusive body by people at the receiving end of its sharp edge is puzzling to say the least. My best guess is that this is a result of a cosy, *entente cordiale* that exists between senior academics in the universities and the management of the NUC. All the more reason for the public concern reflected in this piece. To be fair to the agency, originally, there was a perceived need to have a single authority to coordinate the academic programmes of existing and new institutions to ensure and uphold uniform standards. This is especially so in view of the fact that the universities were, almost invariably, taxpayer funded. However, in 2021, delivery of university education is no longer the preserve of government alone. Churches, consortiums, voluntary organisations and individuals also provide university education for the public. Moreover, the ultimate arbiter of quality education in today's world can no longer be government bureaucrats, it has to be the beneficiaries of qualified graduates from the universities; the employers of labour.

With their clipboard and *Bic* biro to hand, NUC regularly turns up at the door of universities to carry out periodic, in some cases, sporadic inspection of their curricula, checking for conformity to laid-down rules. This has become a huge ceremony, and fanfare, overlaid by enthusiasm and apprehension in varying circumstances. The very fact of a visit by an NUC accreditation team now represents a theatre in which everyone dances to a well-rehearsed tune. They come wielding the big stick of "accrediting" or "de-accrediting" a particular programme, department, faculty, or even an entire institution. They go round; bleary-eyed, ticking boxes like you see election observers do, except

---

234. National Universities Commission Act 1974, ibid.
235. Ibid.

4 · EDUCATION 163

that they carry such awe and such menace on their faces akin to the Gestapos. They delight in probing into every minutiae of a university's programme: how many students have enrolled on a particular course, and a particular unit; over what period of time; the topics being covered in a chronological order; how many textbooks in the tutor's office; how many contact hours with students; classroom space; how much time is taken for tea-break, etc.; pretty mundane and inane. Let us face it, as menacing as they make themselves look at times, there is practically nothing the NUC demands of a resourceful institution that would not miraculously appear in time for an accreditation exercise, even a fresh human skull. Everyone plays to the gallery, of course. NUC officials are good at many things; thinking outside the box is not one of them.

Accreditation exercise (the crown jewel in their armoury), has degenerated into an expensive charade in its manifestation. But, never mind, everyone revels in the ritual anyhow. Nigerians can be so compliant, and are generally too happy to give robotic answers to predictable questions from officialdom. In turn, some Nigerian academics have taken leave of their senses too. Many no longer understand the meaning of the "academic freedom" they profess and cherish so much. Globally, academic freedom is at the core of any university's standing. It has been circumscribed in Nigeria by over-zealous NUC staffers in the name of enforcing uniform standards. Oh, let us not teach this or that, because the NUC team may not approve. Or, this or that course unit has either been ruled out, or not yet sanctioned by the NUC, so, let us not dare expose our students to it, and other similarly mind-numbing banalities. Many have forestalled their own ability for creative thinking and foresight, as a result of their dogmatic, zombie-like approach to NUC's 'criteria', which echo loudly like voices in their heads. Is this a healthy development for the Nigerian academia? Surely not.

In my view, government bureaucrats should not be in the business of dictating course titles and their precise contents to any university. It is a regulatory overreach, and an insult to the more established institutions in Nigeria. Can anyone say that, the likes of University of Lagos, University of Ibadan, Obafemi Awolowo University, Ahmadu Bello University, Bayero University, University of Port Harcourt, University of Nigeria, Nsukka, etc. including the private universities, namely Afe Babalola University, Covenant University, Elizade University, Baze University, Babcock University etc. need some busybody to tell them what to teach and how to teach? There are many more similarly good universities, too numerous to mention. They should not be herded in the same direction. They should be allowed to play to their individual ambitions and strengths. Above all, they should be given maximum leeway to manage their curricula as they deem fit. Most academic courses these days are linked to professional bodies for additional certification anyway. That said, there would still be room for regulatory oversight, but not in the current one-size-fits-all manner. Once granted its corporate licence, a university should be allowed to run its institution free from NUC diktats for a period of ten to twenty years. NUC would reserve the right to revoke the licence anytime, in case of an egregious breach of its mandate. This draconian power would be subject to final arbitration of the courts. NUC would also have the right to conduct an impromptu inspection of any university upon the receipt of a petition from interested parties. This can be described as 'light touch' or 'arms-length' regulation, fit for the 21st century.

Finally, in case you think this piece is unduly harsh on the NUC, this is what the agency cheerfully advertises on its website: "The Commission has recorded a number of successes since its inception. These successes can be attributed to the quality of its leadership, dedication and commitment of the staff, the quality of its Board members, cooperation received from universities and support from the Federal Government". As of today, there is not a single evidence of any of the "successes" referred to in the statement. I rest my case.

Chapter Five

Media

5.01 Why Channels is in the Government's Crosshair

7 September 2021

Channels Television is arguably the most prominent privately-owned television station in Nigeria. It has won several awards for broadcast journalism countless of times, and it is based in the southwest region of Nigeria; birthplace of television broadcasting in Africa.[236] What is the big deal you might ask? It is that a television station dedicated to breaking news has, itself, become the news, of late. It has come under what appears to be a sustained 'attack' by the authorities for not adhering to its commitment to impartial news coverage. A vibrant, 'free press' is the cornerstone of any democratic society. 'Free press' is a relative term though. For good or ill, there is no media outlet without its own institutional bias. At its basic, the press is generally thought to be 'vibrant' and 'free' when it is not subject to government control either in form or in substance. Most media outlets in Africa fall well short of even this modest criterion. Being the "fourth estate of the realm", in Western societies, the concept of a free press is a lot more profound than simply not being under government control; it is about the fundamental (unalloyed) right to free speech, the limit of which is a regular subject of fierce debate and contention as it should be. Free speech by one person can become so stretched that it threatens the liberty of others. It is thus a moving goalpost.

---

236. Mike Egbon, PhD "Western Nigerian Television Service — Oldest in Tropical Africa" Research Article, SAGE Journals, June, 1983 https://journals.sagepub.com/doi/abs/10.1177/107769908306000219?journalCode=jmqb

166   5 · MEDIA

In Africa, debate about the media and free speech is hardly ever anchored around freedom and liberty of the individual; it is mainly anchored around government sensibilities, and the fragility of the post-colonial state. Free press has less profundity in Africa than it does in Western societies. Channels Television is right in the middle of this media trajectory. It is neither tied to government, nor free in essence. It is a station trying hard to exercise its freedom to disseminate information within the context of a rapidly evolving socio-political milieu in a key African country. The media in Africa carries the burden of the fragility of the state to the extreme sometimes. Heaven is always about to cave in on hapless citizens for any 'loose' or 'incendiary' broadcast. It does not take much to shake the fragile state to its foundation in Africa. A little oxygen of publicity given to some renegade political leader or groups, for example, venting their spleen on ethnicity, or, autonomy, nationalism, etc. can set things off violently in a jiffy. So, the media is permanently burdened by the imperative of self-censorship in that regard. For this reason, most African governments believe they know best. They believe they understand what it takes to steady the fragile state; put the media on a tight leash. Channels Television has felt the sharp edge of that of late.

African leaders embrace 'free press' as long as the reportage is done through the prisms of public policy, and 'national security'. Many will stop at nothing until they secure a zombie-like compliance from the media. Some media houses are better at negotiating this than others. It is said that in a society of the blind, a one-eyed man is king. Channels is one of a handful of privately-owned media houses that has become 'mainstream' from which millions of viewers at home and abroad obtain their staple diet of information. It enjoys a degree of trust for its content that the government media house does not, could not, and will probably never match. That is why its programmes attract so much attention from a wide and diverse audience. The irony is that, not everyone thinks Channels is a super brilliant channel in every respect. The manner in which the station sometimes treats its political "VIP" guests with kid gloves is embarrassing. "Sir, please tell us what you think of ..." is one of their favoured, not to say, sheepish line of questioning. The interviewer would often then fold their arms, and watch passively as the interviewee rabbit on, reeling out party lines, and making bland statements totally unconnected to the question asked. Much of that lack of rigor, and pertinent questioning is due to inadequate background preparation by the producers. The media in the UK and US, which we like to emulate here, does not suffer from that type of meekness mainly because the terrain over there is fundamentally different. Society is polarised along clear ideological lines (right, left, centre, moderate, extreme, maverick). News editors

5 · MEDIA   167

and producers set up their anchors and their line of questioning in a way that reflects the polarisation in society as closely as possible. In the absence of ideology, and established political lineage, society like ours remains polarised along primordial and ethnic lines; amplification of which is to be avoided, especially in broadcast media.

What makes this even more problematic in the context of Nigeria is the fact that key government ministers are generally media shy. With the exception of one or two, once appointed, most ministers remain faceless, simply doodling along quietly in the background. They are rarely, if ever, put forward to defend government policy on camera. Does anyone remember ever seeing the Minister of Finance, for instance, being interrogated on TV about the economy? What about the Minister of Defence? Minister of the Interior? Or any of the other over-pampered Federal Government Ministers? The answer, of course, is no. Press officers answer for almost everything in Nigeria. That is not accountability; that is government by spin. This is what the Nigerian Broadcasting Commission (NBC) should be demanding of government to rectify, instead of issuing a pretty infantile 'query' as it did to Channels on the 25th of August 2021, on its 'failure' to balance up the 'anti-government slant' in the interviews conducted by its anchors.[237] That being so, why not let the President himself, or the relevant minister (not press officer, not Minister for 'Communication') provide the counter-narrative? Channels should make a point of inviting relevant government ministers to participate in debates even if they would not accept. The anchors are then able to announce at the conclusion of the exchanges that minister so-and-so was invited but declined to take part.

All said and done, it is not for the NBC to compel television journalists to defend government position on any issue, or rebut an opposition attack on government policy, in the guise of complying with some broadcasting code. Buhari should lead by example, by making himself available for live interview once a month. That way, no ambiguities about any aspect of government policy would linger for too long. It also means less focus on the President's "body language" (No laughing matter). Channels journalists have often been at pains to admonish their guests to 'tone down' or 'moderate' their views on issues many viewers see as mundane, and innocuous. It is something many of them would rather not do, I am sure. Only last week, the station was visibly anxious to accord prominence to a military media spokesperson paying a 'courtesy' visit to its Abuja office, following the ill-advised notice from the NBC. The sol-

---

237. See; "Nigeria's Broadcast Regulator Querries Channels TV Over 'Anti-government interview'" Media Foundation for West Africa. A non-governmental organisation with a base across the 16 West African countries comprising West Africa. https://www.mfwa.org

168   5 · MEDIA

dier had decided to stop by in a show of media 'solidarity' with Channels. Of course, the door to their recording studios was swiftly flung open to him. Channels, please, you do not need the endorsement of a guy in military fatigue with a smug smile on his face, to burnish your image. A written statement of support from the army media corps, read out on air, would have been sufficient. Note, Channels is not in trouble because of its failure to toe the government line, it is in trouble because it is trying too hard to please the establishment.

5.02 Sorry, Servile, Supine State of Nigeria's Media

15 January 2019

For good or ill, the press, also known as the "fourth estate of the realm", being the epitome of power alongside the Legislature, Judiciary and the Executive, is a force to reckon with in any system of government. In a different vein, it has been pejoratively described as embodying "power without responsibility; the prerogative of the harlot down the ages".[238] This is for its ability to hold other people to account, at will, without any corresponding means to hold the press itself to account for its action /omission. 'Press' and 'Media' are used interchangeably in this piece. Celebrities and powerful people love the press when it says nice things about them, but loathe it when it exposes them for wrongdoing or simply portraying them in an unfavourable light. The press has a unique role to play in a democracy; it equally has a unique role to play in a dictatorship. Democracy needs the press to function for mass education, dictatorship wants it to function for mass propaganda, although, where 'education' ends and 'propaganda' starts is not always clear-cut. The main distinguishing factor between the two is that the press is supposedly 'free' in the former, whilst being 'shackled' or 'emasculated' in the latter. In reality though, the idea of a 'free' press is a highly contested concept at the best of times. The beauty, they say, is in the eye of the beholder. The problem with the press in Nigeria is that it is neither free nor shackled; it hovers in an orbit between the extremes. That makes it infinitely more problematic for all concerned. So, what exactly is the issue?

On the question of press freedom, yes, people are free to own publishing houses, and a lot do in this country. Many of those publishing houses are in turn owned by people with partisan political interests. There is no television

---

238. A famous Rudyard Kipling quote https://forum.wordreference.com/threads/power-without-responsibility-the-prerogative-of-harlot-throughout-the-ages.3714217

studio in Nigeria, for instance, whose proprietor is not steeped in partisan politics. Furthermore, there is no print journal in this country whose shares are not heavily owned by active political operatives and business moguls as well. Public media houses are already well known for acting more or less as the propaganda tools for whichever party happens to hold the reins of power in the country. While it may be self-evident that Nigeria has the highest concentration of private media ownership in Africa, it has not translated into truly 'independent' media outlets. Private ownership and independent media are two separate and distinct concepts. "Fox News" television in the US gives us the best example of a private media house that is equally unashamed and unabashed about its extreme right-wing output, even more extreme for a lot of elected Republican lawmakers in Congress to swallow sometimes. The nearest equivalent in Nigeria would be the self-styled "African Independent Television" AIT, which has, overtime, become the communication department for the People's Democratic Party (PDP) in fact. It started as a dream of its founder, Chief Raymond Dokpesi, to become the beacon of hope and an example of independent television beamed across Africa. Initial financial constraint most likely forced the channel to seek accommodation with the power at the centre; the PDP, a couple of years into its launch. No less can be said about the others which have sprung up after them.

Now, then, media houses are one thing, the journalists operating inside them are another. The need to inform and be informed has always existed as the basis for the "social contract" between the governor and the governed in a democratic setting, as well as in a dictatorship (albeit) on a totally different premise. The governor wants the governed to remain ignorant of its shortcomings, he wants only to showcase the 'great work' that he is putting in for the welfare of society, while the governed wants the governor to know precisely where the shoe pinches in order to make amends. As it happens, demands from the governed are infinitesimal, and the resources to take care of them few and far between. The judge, meanwhile, stands ever so ready to pronounce on who is right and who is wrong on disputes and disagreements between the governor and the governed. The oil; the engine oil, that ignites and sustains this interaction is the press. The journalist is hugely important in this. If it fails to perform, then, everything else is in jeopardy. It sometimes fills one with horror not knowing whether the typical journalist in this country fully understands the pivotal role the profession occupies in the whole scheme of things.

Take for instance, the recent "settlement" reached between MTN and CBN over the issue of foreign remittances. The CBN had vowed to make MTN cough up the "illegal" repatriation of funds from Nigeria to overseas branches

170 5 · MEDIA

of the company. It involved a huge sum; $8.1b dollars.[239] This was highlighted on this column last year: ("Forex fiddling: CBN's case against MTN/banks" PUNCH, September 11, 2018), where it was accurately predicted that the end result would see the two sides "moving towards some type of reconciliation and amicable settlement as these things are usually quietly settled in this country". The question for the press is why is the Minister of Finance not under scrutiny over this "settlement" announced a couple of weeks ago? Who is playing what trick on whom in the MTN/CBN 'family quarrel'? If the CBN Governor is not answerable to the Minister of Finance, then, the President should naturally step up to the plate. What this speaks to is the absence of investigative journalism in this country. Our journalists, like our political leaders, are wont to glide over major issues of state and society with reckless abandon. During the first month of this year alone, it has been announced that; Standard Organisation of Nigeria destroyed N23b naira worth of substandard goods entering into the country, that; the Federal Government has earmarked $877m dollars for equipment to fight Boko Haram, which President Muhammadu Buhari said had been "technically defeated" three years ago, that; taxpayers database hit 35 million, that; unemployment is still on a steep curve etc., etc. All we see in the headlines are the travel itinerary of government ministers, or the mudslinging between party apparatchik.

On the rare occasions where government ministers are up for TV interrogation, we are treated to nauseating and banal exchanges, which goes something like; "Thank you for joining us Honourable Minister, what is your view on what is happening"? The minister then gets a free pass to rant and rave about how wonderful a job the government is doing. The journalist then moves on to another guest, just joining them in their Lagos studio to provide another rambling slant on the same subject. Captains of industry too, get the same fluffy and woolly questions from our journalists: "You have heard what so-and-so said; what is your take on it?" This is the most banal of all questions. It sets no parameter for the answer; only a free pass for the interviewee. The journalist on display in this country, on the "news" channels, is no more than a spectator and passive listener for their guests. They make no advance preparation for a particular line of questioning, they appear ill-at ease and befuddled by the answers they get, so, they cross their arms and look on, say thank you and move on to the next item. We call that journalism? Dear media, please let

---

239. The figures in the press vary, but considerable anyhow it is viewed. See; "Nigeria central bank slaps $16m fine on banks for MTN capital repatriation https://www.africanews.com/2018/08/29/nigeria-central-bank-slaps-16m-fine-on-banks-for-mtn-capital-repatriation

5 · MEDIA

us raise the bar and live up to the onerous responsibility society has placed on you. Prove this column wrong, for once, by showing your real mettle in this election year, not caring whose ox is gored.

5.03 Channels TV Interview (Sorry, Torture) of President Buhari

11 January 2022

President Muhammadu Buhari is approaching the end of his second term in office. The taciturn president is known for communicating with the public through his "body language", and also through his press officers, otherwise known as the "spin doctors". In the event of an urgent public policy issue, there is usually the crisp 'statement' from the Presidency clarifying and drawing the line on things. Nigerians often view (in envy) foreign leaders on television and online news being grilled by journalists on topical issues in their domain, and wonder why that is not happening with their own leader at home. Surely, Buhari, with a firm background as a 'law and order' former Nigerian military strongman (1983–1985), who later fought so hard (running in four elections) before finally becoming President in 2015, would have a lot to say about the country's state of affairs on a regular basis once in office. Alas, not. He has been reclusive and keeping his own counsel on most things. A Parliamentary system would not tolerate that from an elected leader even for one week. Parliament and the Executive operate in tandem, daily, and on camera, almost around the clock. In addition, there is little or no ministerial accountability under the Presidential system either. Ministers in the Buhari administration have also taken their cue from the boss; work behind the scenes, and say very little.

This column has pointed out this lacuna on a couple of occasions in the last three months alone. Remember; "Why Channels TV is in government's crosshair". PUNCH September 7 2021? It was stated: "Let the President lead by example, by making himself available for a live interview once a month. That way, no ambiguities about any aspect of government policy would linger for too long". A couple of weeks later, the column took the Minister of Finance, Budget and Planning to task thus: "Zainab Ahmed: Nigeria's featherweight finance minister". PUNCH September 21 2021. It was a critique of the minister's reluctance to submit herself to scrutiny on TV. To her credit, she did exactly that the following week, and spoke eloquently well. She showed the viewers what they had been missing all this while. One was left wondering why the palpably adroit minister has not made a point of defending government policy in media interrogations more often. On his part, President Buhari finally submitted himself to an interview on Channels TV last week, the 5th of January 2022. As it happens, the interview was granted on conditions usually associated with reclusive leaders in authoritarian regimes; no live interrogation, questions submitted in advance, and the whole engagement contained within forty minutes or less. The heavies, (the state security personnel), were seen milling around the TV set inside Aso Rock, watching and keeping a close eye on things.

Despite the restrictions and constrictions designed to protect the President from being found out, the interview was a disaster from start to finish, at least from the point of view of public relations. It was like watching a train wreck. The President looked like a rabbit caught in the headlights throughout. The anchors; Seun Okinbaloye, and Maupe Ogun-Yusuf are usually mild-mannered and courteous interviewers — to a fault at times. Their reputation was also on the line. Be too soft on the President, and risk being viewed as lackeys, or adopt the aggressive, "hardtalk" style, and incur the wrath of the President's handlers. It was such a tightrope. It was a situation of damned if you do, and damned if you do not. In the end, it was not made clear whether Channels retained full editorial control over the content of the broadcast. It would be scandalous if the pre-recorded interview was vetted by the Presidency prior to broadcast. Channels should clear the air on that. Submitting the questions in advance is already bad enough.

Anyway, one would imagine that the President would have been sufficiently coached on what to say on TV, having had the exam questions leaked to him. It was therefore rather unfortunate to see him still looking so befuddled by the mundane (some would say) anodyne line of questioning from the anchors. The advance briefing by his newly appointed Head of the Economic Council, Dr Doyin Salami, appeared to have left an imprint on his mind. It is that only 2.5% of Nigeria's arable land has been cultivated thus far. So when the President was taken to task on the debt stock rising to 32 trillion from the 12 trillion he inherited, inflation rising to 15% from the 9% he inherited, unemployment rising to 32.2% from the 8.9% he inherited, and the exchange rate rising to 400 naira to the dollar from the 197 naira he inherited, he was completely flummoxed. He quickly gathered his thoughts; "we have to go back to the land"…, "only 2.5% arable land cultivated", he emphasised, as if he has found the magic wand for the country's economic recovery. On the farmer-herdsmen conflict, it is a matter of "culture" he said. "Farmers and herders have been co-existing for a long time in Nigeria". Pity he was not taken to task on his wildly premature claim of having "technically defeated" Boko Haram back in December 2015.

On state police, Buhari said: "I don't support state police. Role of traditional rulers must not be undermined". What? As if calculated to rescue him from drowning, the beleaguered President was thrown a lifeline; "What kind of economy do you want to bequeath to Nigerians"? He came back alive, suddenly remembered his talking points: "Free economy, stop the smuggling, stop developed countries dumping goods on our country, make sure we encourage our own industries ..." The anchors then lobbed an additional soft ball at him: "What comes to your mind when you hear PDP? INEC? Young people? 2023 election"? Etc. The President caught the lighter mood, chuckled, and rambled along to the end. What does this all mean you might ask? That the President has no vast knowledge of issues? And that he is not an eloquent speaker? Capital YES to those questions, but what does that matter? Well, it depends. US President, Ronald Reagan (1980–1989) was a Hollywood actor, who developed an age-related degenerative disease leading to lapses in his memory. That did not stop him from becoming a great American President still fondly remembered to this day. Even the current US President, Joe Biden, is not a man known for being particularly bright, as he tends to be verbose and clumsy with his choice of words on important occasions. And at 79, same age as Buhari, his mental state is likely to deteriorate further in the course of his Presidency.

In all, Presidents do not need to be geniuses to be successful; a good and successful leader is propelled by a clear vision and strong moral fibre. Above all, a successful President needs an effective bureaucracy behind him. The "federal character" contortion used in the employment and promotion in the federal civil service in Nigeria undermines merit and competence. Unlike in the West, therefore, a Nigerian President has no guarantee of an effective, politically-neutral civil service to lean on. And, if on top of that, you then have a deficient person in the number one office, you have a recipe for bad governance. Buhari's intellectual ability was known to the APC's hierarchy that connived to put him up as their Presidential candidate in 2015, and 2019. The electorate that twice voted for him en masse did not give a hoot about the depth of his knowledge of current affairs either. Nigeria of today accords no value to knowledgeable leaders in politics. Nigeria of tomorrow would embrace knowledgeable leaders in politics only if the people insist on it. Let Buhari be!

5.04 Why Governments Love (and Loathe) Twitter

27 July 2021

Information is key to the success or failure of government in the modern world. All types of governments and regimes hold this to be self-evidently true. All (without exception) want to control the information citizens can access, and which bits to supress. It is less of a dilemma in a dictatorship than

174   5 · MEDIA

it is in a democracy because of the much vaunted press freedom. Governments in Western democracies have found a convenient way around the imperative of press freedom and their desire to put a 'spin' on news reports of their daily activity. The political and media elites both acknowledge and recognise the mutual respect, sometimes, contempt they have for each other. The creative tension that bubbles up from time to time is often interpreted as evidence of democratic maturity, in sharp contrast to dictatorship and other types of authoritarian rule. The advent of Twitter and other social media outlets in the last couple of decades has been seized upon by Western leaders as the magic wand that would finally prise open the monopoly of information enjoyed by authoritarian regimes they have spent so much time condemning in other countries. What has happened, however, is that social media has also tested and stretched (to a breaking point) the limits of liberal tolerance for undiluted, and unfiltered information. To varying degrees, both liberal and illiberal entities have had an axe to grind against the omnipresence (and governance) of Twitter.

Once upon a time in America, Australia, and United Kingdom, the vast media space was dominated by a single "press baron", the Australian-American, Rupert Murdoch. At one point, he was in direct control of nearly two-thirds of the media outlets in those three significant territories.[240] Across Western Europe and North America, all the major news outlets have been owned by people whose political sympathies could be swayed in exchange for specific campaign promises and policies. Elected officials often kowtowed to the editors' pet hates and dislikes. Political leaders would go the extra mile to assuage their feelings on critical areas of public policy. Such was the power of the mainstream media. They decided what to highlight in the evening news headlines, early morning edition, or the weekend review. Presidents and Prime Ministers fretted over whether their 'message' was cutting through the fog of the sometimes sensational reportage by anxious journalists working to deadlines. Then came the jungle beast, also known as the social 'media', which bypasses the mainstream media and the costly and time-consuming afternoon lunches and evening dinners with the press barons, editors, and media moguls for influence. By far the most potent of the social 'media', as far as politicians are concerned, is of course, Twitter; founded only twenty-years ago in 2006 by the American, Jack Dorsey, who remains the company's Chief Executive Officer.[241]

---

240. See; "How much of the media does Rupert Murdoch own?" No Majesty.com https://nomajesty.com/how-much-of-the-media-does-rupert-murdoch-own

241. He has since resigned from his position, and the company itself has been bought by the billionaire industrialist, Elon Musk, who is yet to finalise details of the takeover.

The genius of Twitter is that it enables the subscriber to build up 'followers' in their thousands and millions. And, with that comes the ability to communicate and disseminate raw information in real time, and across the globe, at minimal cost. It is the most disruptive intervention to the conventional press in modern time. Suddenly, what people get to hear and read no longer emanates from recognised media outlets only; monopoly of information by one source or a group of sources, is now a relic of the past. A lot of Western governments saw this, at first, as a means to open up authoritarian regimes, and so it proved at least in one particular instance; the "Arab Spring" from 2010 and beyond, which challenged authoritarian regimes in the Middle-East. Starting with Tunisia, and expanding to Libya, Egypt, Yemen, Bahrain etc. Hitherto silent and compliant citizens found a voice through social media, and the authoritarian regimes and their edifices began to crumble. Social media can be useful for individual authoritarian leaders too. A section of the Turkish Army attempted a coup against President Recep Tayyip Erdoğan in 2016.[242] With his legion of followers on social media, he rallied support by urging them to come onto the streets in defence of 'democracy'. They responded, and the insurrection quickly fizzled out. More recently, in the United States, the defeated candidate in the 2020 Presidential election, former President Donald Trump, relying on his own unique authoritarian instincts, used his several million of followers on Twitter to try and overturn the result of the election by urging them to march on the Congress, which they did in their thousands, smashing windows and rioting. What turned out to be an uprising was quickly put down, and Trump's account on Twitter was suspended, and later permanently removed for repeatedly going against Twitter's guidelines.[243]

The question that is exercising everyone around the globe at the moment is whether Twitter and the other giant social media outlets should be regulated, or worse, 'cut to size'. If the borderless, information superhighway has rendered that rather cumbersome, should states be able to impose conditions on Twitter within their sovereign territories, even ban it outright if it disseminates or enables 'toxic' information to filter through to their citizens? For instance, why should Jack Dorsey, alone, be the one to decide whether to silence the voice of an elected President of a sovereign state? Social media has become the Achilles' heel for dictators all over the world, as it has provided the chink in their otherwise impenetrable armour, but it is a double-edged sword. Social media can be both a force for good and bad. On balance though, in the field

---

242. See; "Turkey court jails hundreds for life for 2016 coup plot against Erdoğan" BBC November 2020 https://www.bbc.com/news/world-europe-55083955

243. See; "permanent suspension of @realDonaldTrump", Twitter, January 8, 2021 https://blog.twitter.com/en_us/topics/company/2020/suspension

176   5 · MEDIA

of information, most people recognise that the good in social media far outweighs the bad. This is the background within which the ban on Twitter announced by the Buhari administration on the 5th of June 2021 should be contextualised.[244] The ban was imposed following the decision of Twitter to take down a tweet from Buhari that violated its guidelines. On the face of it, the ban looks like an overreaction on the part of the administration. On a careful examination though, and given the consequences of the #EndSARS[245] protests, and the recent history of the "Arab Spring",[246] both of which were facilitated by social media, the administration had good reasons to be jittery.

Social media has become a weapon of mass information and empowerment across Africa and other challenging environments around the world. Twitter in particular has democratised information by facilitating access to the critical mass previously the exclusive preserve of big powerful press barons and their metropolitan editors. The Buhari administration's ban on Twitter has (temporarily) disrupted access to the platform for millions of Nigerians. Nonetheless, the Presidency has learned the wrong lessons from the events of the "Arab Spring", #EndSARS and the like. Rather than being afraid of a social media-inspired 'regime change' lurking around the corner, the administration should seize the moment to re-orientate governance towards the people. And in case they are thinking of borrowing a leaf from China, where social media is heavily censored, they should think again. China does manage to dictate content to social media platforms operating on its shores, because it has acquired the economic/military/industrial muscle to do so without much repercussion. Its centralised political system is complimented by a mixed economy that works. It is a unique Chinese formula, not easily replicated in other sociocultural environments. Not for the first time, Nigerian political leaders like flexing their muscles and wielding power they do not really have. A ban on Twitter hurts Nigerian citizens and its economy more than it does Twitter and its $30 billion market capitalisation.[247] On a final note, a ban is not only an own-goal for Nigeria; it is a brilliant marketing gift for Twitter, whose users in the largest market in Africa will soar in number once the dust settles.

---

244. See; "Nigeria Bans Twitter After President's Tweet Is Deleted", The New York Times, January 5, 2021 https://www.nytimes.com/2021/06/05/world/africa/nigeria-twitter -president.html

245. An acronym for a spontaneous protests by Nigerian youths against police brutality across the country in late 2020 to early 2021.

246. A series of spontaneous uprising and rebellion against authoritarian rule which started in Tunisia, in 2010, and quickly spread across the Arab world.

247. See; Marketcap.com https://companiesmarketcap.com/twitter/marketcap

Chapter Six

Politics

6.01 Why 'Vote Buying' Matters: Why it Does Not

7 August 2018

There is a growing phenomenon trending in the often febrile atmosphere of elections and electioneering in Africa since the beginning of the 1990s. That is the undisputed and inescapable fact of money changing hands, in other words, money being given in exchange for votes, or "vote buying" as it has come to be described. This is not particularly unique to Africa; it happens in most underdeveloped and developing societies in transition. My interest for this column, this week, is a discussion of the trend as it affects continental Africa. The just concluded (July 2018) post-Mugabe general elections in Zimbabwe, and the gubernatorial election in Ekiti State, Nigeria, are only the latest examples of how widespread the phenomenon has become. It is becoming increasingly entrenched. It is now unthinkable to run a competitive election anywhere in Africa without money for votes playing a significant part. The question is, does that really matter? It is my intention to examine the political economy of vote buying from both sides of the argument before proposing a (not so new) way out of the morass.

First, vote buying matters because the idea of giving voters money in exchange for their ballots is utterly repugnant; it is an affront to freedom of choice. Furthermore, it circumvents political debate; the lifeblood of democratic politics. Election time is the opportune period for reflection and contemplation over who to entrust with political power. It is the time when the cut and thrust of ideas and alternative visions for society are supposedly brought under public scrutiny. Above all, it is the time when voters are able to make informed decisions about what party or candidate to favour with their ballot. Now, if the ballot can simply

178 6 · POLITICS

be traded for money, it obviates the need for rigorous scrutiny of candidates for office. It would therefore be open season to all comers. Any bandit, crook, or con artist dressed in a party political garment would not need to worry about being found wanting as long as he is able to negotiate the right price for each ballot. In that case, both the elected and the elector are co-conspirators in a grand scheme of fraud on society.

On the other hand, vote buying does not matter because it is intrinsically redistributive in its impact. It is a unique means of channelling funds from the have to the have-nots. The people doing the "selling" in the main have little else to trade for cash. They are often the army of unemployed, underemployed, un-trained, unconnected, unsophisticated and underclass people who simply want to "cash in" on the only political capital that falls into their laps in an election cycle. Who can blame them? Since the money being redistributed is public funds anyway, so, it could even be seen as their own "dividends of democracy". Apart from that, vote buying actually works if and only if the person voting would not have voted in the particular way he did but for the money. In other words, a vote can be said to have been "bought" only if it would have been freely given to some other candidate or party were it not for the cash inducement. This is an area crying out for political science research, surely. There is a lot of anecdotal evidence to suggest, for instance, that the last Ekiti gubernatorial election, and the one before that in 2014, actually reflected the peoples' will in spite of money changing hands; likewise the outcome of the Zimbabwe election. In this context, vote buying *de jure* occurred only sporadically in both cases. The winning parties paid for ballots that were already destined for their respective camps in any event. In other words, it was more apparent than real. The monetary reward on offer was an insurance premium, just to make sure. In most cases, people were happy to get paid for voting in exactly the way they had contemplated doing anyway. In the absence of solid empirical evidence, the argument that vote buying thwarts democratic value is speculative at best. There is big money influence too in Western democracies, perhaps even on a much larger scale than there is in Africa. Only the mechanics of it are different.

The above notwithstanding, if we are desirous of taking money out of our politics altogether, then, it is a herculean task that may not see the light of day in the lifetime of any currently living African. If, however, we aim to blunt the impact of money in our elections, then, there is the possibility of making a modest progress in that regard by adopting the "Open Ballot System" (OBS) as Africa's unique contribution to political thought. In Nigeria, this was also known as "Option A4", which allows voters to queue behind their candidate's name at polling stations. That way, everyone sees who is voting for whom and in what numbers. This method of voting is not new in the political discourse in Nigeria, as it was successfully adopted in the infamous 1993 elections. Contrary to the fear mongers at the time, there was little or no repercussion for anyone who took part. Voter intimidation was kept at a minimum. The idea that lining up behind the candidate of one's choice in an open ballot system exposes people to negative repercussions is unproven to say the least. "Secret ballot" is a uniquely Western invention; there is nothing sacrosanct about it. After all, we are encouraged to do virtually everything else in the open; dispense justice in the open, worship in the open, hold hands and kiss in the open, take marriage vows in the open, there are even "nudist camps" in many countries in the West where, basically, anything goes. Parliaments function in the open; Conventions are drawn in the open, etc.

For students of international history, World War I was largely precipitated by shady and secret agreements of world leaders. This is what inspired the "Fourteen points" statement of the US President, Woodrow Wilson (1913–1921), to Congress on how to "win the peace" through "open covenants, openly arrived at". It later became known as "open diplomacy openly arrived at", "after which there shall be no private international understandings of any kind", Wilson declared.

Far from being a travesty of democracy, an open ballot system is an exercise in courage and a disincentive to bribery and corruption. This would not ultimately stop people from "buying" votes, of course, but it would render the effect of money on the outcome of an election practically redundant. It would very much be like paying footballers huge bonuses for a particular match. It neither affects the playing field, which remains flat, nor the number of players, which is eleven versus eleven. OBS would empower the citizens as they are able to take control of where power goes, and in what quantum. This level of transparency makes for a more inclusive and accountable system of government. The main credible argument against OBS that I would concede is not one of principle, but one of logistics. How is it possible to queue up behind ten, fifteen, twenty or more candidates at a polling station? Well, that is simple. You isolate the three leading candidates, and get the people to form queues behind them, then, leave one generic queue for all the others. Let us be bold and imaginative in our thinking of befitting solutions to political problems as we see them in Africa; not as they are conceived by Western political thinkers with their incongruous obsession with openness about everything, and secrecy about voting.

6.02 Transition Gap: A Looters' Charter

19 March 2019

Certain things are so palpably, so glaringly wrong and rotten in our system of government in this country, that many often wonder in amazement, shake their heads in disbelief, grin in agony, heave a sigh of anguish while muttering; "oh, this country". First of such is the obnoxious "security vote"; a pot of money totally at the behest of a state governor to spend as he likes. No records need be kept, no account needs be given, and no queries need arise from any auditors. It is a licence and liberty to spend on anything that takes the fancy of the governor. It is to be recalled, a few years back, that Chief (Alhaji) Lamidi Ariyibi Akanji Adedibu, the late godfather of all godfathers in Ibadan, Oyo State, came on the state television to announce his claim on a chunk of the security vote against the wish of the then Governor, Alhaji Rasheed Ladoja, in 2006, and promising to stop him from seeking re-election into a second term in office for his unwillingness to relent. Anyway, so far for the "security vote". What is more of an urgent public policy issue right now, in this moment, is the issue and raison d'être of the mandatory period of transition from one administration to another. This particularly affects the office of the President and more crucially, State Governors.

As things stand, the Governors-elect from the 16th of February elections will not assume office until the 29th of May; a good three months following their election into office. Is this not rather baffling, you might ask? Well, since we are simply here to duplicate what happens in the American Presidential system, which makes provision for such to take place between every administration, it is ipso-facto justifiable enough reason why we do the same here in Nigeria. To say that this foreign import is crass in its conception is no exaggeration; it is a burden and luxury our own system cannot afford. As stipulated by the constitution in America, a President or Governor cannot assume power until he or she has taken the oath of office. Thus, a sitting President or Governor continues to exercise executive power until the oath of office has been administered on his successor. Exactly the same applies in our own system, but which governor of a state in this country needs three months to prepare for office after their election? Which hand-over notes need three months to draw up in many states where the Governor does no more than pay civil service wages? Why on earth do we create this loophole for politicians to tempt fate?

In America, transition politics is a fairly modern phenomenon. It arose in line with the increasingly sophisticated bureaucracy of the US government.

6 · POLITICS

The Presidential Transition Act only came into being in 1963 over there.[248] In a system that runs the most complex capitalist machine on the planet, maybe a period of transition is not unreasonable. After all, Mr President presides over more than $4trillion budget, with more than two million civil service employees, almost two thousand Presidential appointees requiring Senate confirmation, and several thousands more not requiring confirmation, over four hundred federal judicial appointees, close to one million White House staff positions to put in place and more. Remember, it took President Muhammadu Buhari more than six months to appoint a cabinet of forty people in 2015, to preside over a minuscule budget of just over $20 billion US dollars.[249]

The concern on this column, this week, reflects the common knowledge that many state governors have been known to turn the transition period into some kind of bonanza; to clean out the coffers on their way out. Many more have been known to use the hiatus to saddle the in-coming governor with financial burden designed to tie the hands of their successor, especially if he belongs to the opposition party. Loads of employment letters are backdated; many hasty promotions embarked upon; movement of capital through various bank accounts effected; selling off the family silver and other assets; issuing of questionable Certificate of Occupancy (C of O), in respect of land; appropriation of government vehicles and converting such into parting gifts for senior officials etc.. Upon assuming office, some governors simply look the other way and carry on with business as usual. Others embark upon a "probe" of their predecessor, but immediately stands accused of a "witch hunt" and "political vendetta". The "probe" usually turns out to be an exercise in futility as pressure is usually brought to bear on the new governor to let bygone be bygone. "Let us not waste too much time talking about the past governor" is usually the golden word of advice flying across from all quarters to the new governor. So what can and should be done?

There is no magic wand, no quick fix to this intractable problem, but it is useful to consider this. Let it be mandatory on all out-going governors to submit an audit of their administration to be kept by the electoral body (INEC) one month into the start of an election campaign. The audit will then be turned over to the governor-elect alongside his certificate of return. Any governor who fails to submit such an audit will forfeit the right to contest the election, and the state will be subject to direct administration by the Federal Government for the duration and outcome of the election. On this basis, transition is effected

---

248. See; Presidential Transition Act https://presidentialtransition.org/publications/presidential-transition-act-summary

249. Centre for Presidential Transition, ibid.

182   6 · POLITICS

within seven days of the issuance of a certificate of return by the electoral body (INEC). Now, the question some people may be asking is whether seven days are indeed enough to transit from one administration into another? The answer to this is resoundingly yes. Let us remember, there is no "transition" gap as such in a Parliamentary system. The winner is allowed to literally walk into the government house within days. Even where coalition negotiation needs to take place, it is usually concluded within days or a few weeks at the most.

Let us remember Mrs Margaret Thatcher, Prime Minister of the UK between 1979 and 1990, upon being defeated by a vote of her parliamentary colleagues, only had twenty-four hours to pack her bags from Downing Street, her official residence to an address in a residential quarter in town that she was totally unprepared for. Life moved on. Let us stop masquerading as a mature democracy running a genuine presidential system. Let us stop pretending we are like the USA with its economic and military global dominance in need of an orderly transition of power even at the level of our impoverished and Federal Government-dependent states. Let us learn to think for ourselves, take what is good about other people's system of government, ditch what is not quite right for us out of it and, just for once, trim our coat according to our size.

6.03 Yes, Nigeria Needs a Revolution — of the Mind

13 August 2019

If you approach the average man in the street, in any corner of Nigeria, with a choice between two bags in your hand, one labelled "revolution", and the other labelled "rice", with the clear warning that the consequences of his choice will shape the country for generations to come, which of the bags do you imagine would get picked? Let me hazard an educated guess and suggest that the one labelled "rice" would win the day, any time; all the time, in this country. This is precisely the logic that was lost on the leadership of the 'failed' "Revolution Now" project last week.[250] The police and security agencies were all needlessly up in arms about a "revolution" that was pre-announced and widely

---

250. Omoyele Sowore, Publisher of the online media; Sahara Reporters had called for a "Revolution Now" protest, which drew large crowds onto the streets, and fears through the Nigerian security agencies in 2019. For a deeper, academic analysis, see; Vincent Chi Ezenwa. "Symbolism of Omoyele Sowore's "Revolution Now" March Protest to Nigeria's Democratic Process" 'Sapientia Foundation Journal of Education, Sciences and Gender Studies,. Vol 1, No 1, (2019) https://www.sfjesgs.com/index.php/SFJESGS/article/view/10

6 · POLITICS

circulated on social media. My contention in this piece is simply that the security agencies used a sledge hammer to crack a nut last week, with their strong show of force to disperse and disrupt the agitators (not protesters, but agitators). You do not embark upon a revolution to protest, but to uproot and shake things up in a way unrecognisable hitherto. Had they been allowed a free run as it were, it would have fizzled out like a drop of water in a frying pan because, although, there was discontent over the direction of this country on the part of the people generally, before the last election and since, but those concerns have not yet metamorphosed into a mass appetite for a revolution.

To have a successful (non-violent) revolution, you need the presence of two critical elements: mass consciousness and organisation. The leadership of "Revolution Now" had neither, although, they probably convinced themselves and others around them that they already had both, through their presence in metropolitan centres and access to social media. Violent revolution is quite another matter, which we will come to later. That would not require an advance notice to the police or security agencies. In this column's assessment, "Revolution Now" was not aimed at a violent overthrow of government; those behind it had wanted, or were hoping for, a spontaneous uprising against misrule and injustice. That is a totally justifiable and acceptable venture in a democratic setting. The tag "revolution", however, had sent the jitters down the spines of the establishment and the security forces, but there was no need for such overreaction. Bringing Nigeria to the state of a (spontaneous) revolutionary uprising as in the "Arab spring", or to a lesser degree, currently, the Hong Kong protests, is a herculean task. The irony, for us, is the fact that no Arab has suffered onetenth of the suffering Nigerians have endured since independence, and certainly no one in Hong Kong has been subjected to the level of economic hardship suffered daily by ordinary citizens in this country, yet, our propensity to a revolutionary action is minus zero relative to theirs. Why?

To answer the above question, we must first dispel a couple of myths: "Nigerians are just too lazy to fight for their rights". Say that to the former "President" Ibrahim Babangida, or the late General Sani Abacha, and the military in this country and they would be the first to disagree with this assertion. Also, remember, it was a woman (Mrs Ransome-Kuti) also known as, and was indeed, the late Fela Anikulapo-Kuti's mother, who acted and singlehandedly organised the overthrow of an Oba (the Alake of Egbaland) for misrule in the 1940s. She later fought for, and succeeded in establishing Universal Adult Suffrage in this country. Nigerians have never been found wanting for bravery or heroism. Another popular myth is; "Nigeria is a conservative nation". People who say this usually mean the word "Conservative" with capital 'C', meaning that the country is better run along the lines of Western liberal ideology as opposed to embarking on any quick, rapid transformation of society. This is simply an assumption that has no foundation. So, why then are we reluctant to take over government buildings in mass congregations; occupying the streets and setting up barricades for a political end as they do elsewhere?

The answer is because we still have no sense of ownership of the land; Nigeria. You would die protecting and defending what is yours, but would be reluctant to do so for a plot of land whose ownership is still in dispute amongst its beneficiaries. We know and acknowledge ourselves as Nigerians, but visibly lacking in emotional attachment to the land as our joint property; our collective estate. "The Fulanis are the ones holding down this country", "the Yorubas are very treacherous people", "the Ibos have a stranglehold on commerce and the economy too much". All of these are popular myths, of course, but other than singing the national anthem, no one is articulating a different narrative; a common thread that cuts through the ill-informed ethnic prejudices. So, when the metropolitan urban elites in smart suits suddenly wake up mouthing "Revolution Now", it rings hollow and certainly far-fetched in most peoples' reckoning.

As for violent revolutions, there was one involving the "Bolsheviks" in Soviet Russia in 1917. It was a "workers' revolution", which laid the foundation for the former USSR (Union of Soviet Socialist Republics), which collapsed in 1989. There were also other prominent examples around the world: Fidel Castro in Cuba, Samora Machel in Mozambique, Mengistu Mariam in Ethiopia, Rawlings in Ghana, etc. All of them planned and executed by small bands of educated (and in some sense privileged) elites, and all requiring the shedding of blood with no enduring legacies afterwards. A good example of a revolution with an enduring legacy in Africa is, of course, that of the African National Congress (ANC) in South Africa. Following the blockage of legitimate democratic participation, the organisation resorted to an "armed struggle" to overthrow the Apartheid regime in their land. Nigerians participated in kind in their struggle, supplying them with ammunition and money throughout the 1970s. It was a just cause being fought by fellow Africans. The Apartheid regime indeed collapsed and ushered in a new period of democratic dispensation in 1994, which still endures. That said, there is a vocal section of the ANC which does not feel the organisation speaks for the masses anymore. For that reason, some have broken away and formed their own political party (the "Economic Freedom Fighters") to articulate an alternative vision for South Africa. It is going to be a 'long walk to freedom' for them, but they are gradually winning seats in Parliament and gaining traction with the wider electorate.

The people behind the doomed "Revolution Now" in Nigeria last week, meant well, but were rather precipitous in assuming we could usher in the

New Jerusalem in this country, at the stroke of a pen, without first wining the hearts and minds of the people for whom the revolution is sought. One way of achieving a "progressive" change (revolution if you like) is to infiltrate the existing party machines, take them over and drive them along a popular mandate for change. That is called "entry (ism)". It is worth trying, but it has never worked anywhere. Another way is to build a fresh party, raise funds and embark upon a long campaign around a cause, which may or may not be realised in the lifetime of the founding members, but for which future generations will be grateful. That is called a "movement". It has been successful severally in different contexts throughout history, but it takes time. And there is the rub; in building a mass revolutionary consciousness in a rapidly evolving political environment, time is of the essence. Alas, it is something a revolutionary does not have. Yet, in the same context, time is a valuable commodity a revolutionary cannot do without.

6.04 Nigeria: 'Tribalism' and the Nationality Question

17 November 2020

There are two major fallacies Nigerians grow up with about their country; one, that it is composed of many 'tribes' rendering national cohesion difficult, if not impossible. Two, that it has hundreds, perhaps 500+ of 'languages', making the adoption of English as the country's lingua franca not only inevitable, but a *fait accompli*. Although these sweeping statements have been debunked in a few scholarly writings, we, nonetheless, need to explode, and double explode the myths in public fora, again, and again, if possible; till the cows come home. They are patently false, as they are the lingering relics of Nigeria's colonial education. This write up was actually prompted by an interesting encounter I had with a bunch of highly enthusiastic, highly intelligent, teenage university undergraduates recently. I asked them an open question; is Nigeria a country of tribes or nations? It was instantly met with a howl of; tribes, yeah, yes, tribes! Really? I interjected, looking most incredulous. They yelled out the same line over and over again, pretty confidently. Then, I decided to challenge their assertion, since they sounded so settled in it. I asked them to list the characteristics of a tribe alongside that of a nation. Just hold your breath ...

"For a tribe, we have shared language, history, cultural affinity, territory, extended family, food, custom, aesthetics, etc." Fair enough, I said. When they started listing the characteristics of a nation, however, they found themselves almost repeating the same indices as for a tribe. They now became argumentative, dumbfounded, and befuddled. I had made my point. They instinctively knew what a 'tribe' stands for, because, they have been conditioned to live in a world of 'tribes'. But there was no such consensus on what a nation is, because they have no consciousness of living in one. Tribal identity in Africa was a social construct passed on through colonial education that later formed the basis upon which African nations reference each other to this day.

In Nigeria, 'tribe' was even weaved into the old national anthem as a parting gift by the British in 1960; " ... though tribe and tongue may differ, in brotherhood we stand ...", before the Nigerian political leaders suddenly got wise and erased it from the new anthem in 1978. Digging a little deeper into history, the British 'explorers' and other European powers believed they were encountering "savages" and "primitive" civilisation when they embarked upon their mission to colonise the African continent from the 1800s. To them, any thought of the "primitives" and "savages" having well established nations and thousands of years' civilisation potentially rivalling their own was simply unimaginable. It was a denial of the humanity of the African. They needed to advance a theory of racial superiority in order to bolster their notion of Africans as inferior beings. Seeing African territories as fully developed nations (though not yet states) would have elevated those nations unto a position of parity with that of their own, and negated their civilianising mission. Much better for the 'Masters' to proclaim Africans as semi-formed, disjointed little 'tribes' instead. Consequently, centuries-old Kingdoms such as the Kush (Egypt), Aksum (Tunisia), The Mali Empire, Songhai Empire, The Great Zimbabwe, etc. all in the processes of developing into modern states were rudely and brutally interrupted by the forces of imperialism, which turned them into conquered enclaves and latter-day 'tribes'. It was an assault on the collective psyche of Africans.

When it comes to the small European enclaves, then, those were fully formed nations; not "savages". Even the tiniest European country of Liechtenstein, today, with a population of about 40,000 inhabitants (a typical street in Lagos) is recognised as a nation with representation in world bodies. Wales, a constituent part of the United Kingdom, with a population of three million, is a nation with its own flag and representations in major international competitions. Now, what makes these two nations, nations, and the Igbos, the Hausas, the Yorubas in Nigeria, with three thousand years of civilisation, and a combined population of over one hundred million, not qualify as nations, but 'tribes'? The answer is, nothing of substance, aside from the labels. Nigeria, like much of Western Europe, is a conglomerate of nations; not tribes. Tribalism is a parochial attitude found in every culture, in every nation, and in modern societies across racial lines. It neither defines a nation, nor its people. Why then do the ruling elite in this country continue to subscribe to the con-

6 · POLITICS

tortion of 'tribe'? Because to acknowledge Nigeria as comprising nations would be a dangerous concession to the secessionist impulse in some. A claim to nationhood almost invariably leads to a claim to statehood. That is the lesson of history that the ruling elite in this country would not wish to see play out, as it threatens their own survival as a parasitic lot. Is it not the supreme irony, therefore, that the old colonial design of minimising African sense of nationhood is in sync with the Nigerian ruling elite's insatiable appetite for divide and rule?

The same contortion applies to linguistics. It is said, so flippantly, that there are hundreds of 'languages' all over the place, in Nigeria. Not true! Let us look at the three main languages. First, Hausa has so many variations as in Sokoto, the classical Hausa, the Arewa northern dialect, the Zazzaganci in Zazzau of the southern origin, Dauranchi, Kananci etc. Second, Igbo, and its variants located in Anambra, Onitsha, Aba, Delta, Rivers. There are over 30 known variants of Igbo spoken across the south-east, south-south terrain, and beyond. Third, Yoruba has even more variants; Egba, Ibadan, Yewa, Lagos, Igbomina, Ijesha, Ife, Ekiti, Yegba, Owe, Ijumu, Oworo, Itsekiri, extending to Benin Republic, Togo, and modern-day Brazil. If you then multiply these variants further down, they amount to hundreds, for sure. However, these variants are not to be confused for 'languages'. Very thin differences in lexicon and phonology should not be exaggerated and accorded the status of 'language'. This is also playing straight into the narrative of disparate, diverse and disjointed primitive peoples with no real linguistic claim equal to standard European languages. What the Europeans see as "regional accents" in their own yard, we see as 'languages' in our own, thereby emphasising and dwelling on our 'vast' differences. For those who have lived in the United Kingdom, for instance, people in the north of England speak in a way that many in the south would not even understand. Conversely, people from the east-end of London with their "cockney" accent would make any visitor feel like he is listening to a foreign language.

America too, is famous and enriched by the diversity in its linguistic tones. A New Yorker, Mid-Westerner, and a Texan all speak in localised dialects and intonations that do not amount to having several languages in the country. Yes, there are hundred ways of speaking Hausa, Yoruba, and Igbo. That does not equate hundreds of 'languages' spoken in Nigeria. Otherwise, the UK, America, Australia, Canada, and so on, would also qualify as having hundreds of languages by that same logic. Colonial education once taught us that it was Mungo Park (a British explorer) who 'discovered' River Niger, when in fact he was led to the source of the river by a group of obliging local fishermen. The fishermen had no capacity for 'discovery', of course. They were not even really humans in the eyes of the European authors who wrote our history, geography and economics books. See, the essence of a good education is the freedom it gives one to be discerning, but also the foresight to unlearn a distorted narrative from wherever it emanates. Liberating and cleansing our minds of neo-colonial precepts is a pre-requisite for any hope of societal advancement.

6.05 Buhari Should Lance the Boil of Separatism

13 July 2021

Secession from the Federal Republic of Nigeria by any of its constituent units was widely thought to have been banished with the end of the civil war in 1970.[251] Indeed, no one had dared to go anywhere near that topic even in private, as most people had faith in the ability of the country's political and military leaders to steer the ship of state away from such stormy waters. Disagreements over policy, tactics, and strategy have surfaced in the open, sometimes vehemently, but secession was never part of the deal, until now. Something hitherto regarded as taboo has now made its way into the mainstream political discourse. Meanwhile, permutations about the 2023 elections and jockeying for position continue to exercise members of the political class who, like the proverbial ostriches, would rather bury their heads in the sand. The cascading events of the last couple of months focusing on the corporate existence of the country as one unit must be seen as extremely worrying to the wider public inside and outside Nigeria. Suddenly, it seems, talk of Biafra and Yoruba autonomous, even independence status from Nigeria is no longer an 'extremist propaganda'; it is fast becoming a kitchen-table, motor-park discussion. This is being fuelled, no doubt, by the rising cost of living being witnessed by the multitude of citizens up and down the country. Security and heavy-handedness on dissent by the armed forces does nothing to douse the tension either. If anything, harassment and detention of opposition elements, generally and collectively seen as 'suspects', in the separatist agitation only betrays the fragility of the Nigerian state.

The question before the reader, this week, is whether Nigerians have indeed lost faith in the corporate existence of their country so much that they would rather splinter into different 'independent' segments? Let us examine the evidence. From 1970 until 1979, the military was in charge of the country in its effort to rebuild and reconstruct from the aftermath of the civil war. The oil

---

251. Nigeria was plunged into a bloody civil war over the secession of the old Eastern Region from the rest of the Federation between 1967 and 1970

6 · POLITICS

boom of the 1970s gave everyone some stake in the political-economy, and a huge assumption of Nigeria's 'pre-ordained' destiny to 'lead' Africa. No one heard of 'marginalisation' 'nepotism', 'Hausa' 'Fulani', 'Igbo' 'Efik', or anything of the sort. A new civilian government took over from the military under the Presidency of Alhaji Shehu Shagari, between 1979 and 1983 until it was overthrown in a coup d'état led by General Muhammadu Buhari who, himself, was overthrown in a palace coup led by General Ibrahim Babangida, in 1985. Still, 'ethnicity', or 'marginalisation' played almost no role in any of the events. The common enemy was mismanagement and high-level corruption. No one talked about partitioning Nigeria. Subsequently, everybody wanted the military out of government. Everybody had only one project in their front burner; Nigeria, Democracy and Development, in that order. Babangida reluctantly gave in to pressure and organised a general elections in 1992. Nigerians came out in their millions and cast their ballots in favour of the Social Democratic Party candidate, MKO Abiola, a Yoruba Muslim from the southwest, and his running mate, Alhaji Baba Gana Kingibe, a Kanuri Muslim from the north.

Let us note the 'Muslim-Muslim' ticket of the Presidential and Vice-Presidential ticket. It shattered the myth of Christian-Muslim mistrust and disharmony forming the bedrock of the Nigerian political life. What is more, Abiola won the endorsement of the overwhelming majority of Muslims in the North, including, famously defeating the opposition's Republican National Convention's Presidential candidate, Alhaji Bashir Tofa, a Fulani, from Kano, in his own constituency. That, again, shattered the myth of an 'irreconcilable' north-south dichotomy in Nigerian politics. Sadly, the result of the election, though widely known, was never rendered official. It was cowardly, shamefully, and scandalously "annulled" by the outgoing military strongman; General Babangida for being "unacceptable". Nigerians had just taken part in the most peaceful, the freest and most open democratic election in its history, and the military simply tossed it off. Indeed, the military and the person of Babangida in particular, did an untold damage to the wellbeing of Nigeria by so doing. Henceforth, ethnicity made its way into the lexicon of political dialogue in Nigeria, as it was widely believed that the election would not have been annulled but for the winner coming from the southwest region of the country. The military's hierarchy, led by Babangida, could not stomach the thought of handing over power to a man duly chosen by the people irrespective of his ethnicity and religion. A spit in the face for the electorate (north, south, east and west, Christians and Muslims alike) who had turned a blind eye to ethnicity and other forms of bigotry. Was that the pivotal moment when 'one Nigeria' was lost?

The question now is how the same Nigerians who acted in unison, and without prejudice in 1993, then became 'separatists' and 'secessionists' in 2021.

What could have happened to make people disavow the same country they embraced in toto in 1993, to the point where they are now actively seeking separation? The short answer is that the foundation upon which the new democratic dispensation was built by the departing military in 1999 was doomed for failure. It was a military contraption, which the ruling elites have made worse every single year since 1999. It was crafted with the insignia: "We the people ..." That was a blatant lie. The public was not involved. Still, it does not fully explain the clamour for separate nationhood being canvased so openly across the regions. On any objective analysis, the basis for separation or secession does not appear to exist, neither has the political case for it been made or rejected. It is precisely the stifling of democratic debate around this issue that has given rise to the rhetoric and agitation for separation. President Buhari and the APC administration are the ones failing to rise up to the occasion. They ought to call the bluff of the separatist agitators and engage them in debates instead of castigating them as enemies of the state. The more you impose a ban on a political idea, the more attractive it becomes.

To buttress the point, no Igbo leader of any significance has ever associated themselves (at least not openly) with the stance taken by the Indigenous Peoples of Biafra (IPOB),[252] and no widespread support for its objective either. That was until the government proscribed the organisation. Now, no one can claim ignorance of the organisation, its leader and its objective. Conversely, no Yoruba leader of note came out to endorse Sunday Igboho, the Yoruba separatist leader, and no widespread following for him either. That was until the armed forces began to attack him and declared him wanted. By way of analogy, the Scottish Nationalist Party in the UK and the Basque Nationalists in Spain are prime examples of yearnings for a homeland, accommodated and given public space in both countries. The on-going debate in those countries is not without pain and rancour, but it is being countered by superior arguments and deft political moves by the establishment. The Scottish people, for instance, have consistently voted against independence from the UK. The last referendum on the issue was in 2014, which the nationalists lost. How many people would vote for an independent Yoruba (O'odua) Republic or The Republic of Biafra today, for that matter? Most importantly, where on earth would the boundaries of the putative countries be drawn? Which sub-ethnic group would be absorbed, and which would be discarded? Nigeria's unity can, and should be subjected to negotiation. Assuming they eschew violence, let all those nursing political ambition for regional autonomy or independence be un-

---

252. IPOB is a separatist organisation condemned as a terrorist organisation by the federal government

6 · POLITICS 191

banned, come forward, and defend their position in open debate. They must be countered by force of argument, not by force of arms.

6.06 Round-Tripping Politicians: Blessing or Curse?

17 August 2021

For the last twenty years or so, the democratic space in Nigeria has been dominated by familiar faces across all the levels of power; central, state and local. Ministerial power is yet another echelon from which many often emerge to serve. What has become commonplace is the laundering, (or re-cycling), of individuals through different political offices. Term limit was an ingenious devise weaved into the fabrics of the federal system of government from its foundation. It is designed to check the natural impulse of man (and woman) to elongate their stay in power in perpetuity. Term limit in Nigeria, however, has become largely redundant. It has lost its intrinsic value since the person affected can just walk into another office, in a different garb, and set another ball rolling. First, you are a local councillor, then, you move into the State Assembly, and after four years, you move into the National Assembly for two or even three terms, then, move into the Governor's lodge, serve two terms of eight years, then, get a ministerial appointment, cling onto office for four to eight years, after which you move back into the National Assembly, collecting multiple gratuities and pension allowances along the way. This is surely a mockery of the democratic system, but it is nonetheless, the reality of life for a lot of Nigerian politicians. It is classic round-tripping at the expense of the citizens. If ever there was any such thing as 'state capture' by an unproductive and parasitic elite, look no further than Nigeria.

The most egregious examples of round-tripping amongst the political elite in this country are to be found with the "Executive Governors" across different states. At the last election in 2019, there was a rash of former governors taking office as members of the National Assembly. Many were even elected Senators whilst still occupying the governor's seat: Kashim Shettima (Borno), Tanko Almakura (Nasarawa), Ibrahim Geidam (Yobe), Rochas Okorocha (Imo), Ibikunle Amosun (Ogun), Adamu Aliero (Kebbi), Abdulaziz Yari (Zamfara), Seriake Dickson (Bayelsa). The two Olympian round-trippers are: Ibikunle Amosun, and Adamu Aliero. Amosun first represented Ogun Central as Senator, 2003–2007, two-term Governor of the State, 2011–2019, now back in the National Assembly again, as Senator in his old Constituency. Adamu Aliero was a two-term Governor of Kebbi State, 1999–2007, then Senator, 2007–2008, Minister for FCT, 2008–2010, now serves as Senator for Kebbi Central. Orji Kalu was a two-term Governor of Abia State, 1999–2007, ran unsuccessfully for President in 2007, now serves as Senator for Abia North. Ibrahim Shekarau was a two-term Governor of Kano State, 2003–2011, Presidential candidate in 2011, Minister of Education, 2014–2015, now represents Kano Central in the Senate. Gabriel Suswan was a two-term Governor of Benue State, 2007–2015. Before then, he was a Member of the House of Representatives, 1999–2007, now serves as Senator for Benue North-East. Rochas Okorocha was a two-term Governor of Imo State, 2011–2019, now Senator for Imo West. Seriake Dickson, a two-term Governor of Bayelsa State, 2012–2020, now Senator for Bayelsa West.

The above list is clearly not exhaustive; the whole system is riddled with many other serial round-trippers of all hues in the labyrinths of power. Suffice is to highlight the most prominent ones amongst them. It is not going to get any better I hasten to add; it is going to get worse. The allure of political office in Nigeria is too great, and too tempting to cut loose from. It takes a politician of extraordinary convictions to say; 'I quit' in Nigeria. I do not know of one in the horizon. Political office in Nigeria is one of the most lucrative of all careers in the world. It comes with an unrivalled sense of entitlement; humongous salary allowances, outrageous pension and gratuitous benefits, coterie of servants, endless line of aids, security details, bespoke medical entitlements, jet-setting lifestyle and unlimited budget for social and entertainment. The largesse is extended to family and friends, some of whom are incorporated into their 'chop n chop' political orbit as advisers and special assistants, to begin their own tour of the power houses as 'elected leaders' at some point later. What is more, there is no recourse for the electorate against their wrongdoing. Votes are subject to the highest bidding settlement, backroom deals, and outright fraud in places. There is hardly an elected politician in Nigeria whose mandate can pass the litmus test, for clean and honest,. Candidates are usually out to outspend, outfox and, in extreme cases, outgun their opponents.

To this end, you make the playing field as hostile to your opponent as the circumstances permit. Concerned citizens and non-governmental organisations have gone to court on the issue of multiple allowances accruing to politicians across different levels of power, but it has not yielded any concrete result. Sometimes, one shudders when one hears people talk of 'North' versus 'South', and how Nigeria is about to go up in flames. The best counsel is take a deep breath and see whether round-tripping politicians pay attention to north, south, ethnicity, or anything of such. Anyone who thinks any of these political harlots want to burn down Nigeria in an orgy of ethnic violence is living on cloud cuckoo land I am afraid. The politicians are masters of deception and manipulation of ethnic sentiment. They understand and know how to brandish the ethnic joker in an attempt to mobilise and demobilise their 'base'. It is a bargaining chip they deploy often with innocent blood on the streets. Political office in Nigeria is the sumptuous dinner table no one in their right mind would want to flip over even in a fit of pique. My turn, our turn to eat has a powerful resonance with the Nigerian political elite. What is more, the electorate themselves know. Some are even complicit in the grand con; aiding, abetting, facilitating, and providing cover for the boss.

Let us play the devil's advocate for a moment. What about the argument that round-tripping politicians could possibly be a blessing in the sense of their 'vast experience' and longevity being put to good use for their constituents? The immediate answer to that is taking a look at the downward spiral of the Nigerian economy and the near collapse of social services. The proof of the pudding, it is said, is in the eating. Besides, you do not need 'vast experience' to make a difference in public life; you need conviction and moral backbone glaringly absent in the round-tripping politicians. Major political parties are designed to accommodate new entrants; to make contested positions as open as possible, and from time to time, infuse new blood and energy into the party hierarchy. That throws up the good, and sometimes the bad, but, it serves the purpose generally well. In Nigeria, we do not have authentic political parties. What we have are democracy merchants creating special purpose vehicles for power. And, with their access to state funds, they are hell bent on keeping out 'outsiders' whose ideas may conflict with their aim of clinging onto political office. They live in an echo chamber wherein they are content to milk the system for their own self-aggrandisement rather than manage it on behalf of the people. It is a recipe for disaster, of course, but who cares? They are ensconced in a bubble that breeds inertia, and makes democratic renewal nigh impossible. Are they a curse on the country's fledgling democracy? Without doubt. It is precisely their obduracy, and their lack of imagination that, ironically, threatens the survival of Nigeria as a corporate entity. They are the ones who, unwittingly, would end up killing the proverbial goose that lays the golden egg.

6.07 APC, PDP in Disarray: Is There an Alternative?

10 August 2021

Let me share with you an established norm in Western democracies. It is that opposition does not win elections; government loses them. Government provides the electorate with something to vote against *ab initio*. But, as long

194   6 · POLITICS

as it does not slip up, the conventional wisdom is that it is rewarded with power *ad infinitum*. This is so in both Federal and Parliamentary systems. The Christian Democratic Union led by Angela Merkel has been in power in Germany, since 2005. Merkel stands down as Chancellor (Prime Minister) later this year. In France, the 'left of centre' parties led by Francois Holland (French Socialists), and Emmanuel Macron; La République En Marche! (break-away Socialists) have been in power since 2012. Before then, the 'centre right' parties; Rally for the Republic, and Union for a Popular Movement were in power from 1995–2012. Both of these countries practice a mixture of Federal and Parliamentary systems of government. In the United Kingdom, (a Parliamentary system), the Conservatives were kept in power for a combined total of 18 years; Margaret Thatcher (1979–1990), and John Major (1990–1997). Then, the pendulum swung to the Labour Party, who held power for a combined period of 13 years; Tony Blair (1997–2007), then, Gordon Brown (2007–2010). In America, the immediate past President, the Republican Donald Trump, was kicked out after one term in office, largely on account of his personal idiosyncratic behaviour than policy. Before then, Barack Obama (Democrats) was rewarded with two terms (2009–2016), and before then, George W. Bush was likewise kept in power for two terms (2001–2009).

Nigeria appeared ready to follow this trend by rejecting the PDP in 2015. The APC came into office on a hotchpotch, haphazard set of ideas for "change". No one was more surprised than the party's hierarchy to have 'won'. To many observers, it was a clear case of the electorate voting against the ruling PDP, rather than voting for the APC. So, it is more appropriate to say the PDP lost the election, than saying the APC won. Fast forward to 2019, APC did not slip up despite its many shortcomings. The electorate wanted to give the party the benefit of the doubt; to see if it would finally live up to its rhetoric of "change". The party had not been tested long enough for voters to render a definitive judgement it seemed. Besides, it was able to sustain the claim that it was still busy cleaning up 'the mess' left behind by the previous PDP administration. But as time has gone on, APC's failings have become so glaring even to the uninitiated. The party has no one to blame but themselves for the 70 million youth unemployment and the attendant consequences, dilapidated hospitals whilst top government functionaries jet off to Europe and America for medical treatment, workers from all economic sectors taking sporadic strike action, consumer price inflation becoming the order of the day whilst bankers and bureaux de change perpetuate economic sabotage on the country, murder and kidnaping for ransom seen as normal daily life, universities graduating illiterates, road infrastructure and security of life a matter of hit and miss, the stench of corruption in official circles rising to high heavens. No need to go on.

As if all that was not bad enough, the APC appears to be hell bent on pushing the self-destruct button as well. It is riven with factions, and so much discord; it is hard to believe it is the same party that won re-election only a couple of years ago. Because the party has to put up a new candidate for President in 2023, and because there is no obvious, stand-out personality capable of rallying the APC restive troops, it is not surprising that differing coalition of interests are gathering and caucusing. In view of this, control of the internal party structure becomes pivotal. Ward Congresses acquire a deeper significance than it would otherwise be. Whoever manages to hijack the party structure, puts himself at a considerable advantage. The wrangling, the chicanery, and the skulduggery came to a head with the recent controversy surrounding the legal standing of their Caretaker Chairman, Governor of Yobe State, Mai Mala Buni. Those who want him out are just as determined as those standing by him. Whichever faction wins will be in a strong position for the Presidential ticket. So, do not expect the rancour to subside anytime soon. Given all that, you would imagine, this is a spectacular gift for the PDP? The opposition usually benefits from a ruling party clearly in disarray. All the PDP really has to do is sit and watch the APC implode, then quietly, and effortlessly stroll back into power. Sadly for many PDP activists and well-wishers, this is not going to happen. The party is just as riven, if not more riven, with factions than the APC is. PDP is not only haemorrhaging support from prominent party members, its elected leaders are also jumping ship in droves. In the last six months alone, the party has lost three sitting governors to the APC: Governors Ben Ayade (Cross River), Dave Umahi (Ebonyi), and Bello Matawalle (Zamfara). Losing any governor, let alone three, to the APC in one fell swoop, is not only foolhardy; it is reckless in the extreme. Governors in Nigeria are the petrol fuelling party machines; they breathe financial life into them. PDP's embattled Chairman, Prince Uche Secondus is an old hand bereft of ideas. Many in the party believe he is a spent force, long past his sell-by date.

So, readers, when you have the two main political parties in Nigeria being palpably unelectable as things stand, who wins? Sadly, for so many people, aside APC and PDP, there is no other credible party with sufficient organisational and financial muscle to cause a major earthquake in the run up to 2023. We have heard murmurings of a 'Third Force' lurking in the shadows, fronted by Nigeria's brightest and best; the forgotten heroes across the professional divide. They are the familiar household names in the field of finance, economics, industry, law etc. We read about them, and occasionally see a glimpse of their wizardry on television denouncing the rot in the system. They, however, have no snowball chance in hell of taking power this side of the electoral cycle. Long on vision, and rich in ideas, they are lacking in ability to effectively oil a party machine as would become imperative in a serious challenge

196   6 · POLITICS

for power. They have no funds, no organisation, and no wherewithal to assemble a workable party machine ahead of 2023. They are philosopher-kings with no real constituency, and no foot-soldiers aside from distant on-lookers and closeted admirers discreetly egging them on.

Philosophers, says Karl Marx, have analysed the world; the task is to change it. In Nigeria, the philosophers are stuck in the middle of nowhere, they are damned if they put their head above the parapet, and damned if they do not. The political system has made it impossible for them to cut through. A political party is the only recognised vehicle for contesting and winning power under the law.[253] That is precisely the problem. In a quest for high office, citizens ought to be given the choice of organising either as a political party, or stand as independent candidates. It is a fundamental right; the right to vote and be voted for. In the current atmosphere, only an independent candidate with a crossover appeal, free from party shackles, can rally the citizenry and galvanise them to the 'revolution' that would sweep the oligarchs from power. In the absence of that, and given a choice between two evils, the electorate would stick with the devil they know.

6.08 Taliban Victory: Morale Booster for Boko Haram

24 August 2021

The US and its Western military allies had been involved in a twenty-year war with the Taliban in Afghanistan, during which time they trained, equipped and established a new National Army numbering more than 300,000 soldiers,[254] who had also become embroiled in the same war alongside hundreds of thousands of NATO troops. The West went into Afghanistan in 2001, determined to avenge the "9/11" attack on New York. The US, UK, Canada, Australia, France, etc. deployed the most sophisticated weaponry at their disposal, including state-of-the-art communication gadgets against a barely literate improvised Taliban army, numbering less than one hundred

---

253. The electoral law has since been amended to allow for independent candidacy. See; Electoral Act, 2022 https://placng.org/i/wp-content/uploads/2022/02/Electoral-Act-2022.pdf

254. "Remarks by President Biden on the Drawdown of US Forces in Afghanistan" The White House, East Room, July 8, 2021, https://www.whitehouse.gov/briefing-room/speeches -remarks/2021/07/08/remarks-by-president-biden-on-the-drawdown-of-u-s-forces-in -afghanistan

6 · POLITICS

thousand, with a haphazard command structure. Despite this glaring asymmetry of forces, the Taliban fought on, in the hills, and in the mountains, day and night; taking refuge inside caves, digging up trenches with their bare hands, suffering casualties after casualties, but never giving up. In spite of this, and in an eyeball-to-eyeball with the Taliban on the battle field, the better trained, better equipped Afghanistan army blinked first. The Taliban strolled into the capital, Kabul, last Sunday 15 August 2021, without firing a shot. The Western-backed President Ashraf Ghani, having fled the Presidential Palace earlier in the day, to "prevent bloodshed" offered no resistance.[255] If you think this is something that happened in a country that is of no concern to us here, think again. The ramifications for Nigeria are enormous. Emboldened Boko Haram terrorists are rejoicing as you read.

Afghanistan is a country better known for its chequered, and (quite frankly) bloody history. But, the truth is not as bad as has been portrayed lately. The British were there in the 19th century ostensibly to bring civil order to the mountainous enclave. They failed and left in a hurry. The Soviet Union then marched onto the territory with tanks and heavy-duty armoury in the 21st century, stayed for a decade (1979–1989), while attempting to convert the territory into a Soviet-type 'Republic'. The Americans played the mischievous role of sponsoring anti-Soviet guerrilla movement; the bearded Mullahs (Mujahideens), and their foot soldiers, went into battle with the mighty Soviet army. The US not only provided funds for the insurgency attacks against the Soviet army; they supplied them with modern weapons, anti-tank rockets and satellite equipment, which helped drag the Soviets into a quagmire. The US and other Western governments were delighted to see the Soviet army pulled out of Afghanistan with its tail behind its legs in the late 1980s/early 1990s. Afghanistan had suffered several invasions from foreign powers throughout the centuries, but prior to the British and Soviet attempts, the country had been at relative peace, minding its own business in the caves and in the hills. The British and the Soviets taught them violence. Consequently, after the Soviets were driven out in 1989, the Taliban became fidgety and braced themselves for another possible foreign invasion sooner or later. They embraced the al-Qaida terror group for ideological succour and Islamic solidarity, as leading scholars in the West had begun to use their influence to spread the idea of an impending "Clash of Civilisations" that is, to say, a clash between

---

255. See; "Reports of Taliban Violence in Afghanistan As Ghani Denies Theft", by Radio Free Europe/Radio Liberty. August 18, 2021, https://gandhara.rferl.org/a/afghanistan-evacuations-taliban-relations/31416132.html

198   6 · POLITICS

Islamic and Western values as the next frontier in the continuing battle for universal supremacy.

A "Clash of Civilisations" backed up by Western military might is also an extremist agenda that was rapidly gaining ground in policy-making circles. Consequently, it was not totally surprising that the Taliban regime would allow its territory to be used as a safe haven for those avowedly pushing back against the 'infidels' (the US in particular), apparently bent on 'obliterating' Islam. This culminated in the 11th of September 2001 attack on the New York Trade Centre, killing several thousand people. The subsequent invasion of Afghanistan led by US forces and NATO became inevitable. They rooted out al-Qaida and dislodged the Taliban regime within a couple of months. They then decided to embark upon nation-building; to finally remould Afghanistan along the lines of Western values: free press, multiparty democracy, free market, separation of state and religion, free love, etc. The US, alone, committed in excess of two trillion tax dollars as well as the blood of their young men and women to the cause.[256] They embarked upon local recruits of soldiers for the new Afghan army. The objective was to prevent the Taliban from ever coming back to rule over the country again. The Afghan Parliament and a general election completed a job well done. It ushered in a new era of inclusion for women. Many now occupied positions of power for the first time in the nation's history; a truly rude awakening for the Taliban. Women wielding authority, let alone power, is anathema in their (medieval) interpretation of Islam.

Meanwhile, back in the US, public opinion had swung decisively against the continued presence of US troops in Afghanistan. Several US administrations had tried in vain to withdraw from the country. The military's (Pentagon) superior argument against 'precipitous' withdrawal always held sway. President Joe Biden finally decided to grab the bull by the horns earlier this year, and pulled out the US troops without further ado. Contrary to the impression of defeat, the US/NATO alliance in fact, won the battle in Afghanistan, but, lost the war. This is what prompts the question: How come a well-trained, well equipped Afghan army (when it mattered most), simply laid down their sophisticated weapons, their uniforms, and fled in the face of an onslaught from the sandal-wearing, machete-wielding, bearded Taliban

---

256. See; "The War In Afghanistan Cost America $300 Million Per Day For 20 Years, With Big Bills Yet To Come". Forbes, August 16, 2021, https://www.forbes.com/sites /hanktucker/2021/08/16/the-war-in-afghanistan-cost-america-300-million-per-day-for-20 -years-with-big-bills-yet-to-come/?sh=78065a6a7f8d and, "US Costs to Date for the war in Afghanistan, $2.313 trillion in total". Watson Institute, Brown University, USA https://watson .brown.edu/costsofwar/figures/2021/human-and-budgetary-costs-date-us-war-afghanistan -2001-2022

fighters clad in mufti? Well, it is often said that, it is not the size of the dog, but the size of the fight in the dog that counts. But, that raises another question; why was there no fight inside the Afghan army's dog? What is more, Afghanistan was led by the US-backed civilian government of President Ashraf Ghani, a PhD scholar and 'technocrat' with field experience cutting across Harvard-INSEAD, World Bank, DFID, OECD, and other lofty Western finance houses. The good Prof had even written an acclaimed book: "Fixing Failed States", Oxford University Press, 2008,[257] in which there is a blueprint on how to turn around his country and many others in a similar predicament.

The answer to the puzzle is as frightening as it is ominous for us here in Nigeria. Ghani had stated in the book he co-wrote: "only sovereign states — by which we mean states that actually perform the functions that make them sovereign — will allow human progress to continue". The Western-created state of Afghanistan on which administration he presided since 2014, was not seen as an authentic, legitimate state even by its own political leaders and the rank and file soldiers. It was rightly seen as the artificial construct that it was. In other words, it was not worth dying for. The military and civilian personnel it relied on to function supported it as long as it paid their wages. Furthermore, the gulf between the corrupt Afghan military and political top brass and the poorly paid rank and file, told another story. Perhaps, most importantly, the rag-tag Taliban 'army' were fighting for a cause greater than the individual; an Islamic El-Dorado, a Utopia. For them, death is positively embraced as a rite of passage to paradise in the afterlife. On the contrary, for the Afghan army fighting to defend a nominal state, death is an avoidable waste of human life. The comparison between Boko Haram (engaged in a lifelong Jihad) and the Nigerian army (fighting for minimum wage) could not be any starker. The top brass in both the military and civil administration are feeding fat while the 'recruits' starve. So, when push comes to shove would any soldier voluntarily lay down his life in defence of this nominal state?

6.09 Is Nigeria Worth Dying For?

2 October 2018

Nigeria is in the grip of another week of October 1st independence celebrations/reflections again. Time, I thought, for some sobering thoughts on

---

257. Available on Amazon, https://www.amazon.com/Fixing-Failed-States-Framework-Rebuilding/dp/0195398610

the extent of our true feeling for this country, while remembering the painful, and untimely death of a friend and colleague, Chima Ubani, who died "on duty" in a tragic road accident in 2005. Chima was a friend and role model to many in this country and beyond, for his tireless work in the 1990's pro-democracy struggle. His name continues to be a reference point in discussions about Nigerian democracy, citizens' rights and mass movement. I took part in one of such discussions at a soiree, last Sunday, on the eve of Nigeria's Independence day, where the vexed issue of laying one's life down for one's country became the focal point of debate: "No, I cannot die for Nigeria", "Yes, I can die for Nigeria" "You are right" "Hey, you are wrong! What has Nigeria done for me?" etc. Tempers became frail, as the gulf between the opposing camps grew wider and unbridgeable. "Nigeria is worth dying for" was Ubani's last swansong that flashed across my mind as the evening wore on; the floor strewn with a pile of empty bottles of Clarets and plastic wraps of assorted chin-chin. Nothing evokes more raw passion than the thorny issue of life and death, generally, amongst us Africans. For us, death is never a natural occurrence; it is a wrath on the deceased brought by something or someone known or unknown. And when it comes to the question of dying or not dying for Nigeria, there is only a handful of people in this country who can claim to be undecided either way. Why does the issue touch such raw nerves in us, I wonder?

Our discussion is best moderated through the use of personal anecdotes, I think. So, consider the true story of Samuel Okoro (not his real name), who struggled through hardship to send himself to school in this country and found a reasonably well-paid job afterwards. Samuel soon got married and had three children in quick succession. He did what he could to climb up the career ladder as an accountant in a medium-sized company in Lagos. Soon enough, he leveraged his status as a mid-level manager to borrow money from the bank to build a cottage for his family. Since there is no security in his community, he hired his own security men to watch over his gated house, provided his own electricity, his own tap water, sewage system, healthcare, etc. As for schools for his children, the government-run local schools are dilapidated and no teachers on hand; so, he sent his children to private schools. In addition, he installed a satellite dish to watch news from foreign channels. By consequence, therefore, apart from driving in and out of the main roads from home to his workplace, Samuel had virtually no significant contact with the Nigerian state, and vice-versa. For him, therefore, there was no question of dying for Nigeria under any circumstance, he exclaimed and reaffirmed repeatedly. No gainsaying how many millions in our midst, young and old, with Samuel's resolve; 90% of the population? Even more, perhaps?

6 · POLITICS

In the year 2000, though, Samuel's life took a 180° turn when he stumbled on news of the American lottery, one day, on television. Having learnt of how straight forward and open the system operates, he decided to have a go. To cut a long story short, luckily for him, he won and he and his family relocated to Oklahoma, USA, in 2001. However, barely six months after settling down to a new life in America, tragedy struck his adopted country by way of a terrorist attack on the Twin Towers in New York, on September 11, 2001. Samuel rushed to the local army barracks and tried to enlist into the US army. He made three attempts before finally being enlisted as a reservist in the state. He followed that up, much later, by insisting on being sent to Afghanistan to fight (and possibly die) in defence of America. Why?

In case you are wondering, Samuel's story is not so unique; it happens all the time, and not only in America, but in several other countries as well, with fellow Nigerians dedicating their lives to their adopted countries with such zeal and fervour they would not imagine rendering in defence of their country of birth. On an aside, how many military personnel or police would fight to the bitter end in defence of Nigeria? How many soldiers regularly dodge their assignment to fight Boko Haram in the Sambisa forest? The answers to those searching questions are not too difficult to imagine. The question for here and now is what etched the deep feeling for America on Samuel's mind so much, within six months of residence in the country that his previous thirty-five years of existence in Nigeria could not do? Answer: citizenship. This is what triggers the emotional tie to a country in any individual. Citizenship, like in Jean-Jacques Rousseau (1712–1778)'s "social contract", is a collective of people who by their consent enter into a civil society to create the sovereign. Men, he asserts: "are born free, yet everywhere are in chains". The "chains" of civil society suppress the natural birthright of man to physical freedom. The battle to free humans of the "chains" is the story of civilisation itself.

Nations have gone to battle for citizens' rights, they have fought wars to defend the "rights of man"; kings, monarchs and dictators have been displaced to expand the civil space for the populace. The notion of the welfare state, with the safety net to support the have-nots has long been accepted as a minimum obligation on the state vis-à-vis the citizens in Western societies. Thus, it was not too difficult for Samuel to see the extent to which the "chains" of civil society have been loosened up in the USA, compared to how tight the "chains" remained throughout his thirty-five years of existence in Nigeria where, incidentally, the ruling elite has still not found it necessary to seek and obtain "consent" for sovereign authority since the 1914 Amalgamation of Nigeria by colonial power. That said, Rome as they say, was not built in a day. It has taken hundreds of years for the Western European nations and the USA to perfect

202   6 · POLITICS

the social contract. During that time, their societies had evolved through a lot of social strife, but the battle continued until the states in those nations committed themselves to certain minimum standards of living for all, in exchange for the minimum civil obligations on the part of the citizens as well. Samuel lived for thirty-five years as a mere subject of the Nigerian state devoid of citizenship. That is the missing link.

What this is saying is that Nigeria is not beyond redemption. Nigeria of tomorrow, with a little more effort, can replicate the minimum standards that obtain in the West; can act as the guarantor of security of life and property for all; can provide the enabling environment for all to pursue happiness and prosperity. That kind of Nigeria, in my view, would be worth dying for. On the other hand, in Nigeria of today, obedience to the state is obtained through coercion rather than cooperation, there is wanton killing of the innocent, prosperity is held hostage to the connected and the well-heeled, it matters more who you know than what you know, and the gap between the rich and poor is not only growing wider; it is becoming a chasm. The question, therefore, is: Is Nigeria of today worth dying for? Absolutely, categorically, NO, you might be forgiven for saying. The dilemma is, though, Nigeria of today is standing in the way of Nigeria of tomorrow. We cannot have Nigeria of tomorrow without, collectively, fixing Nigeria of today. Nigeria of today cannot be fixed without someone, somewhere, sometime, someday, paying the ultimate price. So, to coin a phrase, if not you, then, who? If not now, then, when?

6.10 Nigeria: A Nation of Lions Led By Donkeys

29 September 2020

Let us take a deep breath as we wade through the content of this piece. It is not as controversial as the impulse from the headline would make you think. There is really nothing new in what is being said here that is not readily acknowledged by most decent people up and down this blessed land called Nigeria. Thus, rather than courting controversy, the piece is aimed at jolting the populace out of their persistent vegetative state. A shock treatment designed to awaken us out of an alarmingly dangerous slumber; a re-statement of an unpalatable truth capable of injecting some sobering thoughts into our collective, felonious acquiescence, and a cold syrup capable of reawakening the boundless energy in us at least for the day. Like the incompetent British generals who led the infantry to defeat in World War I, modern-day Nigerians are lions led by donkeys. This is principally because we are fixated too much

6 · POLITICS

on primordial loyalties: ethnic and clan origins of our leaders, and would-be leaders; their taste and social mores, almost to the exclusion of their purpose and priorities in public office. In aggregate, the loyalties are to the mainstream Hausa, Yoruba, Igbo, but more generally, it goes much deeper from intra-tribal cleavages, to the reification and amplification of communal 'otherness'.

The ethnic animus felt across the divide masks the myth of homogeneity people assume of themselves. Yorubas would not see how hopelessly myopic their sense of self truly is, until there is an attempt at concretising the much vaunted "O'odua Republic", then, they start realising themselves as "Ibadan", "Lagos", "Ondo", "Ekiti" etc. who do not wish to be under the dominance of the 'other'. Neither the Igbos would know who the true Igbos are until there is a similar attempt at rebuilding the "Biafra Republic", then, see whether Delta, for instance, or Port Harcourt, consider themselves Igbo or not. The Hausa would not find out their fragile cohesiveness until they try asking whether their own fiefdom extends beyond the River Niger, and until the Hausa-Fulani question is resolved beyond doubt. All that seems to matter is whether "our guy" (in aggregate terms) is at the helm of affairs; my turn, our turn to 'chop'; to lay a claim to our own salami-sliced portion of the meat. Whether the "guy" eventually goes on to act against the fundamental interest of his ethnicity is a moot point. In other words, given a choice between a lion and a donkey for a leader, the ethnic rosette on their lapels and the one most likely to facilitate the 'chop', wins the day. To be brutally frank, no one goes into public service in Nigeria for nation-building. Why? Because there is neither the reward nor incentive so to do.

There are no monuments to selfless service in this country. Streets and Boulevards are named after crooks, corrupt and murderous leaders and ex-leaders in Nigeria's major metropolis. If in doubt, look no further than the nation's capital, Abuja. The rare individual (from Mars, probably) who lives and breathes patriotism in public office quickly finds himself/herself sailing against a hostile and ferocious wind. He/she must either change course immediately or risks being consumed by the elements. It does not take a genius or a newspaper columnist to uncover the reality of the shallow-mindedness of a lot of Nigeria's public figures. One only needs to look at the membership of the country's National Assembly to see how many are barely literate individuals (the ex "dancing senator", remember him?),[258] who are basically out of their depths and incapable of engaging with the complexity of the legislative

---

258. See former Senator Ademola Adeleke as portrayed in the online media; Sahara Reporters https://saharareporters.com/videos/meet-nigerias-dancing-senator-ademola-adeleke -and-other-dancing-political-gladiators

204 6 · POLITICS

process. By the way, the dancing senator went on to contest (and won) a state-wide gubernatorial election, defeating several men of letters and considerable personal accomplishments who ran against him before he was subsequently out-manoeuvred from the big prize of the governor's lodge. In a similar vein, sometime ago, an urbane and rather conscientious colleague of mine tired of what he saw as 'mediocre' candidates coming forward for election in his home state, angrily went back and began consulting on a possible run for office. He got a rude awakening when he sat with a group of local 'grassroot' party activists, who wearily said to him: "Sir, you are too decent and well educated to enmesh yourself in local politics; it is for the jobless, roadrunners and hungry dogs like ourselves.... we would not like to see you being ridiculed, talk less of being harmed because you are our 'father', we need you".

Now, how many times have we been told of this or that group of 'concerned' citizens coming together to form a political platform and it fizzled out? Nigeria has no shortage of brilliant minds to occupy every level of governance in this country and across the whole of West Africa combined. Why then do we not see them joining government in droves? Because their ideas are out of sync with the desires and priorities of the power brokers at the table. Is this the same as saying there are no brilliant minds in government as of today? Surely not. There are not enough of them to make the critical difference. The few that make it through the door see themselves heavily constrained and restrained by forces beyond their control. How is it then that Western democracies manage to infuse brilliant minds into the echelon of power both in politics and in industry, we might ask? Because their societies have an advanced system of social stratification, where the elites destined for high positions tread a clear path. They know what primary/secondary schools and university to attend and, subsequently, where to look for internship and their first career break. Consequently, top personnel in the civil service, politics and industry self-reproduce (through birth, recruitment criteria, and the old school network); so much that they have sufficient recruits in their ranks, across the board, to keep each other's corrupt instincts in check. This is the magic of the corrupt(less) Western political stability. We do not have the luxury of a settled class hierarchy we can superimpose on our flailing political system to serve a similar purpose.

For us, therefore, it is anything goes, effectively. "Chop and let chop" becomes the norm; the lowest common denominator for the participants in the corridors of power. It is a starker dichotomy than that of the Western democracies. Class mobility is notoriously difficult if not impossible within our own society. At the top end is a tiny few; the oligarchs with 95% of the resources, and at the bottom end is the majority, almost 90% feeding on crumbs from the high table. There is virtually nothing at the middle. In other words, it is statistically insignificant. Based on this, therefore, you would imagine that if any society was ripe for a revolution it would be right here, at home, but still nothing even close in the air. Why? Well, time and space would not permit us to address that thorny issue in detail here and now. But, quite simply, we are a nation of infinite time to burn; of a better tomorrow; a turn-the-other-cheek lot; a delayed gratification dreamers, and a reward-in-heaven pacifists. So, we say, long reign the donkeys!

6.11 Why Millions Join Political Parties in Nigeria

11 May 2021

Last week, the All Progressives' Congress (APC) announced its latest membership tally of forty million members and counting.[259] With its ongoing "revalidation exercise", the People's Democratic Party (PDP) will, no doubt, announce its own membership tally in the millions soon enough.[260] What is going on? What accounts for this new enthusiasm for membership of political parties in this country? It is even conceivable that either APC or PDP will have reached 50 million members by the time of the next Presidential election in 2023. That would mean, in effect, that one quarter of the population belongs to a single political party. It is either that Nigeria has the most politically conscious citizens in the world, or the most ignorant. The astronomical membership figures are at variance with all theories of democracy and democratic norms. Political parties in Nigeria are the antithesis of what they are generally understood to be. Political parties exist to propagate ideas, policy and programme for government. APC's "change", and PDP's "power" hardly count for programmes for government, let alone ideas. Furthermore, at a time of agitation for "restructuring", and a general breakdown of law and order, crippling inflation, decayed infrastructure, and debilitating unemployment, the ruling party is attracting more, not less, members. Something is wrong somewhere it seems. Otherwise, the general feeling that things are going in the wrong direction under the leadership of President Muhammadu Buhari is a

---

259. Flashed across the media outlet. See, for example; "APC largest political party in Africa: Gov Buni," pg People's Gazette, January 13, 2022, https://gazettengr.com/apc-largest-political-party-in-africa-with-41-million-members-gov-buni

260. Efforts to verify the PDP membership proved abortive as at the time of compiling this chapter.

red herring orchestrated by the metropolitan elite and the media. People appear to be endorsing the APC's record in office as they flock to the party in droves. Or not?

To put things in a wider perspective, the Conservative Party in the UK has 200,000 card carrying members, while the Labour Party has a 'massive' (by UK standard), 450,000. Contrast with the USA, the Republican Party has 36 million members, while the Democrats have 48 million. The discrepancy between the two most advanced Western democracies in party membership can be explained in terms of political culture. In the UK, millions of lifelong members of either the Conservative or Labour Party are not, in fact, card-carrying members. They are born into either of the party's tradition and ideology. And they usually remain so, almost invariably, for life. Actual party registration is regarded as superfluous. In the USA, the story is slightly different. Party 'membership' is transient and mostly passive. People simply 'register' as Republicans or Democrats and vote freely either way in different elections, without being accused of "anti-party activities". Besides, whatever million members the Republican and Democrats have locked down have been achieved over a century. For instance, it has taken the Republican Party 167 years to build up its membership to its current level of 36 million, and the Democrats 193 years to do the same for its 48 million members. The parties were founded in 1854 and 1828 respectively. This is compared to the PDP, founded 23 years ago, in 1998, and APC, founded only seven years ago, in 2014. What a rapid turn-around for them both! Is anyone seriously suggesting that the level of political consciousness in Nigeria is far higher than that of the UK or the USA?

The optimist in us may wish to hail the rise in party membership in this country as a triumph, and evidence of a vibrant democracy, but sadly, it is not. It is, in fact, a worrying trend, effectively laying waste to Nigerian democracy. Many of the millions queuing up to collect their party cards are doing so totally oblivious of the party's programme, policy, manifesto or anything of the sort. In fact, they could not care less. Political parties in Nigeria are not parties in the conventional sense; they are open-door, special purpose vehicles. You hop on, and hop off, embark and disembark at random. In a country where nothing seems to work for most people except for the select few, where social services are only extended to the lucky few, where criminality is a recognised means of livelihood for the youth, where access to education and healthcare is curtailed by financial incapacity, where the gap between the have and the have-nots has become a chasm, where poverty is the lot of the majority, and where bribery is as pervasive as the air you breathe in, membership of political parties has become the surest means of accessing state resources, especially where winners usually take all. If the APC is attracting members in their millions ahead of the PDP at the moment, it is because of the belief that it will be victorious at the next election. Both the PDP and APC operate a pyramid structure that trickles down to the grassroots—supposedly.

The big guns at the top are just as important as the lumpen proletariat sitting at the bottom, waiting for the crumbs to drop. The people at the top mobilise and demobilise them at will. There is a symbiotic relationship between the top of the pile and the bottom. Neither can survive without the other. They are bound together by their mutual loss of faith in the system they live under. They are propelled by their mutual sense of fear and vulnerability to the catastrophe the loss of power would bring, or energised by the 'real' prospect of capturing power soon enough. So, the queue for party membership grows longer not to advance governance, but to serve as an escape hatch out of a sinking ship.

The sense of 'if you cannot beat them, join them' is alive and kicking in both the APC and the PDP, which have become surfeited with members of late. Political parties in Western democracies work their socks off to get people to sign up. They would look at the happenings inside the two main parties in Nigeria with some envy, but then, the party managers there know better not to dwell too much on it. The countries normally associated with a hundred million party members are to be found in Cuba, China, and North Korea, which all run authoritarian regimes. Party membership in these countries are the nearest to conscription as you will get. Life is so political in those countries; you can feel it in the air that passes through the lungs. It is in an individual's best interest to belong. If the trend in Nigeria is moving along a similar way, then, party membership and authoritarianism will also become a reality sooner rather than later. Some might even postulate that Nigeria is there already. There is a way out of the morass though. The best way out is to widen political participation by loosening the stranglehold of parties on the electoral system. At the moment, the only route to political office is via a political party.[261] This is not only wrong, it is iniquitous. It goes against a fundamental tenet of democracy; the right to vote and be voted for. A candidate for election ought to be able to present himself directly to the electorate as an independent candidate. That would obviate the need for party membership and would also give the voter a broader pull from the slate, while expanding competition with registered political parties. If implemented, the course of Presidential election in Nigeria would take a dramatic turn for the better.

---

261. Electoral Act 2021 has since amended that to include independent candidacy

6.12 INEC and its 'Independence' Troubles …

20 July 2021

The Independent National Electoral Commission (INEC), the body charged with the conduct and management of elections in Nigeria, has been in the news of late. There is a Bill currently making its way through Parliament aimed at revamping its working structure, supposedly to make it more responsive and compliant. The main bone of contention in the proposed legislation is the conflicting desires of law makers to either include or obviate the need for on-the-spot electronic transmission of results. The People's Democratic Party, the main opposition to the ruling All Progressives Congress, and several others, has been most vociferous about this. Joseph Stalin is widely credited for saying; 'those who cast the votes decide nothing. Those who count the votes decide everything'. Stalin was, of course, a brutal dictator in Soviet Russia. His sardonic take on the value of the ballot was not only prescient for his time; it is perhaps even more so for our time and environment here as well. The Stalinists in the Nigerian Legislature are clearly weary of what an electronic transmission might possibly reveal; the bitter truth. They would rather not take a chance, it seems. That said, some would view the PDP's Johnny-come-lately concern (even obsession) with INEC's independence a trifle hypocritical. The party stood accused of emasculating the electoral umpire throughout its sixteen years in power prior to 2015.[262]

Rest assured, the APC would have been parroting similar uber righteous lines if it was the party in opposition. However, this week's column is not even about the raw sentiments being expressed both inside and outside Parliament, compelling though they may be. Our focus, instead, is on the 'independent' status of INEC as a matter of principle. After all, it is the anchor around which everything else hinges. Why put the tag 'independent' on an organisation which (by any yardstick of fairness) is structured to be anything but?

As an electoral umpire, INEC must not only be independent; it must be seen to be independent. However, to the public at large, the organisation is neither independent, nor seen to be one. How independent can an organisation be if its Chairman and his executives are appointed by a partisan politician (as surely as the President is), working through a National Assembly heavily influenced by him? Furthermore, what, in fact, is the rationale for appending 'independent' onto INEC anyway? Why not simply call it "National Electoral

---

262. Electronic transmission of results has since been included in the Electoral Act 2022

Commission" and then allow it to demonstrate its independence over time, and in the court of public opinion? Let us face it, the tag does not render any organisation truly independent, neither does its omission make it any less so. Independence is a matter of practice, as much as it is a matter of degree. Central Bank of Nigeria is supposedly independent, but it is not (thankfully) tagged as; Independent Central Bank of Nigeria. So too, is the Nigerian Police Force, The Nigerian Stock Exchange, Securities and Exchange Commission, National Judicial Council, Economic and Financial Crimes Commission, and a host of others. The necessity to attach the label 'independent' to INEC is more for psychological comfort and reassurance than it is a legal imperative. It is otherwise meaningless for all practical purposes. It is an organisation whose 'independence' is almost exclusively dependent on a Federal Government superintended by a President, who is invariably, the leader of one of the contenders for power in the political arena. It is like having the chairman of a football club, which has just won a keenly contested league at the end of the season, be the one to appoint the referee, his assistants, and senior administrators for the next season. Even with the best will in the world, how independent could the match officials be afterwards? Above all, would the other participating clubs feel they are taking part in a fair competition?

If the football analogy helps fuel your rage on this topic, then, it should. The idea of having a general election of a country coordinated from the centre by a government-appointed agency is, of itself, profoundly anti-democratic. This is precisely why no equivalent of a national election commission exists in advanced democracies of the West. The more power you allocate to a (political) body at the centre, the more the risk of abuse. Election administration is a devolved matter in Western democracies. As a result of long practice, citizens have developed trust in local officials to conduct and manage voting in their particular localities, which is then independently declared without transmission to an overarching 'collation centre' presided over by an almighty chairman, at the country's capital. Most results are, by custom, 'collated' by the press and civil society groups under the bright lights of the cameras. Projections, permutations, and the post-mortems begin soon after polls close. No room, no inch, given to ballot stuffing, snatching, burning, or anything of the sort. More importantly, the electorate hardly ever bother about the conduct of their local returning officers either. Politics is not seen as a zero-sum game over there, because there is broad agreement on the purpose of government amongst the ruling elite, which prioritises minimal welfare and social security for citizens. It is called the 'social contract' between government and the governed. That is the essence of election in a (liberal) democracy.

Now, do we have anything remotely close to a liberal democracy in Africa? The answer is clearly no. By consequence, politics tends to be all or nothing for the most part. Moreover, since the culture of winning and losing has not yet taken firm roots in Africa, hence, there is a need for a powerful central agency to strike the fear of God into the hearts of contenders for political office. Entrusting local returning officers with the power to deliver equitable results across the board with no regional biases in Africa is an aspiration, and a dream for the longest time. The brouhaha that accompanied the nomination of Lauretta Onochie, as a commissioner on the Board of INEC, a few days ago, highlights the point of this discussion very well. The Senate's rejection of her nomination has been hailed severally as a "victory for democracy". It is not. It is a pyrrhic victory at best. It is more of a setback for the Buhari administration, which will soon be rectified by the appointment of a more hardened APC stalwart, who will not be as careless as Onochie has been in letting slip her partisan mask. That said, the current model of a powerful INEC whose principal officers are appointed by Mr President (who also has a vested interest in the commission's work), is an anomaly that owes its origin to poor legislative drafting. The entire Act should be replaced with one which places emphasis not so much on 'independence', but on even-handedness. For this to happen, composition of the electoral body would be the sole responsibility of a Board of Trustees drawn from members of the civil society, labour union, and retired men (and women) of honour from the civil service and judiciary. In addition, the top three political parties in the last two electoral cycles will also have the right to nominate one representative each onto the board. With that multiple locks clamped in, the soul of the electoral body would be tied to everybody, and to nobody.

6.13 How Religion Enables Gender-Based Violence

9 September 2021

Taken at face value, the deeply religious reader would be forgiven for having a visceral reaction to this topic. The non-religious would heave a sigh of relief as he nods in agreement. Neither of these sentiments helps the discussion too much as they tend to foreclose. The topic is an essay on gender-based violence; a taboo subject for some, and a long overdue conversation for many others. It has been anchored on religion because it might prompt the questioning of some old assumptions, possibly, even lead to a change of mind on the fundamentals. Contrary to conventional wisdom, there is no history of gender-based violence in any African culture.[263] Women have been known to be just as capable of being violent as the men have been throughout history. What is true, however, is the fact that there is a correlation between religion (Islam and Christianity) and women oppression. The more prevalent religion is in a society, the more the incidents of gratuitous violence against women. In fact, there is less documentary evidence of violence against women in societies less influenced by religion (Western countries) than there is in societies where there is prevalence of religion (Africa, Asia, Latin-America and Middle-Eastern countries). These are the most religious, at the same time, most hostile places for women to thrive.

In its simplest form, "Gender-Based Violence" (GBV, as it is known in workshops, seminar rooms, and statutes) refers to the physical pain inflicted on a person mainly on account of their gender. Other elements include; sexual, and psychological. Let us be quite blunt about this, majority of men in this country have had reason to slap, push, or shove their spouse in anger at home, at some point in their relationship, without thinking twice about it. Battery or assault of any kind, inflicted on anyone by whomsoever, is actually unlawful and punishable with severe sanctions. What makes this so tragic is there is a broad acceptance of casual infliction of violence in a relationship as routine, and no big deal. Both the giver and recipient of the 'routine' slap tend not to dwell on it too much. In fact, it is so 'routine' that sometimes, it is done in the open; in the communal yard, alleyways, and even in broad daylight. It is usually done in the course of a man exercising his 'right' to discipline his partner. What is more, people are rarely alarmed at the sight of a man beating on his spouse, except to appeal to him to 'take it easy', and 'calm down'. The subsequent inquisitiveness of neighbours to such an event would often be to find out what the woman could have done to attract the wrath of her man so violently, and probably, offer them prayers. Men have also been known to be at the receiving end of violent attacks by women, but, by and large, that is an aberration; it is still a man's world.

The bulk of violence against women occurs in relationships. In other words, women suffer physical, mental and emotional abuse from people they already know, and with whom they are probably in love. That said, there is a significant amount of violence meted out to women by complete strangers. It is more or less like racial discrimination experienced by black people in Europe, America and other countries. You run into a fellow human being, and attack their person either verbally or physically simply because they are of a different colour

---

263. Although, this is open to debate

to yourself. Gratuitous attack on a person of the opposite sex (especially rape) happens a lot at random as well. GBV is certainly one of the most under-reported public policy dilemmas in this country. This is so in spite of the proliferation of women advocacy groups spread throughout the country. International non-governmental organisations such as the Ford Foundation, have also been involved in creating intervention mechanisms, to develop "Standard Operating Procedures" in curbing GBV. As a country, GBV is criminalised by statute in Nigeria, but it has been left to states to develop their own pro-active measures to arrest the scourge of violence against women and girls. Lagos State is a good example of a state at the forefront of the pushback on GBV. It has one of the toughest laws on domestic violence in the country. It also has several women 'refuge' centres and a specialist court trying domestic violence and sexual assault cases. Other states are also pushing hard on this.

Much of the work done on GBV in Nigeria is carried out by 'women leaders' in the states, particularly, the "First State Ladies", that is to say, wives of state governors, and that of local government chairpersons. Many of them are doing a tremendous job in this area, and deserve more credit than has been given to them hitherto. A notable exemption is Her Excellency, Bisi Adeleye-Fayemi, wife of Ekiti State Governor, who brings her well-earned reputation as a staunch international advocate for women and girls' rights to bear on this issue. She has been compared to Mrs Hillary Rodham-Clinton (a renowned feminist), former Presidential candidate, and wife of the former US President, Bill Clinton, in her tireless effort in this domain. Ekiti State has "Sexual Assault Referral Centre", a 208-bed "Transit Home and Vocational Centre" for women and girls, "Name and Shame" policy, and "Compulsory Treatment and Care for Sexually Abused Minor Law". This law is perhaps the only one of its kind in the country. All of these remedial structures of reference are great. But the point of this piece, as stated earlier, is that we, as a society, are merely dealing with the symptoms of GBV, and not its causes. Religious Houses are particularly good at responding to the victims of GBV brought before them. They not only provide pastoral care; they also provide shelter, welfare, emotional and moral support for them. Nonetheless, the good work they do only masks the evil they themselves perpetrate on the victims of GBV.

Religious Houses are the bastions of chauvinism and women oppression in this country. They exercise not just influence, but real power over the teaming millions of their devotees. The Pastor's, and the Imam's word is unquestioningly taken for gospel by the believer. The church and the mosque commandeer the women folk to be "submissive" to the men folk in all circumstances, then, chastise the woman for not being submissive enough the moment the man turns nasty. There is hardly a dispute between a couple that is not traced to the woman's conduct or misconduct that led up to the attack on them. Both Islam and Christian doctrines reference women as chattels of their men; a nod and a wink to the misogynistic impulse in men. It creates and augments the man's propensity to violence against women. Violence rubber-stamped by Parliament or the constitution can be amended, even abrogated. Violence under the imprimatur of God is permanent and irrevocable. The likes of Mrs Clinton, Mrs Fayemi, and several others understand that GBV is really about power and its overwhelming concentration in men's hands. The patriarchal nature of the state and religious institutions are the real enemy. Some of the antiquarian institutions in this regard need to be dismantled to make way for human progress and for the complete emancipation of women to take place. Many women advocates, nonetheless, shy away from this central tenet of the struggle because they do not wish to be pigeon-holed as 'radical feminists' and 'men haters'. We should be tough on GBV, yes, but should we not also be tough on its root causes?

6.14 Dearth of Female Nigerian Leaders

26 June 2018

"The only condition necessary for the triumph of evil is for good men to do nothing". So says the great Irish philosopher, Edmund Burke (1729–1797). Looking at this enduring aphorism in reverse, one might entertain the thought that, perhaps, the only condition necessary for the perpetuation of misrule by men in Nigeria is for good women to do nothing. How did we arrive at a junction where the minority (i.e. male) are perpetuating misrule and violence on the majority (i.e. female) for so long and with such reckless abandon? How come men in this country (as elsewhere) assume that positions of leadership and dominance are their birthright, while the female folks clasp their palms in resignation? How come our religious leaders in this country continue to preach the virtue of "submissiveness" to the female gender in acquiescence to the perpetrators of violence and oppression against them; the maniac male in their midst?

When it comes to the analysis of gender imbalance in the public square in this country, it is best to start with the sharply contrasting north-south divide. It really is a tale of two cities. The cultural inhibition impeding the career advancement of women in the north is more deeply ingrained than it is in the south, simply because of the prominence of religious indoctrination so pervasive and so regressive in its conception of the women folks as nothing more than appendages of men at best, second class citizens at worst. The "boko

214   6 · POLITICS

haram" phenomenon in the north is an offshoot of the hacking back to ancient religious mores, better suited to the dark ages than it is to modern Nigeria. The colonial influence of Western education in the south allowed for a faster and easier penetration of the white man in that region, but it also accelerated the drive towards mass literacy and a skilled workforce to serve the colonial administration. The north-south divide exemplified in this historical antecedent is still a subject of debate till today. There are those who continue to see a contradiction between being a good Muslim and a well-educated female in many parts of the north. Of course, it is absurd to see, indeed acknowledge, any trade-off between these two values, but the stark choice being given to a whole load of female children in the northern part of Nigeria says something entirely different. The good Muslim girl is one who has little or no social life, gets married in her teenage years and starts producing babies quietly in her husband's house. This, in fact, is the lot of many of our female compatriots in the north.

By contrast, with education, the female child has been able to grow into an economically liberated adult in large parts of the south. But, this has also come at a price, especially with the infiltration of Western consumerism objectifying the female gender and denigrating them as objects of men's lurid desire. This has warped the mind-set of many of the young female school-leavers, whose only purpose in life is hankering after Hollywood, Bollywood and Nollywood soap stars, focusing on their looks and fast cars, with little ambition for positions of leadership in society. The gospel of "submissiveness" has been elevated into a religious edict in almost every household in the south, where women are still being taught to "know your place" in society. Whatever that "place" is, it is not in the realm of leadership. Being Mrs Somebody is still more valuable than having a "BA" or "BSc" behind their name. Signing the family name for the last time remains the crowning achievement for most women in the south as much as it is in the north, of course. Where does this false consciousness stem from anyway? Why do we no longer have befitting female role models going forward in this country?

Did Hajia Gambo Sawaba (1933–2001) not grow up in this same land of ours? A champion of the working people, who rose through the ranks in the defunct Northern Element Progressive Union (NEPU as it was commonly known). How about Margaret Ekpo (1914–2006), a first Republic grassroot political firebrand, who inspired women to take a leading role in public life? And, Hajia Laila Dongoyaro, married off at the age of 12, but fought through life to become president of the National Council of Women's Societies, and a prominent member of the National Party of Nigeria in the 1980s. Let us remember Ameyo Adadevoh, a physician whose great-grand father was Herbert

Macaulay. She not only lived in our time, she put her life on the line combating the spread of the Ebola disease, which later killed her. Adunni Oluwole, founder of the Nigerian Commoners Liberal Party, and a foremost human rights activist, who took part in the famous General Strike of 1945 in Nigeria. Mammy Ochendu, founder of "Mammy Market" at military barracks all over the country, a template that is now part of everyday life in universities and other higher institutions in the country. Princess Adetutu of Ife, Queen Amina, the elder daughter of Queen Bakwa Turunku, founder of the Zau Zau kingdom in the old Zaria. Kudirat Abiola, a foremost pro-democracy activist and wife of the winner of the June 12 1993 Presidential election, MKO Abiola. And of course, the "Lioness of Lisabi", Mrs Funmilayo Ransome-Kuti, better known as "Fela's mother", who fought for the universal adult suffrage now taken for granted in this country.

The above list is not exhaustive by any means. There are many more names that can be plucked from the archives. Suffice it to say that Nigerian women have a distinguished history of activism and public service no less than the men. Why progress for more advancement appears to have stalled is what many people find baffling. As the reader can deduce, I have been careful not to apportion gender blame in this write-up. When it comes to staking claims on leadership positions, women can also sometimes be their own worst enemies by insisting on a level of compliance on other women not uniformly imposed on men. Some women in positions of authority victimise other women even more vociferously than a man in a similar position would dare. "I am the only woman director here", "the only female manager there", "the only member of the executive", and all the other esoteric corners reserved for token female presence. This appears to be the hallmark of accomplishment for some women, who would not lend a hand to others trying to follow in their footsteps. So, what we are talking about is more a societal problem than it is gender-specific.

It is nothing short of scandalous for there not to be a single female governor of any state in this country, let alone a major party leader or a serious Presidential contender of any political hue. Political parties are awash with so-called "women leaders" whose main role is to organise catering and welfare support largely for the convenience of men. Never mind the few infamous women who have also had their hands deep in corruption and looting in this country, it is my contention that the administration and good governance of this country would tilt towards a renaissance with the involvement of more female leaders both in business and in politics. So, to coin a phrase, I say, women of Nigeria, rise up, wake up, you have nothing to lose but your chains.

216   6 · POLITICS

6.15 How #EndSARS Was Lost

27 October 2020

The #EndSARS protest in its current form has come and gone. It is time for the post mortem, soul-searching, and a few sobering thoughts on what just happened, and what it could have been. The most critical aspect of the protest, in my view, was the leadership or leader(less) dimension of the phenomenon. And it was indeed a phenomenon; a moment in history. We were led to believe that the protest was not organised, not coordinated, managed, or directed by any individual or group of individuals; that it simply took a life of its own. How amazing, if only that was exactly true. Having been directly involved in high-octane protests in my time, it goes without saying that someone, some like-minded comrades, somewhere, sat together, planned, and foresaw the outcome. It is like a bomb suddenly going off in the middle of the market, creating mayhem, throwing off people in a stampede, running helter-skelter for cover, and no one claiming responsibility. Quite obviously, someone made the device, and also quite obviously, someone identified the location and timing for its detonation. So, it is not strictly true that no one organised or led the #EndSARS protest; what is true is that the shadowy figures propelling it chose to operate below the radar. No one stepped up to the plate at the critical juncture, when it mattered. That was a strategic blunder.

The media tried in vain to pin down a couple of celebrities here and there, to own up to their involvement in organising it, but to their credit, they declined. The reason for this is not far-fetched. Once a 'leader' or 'leaders' have been so identified, such a person or group of persons become the target of the authorities as agents of influence, even worse, as objects of ridicule and attack. That is the lesson of history. That said, spontaneous or leader(less) uprisings do work with varying degrees of success, under different circumstances. It worked for Poland, in the 1980s. It brought the country's long-serving Communist regime crashing down, following several street battles. Benin Republic in 1990, and Togo the following year, a spontaneous gathering of all sections of the civil society created an unmanageable situation for the sit-tight dictators; Mathew Kérékou (Benin) and General Gnassingbé Eyadéma (Togo) who succumbed to the will of the people as expressed in the streets. Czechoslovakia's spontaneous "Velvet Revolution" righted an historical wrong by splitting the country in two, peacefully, in 1993, having co-existed as culturally diverse, and 'united' entity since 1918. The "Arab Spring" in 2010 and beyond was also spontaneous; it was, more specifically, online inspired just like the #EndSARS was. It led to a series of uprisings across the Arab world, starting with Tunisia, where people protested against authori-

6 · POLITICS

tarian rule, demanded and secured a regime change. All the spontaneous uprisings succeeded without much bloodshed. Can we view the #EndSARS protest in the same breath? After all, the police disbanded SARS, and are now establishing 'SWAT'. How long will it be before we see #EndSWAT? Or should it be strangled at birth anticipating what it too might turn out to be?

Without meaning to play down the spirited effort of the youths, some of whom came out of their cocoons in unprecedented numbers to demand change, the protest was little more than a damp squib I am afraid. Never mind the police clamping down on the SARS issue, and the stomach-churning sight of politicians trying to ingratiate themselves with the protesters. The protest itself has ended in a spectacular failure. Why? Because #EndSARS was not, in substance, a policing issue per se; it was totemic, and a subtext for a much larger demand for fundamental change in the character and shape of government. It was a denunciation of the bad, corrupt, pilfering and insensitive political elite who care for no one but themselves. The youths are tired of living in a country with abundant riches, largely frittered away on law makers' humongous salaries and emoluments. First, they become Commissioners, then Representatives, then, transform into Governors, then, reappear as Senators, then, metamorphose into Honourable Ministers, then, become Party Chieftains in a life-time of political round-tripping. And with uniformed officers doubling as their personal bodyguards, they pick up jumbo pays, collect rents as they laugh all the way to the bank. They then put their cronies and siblings into public and political offices, secure for themselves a life of opulence and splendour in spatial dwellings at home and in choice locations in Dubai and Western cities, whilst the Nigerian youth in this country, with no access, no contact, no connection, go begging for food even after coming out of university with certificates that take them nowhere.

Moreover, the youths are tired of sham and inconsequential elections built on empty campaign promises. They are tired of widespread and endemic corruption that sees no end in sight. Above all, they are tired and fed up to the back teeth of senseless killings of innocent souls and wanton looting of the commonwealth. They are angry seeing their future callously mortgaged to satisfy the unquenchable thirst for self-aggrandisement by politicians. In short, they wanted, and still want regime change; a new Deal in a new Nigeria.

The protest started very well because of its leader(less) colouration, but ended abruptly and badly, ironically, because of its lack of leadership. A leader(less) campaign can only take you so far, dear youths. There comes a point where leaders must emerge from the shadows; where individuals must step forward; where grievances must be properly articulated; where demands must be tabled; where coordination must take place; where the masses must be mobilised to maximum effect. Otherwise, you open room for (sponsored) reactionary elements, with the sole aim of putting their special mark of violence and mayhem on a just cause. The police and the military then step in to restore 'law and order', as state governments are forced to impose dusk-to-dawn curfews. That is exactly what has happened in this case. If one looks at successful, spontaneous uprisings elsewhere, there was not a single one that remained leader(less) for too long. History also tells us that where such protests continue leader(less), the end product is usually bloody. Example of this was first in the Egyptian uprising of January 2011. It was leader(less) at such a critical moment that the military saw an opportunity to stage a coup, shooting hundreds of protesters in cold blood, and installing General Abdel Fattah el-Sisi as the military strongman. He later took off his army fatigue, became a "civilian", contested and won a spurious election in 2014, which transformed him into president to this day.

The other leader(less) uprising that turned bloody was Libya, following the overthrow of Colonel Muammar Gaddafi, in 2011. He had been in power since 1969. Sure enough that many had the feeling that the 'uprising' was fuelled in part by the international (mainly Western) negative media campaign against Gaddafi. It was, nonetheless, popular and greeted with cheers by the populace. In truth, Gaddafi was a benevolent dictator, who overstayed his welcome. The vacuum created by the leader(less) protest in Libya erupted into factions amongst various armed groups, which have since carved up the country into enclaves, and are still at a low-intensity war with each other till this day. The Nigerian military, and President Muhammadu Buhari, a retired army General, would have been well briefed on this. The leadership vacuum left by the #End-SARS protest could well have snowballed into something pretty ugly for the country. The energy it created and the emotion generated clearly struck a chord with the populace, and around the world. Shame it was allowed to peter out without much consequence. But, hey, all is not lost for the gallant youths. Remember, he who fights and runs away, lives to fight another day.

6.16 Imperative (and Myth) of Youth Representation

14 December 2021

Africa has the largest core of talented young population in the world.[264] More than 60% of the continent's population is under the age of 25. As of 2021,

---

264. Figures for this piece culled from "Young People's Potential, the Key to Africa's Sustainable Potential". United Nations, Office of the High Representative for the Least Developed countries, Land Locked Developing Countries and Small Island Developing States.

one of Nigeria's closest neighbours, Niger, has the median age of 15.4 years, the youngest in the world in fact. This is followed by Uganda and Mali (15.8), Angola (15.9), Malawi (16.5); several others down below before getting to Nigeria (18.4). The reasons for this demographic shift in favour of the youth in Africa are varied and prone to several interpretations; high adult mortality rate (8.42 deaths per 1,000) due to the prevalence of hypertension, HIV/AIDS and other severe illnesses, combined with the continent's relatively lower life expectancy rate of 63 years for males and 66 years for females. The average life expectancy globally is currently 71 years for males and 75 for females. In other words, Africans do not have a bunch of older people hanging around for too long; unlike in some other more technologically advanced countries with better health-care facilities. In addition to this, birth rate in Africa is rather high; it currently stands at 32.411 per 1000 people. Many young girls are married off to start giving birth very early. Babies, literally, having babies in Africa is a phenomenon tied to both cultural as well as economic factors. The old not living too long, and the young producing babies early will always translate into a young population overall.

Debate about how to rationalise the statistics has been at the centre of political discourse for some time, especially, in Nigeria. Being the most populous nation in Africa, it has the largest concentration of the youth population. As of last year, 2020, 44% of the Nigerian population was under the age of 14. And almost two thirds of its overall population fall within the brackets of "youth" (i.e. under 35). There have been structures in place to address the youth 'dilemma' in form of the National Youth Service Corps, Citizens and Leadership Training Centre, Federal Ministry of Youth Development and, latterly, Federal Ministry of Youth and Sport Development, National Youth Council of Nigeria, and a few others. Politicians have been quick to jump on the bandwagon as well. Political parties routinely appoint token 'youth leaders' in the same way as they do 'women leaders' into their ranks. For political parties, a 'youth policy' has become a vote winning fad of late, rather than a serious commitment towards youth integration into the echelons of power and decision-making. Otherwise, what better way to respond to the youth exclusion in public life than to lower the age of election to the National Assembly from 35 (for the Senate) and 30 (for the House of Representatives) to 21? Let no one be misled into thinking that old age equals wisdom, although this is a uniquely African mind-set that has been entrenched for a millennium.

Office of the High Representative for the Least Developed Countries, Landlocked Developing Countries and Small Island Developing States

It does not make much sense that Yakubu Gowon became the Head of State of Nigeria aged 32, in 1966, and today, in 2021, with better access to knowledge across the board, the constitution strangely requires a minimum age of 40 to be elected president.[265] It does not make much sense that you can be a semi-illiterate, and be elected to the National Assembly as long as you are aged 30 and above, but you could have solid background in business, academia or community leadership, but still not be eligible for high office because you happen to be under 30 years. It does not make much sense that a young girl of 15 is considered fully grown and ready to raise a family in many northern parts of Nigeria, but the same girl is considered 'immature' for election to high office until she turns 30. It does not make much sense that a young, vibrant man could be enlisted into the army aged 16 and over, yet, the same person is deemed unqualified for high office until he becomes 30 and above. The young 16 year old army recruit can pick up a riffle, go into combat where he makes life and death decisions, but cannot be trusted to serve the public unless and until he is 30 and above. It does not make much sense that Nadia Edith Whittome (British Labour Party), can be a member of the UK Parliament since 2019, aged 23, and Sebastian Kurz "Chancellor" (Prime Minister) of Austria, in 2017, aged 31, both grappling with much more complex economic systems than is the case in Nigeria, where the minimum age for such offices are considerably higher.

The argument for youth inclusion into the structures of governance in the world's most populous black nation, Nigeria, is pretty overwhelming. It has ramifications far beyond the shores of Nigeria itself. The youths should not only be content to be hailed as "leaders of tomorrow", they should insist on being leaders of today, here and now. That said, can we seriously say that Nigerian youths are ready, or even interested in leadership to the same degree that youths in other parts of the world are? The answer to this million dollar question is a depressing NO. Contrary to the popular myth of a systemic youth 'exclusion', Nigerian youths had always been at the forefront of progressive leadership in this country. Those who are old enough or studied widely enough would remember that the fight for independence was spearheaded by the youth, the infamous "Anglo-Nigerian Defence Pact" after independence was inspired by the youth, the Anti-Apartheid struggle was led by the youth, the "Ali Must Go" nationwide protests of the 1970s, and the titanic struggle to rid the country of military rule in the 1990s were led and coordinated by the youth.

The problem now, however, is that today's youths are bone lazy, docile, lethargic, and myopic. Their role models are often in Nollywood and in the entertain-

---

265. This has now been lowered to 35.

ment industry. "Hush-puppy" and his criminal lifestyle have more appeal to the Nigerian youth than a hardworking community youth leader would ever have. They are more interested in the here and now; get-rich-quick mentality of the gangster generation on social media and in the dark alleys. One needs only take a cursory look at the shenanigans inside countless Students' Union Governments in Nigerian public universities to see that they are the mirror image of the decay and corruption they so often decry in the adult population.

The outspoken, highly articulate (political) youths popping up on television screens today, speaking on behalf of the All Progressives Congress, and the Peoples Democratic Party, are self-serving mouthpieces clamouring for inclusion. Fair enough, but they are usually the sons and daughters of the well-connected and the ruling class. They are totally unrepresentative of the wider youth population in the country. They confuse their own craving for relevance for youth 'empowerment'. They are rebels without a cause. A meaningful youth action would focus more on policy, not the headcount of how many are in political offices, doing nothing more than maintain the status quo. At the last US Presidential primaries, one of the youngest candidates, Pete Buttigieg, was 38. He attracted less youth vote than the oldest candidate, Bernie Sanders, did at 79. Why? Because he focussed on policy and what concerned the youths of America. What matters most to the youths in Nigeria are policies on education, IT, family, employment, vocational training, housing, self-employment, etc. Talks on these vital public policy issues are being drowned out in favour of involvement in partisan politics as if it is the panacea to the problem of youth exclusion in Nigeria.

6.17 Warning: Parliamentary System is Brutal and Vicious

28 May 2019

The late Chief Anthony Eromosele Enaharo (1923–2010) dedicated the last two decades of his life on earth not only spearheading the clamour for "restructuring" in this country, but more crucially, for the introduction (some might say re-introduction) of a Parliamentary system of government for the proposed regional governments in a 'New Nigeria'. Parliamentary system of government is particularly appealing to people in the South-West of Nigeria because of the enduring legacy of the late Chief Obafemi Awolowo, who was the first and last Premier of the then Western Region between 1952–1959. He ran an inclusive, transparent and accountable government that was not only the envy of other Nigerian regions, but indeed the world, beating even France to the installation of a nationwide television broadcast medium amongst a glittering list of many firsts in his achievement. He later went on to become Leader of the Opposition to the Tafawa Balewa government in the Federal Parliament from 1959–1963. Awolowo set a standard and benchmark for governance which generations after him still find difficult to match. His successful government has been largely credited to the Parliamentary system of government bequeathed to us by the British hence, the demand for a return to the "good old days" of politics in preference to the expensive and inefficient federal system of government modelled on that of the USA.

Under the US system which we like to follow as and when it suits us, a near-mathematical schedule for assumption and departure from office of elected politicians is pencilled in and assured. The loser is even given the luxury of staying on for a few months after defeat, to 'relax' and catch his breath before finally quitting the stage. He prepares his "hand over" note for his successor, creating as many last-minute financial obligations on his successor as he can get away with. For instance, the general election of February 23rd this year has still not resulted in a change of government as you read this piece. The losers are sitting pretty, in their swivel leather chairs, enjoying the spoils of office — still. The ceremonial handover is not until May 29th of this same year, three months after losing power. This delay to the heeding of the people's voice is thought to be necessary for an orderly transfer of the reins of government. Really?

Spare a thought, then, for Theresa May, the British Prime Minister, who was forced (by her own backbench colleagues in Parliament) to make the announcement for her departure from office at the front of Number 10, Downing Street (Prime Minister's official residence) last Friday, 24th of May . She had just finished putting together a "Brexit Bill", and she had intended to present to Parliament two days earlier. This was her fourth attempt at trying to pass legislation to approve the agreement reached with the other twenty-seven members of the European Union for Britain's departure from the union, otherwise known as "Brexit" after forty-five long years of continued and uninterrupted membership. The Parliamentary arithmetic is not in the Prime Minister's favour. The ruling (should we say governing) Conservative party has no overall majority, and is only hanging on to office with the help of one of the smaller parties. Choking on emotion, and clearly in tears, Mrs May announced her resignation as leader of the Conservative party effective 7th of June, and will quit being Prime Minister as soon as a new leader has been elected by party members. That means, in effect, in a couple of weeks' or so time, no more. The late Prime Minister, Mrs Margaret Thatcher, was Prime Minister from 1979 to 1990, and leader of the Conservative party from 1975

6 · POLITICS   223

to 1990. She was kicked out of office with three days' notice only. There was no lengthy election for her successor, John Major, since he was elected by consensus. Mrs Thatcher too, announced her departure in front of Downing Street in tears, not minding being at the height of her political ascendancy at the time. She had won three general elections in a row, mostly by landslides. But, somehow, something about her continued presence in office was unpalatable to her Parliamentary colleagues. They wanted her out for having become a "liability" for the Conservative party's ambition for a fourth term in office.

Upon her departure from office, Mrs Thatcher was seen scuttling around London frantically searching for a house to buy, and even where exactly to relocate. She had not thought of living anywhere other than the Prime Minister's official residence for more than ten years. No hiatus from being number one citizen to being an 'ordinary' woman in society. No luxury of transition or ceremonial hand-over, parade, or anything of that nature. No theatre, no frills. The fate of the Prime Minister is in the hands of fellow Members of Parliament under a Parliamentary system. It is an important bulwark against abuse of power and tyrannical rule. There is no mathematically enshrined assumption or departure dates. To remain in office, a Prime Minister must enjoy the confidence of his/her colleagues in Parliament or bow out gracefully, or, be pushed out unceremoniously. It is direct, clinical (sometimes messy), and ultimately brutal. Under a Parliamentary system, a government is elected for a term of office, which is usually four-five years at a time. This is just like under a Presidential system, except that the term of office in the latter is fixed, and written in stone. In a Parliamentary democracy, the Prime Minister is *primus inter pares* (first among equal) in respect of his/her colleagues in the Cabinet. Government is a "collective responsibility" of all of them.

This is unlike the Presidential system, where the President is the "executive", the symbol, and personality that embodies the "administration"; not government. The President is only supposed to be running an administration. Governmental authority is supposedly diffused and embedded in the other arms of government 'equally'. So, in theory at least, an administration can be chaotic, and shambolic, but government goes on. In a Parliamentary system, the Prime Minister runs a government, and any semblance of chaos, disunity or mismanagement could precipitate its immediate collapse. This is what renders such a system exceedingly attentive to the feelings of the electorate, echoed through the elected representatives, including the Cabinet. A Prime Minister is willy-nilly, alert and on the ball, mastering and digesting the minutiae of government departments around the clock, practically. From a shooting incident in some remote part of the country, to trade union disputes or prisoner escape, the Prime Minister is thrown straight into the spotlight. A sickly, inattentive, uninformed and lackadaisical political leader will not last long in the post. This is what lies at the core of accountability. It is also what makes the system susceptible to chicanery, and skulduggery of the kind that led to Theresa May's inauspicious exit from government in the UK. So, to my brethren here at home desirous of a Parliamentary system of government, I say, be careful what you wish for; you might get it.

Chapter Seven

Law

7.01 "Panama papers": Lawyers' Ethical Dilemma

31 October 2017

Anyone who has ever set foot on Nigerian Law School premises remembers one thing from their first day to the last. It is that irrespective of how well one does in all the written and oral exams, there is one test that hangs on the head of every student like a sword of Damocles; the "fit and proper" test. It is one you cannot prepare for in advance, neither is it one you can revise for. Past questions, and answers? No use. How about reading and jamming it all in, then, regurgitating later as you do with the other modules? No snowball chance in hell! "Fit and proper" is a value judgement entirely in the gift of the Director General (DG) of the Law School. He, and only he, has to vouch for every single person called to the Bar (in their thousands every year), that he is of good enough character to be admitted into the lofty ranks of barristers and solicitors of the Supreme Court of Nigeria. Why impose this extra endurance of pain on an already overstretched student you might ask? Well, they say it is because law is a "noble" profession; more a vocation than a job; a higher calling of some sort. Also, that lawyers are "ministers in the temple of justice". After all, a lawyer's loyalty is not even to the client paying for his services; his loyalty, ultimately, is to the Court in the common cause of justice. Lawyers are, first and foremost, "officers of the court", so goes the saying. This all sounds and feels rather hogwash to the reasonable mind, I know, but it is actually worse. It is a futile attempt at brainwashing for the uninitiated.

If you think this is a heartrending account of the Law School's effort, well, I invite you to cast your mind to the depressing scenes of the home of senior judges being subjected to dawn raids by the operatives of the Department for

226 7 · LAW

State Security in the last couple of months, for their alleged involvement in corrupt practices. There is mounting anxiety over lawyers' deliberate use of the judiciary to frustrate EFCC's attempt at prosecuting high-level official corruption, so much that the Chief Justice of Nigeria, Justice Onoghen, is currently putting together a special committee capable of cutting through the artificial logjam. Are all of these lawyers not "ministers in the temple of justice"? My guess is that a few will indeed be. Many others would not measure up even if they spent their entire professional life trying. Nonetheless, I am of the conviction that if only ten percent of Nigerian lawyers lived up to the billing of truly being "ministers in the temple of justice", our judiciary would be such an envy of the world that people from across Africa would be clamouring to bring their cases before our judges. A clean judiciary does not require every one of its members to be clean; it only requires the barest critical number to make the barest critical input.

Let it be known, however, that what I am saying here does not amount to identifying yet another "Nigerian problem", far from it. Lawyers' indiscretion and complicity in high crime is a universal phenomenon. It is only noteworthy by its regularity and pervasiveness in our own jurisdiction. The "Panama papers" gives the world a one-in-a-million chance at witnessing lawyers' duplicity in shielding people of questionable character and shady deals from scrutiny. It is the anti-thesis of "minister in the temple of justice". "Mossack Fonseca" is a Panamanian registered law firm founded in 1977 by two friends; Messrs Mossack and Fonseca, to render legal services to corporate clients. The companies on their books soon grew from a dozen to over three hundred thousand within a couple of decades.[266] The two partners were reported to have said in a casual television interview that they had created a "monster". It employs close to one thousand personnel in about forty countries around the world. Their focus is strictly speaking financial services for both corporate and individual clients. They do this by turning liquid investment into cash, put funds into an escrow (third party) account, then, transfer same to an offshore company. They later restructure same to reflect Mossack Fonseca as beneficial owner. All of this, they claim is done within the law, but for many people, it is a classic definition of money laundering (albeit) with a cloak of legitimacy.

Mossack Fonseca is in the fourth top tiers of firms in the world actively engaged in helping people "hide" their wealth. According to the American economist, Gabriel Zucman, about 8% of the world's wealth ($7.6tn) is handled in this way. The loss in global tax revenues is estimated to be about $200bn per

---

266. BVI Company Restorations — mossackfonseca.com. On March 14, 2018, the firm announced that it was shutting down due to the economic and reputational damage inflicted by the disclosure of its role in global tax evasion by the Panama Papers.

year, \$35bn in the US, \$78bn in Europe, \$50bn in Africa, not to talk of Asia, the Middle East and the Caribbean. When the lid was blown off the client accounts of this law firm, it made a staggering revelation of sham companies and offshore accounts held by several figures from poor countries seeking to hide their wealth, to put it far away from the reach of their own economies while the governments in those countries go about with the begging bowl for "foreign assistance" and "foreign aid" of all types. The exposed list of the firm's clients include the 'who and who' of Nigeria's high society, over one hundred in fact. In a situation like this, where does a lawyer's loyalty lie? When a single law firm has three hundred thousand corporate "clients" on its books, many of which are "shell" companies of course, but where does a lawyer draw the line between truth and client confidentiality? Should lawyers go above their call of duty and become moral agents instead of simply applying the law, since they are "ministers in the temple of justice"?

This conflict of loyalties is a dilemma that runs through the life of a lawyer across jurisdictions, but more so, on the continent of Africa with so much scarce resources and a daily struggle for survival by many. As I said earlier, the DG of the Nigerian Law School makes a judgement on every candidate for call to the Bar in this country. He is supposed to vouch for each and every candidate presented to the Benchers for the annual ritual. The 'vouching', of course, is more apparent than real; in other words, it is an illusion. It is difficult enough sometimes to vouch for the moral standing of every member in a nucleus family, not to talk of faithfully doing so for thousands of strangers every year in the Law School. The DG is effectively being put in a position of having to carry the initial burden for the moral turpitude of lawyers later in practice. That is what happens when you vouch for somebody's integrity; it robs off on you if that person is subsequently found wanting. The DG should not be put in this invidious position in my view. The lawyers behind the "Panama papers" represent a challenge to professional standards. Candidates for the Bar should be made to attest to their own honour and personal integrity ab initio, so they live or die by their own sword. The earlier the Law School leaves policing of conscience out of its curriculum, the better for all.

7.02 SEC: Minister's Right to Suspend DG

6 February 2018

The Nigerian Finance Minister, Mrs Kemi Adeosun, gave evidence to the National Assembly last week on the circumstances surrounding the suspension of the Director-General of the Securities and Exchange Commission (SEC),

Mounir H. Gwarzo,[267] who was also there to present his side of the story. The National Assembly performs its oversight function well when it allows issues of this nature to be properly ventilated. The public can only be better informed about such a critical issue of confidence in the country's financial system. SEC being the prime financial regulator in the country, this column has often had reasons to comment on its activities in the recent past. In fact, the on-going hearing highlighted matters of grave public concern this column subjected to a critical review in the December issue of this paper: "SEC's litany of corporate governance lapses" PUNCH, December 5, 2017. It is therefore not necessary to bring up the minutiae of the discussion surrounding the suspension of the DG again here, except in so far as it concerns the singular issue of whether the Minister acted outside her powers in suspending the DG, which some learned colleagues insist she has. This column takes a different view.

It is being said that Gwarzo, not being a 'civil servant' in the conventional sense, is not subject to the Public Service Rules governing the appointment and dismissal of government employees. Therefore, the DG can only be guided or disciplined in accordance with the provisions of the Investment and Securities Act (ISA), 2007, and the staff manual attached to it. As far as I know, the Minister of Finance has not claimed anything contrary to this line of reasoning. Section 5(1) of the Act says the DG "shall be appointed by the President upon the recommendation of the Minister and confirmed by the Senate". In terms of the DG's removal from office, section 8(2) empowers the President "at any time and upon the recommendation of the Minister" to remove the DG. Now, how should these provisions be interpreted? Some lawyers are saying, quite rightly, that while there is express provision for the involvement of the Minister in the DG's removal from office, there is no such provision for her involvement in the DG's suspension. If the Act had wanted the Minister to be involved in this, it would have been stated. If this is the case, then, the Minister has clearly acted *ultra vires,* (i.e. beyond her powers), and Gwarzo should have wasted no time in going to court to obtain a declaration to that effect. Better still, he could simply have gone straight to the President to have the suspension rescinded. The reason he did neither was not because he was just being nice to the Minister; it was because he and his legal team know they do not have a leg to stand on with that.

There is a common problem in this country with lawyers (and Ministers) wilfully sidestepping the extent of ministerial powers in their actions and mode of reasoning. Ministers act at the pleasure of the President. A Minister is the

---

267. Reported in 'Premium Times' and several dozen others, Mounir Gwarzo suspended as DG Securities and Exchange Commission, SEC — Premium Times Nigeria (premiumtimesng.com)

closest the President gets to sitting at the Ministerial desk himself. Ministers are, to all intent and purposes, spokespersons for Mr President at every turn. They do not have the ability to act even in a semi-detached way from the President. That is why sometimes, Ministers, faced with allegations of embezzlement, such as former Ministers under President Goodluck Jonathan, namely; Ibrahim Dasuki and Diezani Alison-Madueke, claimed, and are still claiming vigorously, that they acted with the authority of President Jonathan. Indeed, there is merit in that argument I would say.

The ISA, which Gwarzo and his lawyers are relying on to buttress their case against the Minister of Finance, makes oblique reference to the Minister/President umbilical cord type of relationship. For instance, section 5(1) of the Act does not permit the President to, willy-nilly, pick and choose who becomes DG of SEC. The section empowers the President to appoint the DG only "upon recommendation of the Minister and confirmation by the Senate". Furthermore, section 8(2) of the same Act gives the Minister power to recommend the DG's removal to the President. This is already a good hint of the enormous influence of the Minister in disciplinary matters involving the DG. Moreover, Section 148(1) of the constitution of the Federal Republic of Nigeria, 1999, takes this even further: "The President may, in his discretion, assign to.... any Minister of the Government of the Federation responsibility for any business of the Government of the Federation, including the administration of any department of government". This includes the SEC, which clearly falls within the purview of the Ministry of Finance. By the very appointment of the Minister, he or she acquires delegated authority to act in the name of the President. Suspension is a temporary measure; it should not be confused with removal. It is akin to the President's residual power to wage war in defence of the realm without first seeking Parliamentary approval. A war, once initiated, needs either to be adopted or rejected by the National Assembly subsequently. In a broad sense, ministerial power to suspend an officer under his line of supervision operates very much in a similar way.

Let us be abundantly clear, the Minister of Finance's first obligation to the Federal Republic of Nigeria is the sustainability of the nation's financial health. Capital market is not your run-of-the-mill parastatal; it absorbs and sometimes bleeds billions of Naira in minutes. The President has already assigned the Minister the obligation to act by the very wording of Section 148 (1) of the constitution. Consequently, the argument that the Minister needs an additional instrument specifying her right to suspend the DG is fallacious. It is non-sequitur. For the fastidious lawyer though, nothing short of an insertion of the Minister's right to suspend the DG in the ISA Act would suffice. Consequently, the Minister would have been better off simply recommending the DG's removal to the President right off. However, recommending removal is never the first step in any administrative proceeding. It is usually the last resort in fact. Investigation needs to be conducted and evidence collated in advance. What then is the Minister to do while this is going on? Sit back and allow the DG to remain in post even though it is her view that suspending him was needed to calm a jittery market? The power to suspend has to be implicit in the power to recommend removal because one is much less onerous than the other. Suspension paves the way to see if there is cause to recommend removal. And, if there is not, we go back to status quo ante. That is no more than the Minister has done in this case. It is plain common sense, is it not?

7.03 Why Nigerian Police Relish Parading Suspects

4 December 2018

Ideally, those who are charged with enforcing the law should not, themselves, become law breakers. This statement is simple enough and not given to any controversy, one would imagine? No, not if you are an officer of the Nigerian Police Force, apparently. Section 36 of the constitution of the Federal Republic of Nigeria, Article 7 of the African Charter on Human and Peoples' Rights, as well as a plethora of High Court rulings deprecating the act of parading suspects before trial are as clear as daylight on the protection given to the principle of fair hearing and the presumption of innocence of the accused. The Nigerian police on the other hand, are equally as blatant and downright nonchalant in their disregard of these constitutional safeguards for the citizen. On this fundamental issue of principle and sanctity of the Nigerian justice system, the police beg to differ; they regularly poke a finger in the eye of the law, placing themselves high above the law in this regard, while damning the consequences. What makes this more alarming from this column's standpoint is the seeming acquiescence of society at large about it. Our law makers and the executive branch of government are indifferent, civil society groups respond to it with inertia and the public feel pretty jaded about it all, seeing it as amusing and a piece of theatre to savour. The only people who feel burdened enough to highlight this odious element of our justice system in the media appear to be the odd individual and personalities with prescience and a weight to throw around. Why?

The answer to the above puzzle is traceable to the village-square mind-set of the pre-colonial era that still permeates the Nigerian police thinking in the modern era. In that frictionless communard populated by people aligned to a deep sense of right and wrong, where the sin of the father is usually visited on the sons, daughters and siblings of the wrongdoer, naming and shaming becomes a most potent tool in the hands of those entrusted with the responsibility of enforcing community rules. The mere mentioning of a person's name and the commission of a criminal act in the same sentence carries such opprobrium that the person so-named is shunned by the rest of the community, and is tainted for life thereafter. In the village square, one man's fortune is everybody's fortune. Conversely, one man's misdemeanour is everybody's cross to bear. The village-square mentality is a relic of a bygone order in a bygone culture where the individual is the community, and community the individual. We, nonetheless, and irrespective of the techno drama of the modern life, remain very much by-products of that tradition.

A more utilitarian explanation for the inexcusable police violation of the law in parading suspects is convenience and resources. The police are simply overwhelmed with levels of criminality in society, and little or no incentive for them to do a thorough job of investigating, especially amidst dwindling resources. It is a matter of interest to us in Africa to note that in the West, sometimes, authorities can spend one million dollars to investigate and convict a theft of one thousand dollars. For them, the end always justifies the means. The greater good and health of society requires that no sum is spared in the investigation and punishment of offenders. Here on the continent of Africa, we are yet to arrive at that level of sophisticated administration of justice. What we have, instead, is the law enforcement officers doing what appears to be their 'best' to curtail crime and criminality by harping on the naming and shaming logic of a by-gone age. It appears that the razzmatazz of parading suspects on TV and other media is an end in itself for the police; a wink to the public for marks for effort.

Linked to the question of resources is the police desire to promote deterrence by parading suspects. It is a cheaper and quicker way of achieving that it seems. What baffles right thinking citizens in this country, however, is that every police recruit ought to know that the mere fact of parading someone in public undermines their right to fair hearing. There is no smoke without fire, a lot of people would conclude, which also undermines the presumption of innocence until proven guilty in a court of law. Parading of suspects in Western jurisdiction is anathema to their notion of justice, and would not be countenanced in any way. The main reason for this being that there is a jury trial embedded in their system, which is absent in ours. Jury trial is a process by which twelve people randomly selected from the public where a crime was committed, sit in court, hear the evidence against the accused, and are then asked to pronounce on the person's guilt or innocence following a direction on the law from the judge. This is standard practice in most Western jurisdictions. By contrast, we do not have jury trial in our jurisdiction. A judge, sitting

232 7 · LAW

alone, usually hears the evidence against the accused and pronounces on guilt or innocence after lawyers on both sides have presented their arguments. We do not have jury trial in our jurisdiction for all sorts of reasons, chief amongst which is the problem of mass illiteracy, and inadequate database of citizens up and down the country. These anomalies are not insurmountable, but they are needed to be rectified first, to make jury selection truly neutral and random as it operates elsewhere. The argument runs then, that, under our system, trial by media has a minimal effect, since there is no jury to influence. Judges cannot be influenced by the media. Or can they?

Let us swiftly disabuse the mind of the reader by saying that notwithstanding their antiquarian wigs and gowns, judges are products of the same society which has given them the authority to sit in judgement of others. They too feel what others feel when confronted with the allusion of guilt on the face of a suspect being paraded in the media by police. That said, they, (the judges), ultimately hold the key to resolving this malaise once and for all. Every case brought in front of a judge where the accused is found to have been paraded beforehand ought to be dead on arrival. A police parade of a suspect should be enough to disable a subsequent trial in a court of law in this country, as it is fundamentally prejudicial to a fair hearing. So, no more endless judicial pronouncements on the need to stop the parade of suspects, no more point excoriating senior police officers for parading suspects when, based on the foregoing, the case against the accused is bound to be thrown out later by a judge. No more need to start waging a rear-guard effort endlessly suing the police. We need a hero amongst the judges; we need one ready to put his head above the parapet; one who would, ab initio, treat a case of police parade of a suspect as a jurisdictional issue. It should rank as a solid foundation for a preliminary objection which can be raised at any time during the proceedings. Once established, the judge does no more than throw out the case against the accused who had been paraded hitherto. Let the prosecution appeal against the decision to the Supreme Court, from here until Kingdom come. That would teach them. Above all, it would cut off the head of the marauding snake called police parade of suspects in this country by rendering it a futile exercise.

7.04 Legality of P&ID/$9.6bn award

3 September 2019

Justice Christopher Butcher of the High Court in London, last week, caused an uproar in Nigeria and beyond when he upheld the Court of Arbitration's award of $9.6bn against Nigeria in a case brought by Process and Industrial

Development Ltd (P&ID); a company with which the country entered into a contractual relationship in 2010 for processing and refining natural gas convertible into electrical energy and other domestic use. Nigeria was found to have been in breach of contract by not having followed through with the deal entered into by the administration of the late President Umaru Yar'Adua, and purportedly disowned by current President Muhammadu Buhari. Nigeria was taken to arbitration under the terms of the agreement in 2015, which handed down an original award of $6.6bn. It has since accumulated substantial interest making it $9.6bn as of today. It is the decision of the arbitration which has now been turned into the judgment of the high court. That effectively entitles the applicant, P&ID Ltd, to impound the assets of the Federal Government of Nigeria wherever located in the world, to the value of the award, estimated to be 20% of the country's external reserves. My comment in this write up is written squarely from the perspective of the law, devoid of politics and morality.

Nigeria entered into an agreement with P&ID to build a "state-of-the-art" gas processing plant to refine natural gas. The company (allegedly) then went ahead to commit several millions of dollars of its own money into the project on the expectation of a windfall from the deal later. In international contract negotiations of this nature, the nuts and bolts of the agreement would be trashed out, including what happens in case of a breach. In particular, provision would be made for dispute and method of its resolution should one arise between the parties. The "applicable law" to govern such a resolution and the "forum" (tribunal) where the case would be heard, would also have been worked out. By this very fact, therefore, why is the arbitration of a contract entered into in Nigeria, and designed for performance on Nigerian soil being litigated in the UK instead of Nigeria? The answer is the bargaining position of the parties involved at the time of the contract negotiation. It is commonplace that whichever party is in a stronger position would insist on the "applicable law" and forum being located in their home country. In this particular case, one (P&ID) has technology, the other (Nigeria) has natural resources; judge for yourselves which is stronger.

The next salient point is the appointment of arbitrators to officiate the dispute. What normally happens is that the two parties in a dispute appoint an arbitrator each, then, a chairman is appointed by mutual consent. So, Nigeria appointed Bayo Ojo (SAN), while P&ID appointed its own national, Evans Anthony. They then jointly appointed Lord (Baron) Hoffman as chairman. This is precisely where it all went horribly wrong for Nigeria. Cases of this nature are won and lost prior to the hearing for, process matters much more than substance and actual deliberation. Let me explain with a football analogy.

Imagine a Champions' League football final between a UK football team, say, Arsenal and a Spanish football team, say, Barcelona. Then, further imagine

234 7 · LAW

that the match is not only being played in Spain; the home turf of the opponent, but is also being refereed by a Spaniard. You can bet your bottom dollar that the UK Football Association would protest and kick up a fuss to no end. We can safely say that this scenario would not even be allowed in any event. In the world of commercial arbitration, however, it is routine. By consequence, there-fore, justice may have been done in the P&ID case, but it has clearly not been seen to have been done. That is the first important failure of the Nigerian legal team. If the arbitration must be heard in the UK, then, for heaven's sake, insist on a non-British citizen to preside as Chair. It can be done; indeed, it is done. There is another, even bigger point of failure to highlight.

If you must have your case heard and presided over by a citizen in the coun-try of the other party, then, do your homework on whoever is chairing the panel. Look closely at their judicial record to glean something in their jurispru-dence that could give you a BIG clue as to the likely view they would take in the case at hand. If the Nigerian legal team had asked me to consult for them on a chairman for the arbitration panel, I would have strongly advised against the choice of the highly regarded, but eminently predictable Lord Hoffman based on his past judicial pronouncements. He has recorded several landmark decisions, which would have pointed a smart lawyer to only one conclusion here. The most cited of his landmark rulings came in; **"Investors Compensation Scheme Ltd v West Bromwich Building Society"** [1997] **UKHL 28,** where he set out a "contextual approach" to the issue of a breach of contract based on the following five principles:

1. What a reasonable person having all the background knowledge would have understood
2. Where the background includes anything in the 'matrix of facts' that could affect the language's meaning
3. But excluding prior negotiations, for the policy of reducing litigation
4. Where meaning of words is not to be deduced literally, but contextually
5. On the presumption that people do not easily make linguistic mistakes

Any careful parsing of the above would have set the alarm bell off within the Nigerian legal team for; "a reasonable person having all the background knowl-edge would have understood" really means a Briton, like Lord Hoffman, in effect. Nigeria's special background knowledge, and business environment are of no import to him. So, when people in government now cry blue murder, that the whole contract was a sham, and the circumstances questionable, etc. that is simply whistling in the dark I am afraid. There is also the "presumption", according to Lord Hoffman's formidable judicial mind, that "people do not easily make linguistic mistakes". I beg your pardon, my Lord, people using English language as their second language could fall into a trap here, even if they are otherwise versed in the applicable law. Lord Hoffman ordinarily takes and applies an expansive interpretation of contracts, which should have sounded a high octane alarm on the suggestion of his nomination to chair the arbitration panel.

I would conclude by saying that Nigeria lost the case for want of due diligence. Nigeria has been caught napping before. The case against Cameroon over the resource-rich Bakassi region was lost in a similar fashion of tardiness and inadequate preparation. CBN Governor, Godwin Emefiele, was heard talking tough on this issue a couple of days ago. "The CBN is going to step forward and strongly defend the country and the reserves of the Federal Republic of Nigeria". This is medicine after death, I am afraid. Besides, P&ID are not waiting for a bank transfer from CBN; they are looking out for valuable Nigerian assets anywhere in the world to seize. Nigeria willingly took part in the judicial process, even her counsel on the panel, Bayo Ojo, (SAN), himself found against the government, diverging only on the amount of the fine. That undermines any notion that the process was unfair to Nigeria. All the country can hope and plead for now, on appeal, is a recalibration of the award leading to a massive, and drastic reduction in its quantum. Cancellation in its entirety would make a mockery of the whole judicial process. Meanwhile, P&ID's lawyers have promised to "vigorously enforce" the company's rights. You can hardly blame them for laughing all the way to the bank.

7.05 Politics of P&ID $9.6bn Award

10 September 2019

Last week, we examined the legality of the above humungous award against Nigeria, see; "Legality of P&ID $9.6bn award", PUNCH 03 September, 2019. The analysis in the discussion there was deliberately legalistic for the sake of objectivity. But, as often in this country, we operate in parallel universes; law and lawlessness, peace and conflict, silence and noise, order and chaos operate side by side with surprising ease in daily life. Things do happen in this country that boggles the mind to no end. To the foreign investor desirous of rich pickings in the Nigerian economy, the terrain can seem like one giant casino, where everything is accomplished by a sleight of hand than by canny and genius. How and where does a little-known company (a paper company for all practical purposes), registered in a far-flung remote island, with no tangible assets or record of delivering any large-scale technological or manufacturing projects anywhere in the world; P&ID, suddenly finds itself the beneficiary of a windfall, the size of the budget of West African governments combined, in the guise of an award for a "breach of contract"? It sounds rather like the stuff Nollywood movies are made of, except that this is actually true. We take a little time out in this piece to dissect the poli(tricks) of the award, and what, in broad terms, Nigeria can do to wriggle out of this contract of the century.

If we break down the original arbitration award of $6.6bn in favour of P&ID, it means that the company reckons that it would have made in the region of 200 billion naira a year in earnings from the deal. The owner of the company, Irishman Michael Quinn, who sadly passed away in 2015, must be turning in his grave at the news. What a shame the smartest wheeler-dealer Nigeria has ever known is no longer alive to give evidence of his genius in the court of public opinion in this country. He was the archetypal oligarch, so much a feature of life in Russia after the fall of the Soviet empire in 1989. The oligarch there and then was a man with the nous for a deal involving the combination of politics, money, influence, and natural resources. The oligarch is neither particularly knowledgeable in any field, nor particularly well educated in the conventional sense. All of that matter less than his ability to coax people into believing in the juicy, too-good-to-be-true offer he is dangling in front of them. I witnessed this first hand, working in the region as a consultant for a variety of international organisations at the time. The collapse of the former USSR (Union of Soviet Socialist Republics) was as spectacular as it comes. Egged on by Western financiers and governments, the vast area became a cornfield for all types of chicken to roam about and feed on. Russia, in particular, was badly hit. It had a vast amount of dormant oil and gas fields, which quickly became the target of the capitalist vultures, or venture capitalist, as they are called.

Shoving paper through officialdom and bureaucracy, and literally spewing out loads of cash from the other end was common practice. Plans and plants are built on paper; agreements entered into on behalf of the state with dates for delivery and implementation which never materialised, yet the people involved in the wheeling and dealing become mega millionaires, tycoons and power brokers with private militia guarding them around the clock. Such was the life of the Russian oligarch, until current President, Vladimir Putin, was voted into office with the mandate to clear out the Augean stable in 2000. He went after them with the full force of the state, and overwhelming public support. Putin has since retained power, moving from President to Prime Minister, and back again as President currently. It was also in the 1990s when Nigeria, and Africa in general, were being urged to sell off every government-owned corporation and business to relieve the state of crippling budget deficit, and

7 · LAW

to encourage private entrepreneurs to take the centre stage in economic activity. That was the prescription and new dictum from Washington, which still permeates the mode of public finance in Africa today. Privatisation and corporate greed are inherently good because the whole of society ultimately benefits from the trickle-down economics philosophy it engenders — or so the thinking goes. On this note, and on return to civilian rule in Nigeria in 1999, foreign 'investors' of all hews were invited to come and name their price as it were. It was within this foreign investors-as-saviours mentality that the P&ID contract must be understood. The company came and promised the Federal Government's negotiators pie in the sky technology that would resolve the country's energy woes almost overnight, and they jumped at it. It was a leap in the dark, which needed the connivance of people in high-level political circles to tie up, but hey, there will never be a shortage of citizens in this country willing to sign off their own mothers for a huge bonanza, let alone the interest of the Nigerian state to achieve the same.

There lies the genesis of the P&ID contract. It was cooked up (albeit) with the veneer of legality and uprightness. When you then employ the service of a top (retired) UK judge, Lord (Baron) Hoffman, renowned for his expansive view of contracts to preside over the arbitration panel, you have the proverbial icing on the cake; the missing link in the incredible jigsaw, signed sealed and delivered. Now, the question is, should Nigeria cough up the money to offset the rising penalty of $9.6bn, or not? The legal position was set out in this column last week. The political position is (no surprise) different.

The whole contract could be rescinded and thrown out by the courts if the government proves fraud. To succeed, clear evidence of criminal conspiracy to defraud has to be made out. This is easier said than done, however. It is looking for a needle in a haystack. For a start, the man at the centre of the deal is no longer with us. Moreover, it would depend on what the terms of the agreement say. Besides, if the fraudsters were part of the Nigerian elite that encouraged the deal *ab initio*, that complicates matters even more. On the other hand, Nigeria could file a criminal suit at the High Court, in this country, arguing that the whole scheme was conceived and built on sand from start to finish. Also, that the egregious award is the manifestation of a gigantic corruption snare involving fellow Nigerians colluding with foreign nationals to fleece the nation. There is almost certainly no concrete evidence in place to substantiate this theory, but that is missing the point. The circumstantial evidence to support it should and could be made as strong and effective as it is possible to adduce under the circumstances. So it is over to you, President Buhari. Your administration either keeps it a straightforward civil suit as set out last week, or makes a dash for *gburu-gburu* counter-attack, wipe the smug smile off the faces of the P&ID lawyers, as they retreat from the courtroom with fleas in their ears.[268]

7.06 Legality of Government's Raid on Pension Funds

15 December 2020

Pension funds, by definition, are monies put aside on behalf of employees, which are then paid to them in monthly instalments upon retirement from full time work. For millions of retirees, it's the only source of living in old age. Many have toiled day and night for decades, putting a little on the side for up-keep in the twilight of their lives. The people in charge of the funds; Pension Fund Administrators, owe the utmost 'fiduciary' (i.e. sacred) duty to their members not to do anything that could put the funds in the slightest jeopardy. A breach of that duty quite rightly attracts the severest punishment under the law across all jurisdictions. The funds are to be treated not only with the highest due diligence, but also treated as if millions of lives depended on it, which indeed is the case. For employers, (be it government or company bosses), pension funds are the holy grails of investment savings; they are the nearest thing to God's personal property in the financial world. They are the only 'thing' no government, governor, minister, or company executive wants to dip into, ever. You would sell your own house first, before considering dipping into pension funds for whatever purpose, because it carries such enormous moral burden. So, it came as bewildering that the Nigerian Governors' Forum last week approved a "borrowing" requirement of some 2 trillion naira from the pension funds for "infrastructure". The effortless, breezy nature of the announcement (via a virtual meeting of the governors) was breath-taking, even more so are the ramifications.

Public knowledge or interest in pension funds administration has never been at an all-time high in any jurisdiction, unless, and until some scandal has occurred involving its handling. It is also appropriate to declare my own interest here as a capital markets lawyer. Pension funds play a big role in capital markets. The funds are used not only for the long-term benefits of retirees, but more significantly, for the immediate benefits of the market. A

---

268. The award was set aside by the court on appeal by Nigeria, in September 2020, as widely reported across the international media. For example; Nigeria floors P&ID as UK court grants relief from $10bn fine | TheCable

7 · LAW

retiree would normally expect to receive up to 2/3 of his last final salary on a 'defined benefits' scheme. So-called, because it is specified in the setup. Nowadays, the emphasis is on 'defined contributions' or money purchased scheme, as what an individual takes out depends on how well the contributions have performed in the markets. Pension fund managers are really big players in the markets, the largest of which are linked to state-owned enterprises. The Dutch post office in Europe is one such huge scheme. And CalPERS (the California Public Employees' Retirement System) with assets close to $200 billion is the largest in the world.[269] Pension funds administrators invest in a whole gamut of financial instruments; government and corporate bonds, shares in leading companies, private equity funds, real estates, derivatives, currencies, even loans to companies or what is generally known as the 'credit market'.

In Nigeria, the total pension assets, (market capitalisation), currently stands at N11.65 trillion (or US$ 31 billion) according to data from the National Pension Commission (PenCOM), out of which N7.5 trillion (US$19 billion) has already been used for investment in Federal Government Securities.[270] As if that was not enough exposure, the Federal Executive Council had, in January this year, concluded plans to borrow 2 trillion naira from the funds, gulping close to 80% of the pension funds' market capitalisation.[271] Nigerian Pension Funds are effectively being used as the Federal Government's official piggy bank. It is even more galling that governments in this country are not known for diligently paying their employees' contributions, but one is now so willing to dip into the funds by fiat; as if by entitlement. The hands of the pension fund administrators are willy-nilly tied to the government's apron strings, as they are no longer able to diversify and maximise the funds at their own discretion. Whilst not being illegal, it is a major breach of the administrator's fiduciary obligation. 'Legality' and 'fiduciary' obligations are two different things in law. A fiduciary does not need to have acted illegally to be in breach. That is what makes it such an onerous responsibility, as it extends far beyond the confines of civil or criminal law. Now, can government commandeer, or compel a loan advance from the pension funds? The answer is categorically NO. "Pension Fund Administrator and Pension Fund Custodian shall take

---

269. For a detailed examination of the funds, see; California Public Employees' Retirement System — CalPERS

270. Details obtained from the Pension Commission (PENCOM) National Pension Commission | Regulators of the Nigerian Pension Industry (pencom.gov.ng)

271. From various media reports, which have not been denied. Workers, retirees kick as FG plans N620bn loan from pension funds — Punch Newspapers (punchng.com)

240   7 · LAW

reasonable care to ensure that the management or custody of the pension funds is carried out in the best interests of the retirement savings account holders" (Pension Reform Act, 2014, S. 69(b)).

To buttress this provision even more solidly, section 85(1) of the same Act states: "All contributions made under this Act shall be invested by the Pension Fund Administrators with the objectives of safety and maintenance of fair returns on amount invested". The operative word is "invest", not gratuitous lending to government. It is not the business of pension funds administrators to promote, let alone assist the objective of government. Their only concern is the "best interests of the retirement savings account holders". Government cannot, repeat, CANNOT mandate a loan agreement on pension fund administrators in aid of any infrastructure programme. That is a judgement call for the administrators alone. Then, how could they (the fund administrators) choose to 'invest' in a paper infrastructure programme? The programme only exists as a wish of the governors in cahoots with the Federal Government at this point in time. The guidelines for pension funds administration issued by PenCOM make no reference to government or anyone for that matter, borrowing from the funds. The commission reports directly to the President of the Federal Republic of Nigeria, and can issue fresh guidelines permitting government borrowing from the fund. It is not sure if this has been done. Again, when commercial banks are charging 20–30% interest rate for borrowers, is the government proposed borrowing from the funds at the juicy rate of 9% per annum the fairest deal considering its duration?

Apart from the above technical details, what many people would find most disconcerting about the whole idea of a government's raid on pension funds is simply that it distorts the market by moving money away from industry to government. It is like robbing Peter to pay Paul. As pointed out earlier, when government acquires interest in 80% of the pension funds' total market capitalisation, it leaves the funds overexposed to risk from a singular source. We are told that the funds are to be diverted into the "sovereign wealth" account, which provides guarantee of its security, but that is not the main point. While not being illegal, the cosy deal is illogical, and probably unethical, especially if, and a BIG if, the 'infrastructure' funds are later converted into revenue, or worst, turned into some type of "stomach infrastructure" at the implementation stage. In that scenario, the funds would have metamorphosed from pension to slush funds. I know this sounds rather harsh on the governors who, I am sure, are acting in good faith, but I equally hope they find some illumination in this analysis as well. Having a good intention is not nearly enough when dealing with pension funds. In their fiduciary duty, the fund administrators ought not to be kow-towing to government requests, but should maintain focus on prudential investment at all times. They seem to have taken their eyes off the ball at the moment. It is also not certain whether the relevant National Assembly Committees have taken an interest in this as they should. The raid on the pension funds smacks of desperation on the part of government, but it is also clear evidence of sloppiness on the part of PenCOM.

7.07 Malami's 'Open' Road to Anarchy

25 May 2021

Significant column inches have already been devoted to the intractable issue of 'open grazing' here and elsewhere in the last couple of years, and quite rightly so. It is thus with some reluctance that the topic is being flagged up here again for the umpteenth time. In view of the Attorney General, Abubakar Malami's pronouncement on the issue a few days ago, on the 19th of May 2021, that Fulani herder's right to open grazing is guaranteed under the constitution, it became imperative that this column joins issues with him on the law. It is often said that where law ends, anarchy reigns. The Attorney General of the Federation, and Chief Law Officer to the Buhari Administration has flung the door wide open to anarchy by his inversion of the law on open grazing. The Attorney General said on TV: "It is about constitutionality, within the context of the freedoms enshrined in our constitution, can you deny a right of a Nigerian?" Malami is not a man known for weighing his words carefully, apart from the fact that he lets politics gets in the way of his judicial thinking much too often. Does the right to open grazing apply in equal measure to, say, a pig farmer roaming freely inside the confines of neighbourhood yards, and cities in parts of the north? Or a goat herder trampling on any land he sees fit for his stock? Honourable Attorney General, please note; there is no such thing as an absolute right enshrined anywhere in the constitution of the Federal Republic of Nigeria, not even the right to life itself. There is a problem when the exercise of one person's right infringes on the right and liberty of another.

The second issue is about power over land, and whether the southern governors need to seek to amend the constitution in order to effect a ban on open grazing. That is the view of the AG. He is fundamentally wrong on that too. The Land Use Decree 1978 expressly states: "All land comprised in the territory of each State in the Federation are hereby vested in the Military Governor of that State and such land shall be held in trust and administered for the use and common benefit of all Nigerians in accordance with the provisions of this Decree". We no longer have Military Governors; of course, civilian governors are now walking in their shoes. The Decree has made its way into the fabric of the

242   7 · LAW

constitution, and is now firmly established as an Act of the National Assembly. It has been so woven into the fabric of the constitution that it is almost impossible to amend, let alone overturn. Consequently, governors, be it of the south or north, not only have the right, but an obligation to act as trustees of the land in their territories. It is submitted, therefore, that it is the Attorney General of the Federation (not the governors) who must seek to amend the constitution to nullify the southern governors' collective policy of a ban on open grazing in their territories.

As things stand, cattle herders can ply their trade on any land, anywhere in the country unhindered by anyone, according to Malami. Is the Attorney General saying that cattle herders have an inherent right to trespass on other people's land without consequence? Really? The AG has unwittingly created a state of anarchy where everyone would naturally want to protect and jealously guard his privacy and property. By consequence, they would resort to self-help in order to accomplish that. It is the classic Hobbesian state, where everyone is an island entirely of itself. Cattle herders can migrate from north to south, enter a farmer's backyard at will, graze, and damage crops, then, saunter off as if nothing happened. What about the farmer's exclusive right to his land and livelihood? What is a state governor supposed to do in order to protect life and property in his domain? Fold his arms and send a text to the Attorney General? The AG's public utterances on this and other similarly significant public law events have fallen short of the high standard of reasoning normally associated with the office. He does not appear to see himself principally as a law officer, but rather, as a party hack. He has brought his office to ridicule on a number of occasions (see, for examples; "Malami: Legally incoherent, fundamentally flawed" the PUNCH January 30 2020, and "Maina's disappearance: Albatross around Malami's neck" the PUNCH December 1 2020). On this occasion, the learned silk has sought to draw an analogy between banning open grazing in the southern states with banning the sale of spare parts in the north. Spare part dealers are legitimate traders, but are predominantly of the Igbo ethnic stock. It is clearly a comparison between apples and oranges; a failed attempt at beclouding the issue with an opaque reference to ethnicity. This pedestrian response to the burning issue of the day, from a Senior Advocate of Nigeria, let alone the Attorney General of the Federation, is simply mind-boggling.

It is difficult to pin down exactly whose interest the AG is protecting without opening up a can of worms. It seems clear, however, that he is not upholding the wider public's interest in this instance. What is even more worrying is the fact that the normal checks and balances weaved into the apparatus of governance do not appear to be working in Nigeria. The AG's place at the heart of government is as secure as it has ever been. We do not see reaction, for instance, from the Senate Judiciary Committee, neither do we hear anything from the Bar Council holding the Chief Law Officer to account. Ultimately though, the question, the battle, is not going to be legal but political. It does not matter a dime what the feckless AG does or says; it matters more where the public stand on the issue. Open grazing has become a euphemism for lawlessness, clannishness and brigandage. It is tapping into a dangerous narrative that, in Buhari's Nigeria, there is one law for a section of the population, and another for the others. For the moment at least, the pushback on that is being spearheaded by the political elite themselves. But, soon, it will spill over onto the streets, and the bushes, leaving bloodshed and mayhem in its wake. It is part of a larger ongoing battle for the soul of Nigeria. To ameliorate the outcome, the seventeen governors must not relent; they must up the ante as it were. The collective ban on open grazing must be put into effect forthwith. Otherwise, they will have been exposed to public ridicule themselves with devastating consequences for their reputation and authority. The prediction from this column — for whatever it is worth — is that the open grazing saga will re-energise the push and shove of the north versus south conundrum, but will end in a closing of ranks by the ruling click. Those hoping for more must pitch their tent elsewhere.

Chapter Eight

Military

8.01 Nigeria: Still Under Shadows of Military

13 February 2018

The first generation of voters born under a civilian administration, and who have not tasted a day of military rule ever in this country, will cast their ballot at next year's Presidential election. They, and the generations after them will (hopefully) find any idea of power through the barrel of the gun so repugnant that they will resist any such order with every fibre of their being. It is also hoped that as bad as, and as disillusioned as many of them may feel about the so-called "dividends of democracy" not accruing to them, they will remain resolute in their conviction that to live in poverty under an elected civilian administration is far better than living in luxury under a military dictatorship. The "pro-democracy" struggles so stoutly and remorselessly fought to chase the military out of civilian life in this country feels so distant and so remote to the younger generations now that many would not even know who MKO Abiola or General Ibrahim Badamasi Babangida were, if asked. The era of democratic dispensation is upon us and is apparently here to stay. Or, so it seems, until you realise that although military personnel may no longer be directly running the show from the Presidential Palace, we are, nonetheless, living under the mores and norms of a military regime. It is a kind of civilianised military order. There are two interlocking aspects to this. First, is the intellectual, and second is the symbolism.

It is self-evidently true that we have not made the requisite intellectual shift from thinking military to thinking civilian in this country. For instance, take a look at our constitution, which is a total contraption by the military. Military order dictates that things are run from the omnipresent centre; the man at the top sneezes, and the rest catch cold. Even though we profess to live under a federal system of government, yet decision-making on virtually every aspect of our lives are made from the centre. This extends from community policing to decisions on whether potholes in rural highways are fixed. States were created, but deliberately rendered powerless by the entrenchment of the so-called "exclusive list" of items that can only be dealt with at the Presidency. Civilian life itself has been militarised and remained so that everyone is acting out the script without being conscious of doing so. How many times have people received notices from their permanent secretaries and departmental heads, expecting things to be done with that perpetual military drumbeat: "with immediate effect"? Or the executive blatantly and flagrantly flouting court orders and damning the consequences? Or military personnel on the streets feeling so emboldened to mete out on-the-spot "discipline" on an "unruly" citizen? Or ordinary citizens erecting a structure and pasting "keep out, military zone" on its frontage!? The Land Use Decree of 1978 was an attempt at a land grab by the powerful and mighty; the military. The 1999 constitution made it virtually impossible to repeal it. It is given the same status as a major constitutional amendment requiring all sorts of political and legislative hurdles to overcome. It is the only Act given such a rarefied status in any constitution in the modern world.

If you find the above references a bit heartrending, then, consider the pervasive symbols of the military casting a shadow over our daily lives without anyone even thinking twice about them. We regularly have military and police senior hierarchies popping up on our television screens to, as it were, read the Riot Act on a whole range of public policy issues, when in fact, we have responsible ministers who should be laying out government policy even on live security issues. That is the essence of having a civilian rule. Have you also noticed the conspicuous presence of police "orderlies" standing guard behind Mr President, Governors and High Court judges? Has anyone ever explained why we need to have uniformed personnel on display in such a manner? Are Nigerian political leaders so vain and insecure that they need the presence of uniformed officers to bolster their prestige? What about leaders in advanced countries, who rely on plain-clothed as opposed to uniformed officers hovering above them in public places? Are they any less protected from harm? Perhaps the most ridiculous display of crude power is seen inside the courts with our judges and uniformed officers standing guard behind them. The judges can be adequately protected by plain-clothed police even more effectively than uniformed officers lacking basic communication equipment from what we know. Our political leaders revel in uniformed officers panting and wheezing behind them because it is the ultimate symbol and display of their power and authority. That is a shame though, because the very presence of those officers behind them robs them of substantive leadership. Civilian leadership and authority emanate from the people; not armed uniformed officers.

Against this background, it remains a matter of curiosity that our civilian governors and presidents have found cause to maintain the military tradition of displaying the image of state governors in public buildings in their states alongside that of whoever is the current President of the Federal Republic of Nigeria. What is the rationale behind the gratuitous display of a governor's photograph on public buildings in their state? Is it to accord them respect? God help any governor who needs his image displayed on public buildings in order for him to feel respected. Respect, as a matter of principle, is earned; not demanded, not least by here today, gone tomorrow politicians of all hues. Is it then to engineer adulation and affection of the public? For some, maybe, but these should happen naturally, flowing directly from the performance of the leader. You see, those photographs are put on display for no other rational basis than to generate intimidation and subservience. It also serves as a reminder to the public who is boss. The "constituted authority", one pumped up governor once shamelessly boasted. They are the ones at whose behest we march in and out of those clumsy office buildings. The question is why, in a country of free, independent and proud people, do we need to be tele-guided into an enforced adulation of any public figure? Why has it not occurred to any governor of a state to reject any display of their image on the walls of public buildings? Those governors are not our bosses anyway; they are public servants. Those buildings belong to US; not them.

Finally, Mr President, please lead by example on this. Withdraw all displays of your photograph on public buildings in this country. You do not own any of the structures or the land upon which they are erected. You are only a short-term tenant of one of them; Aso Rock. What is more, we do not need reminding who you really are, neither are we interested in acknowledging your sub-conscious presence in our workplaces every single minute of every working day. Keep your photographs on display for the admiration of your friends and family in your private house and spare us these nauseating images of presidents and governors adorning our public buildings up and down this country once and for all. Thank you!

8.02 Nigerian Military's Conflict of Loyalties

24 November 2020

Take a note of this statement: "I want to humbly express my profound gratitude to Mr President and Commander-in-Chief of the Armed Forces of the Federal Republic of Nigeria, President Muhammadu Buhari GCFR, for his continued and invaluable support to the NA in the discharge of its constitutional roles. Therefore, I wish to pledge the commitment and unalloyed loyalty of officers and soldiers of the NA to the President and the defence of our democracy". Compared to this: "We are unique among militaries. We do not take an oath to a king or a queen, a tyrant or a dictator. We do not take an oath to an individual. No, we do not take an oath to a country, a tribe or religion. We take an oath to the Constitution. And every soldier that is represented in this museum, every sailor, airman, Marine, Coastguardsman, each of us will protect and defend that document, regardless of personal price". No price for guessing; the first statement was issued by the Nigerian Chief of Army Staff, Lieutenant General Tukur Buratai, to the armed forces on November 3 2020. The second was issued by General Mark Miley, Chairman, US Joint Chiefs of Staff, on November 12 2020. It does not take a genius to work out which of the statements reflects core democratic values. It is also interesting to note that the former was issued by a Chief of Army Staff, (not Chief of Defence Staff) who, *de jure*, speaks for the uniformed personnel in Nigeria, and the latter, by the Chairman, Joint Chiefs of Staff who does the same in America.

As stated, in the US, the top military adviser to the President is the Chairman, Joint Chiefs of Staff, known in Nigeria as Chief of Defence Staff, (modelled after the British). The position is currently held by General Abayomi Olonisakin. To the best of my knowledge, he is an obscure figure most Nigerians have never heard of. In normal events, that would be quite rightly so, but in the scheme of things in Nigeria, his reticence is capable of more than one interpretation. Any warnings of 'unrest', 'panic', or 'anxiety' in the rank and file ought to come from the very top. General Olonisakin appears to be the 'boss' in name only. Lieutenant General Buratai has never shied away from taking the centre stage since his appointment. He sees himself as the man with the last word on military affairs; the *de facto* number one. He is a man who would serve and expect all uniformed personnel in Nigeria to sacrifice their lives in a stern defence of his Commander-in-Chief, President Muhammadu Buhari, based on the bespoke motto: my Commander-in-Chief to the last drop of blood. That gives the word sycophancy a whole new meaning. The immediate question then is, does he feel personally (and uniquely) obliged to President Buhari, or would he hold the same stance

8 · MILITARY

regardless of who the Commander-in-Chief is? This is not the first time Buratai has come out for President Buhari with guns blazing. This column has found cause to chastise him on that before. (See; "Armed forces loyalty is to the constitution, not Mr President" the PUNCH, August 6 2019).

In a properly functioning democracy, it is rare and unusual for the top military brass to wade into a politically-charged situation. Outgoing US President Donald Trump, however, has been as erratic as he has ever been since his loss to Joe Biden at the November 3 2020 presidential election. Not surprisingly, therefore, he has been firing and hiring top personnel at random, especially ousting anyone adjudged to hold a view contrary to his, regardless of truth. For Trump, truth is what he says it is at any point in time. His aides often create a set of "alternative facts" for him to dwell on. There is evidence of his intention to rush through a military overhaul in America's theatres of war, especially in Afghanistan, Iraq and others. The top civilian personnel at the Pentagon (US Ministry of Defence) are said to be against what they see as a 'rash' move by the president. Trump has therefore been firing those he considers to be against his authoritarian instincts within the military. Given that he has also refused to concede defeat in the election, all of that combined was enough to force the US top military brass to issue what was effectively a rebuke and a clear warning to the president. Although there was the #EndSARS protests in the Nigerian situation, President Buhari's unexpectedly measured response is a credit to his administration. He towers above the US President in that regard. Who could have imagined? Trump once referred to Buhari as "lifeless", quite uncharitably.[272]

That said, on one side in Nigeria are those protesting police brutality and calling for fundamental change in the overall structure of governance, and on the other, are those desirous of preserving the status quo. Buratai has sought to place the military firmly on the side of the latter, drawing the institution close to the realm of partisan politics. Western military training and doctrine (TRADOC) has its origins both in United States' "West Point", and the Royal Military Academy, Sandhurst, England. Roughly 10% of the recruits at "Sandhurst" are foreigners (many of them Nigerians and people from the Commonwealth countries). There is much emphasis on the importance of the military to subordinate itself to civilian authority. Political power must emanate from

---

272. Covered widely in the media across the globe. For instance; "Trump referred to Buhari as 'lifeless' — Financial Times, 'The Guardian', August 27, 2018. Trump referred to Buhari as 'lifeless' — Financial Times | The Guardian Nigeria News — Nigeria and World News — Nigeria — The Guardian Nigeria News — Nigeria and World News. Also; "Twitter Reacts as Trump Calls Buhari 'Lifeless,'" Twitter Reacts As Trump Calls Buhari 'Lifeless' — The Whistler Newspaper

250 8 · MILITARY

the ballot box; not from the barrel of the gun. In America, the constitution guarantees liberty and freedom of the individual, which the military swear an oath to defend regardless of "personal price". That is firm and unequivocal enough. That of the British is a little more complicated. The British army is not the people's army, since the military belongs to the Monarchy. The clue is in the name; "Royal Military" Academy. This has been so for 800 years of Parliamentary government. Military personnel swear allegiance to the Monarch; the very notion for which Americans went to war against them between 1775 and 1783. It is precisely what General Miley was referencing in his statement; a kind of timely reminder to Donald Trump and people of his ilk.

By insisting on the military's personal pledge of loyalty to President Buhari, Buratai was borrowing a leaf from the British. But, the last time I checked, Buhari is not a Monarch. Or, is he? The Nigerian military has been walking the tightrope of the British and American models almost from inception. The top echelons admire the personal loyalty angle of the British, while at the same time, aspiring to the Republican ideals of the US military. Nigeria sends officers to both training grounds on a continual, regular basis, who then return to occupy the top tiers of the military having acquired the best of both worlds, but within a schizophrenic mind-set. This is what lies at the heart of the conflict of loyalties. The lack of solid doctrinal footing gives the top brass the kind of latitude that is not even open to officers either at West Point, or Sandhurst. It is a dangerous latitude for, it gives Nigerian military leaders a discretion on core democratic principles. Let us also remember that even in Britain, military loyalty to "Queen and country" is anchored on the genius of 'Parliamentary Sovereignty'. The Nigerian military, at the moment, is too detached from the reality (and indeed, imperatives) of democratic accountability. Having only relinquished power in 1999, it still suffers the withdrawal symptoms. It sees itself as the landlord of 'Aso Rock', who reserves the right of re-entry, and repossession. It is an institution operating like an island entire of itself. This cannot go on; it must change.

8.03 AFRICOM: Buhari's White Flag of Surrender

4 May 2021

United States Africa Command (AFRICOM) is one of America's eleven major military bases dotted around the globe for the purpose of protecting and defending America's national security interests, and that of its allies. America, being the leading Western military superpower, has been bearing the brunt of Western security since the end of WWII. The 1960s Cold War ideological rivalry between the former Soviet bloc and the West made it more imperative that America expanded its military operations around the globe to curtail the spread of communism and make the world safe for capitalism. Though Africa has been of strategic interest to the US throughout this period, it did not consider having a coordinated military 'command' focused on the continent. The military operations it ran in Africa, conducted mainly through mercenaries, and with local help from many puppet regimes installed across the continent at the time, went fairly well for the US. Africa had been prevented from falling into the hands of hostile communist regimes from outside the continent. Moreover, the US did not really want to be seen as another Western colonial power, dictating the destiny of the Africans in the way the Europeans did in the 19th and 20th centuries. Remember, America itself had to go through their own "war of independence" (1775–1783). So, the US had maintained a tactical distance from direct military installations on African soil for this very reason. American had fought to dislodge imperialism from its own soil, and did not wish to be seen as a neo-imperialist force, at least, not in broad daylight.

The above calculation changed, suddenly, in the 2000s, a decade after the collapse of the former Soviet bloc. The old Cold War enemy was in retreat, and a "clash of civilisations"[273] took hold, with violent extremism and "Islamic" and "Jihadist" terrorism which began to re-build and re-shape new geo-political alliances. The attack on the Twin Towers in New York trade centre on September 11 2001 crystallised this new reality for US foreign policy and defence establishment. Africa was willy-nilly dragged into the spotlight — again. The continent was no longer staring down the barrel of a communist takeover, but is now, instead, perceived to be vulnerable to Islamic-inspired terrorism, posing a direct threat to vital US interest in Africa. Because the shape of the new threat is disparate and uncoordinated, since there was no identifiable state spearheading the new 'global jihadist' agenda, the hitherto tactical distance the US had maintained in terms of military installation on African soil needed a quick rethink hence, the decision to create AFRICOM to rank amongst others in Europe (EUCOM), Central Command (CENTCOM), Pacific Command (PACOM) and others. What makes AFRICOM so interesting, indeed, so jarring from Nigeria and Africa's point of view is this. In the early 19th century, when European powers decided on the partition of Africa, they summoned

---

273. See Samuel Huntington's provocative book; The Clash of Civilisations and the Remaking of World Order. Simon and Schuster, 1997, The Clash of Civilizations and the Remaking of World Order: Huntington, Samuel P.: 9781451628975: Amazon.com: Books

252   8 · MILITARY

their political and military generals into a cartographic room in Berlin, Germany, to share out portions of Africa that suited their fancy at the infamous "Berlin Conference" in 1885. The Palestinians describe the founding of the Jewish state, Israel, on their land in 1948 as "al Nakba", or the Catastrophe. The Berlin Conference of 1885 was Africa's al-Nakba.

Fast forward to the modern day, when the US made up its mind on a forced military 'supervision' of African territories in 2007; guess where it decided to pitch its tenth? Yes, you guessed it, Stuttgart, Germany; a stone throw away from Berlin. That is not the only coincidence. AFRICOM was established on the 1st of October, Nigeria's Independence Day. You do not have to be a security analyst to see the symbolism involved in these. AFRICOM being physically located in far-away Germany, the US can still avoid being cast in the shadow of an imperial force, which does not sit comfortably with its avowed Republican ideal. For Kwame Nkrumah and his Pan-Africanist disciples, this is a case of 'we told you so, Africa'. Nkrumah was the first directly elected President of Ghana, who fought till his last breath for a united Africa in order to combat external (neo-colonial) aggression. Without unity, he stated time and again, Africa was doomed. Nigeria was one of many 'conservative' voices of opposition to Nkrumah's agenda to 'dominate' Africa. Guess who is dominating Africa now? As if this was not enough of a betrayal, President Muhammadu Buhari, a regional leader in Sub-Saharan Africa, and a leading voice in the new African Continental Free Trade Area (AfCFTA), an arm of the 'African Union', is now appealing to the US to relocate AFRICOM to Africa itself! That clearly is the white flag of surrender and goodbye to any lingering illusion about African unity some people might still be nursing. But why on earth would the Nigerian leader do this? It is either the greatest foreign policy blunder by a Nigerian leader in history, or a masterstroke of tactical genius by the Nigerian President and his advisers, designed to outmanoeuvre the US.

First on the latter, the Nigerian military under President Buhari has been firing blank of late. On the battlefield with domestic terrorism, it has almost lost the will to fight, let alone defeat the enemy. So, how convenient would it be to have the strongest military on earth to suddenly locate its array of sophisticated weapons, I am sure, (Buhari would ultimately prefer), to Katsina,[274] or even better, Maiduguri.[275] In that respect, Boko Haram could be wiped off in a jiffy. And those agitating for "restructuring" could be silenced by the sheer presence of a mini-Pentagon on Nigerian soil, whose preference is always to

---

274. The President's home state.
275. The stronghold of the terrorist outfit; Boko Haram.

preserve the status quo. On a larger plane, the security analysts in Aso Rock might have also made a broad sweep of US military presence in several strategic locations such as: South Korea, Germany, Japan, and the Middle-East, and concluded that Africa should be no exception. America's military presence in those political hotspots have kept the peace at little (direct financial) cost to the host countries. Furthermore, US military presence in Iraq has allowed the ruling clique there to consolidate power at the expense of the vast majority of the population. Same could be said of US military presence in Saudi Arabia and the Philippines. So, there are innumerable examples of places where the US military might have been a force for good they reckon. Why not in Africa? As facile as this reasoning might sound, it is not beyond imagination that it is precisely the premise upon which Buhari had based his appeal to the US. "In my call with US Secretary of State Blinken, I asked the US to consider relocating the AFRICOM HQ from Germany to Africa—near the Theatre of Operation; against the backdrop of growing security challenges in West and Central Africa, Gulf of Guinea, Lake Chad region of the Sahel". Buhari said via Twitter on the 27th of April 2021.

The main problem with this reasoning, is that it is plain wrong. US would not commit its military to any region without a quid-pro-quo. That is to say, America would not give something for nothing. What could that 'something' represent for Africa you might ask? Natural resources of course! What else? If the Chinese are all over Africa with their 'loose cash', and America joins them with their guns and military fatigues, then, who governs Africa? I mean, who would have the last word on the question? Perish the thought, a Nigerian leader? I guarantee many readers of this column would never have thought they would live to see the day when a Nigerian leader would capitulate so meekly to the allure of a recolonised Africa, even in the face of the most desperate political and economic circumstances. Nkrumah must be turning in his grave.

8.04 Africa and the 'Corrective Coup' Syndrome

14 September 2021

That a democratically elected government is the only form of legitimate authority over people has become an incontrovertible mantra for political leaders throughout the developing world, at least in the last twenty years, is not in doubt. It is written in gold in national legal texts, in constitutions, United Nations, and Regional Charters. Echoes of it reverberate in National Assemblies and in military barracks across the continent and beyond. Coup is no longer

254   8 · MILITARY

fashionable, or so it is thought. It has become such an aberration that it is swiftly condemned wherever it occurs. And so, it was that the military coup led by Col Mamady Doumbouya, that ousted the civilian government of President Alpha Condé of the Republic of Guinea, last week, the 5th of September 2021, has been roundly condemned by governments and world bodies. The Nigerian Ministry of Foreign Affairs issued a statement declaring; "The Government of Nigeria strongly condemns and rejects any unconstitutional change of government and therefore calls on those behind this coup to restore constitutional order without delay and protect all lives and property". That sounds good in so far as it goes. It is noteworthy, however, that Nigeria is treating this as a "foreign affairs" matter, not worthy of a direct Presidential intervention, and not minding the fact that one third of the Guinean population is Fulani, and two thirds of the West African regional population are Nigerians.[276] And it is also where Nigeria has toiled day and night for a unified regional bloc since 1975.

Furthermore, that the statement came from the Ministry of Foreign Affairs instead of it coming directly from the Presidency shows how little faith Nigeria still has in the West African regional integration project as a worthy cause. More importantly, it is an indictment of Nigeria's claim to leadership in the sub-region. Where is the 'giant of Africa' at such a critical moment when it was needed? Yes, Nigeria has mobilised other nations in the ECOWAS to suspend Guinea from its membership, but if this is all the energy Nigeria could muster in the face of a brutal attack on constitutional order in its backyard, then, that alone speaks volumes. Nigeria has no claim to the leadership of one inch of land outside its shores. All the other nations in the sub-region will have watched in dismay how the Nigerian army (the largest, and supposedly best equipped in the region) has, for years, glaringly failed to tame the ragtag Boko Haram group of 'bandits' and others. They even mounted a dawn raid on the most elite, heavily guarded, heavily fortified Nigerian Defence Academy with such ease, a couple of weeks ago. Now, is Col Doumbouya having sleepless nights over a possible reaction from Nigeria? You guessed right. Nigeria has no moral standing at any level vis-à-vis its neighbours. All the country can do in a crisis situation like this is huff and puff, throw up its diplomatic hands in horror, then go back to sleep.

Nigeria's low-key reaction to the coup in Guinea also betrays a greater fear that it could happen here too. Democracy is neither a fait accompli, nor a done

---

276. This is easily verified by data from numerous sources. See, for example; Nigeria Population 2022 (Demographics, Maps, Graphs) (worldpopulationreview.com)

deal for anyone on the continent of Africa. The spectre of a 'corrective coup' looms large on the African psyche. It permeates both the military and civilian landscape. The era of forcible change of government will never be over until the era of mass poverty is over. There is not a single country on the continent immune from this societal malaise. For emphasis, it is not a military problem; it is one of society. Let us not forget, whilst the rest of the world mouths righteous condemnation, the coup has been warmly embraced by the opposition and the general population inside Guinea itself. The ousted President is a textbook example of an elected leader gone rogue; a familiar trait in politicians of all hues in Africa. Alpha Condé is a French Ivy-League educated 'pro-democracy activist' with a strong record of fighting for the fundamental rights of Guineans. Lest anyone be confused, there are three countries in Africa sharing the name Guinea; Equatorial Guinea (1.5m), Guinea-Bissau (2m), and the Republic of Guinea (12.5m), the object of this writeup. Condé entered the arena of partisan politics, contested and lost, first, in 1993, and subsequently in 1998, was sent to jail on trumped up charges, before finally winning a democratic mandate in 2010. With that solid pedigree, one would expect Condé to know, and do better.

No sooner did Condé assume power than he began building his own cult of personality, and scheming for tenure elongation; another familiar trait in political leaders in Africa. He was re-elected for a second term in 2015 amidst accusations of voter fraud, suppression, ballot stuffing, intimidation, manipulation, nepotism, registration of minors on the voters' list etc. Again, sounds familiar? Being such patient people, the Guineans accepted their fate with forbearance and stoicism, knowing that the end of Condé's repressive regime would soon be over. The constitution as it stood, forbade him from running again at the end of his second term in 2020. But the eighty-three-year old man's lust for power and the international financiers backing him cooked up the scheme to truncate the country's constitutional safeguard, by securing a yes vote in a dubious 'referendum' organised to "reset" his term in office. He won the October 2020 election for what most people in Guinea considered an illegal and downright fraudulent third term in office with "59.5%" of the vote. The French news organisation, FRANCE 24 released an audio recording of a bribery scandal for mining licence involving the Anglo-Australian Corporation, Rio Tinto, in the wake of the third term scheming operation by the government. Several of Condé's family and friends were implicated in the sordid affair. Guinea is home to half of the world's production of bauxite, among other mineral resources, including oil, gold, diamonds, etc. the bulk of which is frittered away by its pilfering elites.

In a desperate situation like this, and when all other legitimate democratic avenues have been exhausted, a 'corrective coup' may not only be viable, it may be the only option. The African National Congress in South Africa took up arms against the Apartheid regime in their country from the 1970s through to the very early 1990s. Thomas Sankara did likewise against the sit-tight elite in Burkina Faso in 1983. The most prominent of the 'corrective coup' scenario was the Ghanaian experience under the late Flt Lt John Jerry Rawlings (1981–2001). He cleansed the Augean stable by severing the heads of the country's corrupt top politicians. Ghana, with help from international financial institutions, unwound the clock, and started again from scratch. Today, the country is held up as a model of good governance and democracy ahead of most other countries in Africa, certainly ahead of Nigeria in the sub-region. US President, Barack Obama (2008–2016) underlined this by finding time to visit Ghana, but never came to Nigeria. The purist would insist that opposition to military intervention of any kind must remain implacable. Let the Guineans rise up and fight, and fight some more until victory is achieved. Just look up the figures; Guinea has one of the lowest literacy rates in the world, only 41% of the population is literate. Primary school attendance is 40%; there is chronic malnutrition in the wider population, as more than 80% earn a living from subsistence farming. Where is the civic education to empower the people? Who speaks for the downtrodden when the political elite connive to keep them in perpetual servitude? Let us answer these questions clearly and succinctly before condemnation of Col Doumbouya is allowed to grow any louder.

Chapter Nine

Intra-African Affairs

9.01 Zimbabwe: An African Tragedy

21 November 2017

The scene looks eerily familiar and, sadly, all too predictable; it fills one with a deep sense of déjà vu: a frail, flailing tin pot dictator in his nineties, ensconced in his grand and grotesquely opulent Presidential Palace in an impoverished small African state, refusing to give up power even though the writing is clearly on the wall even to the blind. And, just like Saddam Hussein when caught in his bolthole during the uprising in Iraq exclaiming to his captors: "I am the President of Iraq", Mugabe sits tight, and still mouthing expletives to the Generals who had him cornered; "I am the legitimate President of Zimbabwe". Make no mistake about it, Mugabe is out of power. For the army to allow him to re-assume Presidential powers would be suicidal. It would mean a treasonable charge and a sentence of death for everyone who took part in the coup. Laurent Gbagbo before him in Ivory Coast, too, had to be dragged out of his lair in his underwear and frog-marched onto the awaiting prison van outside.

Lest anyone is left in doubt, I am a democrat to the core, and would not condone a military takeover of government under any guise. What happened in Zimbabwe was a textbook example of a "bloodless" or "palace" coup, even though the army tried to dress it up as a routine knock on the door of the Presidential Palace. Forced seizure of power has no place in any civilised society. Claiming power through the barrel of the gun is not only unconscionable; it is an act of the barbarians of a bye-gone age. But there lies the African tragedy; the masses' continuing inability or unwillingness to wrest power from an unwanted leader in Africa and our acquiescence to the men in khaki uniform and guns strolling into the seat of power to "save" us from ourselves. Why?

Because taking a principled stance is awfully painful, and is often accomplished by blood. Remember Fela Kuti's[277] "suffering and smiling": "I no won die", "I won enjoy", "mama dey for house", "papa dey for house" syndrome?

Voices of dissent against the military take-over from inside Zimbabwe are conspicuous by their absence. If this can be explained in terms of fear of a backlash, what about Zimbabweans outside the country? There has been little or no condemnation of the action of the military by any notable figure or social group. Many, in fact, feel a huge sense of relief that this has indeed happened without a shot being fired. The West, and Britain in particular, cannot hide their glee at seeing the demise of their nemesis and tormentor-in-chief for several decades. "We urge both sides to seek a peaceful resolution ..." was the sentiment from all quarters in the West. As a matter of fact, there is no such thing as "both sides" to this. There is only one side; the military and the travesty of the Zimbabwean constitution. Yes, President Robert Mugabe has stayed in power for too long, yes, he banished all official opposition to his rule, and yes, he was attempting to create a family dynasty, by eliminating his long-serving and otherwise loyal Vice President, Emmerson ("crocodile") Mnangagwa, but it is for the people of Zimbabwe to resist tyranny when they see one; not the military to impose themselves on the people however well-intentioned. In that respect, it is a matter of deep consternation that the Zimbabwean elites at home and abroad have decided to be co-conspirators in this military putsch.

No doubt, Mugabe proved himself to be a thorn in the flesh for the British and their white supremacists' kith and kin in Zimbabwe. Initially, he did well, and meant well for his country, but like all other liberation leaders on the continent, soon created a cult of personality around his person. "You are the only one who can hold this country together", "this country will go up in flames without your leadership", "you are the father of the nation", "the teacher", "the leader" etc. etc. Sooner or later, any President would start taking these adulating lines for gospel, and you have the making of authoritarianism and dictatorship in the polity. There is something about being part of the liberation struggle across Africa, which is so alluring and is used to hold country after country to ransom, time and again. There is the "we fought the liberation war" syndrome, which give some people a sense of entitlement to rule for life. No one, no leader in Africa except Nelson Mandela, has ever been willing to "do a Mandela"; serve for one term and gracefully retire, and hand over to others to have a go. Nigeria did not wage a bloody liberation war, but the war psychosis has also permeated

---

277. An Afro-beat musician, for a long time a thorn in the flesh for the Nigerian establishment. He died in 1997.

9 · INTRA-AFRICAN AFFAIRS

their rulers' political thinking from the experience of the civil war and the battle to "keep Nigeria one". Their "war heroes" also think the country is theirs. They have a sentimental attachment to their own notion of "one Nigeria" and would not entertain any attempt at a genuine reform or modernisation.

The other aspect of the African tragedy is that whereas other countries such as the United Kingdom and Spain, have constitutional monarchies within a democratic setting, we have in Africa, hereditary political platforms within an illiberal political setting. Our ruling elites hand down power to their sons, daughters, cousins, concubines, and other extended family relations usually on a platter. Kwara State, in Nigeria, for instance, demonstrates the worst example of a hereditary political platform very well indeed.[278] So too, is most states in the north and the south-west of the country. African leaders have failed again, and again, to anchor power around lasting institutions, they anchor power, instead, around individual personality and family line.

Mugabe has had thirty years to grow and evolve political institutions that would have produced a natural succession, like it is with the Congress Party in India, but he did practically nothing in that regard, but also, given the Western antipathy that greeted his anti-colonial, Marxist leaning, he was hampered from access to international financial and technological sources available to less 'confrontational' African leaders. Granted that, Yuweri Museveni in Uganda, Paul Kagame in Rwanda, Jose Eduardo dos Santos in Angola, Teodoro Obiang in Gabon, Paul Biya in Cameroon, etc. are all similarly to be found in the same cesspit of obdurate, 'me only' political straightjacket of their own making. I do not care how anti-imperialist you may have been, how much you fought the colonial powers to a standstill, how much socialist fire you may have had in your belly, if it led to near starvation for citizens in your country, while you are flown to Singapore[279] for medical attention as and when you need one, and others simply die a needless death in the face of scarcity and dilapidated hospitals at home.

No leader, however brilliant, should ever be allowed to remain in office for one, two, three or more generations as it is common practice, currently, in

---

278. The Saraki family dominated the political landscape in the state for over forty years. See; "The rise and fall of the Saraki dynasty", 'Blueprint', February 27, 2019, The rise and fall of the Saraki dynasty | Blueprint Newspapers Limited: Breaking news happening now in Nigeria and todays latest newspaper headlines

279. A regular spot for hospital treatment for Mugabe, having been barred from entering most Western European countries, for repeated and prolonged human rights abuses of Zimbabweans, and his antagonism towards the European 'settlers' in the country.

Africa. The longer you stay in office, the more seductive power becomes, the deeper your sense of entitlement becomes also, and the more regressive the political system will become. It is up to the people, on the ground, to learn the lesson of resistance to dictatorship and apply it for once. Progress is achieved only through a process of change and renewal, without which stagnation inevitably sets in. On that score alone, comrade Robert Mugabe, his acolytes, and the by-standing elites at home and abroad, all stand accused in the court of public opinion for impeding Zimbabwe's progress. The bigger tragedy for Africa though, is that this particular sorry history is bound to repeat itself.

9.02 How Europe Underdeveloped Africa

12 December 2017

The above is the title of the seminal work by the erudite scholar and revolutionary; Walter Rodney, born in the British West Indies island of Guyana in 1942. He read history in university, culminating in his award of a PhD from SOAS, University of London in 1966. He quickly established his Pan-Africanist credentials with the publications of; "The Groundings with my Brothers" (1969), then, followed by "How Europe Underdeveloped Africa" (1972). This book has remained in print ever since. Sadly, Walter Rodney was assassinated in Guyana, in 1980, aged 38. As a young man still in secondary school in the 1970s, I went through colonial education in Nigeria as many of my contemporaries did, reading history texts written by white authors, discussing African history (I mean their version of it) to the Africans. I was one of those generations taught with the cryptic view of Europeans in pre-independence Africa as "missionaries", "explorers" and "adventurers", not as colonial plunderers, predators and imperialist jackboots many Africans knew they were. I was taught to understand and accept, for instance, that Mungo Park, the British "explorer", was the one who 'discovered' River Niger, and nothing to do with the little boys in the village who actually led him to the source of the river.

We were given the sanitised version of African history; one that exculpates the white Europeans from any atrocity committed as uninvited guests on the shores of Africa. Our school curricula were replete with evidence of the inherent superiority of the European way of life, in contrast to Africa's natural backwardness and savagery. It was the West we needed to mimic in our dealings, since they had the wisdom, knowhow and wherewithal to liberate us from our 'primitiveness'. That was the received wisdom by my contemporaries and myself growing up. Travelling over to the West for higher education did not lessen this lop-sidedness in our mental state; if anything, it reinforced it.

In the West, one quickly sees that frequent talk of aid, famine relief, and other charity fund-raising campaign events usually featured little starving African children with bulging eyes and protruding stomachs on the television screens in Europe. It was the only reference point to Africa that European citizens had access to at the dinner table in their living rooms time after time. As an undergraduate student at the time, I was searching for answers outside my conventional academic training, then, I stumbled on this rare gem of a book: "How Europe Underdeveloped Africa", picked it up and did not let it drop until I had gulped every syllable, dot and comma inside it. It had a profound effect on me; it gave me an unquenchable thirst for more similar literature which, in fullness of time, I found. Rodney's account of European involvement in Africa is one characterized by a deliberate and systematic subjugation of Africa to the apron strings of Europe, in which the continent was to be established as permanent producers of raw materials for the benefit of European industrial development. Other development theories also confirm the account of the 'centre', i.e. Europe, and the USA, and the 'periphery', i.e. Africa', intertwined in the push and pull of prosperity and mass poverty. The underdevelopment of the latter is a condition for the development of the former. This became the second received wisdom by my contemporaries, and myself, and quite justifiably so by all empirical account. Now, Africa has since been freed from direct European rule for over half a century. What, then, is the scorecard?

Our nationalist leaders took over the colonial apparatus of governance, and immediately installed themselves in the former positions occupied by the colonial masters, and continued the exploration and exploitation of African resources, still, for the benefit of the 'centre' in Europe and America. Nonetheless, African leaders gathered together in Addis Ababa, Ethiopia, in 1963, to see if a united front; our own United States of Africa could be established to confront the continued ravaging of our economies to satisfy European and American demands. Notable among those opposed to this novel idea was Nigeria, under Tafawa Balewa (egged on by the British), who vehemently shut down any notion of African unity, and the pooling of sovereignty, espoused by Kwame Nkrumah, the then President of Ghana. Very soon, he was forced out of power in his country and driven into exile, never to return to his homeland again. The irony, of course, is that European leaders subsequently saw an advantage in pooling sovereignty and used that to form the European Union of today. How ironic indeed!

Anyway, not long after the European colonial masters departed, the artificial territorial boundaries they carved up and left behind, became the

262   9 · INTRA-AFRICAN AFFAIRS

lightning rod for ethnic discontentment amongst fellow Africans, who started raining blows on each other at every turn of civil unrest. Having failed to organise as a unified whole, we embarked upon smaller-scale regional integration; East Africa, Southern Africa, West Africa, Arab Africa, etc. This too, has not succeeded as we soon found that each country's tie to former colonial masters in Europe remains stronger than a desire to integrate at the sub-regional level.

African leaders then tried nation-building through nationalisation of industries; a good idea on the surface, given the dominant presence of multinational corporations bent on exploiting Africa for profit to this day. Many industries were indeed taken over by law, and the boardrooms of major industries were suddenly filled with fresh African faces at the table. In Nigeria, this was loftily called; "Indigenisation" and "Nigerianisation" of major industries in the 1970s. Soon enough, the new company executives; the nouveau rich, acquired stupendous wealth, and started leading extravagant lifestyles, buying up choice apartments in, you guess it, European capitals, stashing away money in Swiss bank accounts and offshore centres. How about investing in their home countries? No, not a chance. They became too enmeshed in Western ways to bother. Their taste for Western consumer goods became insatiable to this day. They sent their children to Western schools and lived in gated communities at home. When government functionaries saw that, they too decided to join in the fun by stealing government money and piling such away in foreign banks. And when politicians saw that, they too opted to opt-in and turned political office into money making ventures for themselves, their friends and families, also to this day as we see in front of our eyes.

The late Walter Rodney alongside Kwame Nkrumah before him, wanted a clear revolutionary break from all these in their short, but highly industrious lifetimes. Although their gallant efforts failed, their spirits live on in others across the continent. Rodney, who was buried with copies of his trail-blazing book beside him, would be turning in his grave at the sight of the belly-full Africans lording it over the impoverished and famished masses on the continent with reckless abandon. My guess is he would probably be tempted to write a sequel to the book, appropriately titled; 'How African Leaders Completed the Underdevelopment of Africa'.[280]

---

280. Although, it could be said that the indigenous African leaders that have emerged since independence, themselves, have been helmed into the international capitalist straitjacket from which many have struggled and continue to struggle to disentangle themselves. The point here is that the buck, nonetheless, must stop at the desk of the contemporary African leaders themselves.

9.03 How 'African Time' Is Killing Africa

26 December 2017

Most people reading this column will either have flown or had cause to visit an international airport in the past. The most striking emblem adorning the departure lounge is obviously the giant electronic billboard with its flickering lights on the various departure/arrival times. The planes are expected to run on schedule; no ifs, no buts. If, as often happens, there is a variation to the schedule, it is announced on a separate column beside the original schedule. Time is always of the essence in international flights because it is essentially an integrated service. A departure schedule in one country is intertwined with an arrival schedule in another country. Everybody sings along to the same tune as it were. In advanced economies, the psychology of time keeping has permeated the fabric of everyday life to the point where, even departure/arrival schedules for trains and buses are printed and disseminated a year in advance, allowing passengers to plot and plan their journey right from the comfort of their bedrooms. As it has been written, so it usually is.

Marvelling at the glory of time keeping, the other day, the driver of a fast train (the "Shinkansen" bullet train) in Japan inadvertently left the platform twenty seconds ahead of schedule. The top management of the railway company, Tsukuba Express, had to issue a "sincere apology for the inconvenience caused". They further stated that "the crew did not sufficiently check the departure time and perform the departure operation". You think this is a little over the top? Well, maybe, but it is a clear indication of their aspiration to even greater heights in the future. Generally speaking, in advanced economies, time is money; it dictates the order of life itself. In personal relationships, there is hardly any more casual walk-in to a cousin's or friend's house without their prior knowledge, as they may well have scheduled something different for their own life at that material time. A student registering for a degree course in university is given the schedule for his/her classes for the entire duration in school, up to graduation! How then, is it that time tends to stand still in Africa?

When we turn to the continent of Africa, the contrast could not be more glaring. Let us start with local flight schedules. Some have clear departure and arrival times, but are then heavily subject to variations of hours-long delays, not minutes. Others are simply cancelled at the last minute. Time schedule for trains and buses? Are you kidding me? We are simply grateful to see a train or bus whenever they show up. And what about reporting for duty? Civil servants are the worst in Africa when it comes to 'African time'. Being one, two, three or even four hours late for work is really no big deal for most people.

Some only turn up to sign in and out for the day without batting an eyelid. Combine this attitude with business relationships, it becomes rather alarming. Business appointments are routinely shifted or abandoned with or without notice. It is estimated that 'African time' costs the continent a whopping US$b200 a year in lost revenue.[281] That is an estimated loss of three billion US dollars for each country every single year. It is more than a third of our national budget in this country alone. This is not simply a matter of being a "third world" problem, though there is something about our way of life in Africa that shapes our conception of time in a radically different way to others in the advanced economies of the West.

The problem, first and foremost, is abundance. Africa is the original Garden of Eden. We have crops, and agricultural products sprouting up in people's backyards without anyone having cultivated the land. We even have gold, diamonds and other mineral resources effortlessly dotted across the planes of north-central-south-west and east coasts of Africa, so much that we invite mercenaries from foreign countries to come and loot them. Abundance, of course, creates inertia and ignorance of how scarce these resources indeed are. Planning and timing become the pre-occupation of those who do not have access to those resources in their own countries. Furthermore, time, in Africa, has little relationship to actual events. In English language, for instance, the phrase; "how are you" is no longer a question, but a greeting. Try relaying personal story to the question and you will see the wrench of agony on the face of the questioner immediately. You know he was not the least interested in your tale of woes, as he will often swiftly reply with 'Ok, see ya!' as he saunters off.

Conversely, therefore, the phrase; 'I will see you at 4pm', in Africa, is not a commitment; it is an expression of hope. Similarly, 'I will come to your house next weekend' is not a solid promise of a friendly visit, but an affirmation of goodwill to a familiar person. Fine if the person turns up, and equally fine if he does not. Time in Africa has no definite beginning and no definite end either. It is embedded in our conception of the cycle of life itself. Birth is an arrival as well as a return to Mother Earth. Death is a transition to the ancestral resting space, not the end of life as others see (and fear) it. The dead and the living co-exist in Africa, as it is often possible to consult the dead on crucial matters of state and community at times of danger and need. Time then, in African psyche,

---

281. Accurate data on this is few and far between, but, a good flavour of the problem can be gleaned from; "Running on African Time". 'Stears Business' (Economy), July 29, 2015. Running On African Time — Stears Business (stearsng.com)

is transcendental; it is infinitesimal. While others bemoan a lack of time, we bask in excess of it. While others connect time to scientific and technological innovation, in Africa, we connect time to a luxury we can afford.

This cultural accommodation of laxity and permissiveness makes for a less stressful life for most people in Africa; less cut-throat, and less suicidal deadlines to meet, but it has wrought massive economic ruin to millions of our citizens. Our production level is the worst of any other region of the world, poverty level, infant mortality rate, infrastructure level and human development index, the worst of all others.[282] In our midst, nothing is so important that it cannot wait until tomorrow, the next day, and the day after next. One governor of a provincial state in Nigeria was once asked at a conference whether it would need a massive rebellion by the people to get rid of corrupt politicians in the country. His response was astounding: "If there is a crowd shouting thief, thief, at me as a governor, there will be another section of the crowd who would ask: how much longer does the governor have in office? The answer would inevitably be, two, three or four years. So, the counter to the chanting of thief, thief, would be, well leave him, he will soon go". To echo the late Fela Anikulapo Kuti, we need to knock some truths into our heads, brothers and sisters. We need to wake up from this slumber and regain our sense of urgency on the fundamentals of our lives. Above all, we need to halt the groggy sleepwalk into the abyss, lest the continent becomes a timeless, but ultimately barren land for future generations. There is no such thing as 'African time'; there is only the right time.

9.04 New Scramble for Africa: Not the Chinese, Surely?

20 March 2018

The former Soviet bloc collapsed in a spectacular fashion in 1989. The historical experiment to create a Communist Nirvana; a utopian of all utopian states had lasted for over seventy years, almost to no avail. The West, under the auspices of the United States, rejoiced in triumph; proclaiming what Francis Fukuyama referred to as the "end of history". The ideological rivalry between the "Communist East" and "Capitalist West" had led to the triumph of the

---

282. See; Human Development Index Score of Africa as of 2019, by Country, in 'Statista' Africa: human development index by country 2019 | Statista

latter as the only viable form of organising society. Or so the saying goes. The greatest lesson from the collapse of the Soviet bloc, the big takeaway, appears to be that human beings cannot be organised like robots even in the noble cause of nation-building. Such was the Communist way. For good or ill, individuals and their selfish interests provide the best engine for growth and development under a capitalist system. So too the saying goes. The new free market orthodoxy now rules the waves through the prism of globalisation. Throughout the period of the then "East" versus "West" mode of development, the Chinese took a distinctively unique approach to their relationship with the rest of the world. Under Chairman Mao (1893–1976), they trod the path of Communism with a Chinese face. Backed up with an array of nuclear arsenals, they became a military superpower in their own right, with a permanent seat at the United Nations Security Council, but remained economically backward throughout the period of the Cold War.

The Chinese module was insular, autarky and muscular. They kicked against the export of the revolution doctrine of the Soviet bloc. Democracy then? Oh, no. That is something countries of the West indulged in. The party, the Chinese Communist Party, reigned supreme. Free market? No chance. Central planning and a sort of levelling down was the order of the day for a country of more than one billion citizens. In fact, one out of every four human beings is a Chinese. The country believes itself to be at the centre of human civilisation. It has created empires, lost territories, gained some, conquered and been conquered, finally rebuilding itself again as a modern state within the last century. In contemporary international politics, China has never regarded itself as an influential entity in world affairs, neither has it ever wanted outsiders to meddle in its internal affairs either. It maintains internal order with an iron grip, and considers political rebellions as "anti-state", which is often heavily and ruthlessly dealt with. The Chinese take pride in their own peculiar Eastern civilisation, imbibing Confucianism and its fundamentals. Above all, they are proud of not having taken part in the infamous "scramble for Africa" with the advent of the Portuguese and wider European slave trade across Africa in the seventeenth century, to the partition of Africa at the Berlin Conference in 1885 for the benefit of Western European colonialism, to the Cold War that ran through the 1960s, 1970s and early 1980s. Nowadays, and in a gesture of solidarity, the Chinese whisper to the Africans; hey, guys, we never took part in any of those horrible stuff on your continent. Unlike the other lot, we are clean and untainted by any act of plundering African resources or subjugating its citizens into any form of degradation. We simply want to help reconstruct the continent with our advanced technological know-how, absolutely with no strings attached. Really?

9 · INTRA-AFRICAN AFFAIRS

Indeed, Chinese presence in every part of Africa is undoubted.[283] They are, in fact, the new kid on the block when it comes to construction and infrastructural development on the continent today. From the New National Assembly building in little-known Guinea-Bissau, to the government residence in Uganda, the extensive rail network in Kenya, Zimbabwe, Nigeria, Ghana, Rwanda, Ethiopia, Democratic Republic of Congo, etc. The Chinese are everywhere on the continent, digging, digging and more digging. It has become commonplace to get into a remote part of an African country with very little to show for modern life except the extensive Chinese cranes hanging on tall buildings and skyscrapers, and their assiduous personnel, in rolled up sleeves and khaki shorts, baking in the blazing sun, but diligently supervising engineering work along the roads and on building sites. But why do they appear so committed where others have downed tools in retreat? Are the Chinese such benevolent givers that ought to be given more credit than they currently get?

Let us unpack this by reference to the opening paragraph. Long before the Soviet bloc collapsed in 1989, Chinese authorities had been trying to loosen up on their control of the economy, I suppose, in earnest recognition of the "end of history". For them, the process of loosening up accelerated after 1990, leading to the Chinese Communist Party letting go of its iron grip on the economy.[284] The country then began the gradual process of moving from a hitherto command economy to embrace the dreaded capitalism and market economy instead. This unleashed a flurry of activity and a rapid expansion of production far in excess of domestic consumption. The Chinese enjoyed a significant boost in their overseas trade, profiting from a highly-skilled and highly-educated (but considerably cheap) workforce. The economy expanded and began to generate surpluses that surpassed every expectation.[285] Soon after, the authorities began to play the capitalist's game.

---

283. See a recent report by Peter Stein and Emil Uddhammar. China in Africa: The Role of Trades, Investments, and Loans Amidst Shifting Geopolitical Ambitions. Observer Research Foundation, August 25, 2021. China in Africa: The Role of Trade, Investments, and Loans Amidst Shifting Geopolitical Ambitions | ORF (orfonline.org)

284. The Communist Party at 100: Is Xi Jinping's China on the Right Track?. Financial Times, June 28, 2021. The Communist party at 100: is Xi Jinping's China on the right track? | Financial Times (ft.com)

285. For a more in-depth account, see; Eswar Prasad (Ed) China's Growth and Integration into the World Economy—Prospects and Challenges. International Monetary Funds, Occasional Paper, 232, 2004. China's Growth and Integration into the World Economy: Prospects and Challenges, edited by Eswar Prasad (Occasional Paper No. 232, June 2004) (imf.org)

268   9 · INTRA-AFRICAN AFFAIRS

They took some of the surplus capital and invested in acquiring US bonds; essentially financing the US economy. The Chinese currently hold billions, if not trillions of dollars in US bonds and equities in the capital markets. To reduce their exposure, they decided to look elsewhere, to places like Africa, to invest. It makes economic sense too, since their search for raw materials appears to be insatiable at the moment, and Africa is littered with such, but lacking in infrastructure. At 7% a year, China runs one of the fastest growing economies in the world.[286] It is poised to overtake the US as the largest economy in the world before 2030.

Consequently, just as the 19th century industrial revolution directly led to the scramble for Africa's natural and human resources, the Chinese economic expansion is fuelling the country's quest for raw materials to sustain it as well, but that is where the similarity ends. While China builds bridges in Africa in exchange for raw materials, the Europeans simply took the materials back to the mainland as if they owned them. While Europeans insisted on exploiting Africa's resources through colonialism, the Chinese, on the other hand, maintain the policy of "non-interference" in the internal affairs of African states. Whether their investment in any particular country is directly or indirectly propping up a corrupt regime is absolutely none of their business. They have had enough of being bullied by Western governments over their human right records at home, so, they would not visit same on any of their Africa's newfound "partners". Let us not go into the critique of that approach here and now, for reasons of space. "African concerns are Chinese's concerns, Africa's priorities are China's priorities" says China's Foreign Minister, Wang Yi. This followed Rex Tillerson's (dismissed as US Secretary of State as I was writing this piece) criticism of "China's dollars" being poured into Africa, a trend which he thinks could undermine the sovereignty of African states if the terms are not "carefully considered". Goodness, did he really say that? Listen, America, the USA has been undermining the sovereignty of country after country in Africa for decades. Your government has been sponsoring mercenary missions throughout Africa to protect the flow of resources into the West for decades. How ill-informed can the former Secretary of State be? How ignorant! Sure, there are plenty of criticisms that can rightly be levelled at Chinese investment methods in Africa, but a redundant sermon from a former oil baron turned Secretary of State is not one that resonates with anyone in Africa, let alone China.

---

286. Ibid.

9.05 Who's Afraid of Africa's Free Trade Bloc?

3 April 2018

Imagine a continent-wide free trade zone, comprising of over fifty countries, being able to buy and sell consumer goods in any of the member states without let or hindrance, and without incurring the expense of tariffs and other constraints on the export or import of their merchandise? Imagine the whole of Africa suddenly becoming an open market for the Africans; where only foreigners from outside the continent have to pay money to bring in their wares? Imagine bulky tubers of yam from Makurdi, Benue State, flying across the borders onto people's dinner plates in Egypt, Ethiopia, South Africa etc. and fabrics from Ghana and Togo streaming effortlessly into Nigeria without anyone batting an eyelid? Imagine; imagine the new dawn in African renaissance thereof? You do not really need to let your imagination run too widely for such a new dawn is already upon us. Or so it seems. Two weeks ago, forty-four African states met and agreed a deal for a new Treaty in Kigali, Rwanda: African Continental Free Trade Area, to put the dream into reality. It is the largest of such in the world, but wait a minute, there is a problem. Nigeria and South Africa,[287] the two most prominent economies on the continent have thus far refused to sign up for the deal. The Treaty; really a no-brainer to most people, is the stuff motherhood and apple pie are made of. Who can possibly be against it?

Let us wind back the clock to the year 1963, at Addis Ababa, in Ethiopia, for a cursory look at the historical roots of the deal, and in particular, Nigeria's self-inflicted wound in its trajectory. Addis Ababa was the first gathering of thirty-two newly independent African states in an early attempt to forge a closer link between African states in terms of politics and economics, long before the European Union and other entities developed their own knowledge of economic integration and trade blocs. As it happened, Dr Kwame Nkrumah had become President of the neighbouring Ghana in 1957, when the Northern part of Nigeria kicked against a similar move for independence for our own country. The Southern part was ready and eager to make a dash for independence much sooner than the Northern part could tolerate. Such was the rivalry between north and south that the northern political leaders at the time wanted

---

287. The two countries have since signed up to the agreement. South Africa, May 30, 2019, AfCFTA | South African Revenue Service (sars.gov.za) Nigeria, July 7, 2019, Quantifying the impact on Nigeria of the African Continental Free Trade Area (brookings.edu).

270   9 · INTRA-AFRICAN AFFAIRS

the British to prolong their colonial rule in Nigeria. It sounds rather counterintuitive now, thinking about it, but it is true. We eventually gained independence in 1960 and was immediately caught up in the debate earlier initiated by Nkrumah for a complete unification of all African states without delay. Tafawa Balewa, the new Prime Minister of Nigeria, had the political task of establishing the country's position and standing amongst its peers on the continent and beyond. Nkrumah's ideological quest for the unification of Africa had forced other leaders to take positions either for, or against. Two factions immediately emerged: The "Casablanca Group"[288] comprising, initially; Ghana, Guinea and Mali. They wanted the upcoming 1963 conference in Ethiopia to adopt the motion for the unification of the entire continent under one government. They were later joined by Egypt, Algeria, and Morocco.

The other faction subsequently rallied under the umbrella of the "Monrovia Group". The Casablanca group had met in January 1961, while the Monrovia Group quickly followed with their own meeting in May of the same year. The group, comprising; Liberia, Senegal, Ivory-Coast, Cameroon etc. was led by Nigeria under Prime Minister Balewa. They were against the idea of African unity, Conservative in their politics and pro-West in their worldview. Needless to say that Nkrumah lost the game of numbers at the 1963 conference, as those who were persuaded into adopting the Monrovia Group's position outnumbered those of the Casablanca Group. The sad note, of course, is that Nigeria could have teamed up with Ghana as the founding fathers of a new Africa, but our leaders declined that responsibility. So, instead of ushering in a new Africa, we settled for the clichéd doctrines of "sovereign equality" of member states and respect for the "territorial integrity" of states, and "inalienable right" of the newly liberated countries in Africa to "independent existence". This is despite the fact that these African states were a direct result of European partition of the continent along the lines that suited them; not the Africans. From then on, all efforts at forging any kind of close political and economic links between African states were as good as dead. The newly formed Organisation of African Unity (OAU) in 1963 became no more than a mirage; a talking shop in effect. Nigeria had lost its prime leadership position in Africa for a generation. Fast forward to 2018, with the new Treaty on the table in Rwanda two weeks ago, the chickens of Nigeria's rather timid Conservative stance in the creation of the OAU have now come home to roost. Let me explain.

---

288. For the evolution of both the Casablanca and Monrovia groups see; Bank Group's Evolution | African Development Bank—Building today, a better Africa tomorrow (afdb.org).

9 · INTRA-AFRICAN AFFAIRS

First, a free trade deal of the kind being proposed (in vastly undeveloped and unsophisticated markets) only works if complimented by political integration; the kind of integration akin to that which Nigeria had earlier so vehemently kicked against. Second, a free trade bloc can also only work if the people involved have (home-grown) goods and services to trade. We, in Africa, tend to trade with outsiders more than we do with each other, not necessarily because we loathe each other, but principally because we are all jostling for outside favours from the same low base, low-tech, raw material-generating-agrarian economies. Inter-African trade is less than a fifth of the total traded as a whole, compared to Asia of over half or Europe of over two-thirds traded with each other.[289] We are producers of raw materials which we are now busy giving to the Chinese in exchange for constructing our dilapidated road network. It follows, therefore, that Nigeria, being the largest economy on the continent, has the advantage of first, economy of scale (it can locate factories across different territories in Africa. Ask Alhaji Aliko Dangote). Second, it already has the capacity to sell its products to neighbouring states in West Africa and beyond at a competitive advantage. South Africa is exactly in the same position. I can hear some people reading this and saying; yes, what is the big deal in signing the deal that would allow all Africans to bring in goods and services onto each other's shores? It is a good deal in principle, no doubt. Other smaller African states already constitute the bulk of the market for Nigerian goods. We have a lot more to sell to them than they have to sell to us. A tariff free zone would mean an invitation for outsiders to relocate to those countries, register their companies under local labels, then, ship their goods to Africa's largest market; Nigeria. The advantage of the free trade zone for the Africans would have been effectively lost, as it will under this new deal.

The real tragedy, though, is that Nigeria could have taken a frontline; leadership role in shaping the African (economic) unity the country is now so afraid of, if only Nkrumah had not been thrown under the bus as our country and other African leaders shamelessly did back in the sixties. We had an open goal then, and still missed! The politics of the continent could have been dotted with Nigeria's footprints all over it for posterity. Our reluctance to recognise the necessity for the coming together of Africans upon independence allowed outsiders to continue their story of exploitation of Africa's human and natural resources. A free economic trade zone among "independent" and "sovereign" African states without some sort of economic convergence and political

---

289. "Intra-Africa trade: A path to economic diversification and inclusion"—A Report. Brookings, January 11, 2019, Intra-African trade: A path to economic diversification and inclusion (brookings.edu)

272   9 · INTRA-AFRICAN AFFAIRS

integration is simply not feasible in the modern world. Nigeria had failed to seize the moment when it was offered on a platter in 1963. Right now, there is no viable political structure in place to compliment the move for economic union. Nigerian economy would be open for rich pickings with the new deal. Dumping of foreign goods in the guise of local labels from neighbouring countries represents an existential threat to our indigenous industries. Not embracing further moves for a deeper African union represents an even bigger threat to all Africans.

9.06 Why We Celebrate (Not Jail) Corrupt Leaders In Africa (I)

1 May 2018

In case you have missed it, there is something interesting trending of late in the world of politics, governance, and accountability. It is the sight of prominent former Heads of State and Prime Ministers helping police with their enquiries, and subsequently being escorted to serve various jail terms, having been convicted of grand larceny and other high crimes, in various courts of law, during their tenure in office. Where on earth is this happening you might be wondering? Must be on another planet it seems? Of course not, it is happening right here on earth; on the other side of the Atlantic in fact. Well, then, let us see what is really happening in those countries and continents where they are busy sending their former corrupt leaders to jail. They may have something to learn from us Africans, who tend to celebrate and hero-worship such people. We shower them with boulevards and monuments across our towns and cities, you know? So, who the hell has the audacity to send corrupt former leaders to jail? And what exactly is wrong with the system there that would allow such a thing to happen?

First, imagine a one time "people's President", who rose through extreme poverty to become a skilled metal worker, then, worked his way to the top of the leadership of one of his country's trade unions, and subsequently being elected to Parliament before campaigning for the Presidency, which he won. Also imagine, after becoming President, he dedicated the whole of his Presidency to improving the lot of the working people, spending vast amounts of money on education and infrastructure, lifting thirty million of the country's poor citizens out of poverty. Former US President, Ronald Reagan (1981–1989), famously said that the ultimate question to ask of a President seeking re-election is: "are you better off than you were four years ago?" If you are not, then, the President does not deserve to be re-elected, and if you are, then, you

9 · INTRA-AFRICAN AFFAIRS 273

may consider re-electing him. There is no doubt that, eight years after Luiz Inácio Lula da Silva first became President of Brazil (2003–2011), his country was a much better place than it was before his election. He was lauded by just about every international financial institution for his prudent management of the Brazilian economy, making it a lot more inclusive than it previously was. His country was one of the last to go into recession in 2008, and quickly came out of it a year later in 2009, as one of the first to do so. He expanded access to higher education for the poor, raised minimum wage, initiated the "Bolsa Família Programme" covering at least twelve million families, which provided them with life-changing sums of money in return for keeping their children in school. Former US President, Barack Obama, once dubbed him the "most popular head of state in the world". A man with no known enemy, he handed his successor a booming economy and a positive outlook for the country, becoming the most popular President in Brazil's history.

Imagine then, that in spite of the above, the state prosecutor in Brazil somehow managed to put together a corruption case against the man affectionately known as "Lula". The charges, by our standards in Africa, are kindergarten stuff: that he used state resources to make improvements to his family farm, and that he was later discovered to have been given a swanky apartment on the Sao Paulo Coast as a kickback from an inflated contract. He was sentenced to twelve years in prison. He is now in custody. Now, how much money has been alleged to have been siphoned away from the Nigerian Treasury by the former Minister for Petroleum Resources, Mrs Diezani Alison-Madueke? Or her counterpart, Colonel Sambo Dasuki (retd) in the on-going arms probe? The amount runs into billions of US dollars in both cases. One of the allegations levelled against the former Brazilian President was his indirect involvement in the "Petrobras scandal" involving kickbacks from corporations to government officials. Like the Nigerian National Petroleum Corporation (NNPC), Petrobras is also a largely state-owned corporation, through which billions of dollars were alleged to have been frittered away by corrupt means. The investigation, which started in 2014, after "Lula" had left office quickly engulfed his successor in office, President Dilma Rousseff, and later Lula himself became embroiled in it as the prosecution stated: "besides being party leader, he (Lula) was the one ultimately responsible for the decision on who would be the directors of Petrobras and was one of the main beneficiaries of these crimes". Has anyone reminded former President Goodluck Jonathan under whose watch billions of dollars were taken out of the Treasury in Nigeria, that he too, was ultimately responsible? How about former President Obasanjo and the numerous scandals under his watch (Halliburton bribes, Transcorp shares,) to mention but two? Going further still, how about military "President" Babangida before them? The scandals involving

274   9 · INTRA-AFRICAN AFFAIRS

him even included allegations of complicity in murder of Nigerian citizens. No probes, no inquiries, no investigations of these individuals, nada!

Earlier this month, Park Geun-hye, South Korea's ex-President (2013–2017), was jailed for corruption for 24 years, having been found guilty of "abuse of power and coercion". The trial and the verdict were broadcast live on television. She was said to have caused "massive chaos" for which she should be held accountable. What about the charismatic, action man, President Alberto Fujimori, President of Peru (1990–2000). He was noted for confronting organised crimes and fighting official corruption. His popularity in the opinion polls rose dramatically as he established himself as one of the most efficient politicians the country had ever known. He, nonetheless, was later prosecuted, convicted and sentenced to 25 years in jail for human rights abuses in 2009, including ordering massacres and embezzlement of state funds. What is interesting about this particular case is that Fujimori actually had the opportunity to stay away from Peru, having flown out to Japan, his ancestral home, whilst he was being prosecuted in court. He, nevertheless, chose to come back to face justice. He has recently been released on compassionate grounds, in 2017. Alfonso Portillo was President of Guatemala from 2000–2004. He was detained in 2010 and extradited to the USA, where he was sentenced to 5 years and 10 months for money laundering. Ehud Olmert was President of Israel (2006–2009). He was jailed in 2016 for taking bribes, fraud, corruption and obstruction of justice.

9.07 Why We Celebrate (Not Jail) Corrupt Leaders in Africa (II)

8 May 2018

How about former heads of states in Europe? Ivo Sanader was Prime Minister of Croatia (2003–2009). He was arrested late 2010 on charges of corruption, embezzlement and abuse of power. He was later convicted and sent to prison. Jose Socrates was the Socialist Prime Minister of Portugal (2005–2011). He spent almost one year in temporary detention, then, placed under house arrest, having been charged with bribery and other crimes including money laundering, tax fraud and falsification of documents. Adrian Năstase was the Social Democrat Prime Minister of Romania (2000–2004). He was sentenced to four and a half years for corruption in 2012. Svetozar Marović was President of Serbia and Montenegro (2003–2006). He was sentenced to three years jail in 2016 for corruption and related offenses. The list goes on, but I think you understand what I am saying.

9 · INTRA-AFRICAN AFFAIRS 275

When it comes to the continent of Africa, Banana Canaan was the first (ceremonial) President of Zimbabwe (1980–1987). In case you are wondering, 'Banana' was truly his name; Canaan Sodindo Banana was charged and convicted of sodomy in 1997, following the murder trial of his bodyguard. He fled to South Africa, but was persuaded to give himself up upon meeting and having an audience with Nelson Mandela. He served term in an open prison from 1999 until 2001, and died two years later in 2003. Ben Bella, Ahmed was President of Algeria (1963–1965). He was placed under house arrest from 1965–1980, no charges filed. Bokassa, Jean-Bédel, was President of Central African Republic (1966–1976), and the country's "Emperor" (1976–1979). Bokassa was a megalomaniac personified, he turned the country into his own personal fiefdom, maiming and killing anyone with a contrary view to his. To say that he was corrupt would be an understatement. He owned the country and could do no wrong. The French finally launched an invasion of the country and got rid of him in 1979. He fled into exile in France, was tried for treason and murder and sentenced to death in absentia. Latterly, Jacob Zuma, President of the Republic of South Africa (2009–2018), has been charged with involvement in a multi-billion dollar arms deal from the 1990s, alongside a string of bribery and embezzlement charges that have dogged his Presidency almost from the start. If convicted and sent to jail, he would be the first of such leader to go to prison, for corruption-related crimes on the continent of Africa. My guess is that the seventy-five year old rugged politician would not be incarcerated; it is simply not the African way. Here is why.[290]

The colonial legacy. For those who may have heard me make this point before, I apologise, but it is worth re-stating. During the independence struggle across the continent, the nationalist leaders were bundled into colonial jails in their dozens on a daily basis. Jomo Kenyatta (Kenya), Sékou Touré (Guinea), Ahmed Ben Bella (Algeria), Robert Mugabe (Zimbabwe), Kwame Nkrumah (Ghana) etc. were all inmates in colonial jails, as were numerous more like them. The irony, of course, is that the more the leaders were thrown into jails, the more popular they became. They were all fighting a common enemy: European colonial presence on African soil. Over time, incidents of political leaders going to jail lost its shock value. It even became a badge of honour (and a rite of passage) for the prisoners, who later assumed the mantle of leadership in their respective countries. During the long independence struggle, the state in Africa was the archetypal colonial state; foreign to the

---

290. Zuma was in fact sent to jail in the Kwazulu-Natal Province, in 2021, but not for corruption, but, for contempt of court.

subjects upon whom they exercised authority. 'The state' was therefore conceived of, and related to, as the tool of exploitation, subjugation and harassment that needed not only to be resisted, but ultimately brought down. Government property, money, investment, infrastructure and the like, became legitimate targets for ventilating anger and people's frustration. Stealing from the state became a patriotic obligation on the part of those with the means so to do. Anyone returning to one's village with a horde of loot from the government would be met with a dance troupe and a chieftaincy title to match. The tragedy is though, that more than sixty years after independence in most African states, attitude to the state does not appear to have shifted in any appreciable degree. Again, here is why.

The post-independence leaders who took over the reins of power throughout Africa did so as if they had just acquired their own kingdoms. Rather than dismantle the apparatus of oppression represented in the colonial state, they simply took it over and used it to suppress their own people with even more vigour than the colonial masters did to them. Consequently, people's alienation from the oppressive state intensified despite now having indigenous Africans in the seat of power. One more time, here is why.

The state is an essentially problematic instrument in Africa for a very important reason. The colonial partition of Africa at the Berlin Conference in 1885 completely disregarded historical and cultural affiliations of the indigenous people, and carved out areas of land that merged and lumped people together in the artificially created colonial state. The state was created before the people's national consciousness could be established. Modern states such as the Palestinians see and feel themselves as a nation first, before fighting for an independent state of their own. So too, is Taiwan, Catalan, Scotland etc. In Africa, we got the state first before getting to know who we were to share its structure and powers with. And, in many cases, fighting broke out once people found out the gulf in cultural disparities and ambitions of the various ethnic elements that constitute the new state. Consequently, there is still no sense of ownership of the established state in much of Africa. Very few people conceive of their state as being worth dying for in Africa, the concomitant of which is that its commonwealth is not worth watching over by active citizens. When political leaders steal in Africa, they do so in their own name, but when faced with a charge for stealing, his ethnicity immediately becomes the issue. They get succour from their kith and kin with some absurd ripostes such as: "Yes, he may have stolen money, but others have stolen money too", "even if he is indeed a thief, he is, nevertheless, our son", "they are using the charges to persecute, suppress and humiliate his ethnic base", "at least he used the loot well for his people", "is he the only corrupt leader out there?" etc.

The state is still the alien enemy to devour and strip of its assets. Corruption has become so ethnicised that there are many corrupt ex-heads of state and governments across Africa, who no prosecutor dares touch for fear of igniting an ethnic war, or for fear of "heating up the polity" as they say in political elite circles in Nigeria. Many such corrupt leaders have streets named after them, they go about leading delegations to promote reconciliation and democracy as ex-leaders in other countries, rather than spending time in jail as other people would have them do. In Africa, if you are a political leader and found yourself unlucky to be convicted and sent to jail, rest assured your 'pardon' is being negotiated even as you take the first step into detention. If not, your time in jail will soon be reduced so drastically on appeal that you will be released for time already spent in custody. The opprobrium other people attach to jail in respect of high level officials does not apply in Africa, since colonial use of indiscriminate detention for political leaders all those years ago has desensitized the public to elite prison 'shame' to this day. What works in Africa is the loss of assets. Given the choice, a public official found guilty of corruption would accept a temporary loss of his liberty than a loss of a single kilogramme of his assets. As an alternative to a custodial sentence, therefore, it is time to consider asset-stripping those who wantonly asset-strip the state in Africa.

9.08 What "Brexit" Means for Africa

16 October 2018

On the 29th of March 2019, the United Kingdom will cease to be a member of the most successful trade bloc in the world, namely, the European Union. It will no longer be a voice to reckon with within the labyrinths of the European super state called the European Commission in Brussels. A new leaf in the history of the United Kingdom and her relationship with continental Europe will be turned. It is this long, arduous, and painstaking process that has been dubbed "Brexit". It is funny sometimes, to outsiders, to hear people in the UK refer to continental Europe as if it belongs in another place. They would constantly make reference to "us and them", "UK and Europe" as if to underline the assumption that the UK is not actually in Europe. The UK, it is often thought, is an island cut adrift from continental Europe, and only recently linked by rail through the small strip of river called the "Channel", underneath of which passes the rail link to France from UK's port of Dover. If the EU is such a successful trade bloc, which it is, and countries in and around European mainland are queuing up for membership, why would any existing member want out?

278   9 · INTRA-AFRICAN AFFAIRS

The answer to the above question lies in the understanding of a unique British attitude and its identity in the modern world. The EU, formerly known as EEC (European Economic Community), was established by the Treaty of Rome in 1957 as an "economic" community, but was renamed the European Union, EU in 1993, its initial object having evolved from an economic entity into socio-political, economic, quasi European government over the decades through the wishes of its now 28 members. It will be reduced to 27 upon Britain's exist next year. It is important to note that the UK was not part of its foundation members. She applied to become a member in 1961, but the then French President, Charles de Gaulle, applied the French veto on UK's membership, suspicious of her ulterior motive. The "special relationship" between Britain and the USA was thought to pose a threat to the "European project" of an independent, counter influence on world affairs envisioned by the founding members. It was feared then that the UK would be in the club as a stooge for the Americans, therefore wielding a negative influence on the organisation. But, after prolonged political manoeuvrings and changes in world affairs, the UK was finally admitted in 1974, following a bitterly divisive referendum. Why was it such a big deal?

Well, opposition to EU membership in the UK cuts across the 'Left' and 'Right' divide. Politicians on the Left of the political spectrum were deeply suspicious of the EU becoming a club for the rich and business elite across Europe, while politicians on the Right of the political spectrum feared that the EU was a fundamental threat to Britain's Parliamentary democracy, as more and more powers were being ceded to the EU, whose decisions were becoming increasingly binding and non-negotiable. It has been left to politicians in the middle, the so-called "moderates", within UK's main political parties to steer the debate along a consensus. The 'consensus' was that the EU is more of a force for good than bad. Opposition to EU grew increasingly vociferous amongst the politicians on the political Right in the 1980s because of two things: The rise and influence of Germany as the dominant economic force in Europe, and the increasingly "social" or "socialistic" dimension of the Union in terms of employment and social services provisions. What is more galling for "Right-wing" politician in the UK was the relics of history, which had witnessed how the UK under Winston Church stood up to, and defeated "Nazi" Germany in World War II. Germany had indeed been defeated and its economy in ruins. It was rebuilt through help from America and the UK, which had banished Germany from ever rising to the status of military power again. It worked.

What then happened, though, was that Germany's focus on economics and technology saw it rise to the status of global economic power, surpassing the UK and all other European countries. The Right-wing now feared the prospect

9 · INTRA-AFRICAN AFFAIRS

of Germany achieving in peace time, what it had failed to achieve through war, that is, European 'domination'. The campaign to take Britain out of the EU had taken almost three decades to achieve; it was dominated by nationalist fervour on the Right, and on the Left, it was welcomed as a relief from the "shackles of Brussels". Politics, rather than economics, had won the day. The UK may well rue the day they left the EU, and to forestall a calamitous outcome to Brexit, Africa has now become the new darling to be wooed and embraced as UK's newest trading partners. How ironic for a country that colonised much of the land in Africa, then, neglected it in pursuit of European influence, then, saw China become Africa's biggest foreign investors and trading partner. The UK is now rushing back to Africa to recover lost ground.

It is in this context that UK Prime Minister, Theresa May's recent whirlwind tour of three African states (Kenya, South Africa and Nigeria) must be understood. The trip last August, 2018, was billed by the Prime Minister (who had never been to sub-Saharan Africa before), as a "unique opportunity at a unique time for the UK". The UK wants "to deepen and strengthen its global partnerships as it leaves the EU in 2019" she says. It was the first time a British Prime Minister would visit Africa since 2013. UK's visibility on the continent has been clearly in decline at the same time as that of France, Turkey, Japan and most especially China have been on the rise. The Prime Minister was accompanied by a bevy of trade negotiators on a chartered RAF (Royal Air Force) "Voyager" transport plane to try and sign as many deals as they could possibly muster. The UK had earlier hosted the Somalia Conference in London last year, in 2017. The Minister of Finance, Philip Hammond, International Trade Secretary, Liam Fox, and Foreign Secretary, Boris Johnson, had been criss-crossing Africa, frantically building or should I say rebuilding friendship in the last couple of years. Nigeria and South Africa, however, remain the main targets of their efforts for obvious reasons. They are the UK's largest trading partners, worth $3.3 billion and $8.7 billion respectively,[291] all of which are in favour of British export into the countries, of course. President Uhuru Kenyatta said, when challenged about the growing Chinese influence in his country: "We are not looking to China, China is looking to us". The same could be said of the UK's renewed interest in Nigeria and Africa in general. The question is that, are we going to be wise enough to dictate the terms of UK's engagement with us this time round?

---

291. According to the UK's department for international trade, total trade in goods and services (exports plus imports) between the UK and Nigeria was £4.1bn in the four quarters to the end of Q4 2021 Trade and Investment Factsheet (publishing.service.gov.uk) And, the Reuters Report; "Britain agrees post-Brexit deal with South Africa" September 11, 2019. Britain agrees post-Brexit trade deal with southern Africa | Reuters

9.09 South Africa: False Narrative of Xenophobic Attacks

17 September 2019

The world has witnessed a spate of attacks on "foreign" workers in South Africa almost since the day after the end of apartheid in that country, in 1994. It has become particularly acute in the last few years as levels of unemployment and deprivation have reached new heights amidst allegations of corruption and "state capture" levelled at the former President, Jacob Zuma. The media, both in Nigeria and elsewhere, have portrayed dreadful scenes of "black-on-black violence" taking place at regular intervals especially in Johannesburg and Pretoria as a uniquely black African phenomenon. Nigerians have been especially singled out for direct attacks and lynching, in some cases, even more inhumane than the white minority regime used to mete out to the blacks under apartheid. Some say it is because Nigerians and other fellow Africans have come to "steal" local jobs, others claim it is because of the involvement of Nigerians in criminality that they are being targeted. Others, still, claim it is a combination of both. My contention, in this piece, is that the widespread account of blacks turning on other ("foreign") blacks in frenzied "xenophobic" attacks in South Africa appears true on the surface, but it is a fundamentally flawed rationale. Here is why.

There is no hate blood flowing from the veins of one set of blacks onto another in South Africa. The root cause of the violent attacks lies in economic inequality, not xenophobia. South Africa's economy grew by 1.3% in 2017, and a dismal 0.8% in 2018. Growth projection for 2019 is 1.3% nudging up to 1.7% in 2020, according to the World Bank.[292] Per capita (income per head of the population) growth has come to a screeching halt since 2014, leaving little or no room for poverty reduction in the wider sense. More than twenty-five years after the end of apartheid, South Africa has become the most unequal society in the world.[293] The country is followed in the league of inequality, by Namibia, Botswana, and Zambia. South Africa is at thirty places above Nigeria on this particular score. The nation's wealth remains ensconced and unabashedly in the hands of a very few, super-connected elite. The top 1% of the

---

292. South Africa "Overview", World Bank, (Updated April 14, 2022), South Africa Overview: Development news, research, data | World Bank

293. Ibid. See also one of numerous international news headlines: "World Bank—South Africa is the most unequal country in the world". World Bank: South Africa is the most unequal country in the world | Africanews

population owns and controls over 70% of the net assets, leaving the bottom 60% in control of 7% of the remnants. High inequality is perpetuated by a legacy of exclusion, and the nature of the anti-people, lopsided economic policy spearheaded by the ruling African National Congress (ANC); not some "foreigners". Intergenerational mobility in South Africa is abysmally low, meaning the poverty disease is passed down through the generations with little change in that condition on the horizon anytime soon.

This scale of mass economic deprivation could only be rationalised if examined through the prism of apartheid, when the majority blacks were kept in bondage by the minority whites. The greatest achievement of the post-apartheid settlement, from the point of view of the whites, has been the preservation of the old structures of power in the hands of a tiny few, of which a significant number of blacks have now been invited to join. It is these urban black nouveau rich who are now being thrust forward as the modern faces of domination and oppression. Income inequality has worsened on the watch of the new black landlords, as oppression is no longer associated with race, but class. To buttress this point, in the last decade alone, white middle class grew by only 15%, while black middle class grew by a whopping 78%.[294] The latter now constitutes the privileged few occupying the citadels of power and influence; once the exclusive preserve of the white minority regime. The radicals of yesteryears have now become the reactionaries of today, united in their determination to maintain the status quo by force and propaganda. They are the ones with significant influence over the media, culture and other means of communication spreading falsehoods (like a bushfire), about "foreign invasion" and "foreign criminality" as a way of tapering down on the peoples' revolutionary impulse against the inherited oppressive system the black elites are now using to keep them down. With their access to, and control of the media, they spread the poisonous idea of "otherness" and "territoriality" in the minds of the poor, unemployed and 'wretched of the society' who, in turn, move against their brethren in what appears to be spontaneous attacks provoked by joblessness and criminality. In all, it is the poor being whipped up to fight the poor in a mad scramble for crumbs at the feet of the elite.

Have you ever wondered why, despite the overwhelming presence of Nigerian bankers, professors, scientists, doctors, lawyers and other top business executives thriving in the same South African economy, there is no simultaneous uprising against them, and other white-collar "foreigners"? How many poor people even understand the word "xenophobia" anyway? The black elites roaming the cor-

---

294. World Bank, ibid.

ridors of power in South Africa clearly do not wish to amplify the message of economic inequality too loudly for fear of a reprisal and a mass uprising against their own privileged lifestyles. So, what better way to divert the people's frustration than towards the bogey "foreigners" in their midst? In a way, what we are witnessing in South Africa is not really different to what happened elsewhere in Africa in the 1960s when most of the continent achieved independence. The elites who took over the reins of power in various African countries devoted much of their energy into consolidating their hold on power at the expense of the poor and downtrodden. They entrenched inequality rather than embarked upon a radical transformation of society. They did this by turning villagers against villagers, ethnic groups against ethnic groups and communities against communities. South Africa elites are doing exactly the same thing, this time, by diverting attention away from their own shortcomings as self-centred egoistic rulers, and instead focusing the peoples' mind on the "foreigners" taking over their jobs.

In the final analysis, though, when we live in a world that insists on "trickledown economics" as the only means of organising society, majority of the citizens are bound to be kept at bay violently, it appears, as they wait for the fruits of the elusive economic growth to manifest in their communities. Despite being the most advanced economy in Africa, South Africa (alone and by herself), cannot and will never be able to secure the liberation of her citizens from perpetual economic bondage and the internecine warfare that flows from that. Concomitantly, despite being the largest economy on the continent, Nigeria too will never secure the liberation of her citizens from poverty and hunger singularly and alone. The two countries will only be able to achieve this through economic and political union with the rest of the continent. This, without doubt, is the only viable option in the long term. Let us remember one of the sayings of the late sage; Chief Obafemi Awolowo: "wherever there are only two bones for three dogs, there can never be peace in the kennel". What a salutary, if ominous lesson, and a timely reminder that Africans must either hang together, or hang separately.

9.10 Nigeria's Muddled Policy on Western Sahara

24 September 2019

The territory is a remote, tiny plot of land on the tip of the West African coast, with about 600,000 Arab-speaking Muslim inhabitants, involved in a struggle for independence for over forty years. Africa Union (AU) refers to it as the last vestige of colonialism on African soil. Morocco, the colonial master,

9 · INTRA-AFRICAN AFFAIRS

vehemently disagrees. It sees the agitation for independence as illegitimate, as the territory "historically" belongs to them. Historic claims to such apparently 'barren' lands abound all over Africa, indeed, the world. The last major dispute of this kind in world politics occurred in East Timor; an oasis of about 1 million inhabitants, on the southern edge of Indonesia (Southeast Asia). When the Revolutionary Front for an Independent East Timor (Fretilin) proclaimed independence for the island as the colonial power, Portugal (still reeling from an internal military coup the previous year), literally packed out in a hurry in 1975, the island's big brother, Indonesia (over 200 million inhabitants), promptly proclaimed its "historic" claim on the island and declared it the "27th province" of the motherland. There ensued a David and Goliath situation culminating in a war of attrition which lasted until Indonesia succumbed to the will of the people, following a UN-sponsored referendum to determine the island's future in 1999. The East Timorese, of course, had voted overwhelmingly for independence. The parallel with the current Western Sahara problem is stark, and Nigeria's ambivalence towards the territory is troubling to say the least.

In 1976, the following year after Fretilin had declared independence from Indonesia, the indigenous people in Western Sahara too proclaimed the Sahrawi Arab Democratic Republic (SADR), which was recognised by many African countries and beyond, including the then OAU. SADR proceeded to set up a government in exile in Algeria, which still endures. There ensued another David and Goliath situation, this time, involving Western Sahara (600,000 inhabitants) and the Kingdom of Morocco (36 million inhabitants). Morocco subsequently annexed almost the entire territory of Western Sahara, and has held onto it till today. SADR, in retaliation, embarked on a guerrilla war with Morocco ending with a UN-brokered cease-fire agreement in 1991. Morocco has subsequently reneged on allowing a referendum of the people in the territory to determine their own future in a clear defiance of the UN and AU. While the uprising in East Timor was eventually settled in 1999; the island became the newest independent nation of the 21st century to join the United Nations in 2002, the struggle to achieve the same thing for Western Sahara, however, has remained elusive for SADR. Why?

To answer this question requires us to cast our minds back to what happened after the independence referendum in East Timor. There were more than 10,000-strong UN peacekeeping troop assembled and stationed on the island; the largest of such operation in the history of the UN.[295] The number

---

295. East Timor UN peacekeeping background UNMISET: United Nations Mission of Support in East Timor—Background

284   9 · INTRA-AFRICAN AFFAIRS

of UN police, the blue helmets, tripled that of the military, then, civilian personnel from Portugal, Indonesia, Australia, the USA, Canada, UK, etc. ran into several thousands, not to talk of Western casual workers in their hundreds of thousands milling around the lush island to render any type of help. Just wonder, such a huge influx of foreign 'expats' for a tiny island of 1 million people? Well, no price for guessing; it is oil. The keenly supervised referendum on the island happened in the wake of the discovery of megatons of oil along some of the world's richest reefs and marine life, that its southern neighbour, Australia, backed by the US, was keen to get involved in. Security Council resolution authorising the deployment came without objection, as it happens. On the contrary, Western Sahara can only boast of having phosphate although in vast quantities, but not enough to attract the deployment of 10,000 UN troops, and hundreds of thousands of Western 'aid workers'. There is no free lunch in Western capitalism, remember. There is, nonetheless, the potential for oil deposits on the seashore, deep inside Western Sahara, but that is yet to be explored. Furthermore, the territory's only regional power, Nigeria, neither has the military nor political weight to throw around, not even a clear strategic interest to exhibit as Australia managed to do vis-à-vis East Timor.

In addition to all this, is the disarray and a glaring lack of direction on the part of the AU. Its predecessor, the OAU, had admitted SADR as a member back in 1984, following which Morocco quit the organisation in protest. It was readmitted in 2017 while still occupying Western Sahara. Nigeria could have mobilised fellow Africans against Morocco's readmission, but the internal political squabbles between PDP, APC, election Tribunals, the Courts, defections, incumbency, political witch hunts etc. got the Presidency blindsided about this. Morocco now effectively feels in control of the agenda in Western Sahara despite the continuing involvement of the UN and AU. It is the first time an occupying force is allowed to dictate the terms of its own withdrawal from a territory hitherto recognised as 'independent' by Africa's only political organ; the AU.

To point out how history is repeating itself on this issue, the Southern African Development Community (SADC) attempted to give a fillip to the talks by African diplomats by organising a "solidarity conference" in March earlier this year, in Pretoria, South Africa. It was attended by more than 20 countries, including civil society and other political bodies, who were clearly pro-independence for Western Sahara. Upon hearing that initiative, Morocco hurriedly assembled its own parallel conference in Marrakesh, which attracted representatives from 36 African countries including; Cameroon, Cote d'Ivoire, Ethiopia, Liberia and Nigeria. This parallel meeting was designed to frustrate that of SADC, of course. And, Nigeria, once again, was found sitting on the wrong side of history. Is it not said that those who fail to learn the lesson of history are doomed to repeat it? Prior to the OAU's formation in 1963, there was agitation by some of the new African leaders to embarked upon an immediate unification agenda for the entire continent, led by the late Dr Kwame Nkrumah of Ghana. They held a meeting in, surprise-surprise, Casablanca, Morocco, in 1961. On the opposing 'conservative', status quo agenda was a parallel meeting hurriedly arranged, which took place in Monrovia, Liberia, a few months later. Prominent amongst them was, of course, Nigeria, vehemently opposed to any idea of African unity.

The OAU was indeed formed two years later in 1963, but largely became an empty talking shop until African leaders suddenly woke up with a dream of a united Africa in 2002, 47 years after Nkrumah's vision was strangled at birth. They agreed on the new name; African Union, to reflect their late (half-hearted) conversion to the cause. Then, having declared Western Sahara "the only territory in Africa under colonial rule", the AU leaders in their wisdom then went on to elect Morocco, the same colonial ruler they are busy denouncing, onto its Peace and Security Council (PSC). This is putting Dracula in charge of the blood bank, surely? It was painful to watch a representative of SADR on a Nigerian TV channel the other day, trying not to say anything offensive to Nigeria when questioned repeatedly about companies trading in Western Sahara's mineral resources on Nigerian soil in an apparent collaboration with Moroccan companies, and contrary to all international conventions. In terms of foreign policy objectives, the Western Sahara mess has to rank as a failure to articulate and demonstrate Nigeria's vital strategic interest at an important moment in history. The question now is, if Western Sahara's big uncle, Nigeria, would not speak for the fundamental rights of the Sahrawi people in its own backyard, then, who will?

9.11 Adesina's Re-election: Slap in the Face for America

1 September 2020

In the normal run of things, the election of President of the African Development Bank would be a non-event. Nothing particularly newsworthy to the world at large, especially coming from what the President of the United States, Donald Trump, has disparagingly described as "shithole countries". The re-election of the Nigerian, Dr Akinwumi Adesina, for a second term of five years as President of the bank last Thursday, the 27th of August 2020, caused ripples around the world of finance and politics in Washington, Africa, and beyond. Why, you might ask? Because the US fought tooth and nail to prevent Adesina

286   9 · INTRA-AFRICAN AFFAIRS

from being re-elected. The Trump administration deployed all the diplomatic and financial muscle at its disposal to block his unopposed nomination by the bank's Board of Directors.[296] By making it such a critical issue of principle, the administration placed the weight and prestige of its diplomatic leverage on the line, and came up short. The question is why the US spent so much political capital on an apparently minor office in a far-away land? And, given that Adesina received the unanimous (100%) backing of all regional (54) and non-regional (26) members of the Board for a second term, what did they see in the candidate that America did not? Why was there so much American angst over an otherwise innocuous process, and how did they misjudge the mood of the stakeholders, and got the outcome so spectacularly wrong?

We cannot understand America's keen interest in the Presidency of the bank in a "shithole country" without a broad understanding of international capitalism that informs it. Since the end of World War II, in 1945, the centre of gravity for international finance shifted onto the US from Europe and from the UK in particular. America was called upon to help rebuild Europe from the ruins of the war, which it did with aplomb, but at a price. Control of international finance was to be led henceforth, by the US, through the "Bretton Woods" institutions in Washington: World Bank, IMF, and the World Trade. The World Bank was to be (permanently) run by an American, and the IMF run in the same breath by Western Europe with US approval. World Trade was to be organised around "American values" of cut-throat competition and "free trade" in which it had become dominant. Thus, America became leader of the "free world", which needed to be protected, where necessary, by gunboat diplomacy and blood. Unfortunately for the US, but fortunately for the rest of the world, that consensus has been shattered by the expansion of international commerce beyond borders. China's rise to the summit of international trade has been accompanied by US decline in economic and political influence. This is one of the consequences of the Trump administration's penchant for up-ending international norms in the area of collective defence and economic co-operation, which is winning applause at home, but gradually eroding America's grip on global capitalism. It is this realisation that is making American officials jittery. It is what has made an otherwise inconsequential bank in an economic backwater of Ivory Coast, suddenly become so consequential.

---

296. See; "Why the US opposes Akinwumi Adesina's re-election as African Development Bank's president". 'African Courier' (Reporting Africa and its Diaspora) May 27, 2020. Why the US opposes Akinwumi Adesina's re-election as African Development Bank's president — THE AFRICAN COURIER. Reporting Africa and its Diaspora!

9 · INTRA-AFRICAN AFFAIRS

The supreme irony of this, is that Adesina is an apogee of Donald Trump; a disrupter per excellence, whom the Trump administration should readily be carrying shoulder high. He is a colourful, gregarious, larger-than-life character, who has no time for conventions and customs. He has proven that in his previous careers, and in particular as Minister of Agriculture in Nigeria prior to his appointment as President of the bank in 2015. As an illustration, for almost fifty years, Nigeria's staple diet; rice, was comfortably supplied by other countries in Asia and beyond. Adesina came in and famously proclaimed: "Nigeria has no business importing rice". The effect of that is now seen in the closing down of major rice factories in Asia, and a corresponding boom in its production in Nigeria. It has also led to the temporary closure of Nigerian land borders to prevent the hitherto lucrative rice smuggling into the country. It came as no surprise, therefore, that Adesina's first major move at the African Development Bank was to embolden and empower the bank by 'recapitalising' it. It used to be worth a paltry $93bn, it is now worth $208bn. And rather than sheepishly following Washington's economic precepts, it is now aggressively living up to its founding mission: development, especially in the field of education, energy, agriculture and infrastructure. The financial ratings agency; S&P, gave the bank its 'triple A' for an outstanding performance in 2019.[297] But, that notwithstanding, America no longer considers it a 'reliable' partner. Consequently, Adesina had to go in order to align the bank with the Trump administration's economic world view more pointedly. How ironic is that?

Americans used to have the smartest tactics for removing an unwanted head of any global institution; tar the person with a brush of "scandal" or "corruption" and rely on Western allies to fall in line. It is the manifestation of US "soft power" which has been eroded in recent times, not least by the Trump administration itself. Thus, in his bid for a second term, Adesina was suddenly ambushed by a litany of allegations of "corruption" and "nepotism" by an anonymous employee of the bank; a whistleblower. The bank's internal Ethics Committee immediately smelt a rat. It investigated the complaints and promptly cleared Adesina of any wrongdoing. America, the second largest shareholder of the bank after Nigeria, kicked against the committee's conclusions and insisted on an "independent" investigation of the allegations. The Board of the bank felt slighted by this demand, but gave in, and mandated a "High-Level Panel of Independent Experts"

---

297. "Our ratings on AfDB reflect its important role in Africa ..." S&P, 2019. S&P Global affirms African Development Bank's AAA rating with stable outlook | African Development Bank — Building today, a better Africa tomorrow (afdb.org)

to carry out a review of its Ethics Committee's clearance of Adesina. It was headed by Professor Mary Robinson, former President of the Republic of Ireland. Its verdict was as compelling as it comes: "It has considered the President's submissions on their face and finds them consistent with his innocence and to be persuasive. Complaints were correctly dismissed at the stage of preliminary examination". Most damning of all, it concluded that the "complaints did not satisfy the threshold of credibility and substantiation".

With that clean bill of health, Adesina was confirmed for a second term. The US Treasury Secretary, Steve Mnuchin, who had spearheaded the fierce opposition to Adesina's re-election, went back home with his tale between his legs. China, the main beneficiary of any US humiliation on that front, has remained tight-lipped and in the shadows all along. Chinese officials must be wringing their hands with glee at the comeuppance for America. The bank's new capitalisation, $208bn, though substantial, is only equal to the level of China's sprawling investment on the continent. The looser America's economic grip becomes, the better for China's influence. It is probably an inevitable consequence of America's persistent attempt to have its cake and eat it too on the global stage. This is where "America first" doctrine comes face-to-face (and indeed) collides with reality. Necessity for multilateralism and respect for traditional allies (anathema in Donald Trump's worldview) are, nevertheless, paramount for success. It is not too late for America though. It can, and will bounce back from its go-it-alone, debilitating, attitude only if it stops banging on how much the rest of the world owes 'us', and realises how it needs the rest of the world to help salvage something from its rapidly dwindling global economic dominance.

9.12 Africans Hiding Wealth in Offshore Accounts Are Traitors

12 October 2021

Revelations after revelations from the "Pandora Papers"[298] unearthed by the International Consortium of Investigative Journalists (a consortium of some 300 journalists around the world) have been splashed through print and broadcast media, nonstop, throughout last week. The revelations are extracts from the financial details of some very prominent and wealthy individuals

---

298. See the International Consortium of Investigative Journalists (ICIJ) uncovering of Pandora Papers, Pandora Papers — ICIJ

9 · INTRA-AFRICAN AFFAIRS   289

around the world, and their hitherto concealed wealth. It follows a leak of 12 million files exposing their offshore dealings. For clarity, an "offshore" dealing or account is a method of hiding wealth in an account in one of several "tax havens", usually a remote island in the Caribbean, Latin America, and Europe, away from the prying eyes of the tax authorities in their home countries. Put simply, an individual with loads of cash at their disposal, who does not want ownership to be traced to him, would approach an agency specialising in hiding wealth overseas, far removed from their home jurisdiction, create fictitious companies with fictitious directors on some remote Island, where no tax deductions are payable. Once established, the beneficial owner of the wealth can begin to enjoy the proceeds by giving instructions to the agent on where and how to dispose of the wealth, usually by buying properties in choice locations in Western capitals.

The fictitious companies give the appearance of legitimate businesses, able to buy and sell properties, as well as move cash around major financial hubs in Europe and America, anonymously, and completely legally. You are spending money, accumulating properties, but, no one knows your identity. No one knows you are the shadowy figure behind the fictitious (or shell) companies. It sounds murky, cloak and dagger(ish), but that is capitalism at its worst. Fabulously rich individuals from the system do not fancy surrendering too much of their wealth to their country's tax authorities. There are three principal reasons why a person might want to hide wealth in an offshore account. First, is to avoid paying income and inheritance taxes. Remember, there is a difference between tax avoidance and tax evasion. One is legal, the other is illegal. So, people hiding wealth to avoid paying taxes though morally culpable, are totally legit. The second reason people use offshore accounts is anonymity. Not every wealthy individual is comfortable with the source of their wealth being scrutinised in the media. The third and final reason why this method is adopted is criminality. That is, for the purpose of money laundering. People who have come into sudden wealth through bribery or theft find it a convenient way of moving cash around the world, gobbling up luxury yachts, fancy apartments in central London, Manhattan, New York, and Dubai without fanfare.

Since the revelations, many countries have been combing through the documents, looking to see if any of their citizens are highlighted. Indeed, many are, including from the 'usual suspects'; Russia, India, Pakistan, Brazil, but, also, Spain, UK, USA, Australia, and several others. With specific reference to Africa, what boggles the mind is the thought that, with such a level of underdevelopment, and endless borrowing requirements from wealthy countries, any African citizen would embark upon taking money from the continent for hiding in secret locations, contributing to the development of other countries at the expense of theirs. It is even more galling to imagine that any political figure in Africa would stash their wealth away in foreign lands, whilst implementing policy that creates economic hardship for their compatriots at home. Above all, it is sickening to imagine that anyone in position of authority in Africa would be busy buying up pricey properties in Western capitals while the rest of the population live in shanty towns and in slums around major cities as a result of government inability or unwillingness to spread the wealth around in their own countries.

Do we have prominent Africans amongst the revelations? Of course, we do. Perhaps the most prominent names that have come up are President Uhuru Kenyatta of Kenya, and in Nigeria, former Governor Peter Obi, and Senator Stella Oduah, both from Anambra state. The authenticity of all of the documents in the leak has never been questioned. For instance, the shell companies associated with the transactions linked with Obi and Oduah and the various properties bought overseas are precise and detailed. There is no escape from the cold truth. Be it Kenyatta, Obi, Oduah, or anyone of their ilk, it is an unforgivable betrayal of public trust. It is nothing but treachery. There is an urgent need for anyone standing for office in Africa to make a declaration about their interest in any offshore accounts. The public have the right to this information prior to an election for, it should be an automatic disqualification from office. How can anyone seek to rule over an African country in whose financial regime they do not, themselves, have confidence?

Furthermore, no one seeking position of power and authority in any African country should be permitted to basically stick up two fingers to millions of their impoverished citizens, more or less saying; "Up yours! My (mostly) illgotten wealth is accumulating even more wealth for me out there in foreign lands." Assuming the monies in those offshore accounts are even legally held, they, nonetheless, constitute an affront to all sense of moral decency of the African. Kenyatta, Obi, Oduah & Co, are by consequence, unfit for office. What is more, they and others like them should be held to account for the humongous amount of wealth stashed away for them and their families offshore. How could accountability possibly happen without having to prove criminality, a notorious route to recovering stolen assets? Incidentally, the UK (the one time favourite destination for looted cash from the continent) is now the leading thorn in the flesh for Africa's "Politically Exposed Persons" and their illegal assets. "Scotland Yard" (the Metropolitan Police), in conjunction with Her Majesty's Civil Service, Assets Forfeiture Team, have spared no efforts in tackling the rising tide of money laundering emanating from this continent in the last twenty years. This is far more than Nigerian or any other government in Africa has managed in the same time frame.

The UK's Proceeds of Crimes Act 2002, permits the confiscation of criminal property using a lower "civil" standard of proof. This was, however, limited to exceptional cases where prospect of criminal prosecution was unavailable or undesirable, particularly in the African situation where the suspects are usually part of the establishment relied upon to assist. This column came up with a novel idea of creating a 'trust' relationship between a public office holder, and the government property at his disposal. The 'trust' element obviates the need for anti-corruption agencies to proof wrongdoing before confiscation. This was deemed too draconian in the context of the UK. See; "Money Laundering Regulation and the African PEP: Case for tougher civil remedy options", in 'Journal of Money Laundering Control', Vol 9, 1, 2012. Not satisfied to rest on their oars, the UK government later came up with an innovative legislative hammer of their own in form of "Unexplained Wealth Orders", included in the Criminal Finances Act 2017. It was targeted at people linked with serious crime or who hold public office outside the EU, in other words, political office holders here, in Africa, and elsewhere. It took effect from January 2018. Two things left to accomplish: "Unexplained Wealth Orders" should transform into a UN Convention. Then, it should be domesticated in home countries, subsequently, across Africa. No offence, no crime would have been committed before the likes of Kenyatta, Obi, Oduah, etc. are requested to account. Never mind offshore accounts, this would be a game changer in the fight against official corruption on African shores.

9.13 Thomas Sankara: Africa's Finest, Gunned Down Too Soon

19 October 2021

That there is a huge discrepancy between the potential wealth, and the reality of poverty in African states, is uncontested. The continent is endowed with abundant human and natural resources from the north; petroleum and gas, to the east; gold, gas, uranium, copper, etc. To the west; iron-ore, phosphate, titanium, gold, timber, diamonds, petroleum. To the equator; timber, petroleum. To the centre; diamonds, cobalt, uranium, petroleum. To the south; aluminium, gas, platinum, gold, etc. To crown it all, the continent has the largest youth population in the world; a ready pool of technically-adept workforce.[299] Despite the oft mentioned widespread economic hardship, Africa is

---

299. Data readily available from the Mo Ibrahim Foundation as well as multiple other sources international-youth-day-research-brief.pdf (ibrahim.foundation)

the fastest growing region for Foreign Direct Investment in the world.[300] Furthermore, Africa has the largest arable land mass in the world, one third of the earth's remaining resources are located in Africa.[301] Yet these vast natural and human resources do not translate into economic value for the citizens. Much of the resources (70%) are extracted for shipment to Europe, America, and the rest of the world, who then turn them into finished products for export and consumption back to Africa. The continent is still riven by internecine war in places. With little manufacturing capacity, it is dependent on outsiders for virtually all its technical needs. The division between 'Francophone' and 'Anglophone' Africa is entrenched and deepening. With the exception of Haiti, Tajikistan, Yemen and Afghanistan, the poorest nations on earth are in Africa, starting with the very bottom; Burundi with a paltry GDP of US$263 dollars; South Sudan, US$303; Malawi, US$399; Mozambique, US$455; and Democratic Republic of Congo, US456.[302]

Compare the above figures to those of the top three richest nations on earth, starting with Luxembourg with a GDP of US$118,359 dollars, Singapore; US$98,526, Ireland; 93,612.[303] Neither of these countries boasts of natural resources. Of the ten topmost technologically advanced countries in the world; Japan, South Korea, China, US, Germany, Russia, UK, Singapore, Israel, and Switzerland, only three; Russia, China, and US have natural resources. The others have to make do with imports from Africa and the rest of the world, which they then convert into technology and economic advantage. Why Africa remains forever stagnant, famished, and impoverished amidst plenty has been the unanswered and unanswerable question of our time. Some blame the very abundance of resources as a curse; others blame it on poor leadership. Others, still, see a combination of poor leadership and imperialism as the source of the continent's malaise. Those who take this last stance never make it to the seat of power, and the handful who did, had not lasted. They were assassinated. Patrice Lumumba of the Democratic Republic of Congo, and Kwame Nkrumah of Ghana are two names flashing through the mind. And so it was, that Thomas (Isidore Noel) Sankara (1949–1987), came to power in a military coup in Burk-

---

300. See; "Foreign Direct Investment to Africa defies global slump, rises 11%". United Nations Commission for Trade and Development (UNCTAD), June 2019. Foreign direct investment to Africa defies global slump, rises 11% | UNCTAD

301. World Bank Data, Arable land (% of land area) | Data (worldbank.org)

302. See; World Population Review's "Poorest countries in the world 2022". Poorest Countries in the World 2022 (worldpopulationreview.com)

303. See; Worlddata.info's "The 50 richest countries in the world" 2022. The richest countries in the world (worlddata.info)

9 · INTRA-AFRICAN AFFAIRS 293

ina Faso (formerly Upper Volta) in 1983, aged 33, with a clear mind and focus on what needed to be done; pursue a people-oriented, self-sufficient economic programme, which defy the logic of dependency.

Military coups are, (or were), common in Africa in Sankara's time. Such coups are often rabble-rousing and opportunistic. There have been a few that could be described as ideological, or 'revolutionary' if you prefer. The military regime of Sankara was quintessentially the 'root and branch', fundamental change, type. The only other parallel in Africa was Egypt under Gamal Abdel Nasser, in 1952, which overthrew the country's Monarchy. If ever there was any such thing as a good military intervention and takeover of government anywhere, look no further than these two prime examples. Purists would argue from-dawn-to-dusk that military coups are inherently bad, and must be condemned. In principle, they are right. Nonetheless, on very rare occasions, the end ought to justify the means. When Sankara came to power, literacy rate in the country was 13%. It went up to 73% at his death. He embarked upon a programme of mass vaccination against meningitis, yellow fever and measles, protecting over two million children, and reducing infant mortality rate from 20.8% to 14.5%, redistributed land to the poor, who then planted crops which transformed the country from dependent to self-sufficient in food overnight, planted 10 million trees, championed the cause of women, opening up the military ranks to them, invested in the textile industry thereby cutting off the reliance on foreign clothes, no portrait of the head of state on office walls, banned the fleet of official luxury cars in favour of the modest (and cheap) Renault 5, cut his own salary in half and that of top government functionaries in solidarity with the have-nots. The list goes on.[304]

Having firmly established his domestic agenda, and realising that his country could not truly succeed as an island entirely of itself, Sankara sought a bigger, (Africa-wide), platform to articulate his vision, and persuade fellow Africans to join hands in the fight against imperialism and neo-colonialism, which he believed would never allow his country to reach its full potential despite the considerable progress achieved thus far. Unbeknown to him, though, the vultures were already circling. His unapologetic brand of national self-pride and cultural awakening had caused upset in the circles of the rich and conservative reactionaries not happy with losing their economic preponderance. Sankara was unusually articulate and eloquent for a military man; extremely well informed, and unabashed in his quest for the total liberation of the African continent. He was

---

304. See; "Facts about Thomas Sankara" (www.thomassankara.net), Facts about Thomas Sankara in Burkina Faso | My Blog

294   9 · INTRA-AFRICAN AFFAIRS

not only advanced for his age, he was well ahead of time on some of his pro-nouncements. He could hold his own in any intellectual discourse with the think tanks, brain boxes and sundry, any day. A level-headed, visionary African leader with the military at his beck and call is the neo-colonialist's worst nightmare. This *enfant terrible* must be dealt with. The big platform duly presented itself at the OAU Summit in Addis Ababa, Ethiopia in July 1987. Sankara went into the Summit, stepped onto the podium, and delivered a most compelling, riveting argument against the payment of debilitating, and crippling external debts supposedly owed by chronically poor African states.

Sankara had titled his speech; "A United Front against Debt", and urged fellow delegates to respond to the burning issue of the day as a united bloc. 'Debt is neo-colonialism, in which colonizers have transformed themselves into "technical assistants". We should say "technical assassins". Debt cannot be repaid. Those who led us into indebtedness gambled as if in a casino. Now, that they have suffered losses, they demand repayment'. The African debts were mainly owed to Western financial houses, including the IMF. Delegates at the conference looked and listened in awe of Sankara's bravery and mesmerising oratory. As if in a premonition, he said in conclusion: "If Burkina Faso stands alone in refusing to pay, I will not be here for the next conference". He was gunned down as he led a training workshop in the country's capital, Ouagadougou, in October 1987, barely three months after the Summit. The 'rebel soldiers' who carried out the assassination was led by his best friend, and close confidant, Blaise Compaoré who took over and remained in power for 27 years subsequently. He did all he could to undo and besmirch Sankara's work and legacy. He had envisaged being in power for life, but was finally forced out in a mass revolt in 2014. He fled into exile in Ivory Coast. He is now being tried in absentia at home, along with 13 others for the brutal and cowardly murder of Sankara 34 years after the event. The irony of it all is that the debts were indeed cancelled for African states, partially and in whole, following a sustained, worldwide campaign from the late 1990s to early 2000s. Oh, Africa!

9.14 King Mswati III: Africa's Last Maximum Ruler

2 November 2021

The Kingdom of Eswatini (or Eswatini as it is interchangeably referred to) is a tiny country of just over one million, located in Southern Africa, sandwiched between Mozambique and South Africa. It is as landlocked as it is completely encircled by big brother, South Africa, to which its currency is pegged. It is ruled by 53 year old King Mswati III, who acceded to the throne in 1986, aged 18. It will come as a rude awakening to many people in Africa that, in the era of continuing agitation for inclusive governance, there is a country on the continent whose citizens still toil under maximum rule. Nonetheless, Eswatini is a full-fledged independent sovereign state, with membership of the African Union, Southern African Development Community, and the United Nations. Prior to the scramble for Africa in the 1880s, the land was occupied by the Swazis, and they were content to be governed through traditional institutions. It was also the time when smaller empires and kingdoms were dissolving and merging with bigger, and more powerful ones across Africa, so who knows what might have happened had European colonialism not taken place as it did, with Britain gaining the upper hand and taking hold of the territory in 1907. Would the kingdom have been absorbed by some other neighbouring forces in the region? Anyway, that is an interesting conjecture that applies across other empires throughout Africa. The British did well to recognise King Sobhuza II in 1921, through whom colonial orders were passed down until the country gained independence in 1968.

Unlike other African states, where several political associations were formed along ethnic lines, who then fought alongside each other against the common enemy, Eswatini is almost homogenous, where no ethnic tensions had existed. The fight, and negotiation for independence did not become as protracted as it did in Nigeria, for example, where different regional leaders had different political priorities. Rather than take the country in whole to himself, King Sobhuza was prevailed upon to allow political parties to form and campaign for power. The new constitution established the House of Assembly and the Senate in 1967, a year prior to the granting of independence, but the King swept that away six years later, in favour of a hand-picked, rubber-stamped Parliament, which has endured in some form or another to this day. The fight against the Apartheid regime in South Africa during this time meant little attention was paid to questions of democracy in its neighbouring countries. The greater evil was apartheid, which drew the ire of everyone. Upon independence in 1968, however, King Sobhuza moved swiftly to entrench and perpetuate the monarchy by creating a Fund: "Tibiyo Taka Ngwane" (Tibiyo for short), a Sovereign Wealth Fund ostensibly for the benefit of his people, but in reality, for the nourishment and aggrandisement of the monarchy.[305] Revenues from the

---

305. Based on the analysis in "Towards Equal Opportunity: Accelerating Inclusion and Poverty Reduction — A Systematic Country Diagnostic". The World Bank Group, Eswatini Country Team, Africa Region, December 14, 2010.

296 9 · INTRA-AFRICAN AFFAIRS

mining industry in the country were channelled through the Fund, and it has grown exponentially in leaps and bounds since. It is the financial foundation for maximum rule.[306]

The King had hoped to live for ever, of course. But he died ('transitioned' in African parlance) in 1982, having ruled for 82 years and 254 days, thereby cementing the historical foundation for maximum rule. An incredibly long reign for which there is no comparison in modern world history. King Sobhuza's death in 1982 left a dangerous power vacuum though. The heir to the throne, the current King Mswati III was only 14 years old, and still in school in England. The tradition was that the successor needed to be at least 21 before being crowned. Sensing a chance for power grab, a group of political activists quickly formed the "People's United Democratic Movement" (PUDEMO) in 1983, and immediately tabled a list of demands aimed at ushering in a new democratic and inclusive governance. This alarmed the royalists and reactionary forces desirous of maintaining the status quo. Consequently, upon attaining the age of 18, Prince Makhosetive's coronation was brought forward at the expense of his education, and was crowned King Mswati III in 1986. He has both history and the Fund established by King Sobhuza to legitimise and entrench his reign. If you think being young, and of the modern age, might have helped the new King develop a different outlook for the country, you would be mistaken. King Mswati is a man living large, in opulence, with his political accolades, and a recently acquired private jet,[307] in a country virtually surviving on charities from foreign donors, with one of the world's highest rates of HIV infections, and where life expectancy has dropped to below 40 years.

Subtle pressure was put on the king to open up the country's political system, but, nothing fundamental has changed. On the contrary, it has been one step forward, and three steps backward on that front. The inevitable financial crisis hit the country in 2011, forcing the King to appeal to South Africa and the IMF for a bailout. Meanwhile, "Tibiyo" (remember?) has accumulated capital in excess of US$10 billion dollars, double the country's GDP, and the King's personal fortune is estimated to be in excess of US$100 million dollars. Surely, no point borrowing from anyone when there's ready-made cash to draw from? Well, there lies the puzzle. Indeed, we have been there before. A

---

306. To buttress this point, see; "Anti-Money Laundering and Counter-Terrorist Financing Measures — Eswatini. Eastern and Southern Africa Anti-Money Laundering Group, Mutual Evaluation Report, June 2022. https://www.fatf-gafi.org/media/fatf/documents/reports/mer-fsrb/ESAAMLG-Mutual-Evaluation-Report-Eswatini-2022.pdf

307. See; "Eswatini: Secrecy over cost of King's new jet". Allafrica.com, April 18, 2018 https://allafrica.com/stories/201804190210.html

9 · INTRA-AFRICAN AFFAIRS

leader's personal fortune being higher than his country's GDP is not strange in Africa. The late Mobutu Sese Seko of the Democratic Republic of Congo, Omar Bongo, also late President of Gabon, and current President of Equatorial Guinea, Teodoro Nguema Obiang Mangue are other prime examples. King Mswati is therefore in good company. And when you are in the middle of an economic downturn with mounting political pressure, what do you do to change the narrative? You change the country's name from Swaziland to Eswatini. This is exactly what King Mswati did in 2018, single-handedly. 'Swaziland', he claims, is a relic of colonialism.

Removing vestiges of colonialism is not new in Africa. After all, upon independence, "Gold Coast" became Ghana, "Bechuanaland" became Botswana, "Nyasaland" became Malawi, "Northern Rhodesia" became Zambia, and latterly, "Zaire" became DRC, while "Upper-Volta" became Burkina Faso etc. But why wait 50 years? More so, Eswatini translates as 'land of the Swazis', exactly the same meaning as the Swaziland you have just abandoned. For King Mswati, it was a calculated move to divert public attention away from politics. In addition, the King also makes a big deal of the ritual of the "Reed Dance" (or Umhlanga), involving a parade of bare-breasted (mostly pretty) young girls and women in the courtyard of the Royal Palace annually. This cultural, open celebration of 'chastity' and 'virginity', though a major national event in Eswatini, was deemed so offensive by Western critics that the video clips of it were banned from YouTube, for promoting "nudity". However, after a barrage of protests from several angles about "cultural imperialism", YouTube reversed itself. The ritual has now been judged "culturally relevant and properly contextualised", much to the delight of the King, who is at liberty to pick any of the spring chickens on display in his courtyard every year, as an addition to his burgeoning (13) consorts. His late father had 70 and more than 200 offspring. At only 53, King Mswati has already had a full, fulfilled and adventurous life with real estate dotted around the world, private jet, and millions of dollars in personal fortune hidden away in safe locations. He can quit and retire into a life of luxury, but he would not; at least, not voluntarily. It is said; there is always enough for a man's want, but never enough for his greed.

Chapter Ten

International Affairs

10.01 Hypocrisy of Foreign Election Observers

12 February 2019

The presence of international election observers has become a regular feature of life in this country as elsewhere in Africa, for the best part of twenty five years, if not more. It is a phenomenon that our political leaders and electorate alike have not only come to expect in general elections, but have now tended to accept as part and parcel of the package. Nowadays, it seems, no general elections will be deemed complete without the prying eyes of individuals and groups of individuals from mainland Europe and America for starters, and others from different parts of the world, and organisations dedicated to observing elections. Indeed, election observation has developed into a career and profession for certain groups of people in these countries that they make comfortable living out of it. They become established and experienced in observing elections, get promotion and recognition as 'professionals' and 'experts' in the field so much that people struggle to get their names included in the "core team" of election observers by the funding organisations in Europe and America. They, therefore, will always see the need to observe elections in overseas countries because they have now developed a vested interest of their own in the exercise.

It used to be merely an altruistic exercise on the part of European and American retirees and election tourists eager for an all-expenses paid vacation to exotic locations around the world; the bulk of which they still are. But more importantly, election "missions" have seen the creation and steady rise of professional cadres and the concomitant need for perpetuation and self-preservation; a trade union of sort.

The above background is given not as an argument against foreign election observers, but to put the rest of this write up in a better perspective. It is equally important to state at the outset, that the term "international" observers as used here precludes the countries of Africa and fellow Africans coming to observe elections in Nigeria. Their participation, history and structure are fundamentally different from that of the funding bodies from Europe and America. In fact, observer missions from Africa are viewed as "peer-review" and in some sense, 'internal', than the ones from Europe and America, sometimes seen as meddlesome and extraneous. The main rationale for European and American election observer missions in this part of the world is essentially to deter fraud and promote transparency. Since political power offers untrammelled access to state resources in Africa, whoever emerges winner and loser has everything to gain and lose respectively from any election. Ultimately, the margin between winning and losing often makes the difference between economic survival and ruin for the country concerned. Let us not forget, European and American monies are heavily invested across the continent of Africa as well. That being so, economic ruin in any of the fifty-three states on the continent could result in an extra flow of refugees to Europe and America. So, does that also give them a vested interest in the process of elections in Nigeria, and Africa in general? You bet it does, it is a two-way traffic.

It is precisely the European and American vested interest just referred to that forms the basis of their weak standing on the election process in Africa. European and American experts are bent on making us clones of their respective electoral processes in their home countries. Their insistence on multiparty democracy, for instance, leads to fragmentation in many homogenous African settings. For instance, when such experiment was first attempted in Guinea-Bissau almost twenty years ago, it literally led to communities fighting communities, and family clans fighting family clans, because, with a population of just over one million, everybody was related to each other in one way or another. So, once you insist that they must organise into different parties overnight, you have brothers and sisters suddenly campaigning against each other from different sides of the party game. It was a recipe for disaster for the country, which has continued to this day. Another thing is the insistence on "free press" without taking account of the lack of resources in private hands to make that a realistic option in Africa. Consequently, when, as a European or American observer, you view the media in Africa through the rose-tinted goggles of a free press from your home country, you are bound to see the unimaginable and the bizarre, upon which you draw conclusions. Contrary to widespread belief, many people love, and subscribe to the ideal of democracy in Africa. As a matter of fact, democratic accountability in African societies was better pronounced, and much deep-rooted before the advent of colonialism, than it has been with the so-called 'modern' Parliamentary and Presidential systems foisted on the continent by the West.

Do election observation funding agencies in the West have something to teach Africans about democracy? The answer is emphatically NO, unless you think that the process alone is substitute for substance, as many Western experts inside the International Monetary Fund, European Union, and Washington apparently do. It was indeed these renowned institutions which once gave succour and protection to sit-tight dictators and military coups across Africa in the 1960s, 1970s and early 1980s for fear of Communist take-over of the continent. Kwame Nkrumah won a popular, democratic election in 1957, and had embarked on a people-oriented transformation of Ghana before he was bundled out by Western imperialist agents-cum autocrats who had held the country down for years. Similarly, Patrice Lumumba won a decisive democratic election in the Congo in 1960 before a CIA-sponsored coup installed the despotic regime of Mobutu Sese Seko to power and kept him there for over three decades while multinational corporations plundered the country's natural resources. Before long, Africa was strewn with puppet regime after puppet regime on every corner of the continent, which also went on to plunder the resources of the continent, leading to the rush of economic refugees into Western countries. Western donor agencies then suddenly realised the need for 'democracy' and an end to sit-tight dictators that their own policy had hitherto created across Africa.

For the avoidance of doubt, nothing that has been said thus far represents a rejection of, or hostility towards Western election observers. Most of the personnel involved in the exercise are ignorant of the historical records highlighted in this piece. Many more simply seize on the opportunity to do good for people in the "Third World" as they see it. In that respect, they are neither to be vilified nor castigated for making an honest living out of the cyclical jamboree. That being said, there is a lot to be desired at the policy and state levels in their home countries. It is particularly galling to hear, for instance, representatives of American government wagging their fingers and warning us of "consequences" if the election process falls short of their own expectation. Was it not the current US President, Donald Trump, who talked repeatedly, in his 2016 Presidential campaign, of how the US electoral system had been "rigged" against political outsiders like himself? Is the US not guilty of systematic suppression of black votes in some US states? The election of the first black US President, Barack Obama (2008–2016), witnessed a rise in violence and killing of innocent black people by police in America. Against that background, how should the world view the issue of post-election violence in the country? US diplomats in

Nigeria represent and speak for Donald Trump; a man who has no moral authority to lecture others in "hate speech" (he does a lot of that himself) and racism or ethnicity as it is known here (he exhibits tons of that himself). Please, remember, when you are pointing one finger, the remaining four are pointing straight back at you.

10.02 Why Trump Supporters Are So Wrong

11 February 2020

In an off-the-cuff remark regarding the Nicaraguan dictator, Anastasio Somoza (1937–1947, 1950–1956), the US President, Franklin D. Roosevelt (1933–1945) said something about Somoza, who had lived in the United States before returning to his country to lead a US-backed coup which toppled President Adolfo Diaz. Thereafter, Somoza captured and ruled Nicaragua with an iron grip, so brutal that it attracted rare condemnations across the normally placid neighbouring Latin American countries and beyond. Somoza had been hellbent on turning Nicaragua into an outpost of the United States. However, when the disquiet and murmuring about him started swirling around the corridors of power in Washington too much, Roosevelt was said to have snapped: "He may be a son-of-a-bitch, but he is our son-of-a-bitch". Today, in America, there are many people within and outside the Liberal establishment, who are so disdainful of current US President, Donald Trump, so much that they see his cantankerous approach to political debate, and his lackadaisical attitude towards national security matters as simply madness. Meanwhile, conservative America; the hinterland in the suburbs, and the few dedicated core of Trump's "Right-Wing" supporters; his "base", understand the tempestuous streak in him. They see a method in the 'madness', and would not be swayed from their resolute loyalty. A case of; 'He may be mad, but he is our mad man'? They see through the dusty political wind blowing across their faces, and are happy with what they view as the bold steps Trump is taking to "make America great again". They are wrong.

First, let us highlight some of Donald Trump's notable achievements and see how they represent a vindication of the loyal support he enjoys. His anti-immigration rhetoric during the election has been given effect in the building of a partial wall along the US-Mexico borderland. He has relentlessly and deliberately been reversing almost all of his predecessor (President Barack Obama)'s signature achievements: path to citizenship for undocumented immigrants, tighter regulation of the financial markets, Paris Climate Change

Accord, the Iran Nuclear Deal Agreement, etc. The Administration has tried severally but failed to dismantle the "Affordable Care Act", widely seen as the most audacious legislative act in America this century, and President Obama's most important accomplishment in office. It guarantees health coverage for millions of Americans previously left out. Trump has given license to oil companies to continue digging for new oilfields, contrary to the stance taken by the previous Administration. He has aligned himself with Saudi Arabia, culminating in a multi-billion dollar arms deal, and creating thousands of jobs for Americans. He stopped short of condemning the Saudis for the wanton killing of one of their own citizens; the US-based Washington Post correspondent, Jamal Khashoggi, pulled US troops out of Syria without consulting allies, renegotiated trade deals with Canada, and Mexico, tearing up the previous North Atlantic Free Trade Agreement negotiated by his two predecessors, slammed high tariffs on China for "taking advantage of America" by building trade surplus to the detriment of US workers, nominated and pushed through the appointments of conservative justices onto the Supreme Court, with the view to reversing the US liberal abortion laws at some point in the future. Most of all, he drove a major tax cut legislation through the formerly Republican-led Congress, largely favouring the top 3% of earners in a "trickle down" economic strategy.

The US economy has since been booming, creating jobs, and the stock market skyrocketing, although 45% of Americans do not own stocks. The tax cut has pushed up the country's budget deficit from 19 to 22 trillion dollars. This used to be a major point of fierce economic debate under the previous Administration, but now, no one really cares, it seems. Tax receipts from the booming economy will eventually help offset the budget gap, so the thinking goes. Only last week, the Trump Administration announced an end to "birth tourism"; a liberal visa regime, which basically allowed pregnant women from any part of the globe to enter the US for the sole purpose of giving birth, leading to automatic citizenship as it does, to anyone born on American soil. All of these policy initiatives are what make Donald Trump unimpeachable in the eyes of his supporters, even if he was caught at a crime scene with his hand soaked in the victim's blood.

Surprisingly, Trump is not short of admirers amongst Africans, and even amongst African-Americans in the United States itself, in spite of his unabashed racist utterances. Despite trashing the African continent as "shithole", including talking of how "lifeless" Nigerian President Muhammadu Buhari looked on his visit to the White House last year, he has, nonetheless, built up a sizable fan base amongst the African political and business elites. Why is this? The reason is simpler than it appears. Trump's faults aside, he has managed to tap into the African nostalgic yearning for patriotic leadership; one who would act to put their country first, hence, their willingness to forgive what they see as his 'loose tongue' on occasions. The US President had once boasted that he could stand on 1600, Pennsylvania Avenue (the White House), shoot someone dead, and he would get away with it. Something, somehow, makes this crass conjecture possible. This is a President who was impeached by the House of Representatives, but acquitted by the Senate last week of the most egregious breaches of national security and abuse of power in US history. If this was happening in Africa, we would naturally put it down to financial "settlements" of the protagonists, or "silencing" of the opposition. This is clearly not the case in the US. So, why is it proving difficult to hold Trump to account for his numerous misdeeds?

The answer lies in how individuals conceive the United States of America. America is a country, but it is also an idea. America as a country; "rags to riches" mind-set, self-interested individualism; "America first" syndrome, is what Trump (who built a life-long career in real-estate), is marketing to his compatriots and the rest of the world. America as an idea; Republicanism and Constitutionalism, does not resonate with Trump whatsoever. The rule of law, separation of powers, checks and balances, restraint on executive discretion are time-honoured Republican ideals for which Donald Trump has no patience. Also the idea of America as a "shiny city on a hill", beacon of hope and liberty; American exceptionalism, are all rooted in its enduring constitution. The Statue of Liberty on prominent display in the New York harbour says it all.

Supporters of Donald Trump conflate America as a country and America as an idea. That is a tragic mistake. They have been sold only the spirit of, and indeed, bought into America as a country. America as an idea is a bitter pill to swallow for the core Trump supporters especially at times of economic hardship. And for a transactional President such as Trump, it is easier to lead America as a country, than it is to lead America as an idea. In an ideal world though, a combination of both is what the Presidency should be all about. It requires tenacity to principles and high moral values which cannot easily be reduced to the outcomes of today's trade negotiations, and commercial agreements. It also requires painful sacrifices for the higher goal of liberty and individual freedom across borders. Trump and his legion of supporters clearly think there is a trade-off between the two. In so doing, America has become just another country in some part of the world. That is a pity, because attempts by successive US Administrations to acknowledge, if not live up to, the founding of America and its timeless values is precisely what makes it greater than any other.

10.03 USA: Why Trump Must (and will) Be Defeated

3 November 2020

It is that time of the year in the electoral cycle, when Americans go to the polls to elect the country's 46th President this same day, the 3rd of November 2020. America's Presidential elections are set in stone; on the first Tuesday after the 1st of November every four years. Thus, even the date of the next general elections for the 47th president is already known, including the swearing-in date; the 20th of January. There is no commission or body sitting on their high horse to "announce" the date of the elections. Peaceful transfer of power has been the hallmark of American democracy since 1797. Unlike in other republics, the constitution cannot be hurriedly altered, or amended to accommodate the ambition of a sitting president who suddenly discovers he is indispensable, and feels obliged to answer the 'popular demand' to extend his stay in office, as the country cannot possibly cope without his leadership. Spare a thought for; Yoweri Museveni (Uganda), Pierre Nkurunziza (Burundi), Paul Kagame (Rwanda), Vladimir Putin (Russia), and as you read, ballots still counting, Alassane Ouattara (Ivory Coast) to mention but a few. Even here, in Nigeria, there was an audacious attempt by former President Olusegun Obasanjo to gain an unconstitutional third term in 2007, which was stoutly resisted. To everyone's relief, he backed down and bowed out.

In one of his rhetorical flourishes, President Trump has indicated that he might not leave the White House if his loss could be attributed to "irregularities" in the voting process. Let us be absolutely clear, Trump will leave office, willy-nilly, come rain or shine if, as expected, he loses. America is not a banana republic — yet. President Trump talks through his hat quite a lot, and people generally know it, even if they find that extremely disconcerting. One striking feature of the elections is that Americans do not elect their presidents directly. Voters go to the polls not to vote for president, but to elect "delegates" who will proceed to the "electoral college" to determine the president. The "college" is not a physical structure; it is an assumption in the minds of the delegates who could, in theory, overturn the will of the electorate and declare support for a candidate other than the one who actually won. That exists only in the realm of fantasy though. Winners and losers are decided and declared on a state-by-state basis, whose mandates are carried forward to the "college". The will of the people ultimately prevails.

To be successful, a candidate needs to win more than half the total delegates; 270. Thus, a candidate may not have the popular mandate and still become president, as happened with Donald Trump, who lost to Hillary Clinton, his Democratic challenger, by a whopping 3 million votes in 2016. Clinton could not, however, muster enough delegates in the so-called "swing states" to secure victory. Can you imagine that scenario playing out peacefully anywhere else? It is one of the quirks of America's presidential politics. The states in the union are allocated delegates depending on their size; the larger a state, the larger the delegates. This was deliberately done from the onset to keep the larger states in the tent, so, none ever thinks of seceding due to 'marginalisation' or anything of the sort. Whether or not this is still necessary in the modern age is a moot point. Lest I forget, there is provision for early voting in America too. "Election day" in the context of America, is a misnomer. Early voting exists in states that choose to start voting early. Over ninety million (or 2/3) have already cast their ballots prior to today as a matter of fact. There is no centralised electoral body running the show like Nigeria's Independent National Electoral Commission. Each state conducts its own elections and can adjust the national time table for its own convenience. This sounds weird to a lot of people in this part of the world, but it is open democracy in action. It is one of the enduring layers of American exceptionalism.

This column has been highly critical of the Trump's presidency from the get go. So, it should not come as anything surprising to be reading this. Doubtful it will influence the voting in America, but it sure will inform public opinion at home and abroad. Trump is by far the most polarising American president of this century. Nonetheless, as much as this column has been critical of him, so too many others have been vociferous in their support of him, including people living in Trump's "shithole countries". They see in him a deeply flawed character, but they also see a man who says it as it is. A man who is not trying to pull the wool over anybody's eyes like the conventional politicians are wont to do. But neither can he stop the smooth-talking bluster of a salesman that he was in another life. Trump is a man who has no time for political correctness when others spend a lifetime spinning, and dancing on the head of a pin. Given the weight of the mainstream media's scrutiny of him all along, it is even amazing that he was still in contention at all. He has done a remarkable job of helping American businesses stay competitive. He introduced a tax cut which helped pump money into the economy, and boosted employment across the board, but at the expense of increased budget deficit now standing at $1trillion, and US public debt of almost $25 trillion, up from $21 trillion when he took office. None of these economic numbers will count in the election. Trump's mishandling of the coronavirus pandemic from which 250,000 Americans have died (a quarter of the world's total with only 4% of the world population), has become pivotal in an election that has turned into a referendum on the issue.

Coronavirus will do to Donald Trump what the economy did to President George H.W. Bush, the 41st president of the US in 1993. Bush had been riding high in the opinion polls, having defeated Saddam Hussein in his attempt to annex the neighbouring Kuwait in an ill-advised invasion of the country in August 1990. Bush was widely admired and lauded on the international stage for his statesmanship. His re-election to a second term on the back of his numerous foreign policy triumphs was seen as a foregone conclusion until his Democratic challenger, Bill Clinton, a young, brash, inexperienced and 'unknown' quantity, turned the table, famously declaring; "it's the economy, stupid!". This time, for Trump, Democrats and the mainstream media have saturated the airwaves with the subtle equivalent; 'it's the coronavirus, stupid!' Trump's appointment of an ultra-conservative justice Amy Coney Barrett onto the US Supreme Court last week will not be enough to save him from defeat. On the contrary, it will embolden the anti-Trump Republicans to vote for his opponent, Joe Biden, safe in the knowledge that the Supreme Court is secured for the conservatives for a generation.

By presenting himself as the mouthpiece of the common man, Trump played on, and pandered to the worst instincts in humanity; selfish, egocentric, hedonistic, narcissistic, me, my taste, my preference above all others. He paints and glories in a dreary notion of a society that does not, and should not exist. Finally, as Trump stares down the barrel of defeat, an American expat, resident in Nigeria, who only knows me through this column, took exception to my "harsh" characterisation of the US President in a previous write-up, a while back. He then challenged me to a $100 dollar bet on the president's re-election, which I quickly doubled in a counter-offer. Well, if you are reading this, my friend, tonight's champagne in my yard is on you.

10.04 What Makes a Country 'Third World'?

13 April 2021

Ask whether Nigeria is a 'Third World' country, an average Nigerian would probably say yes, of course! It is a label many people grew up with, and accept as reality. To them, the term equates poverty, corruption, unemployment, kidnapping, wanton murder, mismanagement, electoral fraud, nepotism, graft, etc. All of these are axiomatic of their belief in its substance. It has become so commonplace that, I am sure some readers would even be wondering what the fuss is all about. Well, it is being made into an issue because it is not only a redundant term, it has never had any objective (rational) foundation. I was at a conference discussing development and globalisation recently, when, during the tea break, I asked a bunch of young, highly educated participants whether they thought Nigeria was a 'Third World' country. Instantly, and simultaneously, they yelled; "yeah we are, yes!" Really? I interjected, completely taken aback. Their voices grew even louder; "Yes, we are, yes, we are." following which I challenged them to explain what that entails in substance. The answer, this time, astounded me beyond belief; "we are inferior to the advanced countries", "oh yes, we are", they kept blurting out. Inferior? I asked, grim-faced. They repeated the same line over and over, with conviction. What is even more alarming was the fact that their team leader, a university lecturer in political science in this country, compounded my frustration by saying; "honestly, I really don't understand your position. Economically, politically and technologically, are you saying Nigeria, for example, is not inferior to Western advanced countries?"

If a political scientist, in charge of training Nigeria's future leaders can be this warped in his thinking, then, God help the rest of the country. More so, this particular academic got his training from a top Nigerian university, which he is presumably passing onto his own students, who will also pass same logic onto their friends, relatives, co-workers, and perhaps, their own future students as well. And if this is shared across social science faculties in the country, you can imagine what a big dilemma that poses. Imagine hundreds, if not thousands of university graduates leaving the campus believing they are, in fact, "inferior" to "Western advanced countries"? I once taught in Europe and the USA myself, and I remember the fierce debate scholars of all hues engaged in over the academic validity of any undergraduate course with 'Third World' in its title. It was not only thought to be an anachronism, it was widely accepted that it lacked academic merit. It was gradually, and quietly withdrawn from the curricula. That was more than twenty-five years ago. Similarly, the study of literature in the university curriculum in this country used to assume that only English literature was worth studying, until the academia got wise. Yoruba, Hausa, Igbo also have literature worth studying hence, the re-designation of the relevant department from 'English Literature' to Literature in English, marking a clear acknowledgment of the fact. Today, in 2021, the National Universities Commission is still sanctioning "Third World Study" as a significant building block of knowledge. How embarrassing.

The term 'Third World' was first used in an obscure text written by the French demographer, Alfred Sauvy, in a newspaper article in 1952. He did not intend it to be used in the way it subsequently developed. He used it to describe

10 · INTERNATIONAL AFFAIRS

a bi-polar Cold War, where most nations found themselves to be either in the Soviet camp, or the Western camp. What about the rest of the (non-aligned) world? It was precisely for this anomaly that he referenced 'Third World' in his write-up. It has since taken a whole new meaning by those desirous of finding a convenient label for the group of countries in Africa, South Asia and Latin America, who were outside the Cold War geo-political division. Given that much of these countries were former colonial outlets of the European powers, and given that they were also in the first stage of the industrial revolution and, above all, given that they supplied the resources for the Western industrial advancement, and are broadly non-white, 'Third World' seemed a convenient epitaph to categorise them all. Western intellectuals were subsequently quick to discover a new area of scholarship for study. This, in a nutshell, is the origin of the term. It appealed to Western governments mainly because it stopped them having to study the disparate countries and continent individually; in their own rights and because it played to the conception of racial superiority harboured by many of them. 'Third World' study became entrenched in Western education which also found its way onto the curricula in Africa, Asia and Latin-America. It has since been debunked, discredited and largely discontinued; except, apparently, in Nigerian universities.

Many of the countries formerly lumped together as 'Third World' have been shown to possess differing levels of economic and technological advancement. For instance, 'Third World' India, Singapore, Malaysia, Brazil etc. are industrial and technological giants rivalling any in the world. 'Third World' Qatar has the highest GDP per capita in the world; it is so rich that the state does not even collect income tax. 'First World' Greece is one of the poorest in Europe. The country had to be bailed out of its unsustainable debts a couple of years ago. 'Third' or 'Second' world China is about to overtake the USA as the largest economy in the world. 'First World' USA is the murder capital of the world. It harbours one quarter of the world's prison population, racial hatred, sporadic shootings, and killing by lunatics is an everyday affair. Drug addiction and homelessness is rampant, and even electoral fraud has become commonplace. You see the contradictions?

Aside from the above, if there was any such thing as first, second, or third world, then, Africa would be first. It is the cradle of humanity. The first humans emerged from African soil before curiosity and survival instincts drove the rest to different parts of the earth for settlements. This is a universally accepted scientific fact. So, in terms of geography and archaeological history, the term makes no sense. My interlocutor, the university don mentioned earlier, who casually based his concept of Nigerian inferiority in the "economic, political, and technological" fields clearly needs re-education. The economies of African states have been so inter-woven with that of the West for a century. Development of one perpetuates the underdevelopment of the other. This has nothing to do with "superiority" or "inferiority"; it is the logic of international capitalism. On the terrain of politics, Western powers expended so much resources throughout the Cold War period to destabilise Africa, and Latin American countries, fomenting internecine wars, military coups and regime change in order to prevent 'communist infiltration' of the African continent; the source of their raw materials. Yes, African countries are playing catch up on the technological front, but the gap between them and the West on this and other indices are not owed to some notion of "inferiority". It is wrong to assume (let alone teach) such baloney. Africa, Asia, and Latin America are palpably different in their socio-economic-political outlook from Western societies, but certainly NOT inferior. Inferiority is a state of mind. A university lecturer ought to know better although, less so a bunch of highly impressionable youngsters, who are still learning the ropes. 'Third World' as an academic title has long been jettisoned in the elite universities in the West. Even the international financial institutions would only reference "highly indebted", "developing", "less developed", "lower income" "middle income" or "emerging" economies in lieu of the meaningless 'Third World'. Why then would any African, Asian or Latin-American insist on the puny label? Answer please to the editor.

10.05 Why G7 Disavow 'Race to Bottom' Tax Incentive

15 June 2021

From the period after World War II, in 1945, the "Washington Consensus" had revolved around the need to commit public money to build some aspects of the economy. This was underlined by America's "Marshall Plan" (European Recovery Programme), aimed at reviving Western European economies from the ruins of the war. It was underwritten with US15bn dollars, and enacted into law by US Congress in 1948. Western economies would be run on the basis of free market, with minimal government intervention targeted at infrastructure and social services. Government annual deficit could be offset by 'limited' borrowing. Inflation could rise a little, but that was preferable to rising unemployment. A cosy, middle-of-the road, mixed economy type philosophy you might say, but it worked. The "consensus" remained the orthodoxy until it came under sustained assault by the apostles of (ultra) free market, the 'supply-side' (lower taxes, minimal regulation, and free trade) economists, from the late 1960s

10 · INTERNATIONAL AFFAIRS

through to the 1980s. Accumulation of public debt, bureaucracy, inflation, even stagflation in some cases, and a steady decline in manufacturing capacities, made the point for them succinctly. The supply-side economists had won the intellectual argument by the end of the 1970s, but needed political power to put their ideas into practice. Then, came Britain's first woman Prime Minister, ("Iron Lady"), Mrs Margaret Thatcher (1979–1990), followed by US President Ronald Reagan (1981–1989). Together, they pushed for low taxes, low inflation, deregulation, and smaller government with an evangelical zeal. It caught fire, and a new orthodoxy was established, until the G7 "historic" agreement at a meeting of its finance ministers in London on the 5th of June 2021.

The G7 countries are a collection of seven of the most advanced economies in the world: USA, UK, France, Germany, Canada, Italy and Japan. The odd thing about this is that France, Germany and Italy are also economically and politically tied to the EU. It is for this reason that there is, in addition, a seat at the table for the President of the European Council as well. The original G7 in fact started as the G6, at their first meeting in Rambouillet, in the suburb of Paris, in 1975. Canada was invited to join the club in 1976, when it morphed into the G7. The 1970s "oil shock", recession and negative growth had propelled the group to meet up and chart a new economic path for themselves and (by extension), the rest of the world. It was also against the background of the collapse of the "Washington Consensus" fashioned on a stable exchange rate under the auspices of the "Bretton Woods" Agreement. Also, as stated earlier, the supply-side economists had crystallised their ideas and were pushing hard for a pivot to monetarism as an alternative to the too cosy "Washington Consensus". The G7 group slowly and steadily built on the policy precepts of the supply-side economists, gradually making it the new orthodoxy under Thatcher and Reagan's watch.

Consequently, throughout the 1980s and 1990s, the Trojan Horse of low taxation, low inflation, and low interest rate, was built to push back the "frontiers of the state", and to make for smaller, leaner governance throughout the Western world. Developing nations were helmed into the new dawn of state belt-tightening, economic efficiency and the 'greed is good' philosophy of the "Young Urban Professionals" ("Yuppies" in the popular press). Russia was subsequently invited to come on board in 1998, to transform the group into the G8, until it invaded its neighbouring country, Ukraine, and annexed the region of Crimea in 2014. The club reverted back to G7, following Russia's exclusion. Curiously though, China, the second largest economy, with the largest population in the world, is not a member, and probably never will be. Well, you not only have to be a rich country to become a member of the exclusive club, you also have to be a democracy as well. China is not, and probably never

312   10 · INTERNATIONAL AFFAIRS

will be a (liberal) democracy. Russia is not a (liberal) democracy either, but had been tolerated for strategic reasons to the Western Alliance. Would China be invited to join one day for similar reasons? It is a remote possibility only in the longest of time in the future. For starters, China (soon to be largest economy in the world) has no immediate need to belong. Besides, its leaders' strategic ambition is to reconstruct the world economy in the country's image, not to sheepishly follow the Western model.

Low taxation has been an article of faith for members of the G7 for over 40 years. The online and tech giants: Google, Facebook, Instagram, Twitter, Apple, Microsoft, and retail companies such as Amazon, have exploited this to the full all along. They shop around for any country willing to offer the lowest corporate tax, stable legal regime, and modern infrastructure at the same time. The smaller European countries such as the Republic of Ireland, Cyprus, and others fit the bill nicely. They offer 12.5%% corporate tax compared to the EU average of 20.71%, and global average of 23.65%. US Treasury Secretary, Janet Yellen, described the tactic of offering low taxes to gain advantage over rival economies as a "race to the bottom". Yes, that may well be, Madam Secretary, but since when has it become fashionable for Western economic leaders to sniff at low taxation? Her British counterpart, Rishi Sunak, describes the current international tax regime as being designed in the "1920s" and no longer fit for purpose. It is poignant that the meeting of the G7 countries took place in the country of Adam Smith, whose 18th century free market ideas have underlined modern economic policies around the world to this day. Is Mr Sunak willing to disavow those as well? Sunak's highly seductive soundbite on this issue clearly defies logic too.

The G7's sudden self-immolation over low tax is totally bewildering to the rest of the world, which has long endured a perpetual struggle and, indeed, race to the bottom; trying to curry favour with Foreign Direct Investors, not least, on the prompting of the G7 countries themselves! Corporate tax rate has been the weapon of choice for foreign investors, using it to bully developing countries into agreeing to all sorts of unfavourable demands. Right now, the West is willing to jettison a core economic principle for pragmatic (some would say cynical) short-term objective of shoring up their Treasury coffers. If you fervently believe in free market, and low taxation at its core, why whinge about companies setting their stalls in tax efficient economies? A race to the bottom is precisely what the Libertarians amongst them would welcome. As a matter of principle, the less government takes in taxation the better for the cause of liberty.

The G7's reversal of a favoured economic doctrine will be endorsed at the G20 meeting coming up in July. They are expected to ratify the new 15% minimum corporation tax agreed at the G7 meeting. Thereafter, as a rule, no company will be allowed to pay less than the minimum. It is difficult to see this measure standing the test of time though, as every solution in this domain produces its own unique snags. Nonetheless, the problem for Africa and much of the developing countries is that multinational corporations pay virtually no tax at all for years on end as a condition for investing. They negotiate numerous 'tax holidays' and dubious 'exemptions', relieving themselves of tax obligations over and over again. In addition, multinational corporations are the consumers of Africa's natural resources. They (the buyers) also determine the price for extracting African mineral resources. Granted that the G7 exists primarily to further its members' interests; so, kudos to them for driving a hard bargain. The question is who will speak for Africa?

Conclusion

With a heavy reliance on empirical data and a set of theoretical assumptions, this book sets out to dissect public policy in an emerging economy as it happens. It is a radical departure from the conventional method of engaging with scholarly works on the subject-matters, which normally falls within the pattern of a narrative based on a theoretical framework, central argument, recommendations and proposal for further research. Here, the reader was invited to sit in the cockpit of a light aircraft listening and watching the pilot's live commentary on events as they unfold on the ground. The intention was not to elicit instant conclusions, but to ascertain the extent to which key events bear out conventional wisdom and theoretical knowledge. Nigeria's handling of its "Vision 20:2020" grand plan offers a useful insight into this methodological approach. It upends all attempts to encapsulate the Nigerian development paradox in a single narrative.

The whole fabric of the country was mobilised for it to become the top 20th economy in the world by the year 2020.[308] The drumbeat of this audacious goal had entertained and grabbed public imagination in the ten years prior, but quietened down in the last two, because of the realisation that the goal would not be met. Why? And what went wrong? The entire government of Nigeria embarked upon the ambition to "position Nigeria to become one of the top 20 economies in the world by 2020, by linking the objectives of the NEEDS programme (2004–2007),[309] the NEEDS 2[310] programme, and

---

308. The full text of the plan is contained in "Nigeria — Vision 20;2020. Economic Transformation Blueprint". London School of Economics Papers https://www.lse.ac.uk/Grantham Institute/wp-content/uploads/laws/1516.pdf

309. Nigeria: National Economic Empowerment and Development Strategy. Central Bank of Nigeria Publications, March 2004 https://www.cbn.gov.ng/out/publications/communique /guidelines/rd/2004/needs.pdf

310. See; "Nigeria — National Economic Empowerment and Development Strategy. Joint IDA-IMF Advisory note". The World Bank Publication/documents https://documents

316 CONCLUSION

the Seven-Point Agenda". The Nigerian government and key Vision 2020 stakeholder groups took concrete steps towards the development of the vision such as: budget allocation, development of sectoral strategies by Ministries, Departments and Agencies (MDAs), CBN Financial Sector Strategy 2020, Federal Inland Revenue 2020 strategy, constitution and inauguration of the Business Support Group intended to engender private sector support for the vision under the auspices of the National Steering Committee. In addition, the National Planning Commission and the Vision 2020 Secretariat, which houses the Steering Committee, were mandated by the Federal Executive Council to produce the Vision 2020 plan for launching by the President of the Federal Republic of Nigeria by the 1st of October 2009.[311] All of that was put in place and much more.

An institutional framework was established to oversee the country's arrival at the top table of the 20 largest economies in the world by this same year 2020. National Council on Vision 2020, National Steering Committee, Project Steering Committee, National Technical Working Groups, Business Support Groups, Programme Coordination Office, Vision 2020 Stakeholder Development Committee, State Governments, Ministries, Department and Agencies, Special Interest Groups, etc. all co-opted into this humongous vision expected to touch on the key parameters of: quality education, which provides "the opportunity for maximum potential, adequate and competent manpower", infrastructure to "support the full mobilisation of all economic sectors", manufacturing to deliver a "vibrant and globally competitive manufacturing sector that contributes significantly to GDP with a manufacturing value added of not less than 40%", health sector that "supports and sustains life expectancy of not less than 70 years and reduces to the barest minimum, the burden of infectious and other debilitating diseases", and last but not least, "a modern technologically enabled agricultural sector that fully exploits the vast agricultural resources of the country, ensures national food security and contributes to foreign exchange earnings". All of the above are expected to be achieved, according to the blueprint, in a "peaceful, harmonious and a stable democracy".[312]

.worldbank.org/en/publication/documents-reports/documentdetail/234301468290438608 /nigeria-national-economic-empowerment-and-development-strategy-and-joint-ida-imf -staff-advisory-note

311. See; "Vision 20-2020 Still Being Articulated, says FG", AllAfrica.com, April 20, 2009 https://allafrica.com/stories/200904201326.html

312. See the abridged version of the plan issued by the Federal Government https://www.nigerianstat.gov.ng/pdfuploads/Abridged_Version_of_Nigeria%20Vision %202020.pdf

CONCLUSION

We do not have the exact financial cost of this welcome party, but it is safe to assume that it is in billions of naira, involving the recruitment of experts, domestic and international consultants, thousands of support staff up and down the country. To coin a phrase, never has so much resources been committed by so many to such a scanty outcome. As of today, Nigeria is the 27th largest economy in the world by GDP of under $US500 dollars.[313] It will take another 20 years, at least, to attain the position of the 20th largest economy in the world if at all. Meanwhile, income inequality has widened since the vision was launched, human development index has fallen, at 0.534 as of 2018, putting the country in one of the lowest categories in the world; 158 out of 189 countries and territories, according to the UNDP.[314] The economy, which grew at close to 8% in 2009, has since contracted (i.e. shrunk) to less than 2%, and future prognosis is even more depressing to contemplate. This concluding segment is not offering a comprehensive review of the Vision 20: 2020 project; sector by sector analysis and all that. We are interested in the grand aim, which has spectacularly fallen out of reach, leading any rational observer to call the whole vision into question. Just like the top-flight football manager, an ambitious target is set by the club and the manager is judged by results. Was the ambition too high for Nigeria in the first place? Or was there not enough commitment to back it up?

To be fair, Nigeria is not alone in declaring audacious ambitions. China's "Great Leap Forward" campaign in 1958 under Chairman Mao-Zedong was an attempt to transform the country from an agrarian to a communist nirvana by organising society into "communes" in an effort to increase yield production and eradicate the urban-rural divide across the nation. Far from the increase surplus envisaged by the goal, agricultural production declined significantly, leading to mass starvation. In short, the "Great Leap Forward" turned into the "Great Chinese Famine" before long. The "Bolshevik revolution" in Russia in 1917. They wanted to transform society into a utopian communist Eldorado. The revolutionaries transformed into the Communist party several years later, culminating in the eventual formation of the Union of Soviet Socialist Republics (USSR) in 1922. The aim was first, to "catch up" with the West, and overtake it in human, technological and scientific development. The USSR sur-

---

313. Slipped further back to 32 as at the time of writing. https://countryeconomy .com/gdp/nigeria#:~:text=The%20GDP%20figure%20in%202020,million%20with%20 respect%20to%202019.

314. Nigeria—Human Development Report, 2020. UNDP, https://hdr.undp.org/sites /default/files/Country-Profiles/NGA.pdf

318 CONCLUSION

vived for over seventy years before collapsing under the weight of its internal contradictions in 1989 without ever achieving any of its lofty aims. Japan was an imperial power destroyed by America's dropping of atomic bombs on the cities of Hiroshima and Nagasaki on the 6th and 7th of August 1947 at the height of the Second World War. It led to Japan's surrender on the promise to the Americans never to be a military threat again. Without further ado, the country with little or no resources quietly went underground, rebuilding their society along education and technology with no grandiose "visions" to boast of. It has since risen to be the third largest economy in the world. There is no household in the world without at least one electronic item made in Japan.

Germany under Adolf Hitler went through a similar scenario following defeat after World War Two. No ambitious economic plans or dreams of surpassing anyone on the technological front, only a desire to rebuild a war-ravaged economy. Germany has since also risen to become the largest economy in Europe and fourth largest in the world. Malaysia and Singapore went through a period of colonial repression under the British, got their independence in 1957 and 1963 respectively. The two countries once tried to merge into one entity, but went about their separate ways to become the leading lights in the creation of the so-called "Asian Tiger economies" almost literally from the ashes, and without grandiose visions beyond hard work, dedication and forthrightness. What do these analogies from the outside world tell us here in Nigeria? That you can have big dreams on paper and indeed by intention such as the old USSR and China, but without the backing and collective will of the people, it is doomed to failure as it did for those two countries. On the other hand, you can nurse big dreams to become successful as indeed happened in the cases of Japan, Germany, Singapore and Malaysia, if the people plug into the same aspiration as the government pushing it. Nigeria's "vision 20:2020" was long on ambition, but short on commitment of the people.

So much for having a vision; it appears and disappears almost as quickly as it is conceived. Nigeria's tolerance for public policy failure has proven to be elastic over time. It should come as no surprise, therefore, that proposals and ideas conceived on a new vision 3030, 4040, even 5050 are already being contemplated by some in the corridors of power. As we have demonstrated throughout this volume, Nigeria has embarked upon many questionable public policy initiatives over the years, but, it is also palpable that the country has no shortage of viable public policy alternatives and progressive ideas for nation-building. A great number of such policies and ideas have been brought under the spotlight in this collection. Nonetheless, in the end, the grand narrative from the foregoing, and indeed this book, perhaps, is that there is no grand narrative around which to anchor the Nigerian phenomenon. It is time to stop looking at Nigeria as a puzzle to unravel. Nigeria is what it is because that is how Nigerians chose to have it. Nigeria will become different when, and only when, Nigerians choose a different path.

Index

Note: Page number followed by 'n' refer to notes

A

Academic Staff Union of Universities (ASUU), 153–155

Accountability, 42, 43, 74, 123, 124, 145, 150, 167, 224, 272, 290

Accreditation exercise, 163

Activist investors, 78–80

Adeosun, Kemi, 4, 17, 113

Adesina, Akinwumi, 14, 285–288

Advanced economies, 7, 12, 18, 23, 28, 46, 52, 110, 263, 264, 282

Afghanistan, 10, 102, 196–199, 201, 249, 292

Africa, 253
and "corrective coup" syndrome, 253–256

"Africa Continental Free Trade Area" (AfCFTA) agreement, 121

African Development Bank, 14, 53, 285, 287

African finance powerhouse, 69

African National Congress, 184, 256

African states, 124, 139, 268–271, 276, 279, 291, 294, 295

African Union Summit, 145

AFRICOM, 250–252

American financial assets, 105, 106

Anchors, 167, 172, 173, 208, 319

Anglo-Nigerian Defence Pact, 220

Arab Spring, 175, 176, 183

Aramco, 56–58

Arik Air, 21

Arrests, 138, 139, 141, 212

Artificial scarcity, 15, 85

Asian Tiger economies, 18, 19, 59, 318

Asset management, 23

Asset Management Corporation of Nigeria (AMCON), 19, 21–23, 60, 61, 109
dubious economic function, 19–22

Assiduousness, 23

Automated Teller Machines (ATMs), 92

B

Bagehot, Walter, 109

Bancarotta, 108

Bank of Credit and Commerce International (BCCI), 74

Bankers, 22, 64, 86, 87, 92, 107, 134, 194

Bankruptcy, 22, 60, 108

Ben Bella, Ahmed, 275

Biden, Joe, 107, 173, 249, 307

Big multinational corporations, 31

Black market, 4–6

Blair, Tony, 194

Bloomberg, 59

Bokassa, Jean-Bédel, 275

Bolshevik revolution, 49, 317

Bookrunners, 56

Borrowing, 4–6, 27–29, 51–53, 61, 63, 84, 104, 105, 240

Bretton Woods institutions, 50, 103, 104, 286

Bribery, 136, 140, 148, 179, 206, 274, 275, 289

Brown, Gordon, 194

Budget, 11, 51, 78, 88, 89, 134, 171, 181, 236

    crisis, 51

    deficit, 29, 37, 150

Budget 2017, 88–90

Buhari, Muhammadu, 4, 15, 17

Bureaucracy, 29, 44, 64, 77, 95, 99, 173, 180, 236, 311

Burke, Edmund, 213

Bush, George W., 194

Business failure, resurrect, 33–35

C

Cadbury Report, 124

Canaan, Banana, 275

Capital

    expenditure, 11

    imperatives, 90

markets, 24, 79–81, 84, 87–90, 111, 112, 116, 118, 119, 122

resource, 4

Capitalism, 20, 24, 32, 38, 60, 79, 80, 92, 129, 251, 289

Central Bank of Nigeria (CBN), 4–7, 17, 19, 34, 39, 44, 47, 75–76, 84, 85, 92, 96, 109, 110, 113, 116, 132–134, 169, 235

China, generous lender, 125–128

China and African Development Bank, 53

Civic obligation, 25

Civil enforcement powers, 82

Colonialism, 268, 282, 297, 301

Commercial banks, 4–6, 83–86, 108, 110, 129, 132

Companies, public, 53–58

Companies and Allied Matters Act (CAMA), 75, 118

Company valuation, 54

Concealed state capitalism, 68

Consumer Price Index, 62

Consumer Protection Act, 21

Contracts, 11, 115, 135, 136, 144, 148, 233–237

Corbyn, Jeremy, 32

Corporate Affairs Commission (CAC), 75

Corporate governance, 70–77, 113–115, 122–125

    Codes of, 70, 72–74, 76, 122

    Lapses, 113, 228

Corporate Governance and Regulatory overreach, 70, 73, 75

Corporate Social Responsibility (CSR), 76

"Corrective coup" syndrome, 253–256

INDEX

Corruption, 132, 135, 136, 138–140, 145, 148, 149, 274, 277, 280, 287
Cost of borrowing, 4, 27–30
Country's debt, crisis, 50–53
Credit economy, 30
Criminality, 20, 206, 231, 280, 281, 289
Crisis, 24, 50–53, 118
Critical sectors, 18, 21, 33, 84
Cui bono, 67–70
Currency swaps, 118, 119

D

Death penalty, 98
Debt management office (DMO), 22–24
Debts, 22–24, 50–52, 61, 105, 117, 118, 294
    management, 22–24
    obligations, 105
Deficit finance, 52
Democracy, 20, 80, 168, 174, 175, 205, 207, 209, 248, 249, 254, 300, 301, 311, 312
Democratic accountability, 22, 65, 250, 301
Democratic space, 79, 191
Democrats, 8, 194, 206, 257, 307
Devaluation, 7
Developed economies, 28, 30, 68
Diaspora bonds, 24
Dictatorship, 78, 168, 169, 173, 174, 258, 260
Dividends, 53, 56, 74, 79, 89, 116, 118
Dodd-Frank Act, 81
Dodd-Frank Wall Street Reform, 21
Dollar morass, 106
Dollar-naira parity, 101, 120
Dollar trap, 106
Domestic market, 119
Domestic ramifications, 105

E

East African trade pact, 31
Economic and financial crime
    Courts, stolen funds, and legal technicality, 135–137
    Economic and Financial Crimes Commission (EFCC), 135–143
    Kleptocracy Assets Recovery Initiative (KARI), 144–146
    Legalism, cobweb of, 149–151
    Transparency International (TI) and game of numbers, 138–140
    White collar crime and business efficacy, 146–149
Economic and Financial Crimes Commission (EFCC), 135–143, 149–151
    Criminal assets forfeiture, failure, 141–143
Economic/economy
    benefit, 8
    consensus, 63
    destiny, 38, 52, 58
    diversifying or decentralising, Nigeria, 16–19
    emergency, 89
    foreign (direct) investment, Nigeria, 11–13
    freedom, 78
    growth, 7, 9, 29, 30, 36, 128, 282
    law, 53
    model, 32
    Nigeria's interest rates/forex quagmire, 3–7
    pluralism, 78
    policy, 17, 20, 64, 104
    recession, Nigeria, 8–10
    rice import, Nigeria, 13–16
    space, 78

Economic Recovery and Growth Plan (ERGP), 36
ECOWAS, 31, 254
Education
  academics, moral agents, 156–158
  National Universities Commission (NUC), 161–164
  Nigerian Universities, illiterates, 153–156
  "VC" position, contested in Nigeria, 158–161
Education establishments, 154
Ekpo, Margaret, 214
Emefiele, Godwin, 85
Enaharo, Anthony Eromosele, 221
Entrepreneurial skills, 72
Ethical investors, 131
Ethiopia, 49, 126, 184, 261, 267, 269, 270, 284, 294
Exchange rate mechanism (ERM), 109

F
Fayemi, Kayode, 18
Federal Allocation Account Committee (FAAC), 42–45
Federal Republic of Nigeria, 20, 22, 50, 114, 229, 230, 235, 240, 241, 247, 248
Federation Account Allocation Committee, 39
Federation of International Football Associations (FIFA), 95
FGN Savings Bond, 24
Finance/capital markets, 84
  activist investors, 78–80
  bank failures, 107–110
  banks and economic saboteurs, 131–134
  budget 2017, 88–90

"bureau de change" (BDC), 131–134
capital markets, 88–90
corporate governance, 70–77
corporate greed and corporate governance, combating, 122–125
Financial Reporting Council of Nigeria (FRCN), 70–77
Nigeria's banking services, 90–93
Nigeria's currency "swap" with China, 118–121
Non-interest (Islamic) banking, 128–131
pro-democracy activists, 78–80
regulatory overreach, 70–77
sovereign wealth fund, 67–70
stock exchange and mechanics of markets, 96–99
US dollar (USD), 99–107
Financial assets, 106
Financial crisis, 23, 105, 122
Financial instruments, 24, 119, 133, 239
Financial intelligence, 94
Financial irregularities, 73
Financial Reporting Council of Nigeria (FRCN), 70–77
Financial reporting standards, 76, 77
Financial stakeholders, 22
Financial statement, 77
First law of development, 30–32
Fiscal consolidation, 37
Fiscal policies, 29, 64
Forced military, 252
Foreign aids, 20, 145, 227
"Foreign Corrupt Practices Act" (FCPA), 147
Foreign direct investment, 11, 32, 33, 292

INDEX

Foreign exchange (forex) market, 83–85
  CBN governor's parallel universe, 83–85
  Nigerian banks, 86–87
Foreign investors, 9–13, 32, 34, 42, 105, 279, 312
Foreign-made motorbikes, 55
Foreign portfolio investor, 12
Forex, 83–87, 131, 133, 134
  fraud, 86, 87, 134
  guidelines, 85
  transaction, 87
Franklin, Benjamin, 25
Free market, 20, 21, 24, 32, 48, 59, 122, 198, 266, 310, 312
  economics, 48
Free press, 166
Free trade, 15, 16, 31, 32, 38, 59, 286, 310
Fujimori, Alberto, 274
Funding gap, 52, 105
Funds, 42–44, 67–70, 82, 83, 119, 196, 238–240, 296

G

Gender-based violence (GBV), 210–213
Geun-hye, Park, 274
Giant of Africa, 101, 254
Globalisation, 12, 31, 32, 110, 266, 308
Government expenditures, 29
Government interference, 59
Government policy, 14, 167, 171, 246
Government spending, 31, 38, 63
Grand larceny, 39, 42, 86, 132, 272
"Great Leap Forward" campaign, 317
Grenada, 49

Gross domestic product (GDP), 50–52, 58, 62, 292, 316, 317
Guinea, 253–256, 270, 275
Gwarzo, Mounir H., 113, 114, 228, 229

H

Haram, Boko, 15
Headline inflation, 45, 62
High debt profile, 51
High inflation, 5, 45–47, 62
High-level corruption, 45–47, 189
Holland, Francois, 194
Home countries, 79, 108, 233, 262, 289, 291, 300, 301
Hussein, Saddam, 8

I

Ibrahim Babangida (IBB), 7
Import Substitution Industrialisation (ISI), 15, 16
Indebtedness, 127, 294
Industrial revolution, 102, 268, 309
Inflation, 7, 29, 30, 37, 45–47, 62, 63, 310, 311
Informants, 45
Information, 54, 55, 95, 96, 98, 113, 114, 138, 166, 173–176
Initial Public Offering (IPO), 54
Insider knowledge, 55
Institutional investors, 89, 108, 130
Inter-bank rate, 3n2
Interest rates, 3–7, 27–30, 109, 119
Interest repayment, 28
International affairs
  foreign election observers, hypocrisy, 299–302
  G7 countries and tax incentive, 310–313
  "Third World" country, Nigeria, 307–310

326 INDEX

Trump supporters, 302–304
USA, Trump defeated, 305–307
International economic order, 37
International finance, 11, 69, 95, 110, 286
International financial institutions, 20, 40, 95, 105, 256, 273, 310
International Monetary Fund (IMF), 7, 20, 35–40, 91, 103, 301
Intra-African affairs
Adesina's re-election, 285–288
African time, 263–265
Africa's free trade bloc, 269–272
"Brexit," Africa, 277–279
Celebrate corrupt leaders, Africa, 272–277
Europe underdeveloped Africa, 260–262
king Mswati III, last maximum ruler, 294–297
new scramble, Africa, 265–268
Thomas Sankara and, 291–294
traitors, hiding wealth, 288–291
Western Sahara, Nigeria's muddled policy, 282–285
xenophobic attacks, false narrative, 280–282
Zimbabwe, African tragedy, 257–260
Investment activism, 79
"Investors Compensation Scheme Ltd v West Bromwich Building Society" [1997] UKHL 28, 234
Islamic finance, 24, 129, 130
Israeli-Arab conflict, 6

J
Jaiz Bank, 128–130
Joint Operations Agreement, 40

Jonathan, Goodluck, 16
Jurisdictions, 119, 137, 226, 227, 231, 232, 238
Justice, 77, 135, 145, 146, 225–227, 231, 234, 274

K
Kachikwu, Ibe, 44
Kleptocracy Assets Recovery Initiative (KARI), 144–146

L
Lagarde, Madame Christine, 64
Lagos Stock Exchange, 97
Laissez-faire, 78, 98
Languages, 37, 185, 187
Largest economy, 9, 45, 63, 93, 268, 271, 309, 312, 316–318
Law
Malami's "open" road to anarchy, 241–243
Nigerian police relish parading suspects, 230–232
"Panama papers," lawyers' ethical dilemma, 225–227
pension funds, government's raid, 238–241
Process and Industrial Development Ltd (P&ID) award, 232–238
Less developed countries (LDCs), 6, 7
Liberal economic policy, 20
Liquid market, 99
Liquidity, 81, 99
Lula da Silva, Luiz Inácio, 273

M
Machel, Samora, 49, 184
Macro-economic strategy, 6
Macron, Emmanuel, 90, 194

INDEX

Major, John, 194
Marginal profitability, 61
Market, 45, 55, 56, 59, 63, 80, 81, 83, 99, 101, 111–113, 119, 120, 239
    capitalisation, 176, 239
    infractions, 80–83, 99
Marović, Svetozar, 274
Marx, Karl, 48
Marxist-Leninist Derg, 49
Massive budget deficit, 38
Massive debt forgiveness, 23
Mechanics of markets, 96, 120
Media, 165–175, 230–232, 281
    channels and government, 165–168
    channels TV interview, Buhari, 171–173
    governments and Twitter, 173–176
    servile, supine state of, 168–171
Medium-sized enterprises, 84, 87
Merkel, Angela, 194
Military, 158, 182, 189, 199, 218, 245, 246, 248–250, 252, 253, 255, 258, 284
    Africa and "corrective coup" syndrome, 253–256
    Buhari's white flag of surrender, 250–253
    conflict of loyalties, 248–250
    dictatorship, 20, 78, 158, 245
    still under shadows, Nigeria, 245–247
    United States Africa Command (AFRICOM), 250–253
Minimum wage, 47–49, 199
Monetary policy, 29, 104
Monetary tool, 63
Money changers, 107
Morality, 68, 157, 158, 233
Mozambique, 49, 184, 292

Multinational companies, 40, 148
Multinational oil contracts, 39–42
Multinationals, 40–42
Multi-party democracy, 20
Mushroom banks, 92
Musk, Elon, 174n241
Muslims, 130, 131, 157, 189

N

Naira, 3n3, 5, 6, 24, 50, 51, 84, 85, 98, 99, 101, 107, 111, 120, 133, 172
    market capitalisation, 97
Năstase, Adrian, 274
National Bureau of Statistics (NBS), 45, 46
National Code of Corporate Governance (NCCG), 70, 75
National Tax Policy review committee, 26
National Universities Commission (NUC), 161–164
NEEDS programme, 315
Nigerian banks, 28, 29, 55, 84, 86, 87, 107, 109, 110, 116, 133
Nigerian Broadcasting Commission (NBC), 167
Nigerian citizens, 11, 101, 274
Nigerian democracy, 200, 206
Nigerian Enterprises Promotion Decree, 13
Nigerian Football Association (NFA), 95
Nigerian Inter-Bank Offered Rate (NIBOR), 4, 5
Nigerian manufacturing sector, 120, 121
Nigerian National Petroleum Company, 56

328 INDEX

Nigerian National Petroleum Corporation (NNPC), 39–45, 56, 273
Nigerian police, 151, 230
Nigerian Police Force, 209, 230
Nigerian population, 219
Nigerian Stock Exchange, 5, 54, 75, 97, 99, 110, 113, 125, 209
Nigerian telecommunications industry, 33
Nigerian universities, 153, 155, 156, 159, 162, 309
Nigerian workers, wage, 47–50
Nigeria's banking services, 90–93
Nigeria's capital market, 89, 114
Nigeria's Companies and Allied Matters Act, 72
Nigeria's Financial Intelligence Unit (NFIU), 94–96
Nigeria's Independence Day, 200, 252
Nigeria Sovereign Investment Authority Bill, 67
9Mobile, 33–35, 116, 118
shareholders, 116–118
Non-performing loan assets, 19

O

Obama, Barack, 256, 301
Ogbe, Audu, 15
Oil companies, 114, 303
Olmert, Ehud, 274
Online experts, 88
"Open Ballot System" (OBS), 178, 179
Openness, 98, 179
Option A4, 178

P

Parallel market, 84, 85, 87, 133
Partnership Investment Company Limited (PICL), 82
Party membership, 206, 207

Pensioners, 105
Pension funds, 89, 238–240
People's Democratic Party (PDP), 62, 169, 173, 193–195, 205–207, 284
Petrol Profit Tax (PPT), 43
Policy makers, 90, 92, 121, 139
Political acolytes, 23
Political discourse, 47, 179, 188, 219
Political expediency, 87
Political freedom, 78
Political interference, 94
Political intrigue, 115
Politically Exposed Persons (PEPs), 149–151
Politics
APC and PDP, 193–196
Buhari and separatism, 188–191
#EndSARS protest, 216–218
female Nigerian leaders, dearth, 213–215
gender-based violence and religion, 210–213
independent National Electoral commission (INEC) and, 208–210
Nigerian democracy, 200
parliamentary system, brutal and vicious, 221–224
political parties, joining, 205–207
primordial loyalties, 203
revolution of mind, Nigeria, 182–185
round-tripping politicians, 191–193
Taliban victory and Boko Haram, 196–199
transition gap, looters' charter, 180–182
tribalism and nationality question, Nigeria, 185–188

INDEX

vegetative state, 202
vote buying and, 177–179
youth representation, imperative, 218–221
Potential negative consequences, 48
Private companies, 35, 70, 71, 76, 77, 120
Private enterprises, 20, 21, 122, 123
Private investors, 37, 38
Private placement, 117, 128, 130
Process and Industrial Development Ltd (P&ID) award, 232–238
legality of, 232–235
politics of, 235–238
Processing fees, 112
Pro-democracy activism, 79
Pro-democracy activists, 78–80, 215, 255
Production sharing contracts (PSC), 40
Profit-making company, 117
Profit maximisation, 31, 123
Pro-investment activists, 78
Public debt, 6, 20, 23, 104, 306, 311
profile, 104, 106
Public expenditure, 16
Public finance, 22, 43, 237
Public interest entities, 77
Public limited company (PLC), 53
Public money, 60, 310
Public policy, Nigeria, 3
Public policy discourse, 53
Public universities, 154, 159–161, 221

Q

Quagmire, 3–8, 133

R

Rawlings, John Jerry, 256
Reagan, Ronald, 123, 173, 272, 311

Real petrol economies, 17, 18
Receiver, 34, 35
Receivership, 34, 35
Republic of South Vietnam, 49
Rescue mission, 34
Revelations, 26, 39, 149, 288–290
Revolution, 7, 49, 63, 80, 123, 182–185, 196, 205
Right-wing political ideologues, 78
Roosevelt, Franklin D., 302
Rousseau, Jean-Jacques, 201

S

Sahrawi Arab Democratic Republic (SADR), 283–285
Sanader, Ivo, 274
Sankara, Thomas, 291–294
Saudi Arabia, 17, 18, 56–58, 253, 303
Sawaba, Hajia Gambo, 214
Schizophrenic imbalance, 39
Securities, 18, 27, 54, 113, 125, 147, 188, 194, 200, 202, 240
Securities and Exchange Commission (SEC), 54, 75, 80–83, 96, 110, 113, 209, 227
corporate governance lapses, litany of, 113–115
Minister's Right to Suspend DG, 227–230
new "derivatives" platform, 110–113
Self-fulfilling prophesy, 80
Self-preservation, 48, 299
Severance payment, 113
Sex for marks controversy, 53
Shagari, Shehu, 91
Shareholders, 35, 39, 56, 71, 73–75, 89, 91, 116, 117, 124
Shithole countries, 285, 286, 306

INDEX

Small-scale enterprises, 84
Smith, Adam, 71, 122
Social media, 154, 174–176, 183, 221
Socrates, Jose, 274
Soludo, Charles, 17, 92
Somoza, Anastasio, 302
Southern African Development Community, 284, 295
Sovereignty, 125, 126, 128, 261, 268
Sovereign wealth fund (SWF), 67–70, 106, 295
Speculative trading, 98, 119
Stagflation, 62–65, 311
State capitalism, 18–19, 120
State capitals, 45
Stock exchange, 54, 72, 96, 97, 99, 110, 112, 119
Structural Adjustment Programme (SAP), 7

T

Taxes, 25–27, 29, 37, 59, 61, 303, 306, 312, 313
    avoidance, 25, 26, 289
    compliance, 27
    havens, 25, 289
    incentives, 13, 38
    obligations, 26, 313
    receipts, 29, 303
    revenue, elusive quest, 25–27
Technocrats, 65
Thatcher, Margaret, 123, 194, 311
Thatcher revolution, 72
Third World, 43, 104, 301, 307–310
Third World Syndrome, 44
Top government functionary, 55, 147, 148, 293
Transparency, 22, 55, 74, 145, 150, 179, 300
Transportation, 38, 49, 125

Treasury bills, 47, 93, 104, 106
"Treasury Single Account" (TSA), 29
Tribes, 185–187, 248
Trump, Donald J., 8, 25

U

Udoji Award, 6
Union leaders, 47, 49, 50
University education, 162
Uruguay round of agreements, 31
US dollar (USD), 83, 84, 99–107, 132, 181, 264, 273
US military, 250, 253

V

Violence, 190, 197, 211–213, 218, 301
Vote, 39, 41, 177, 178, 190, 192, 193, 196, 206–208, 255, 305–307

W

Wall Street Crash, 20n36
War of independence, 251
Washington-based International Monetary Fund, 59
Wealth, 32, 71, 72, 78, 79, 131, 138, 226, 227, 289, 290
Welfare state, 123, 201
West Africa, 204, 262, 271
West African trade pact, 31
Western economies, 30, 38, 71, 123, 131, 310
Western Sahara, 282–285
Wilson, Woodrow, 179
Wolfowitz, Paul, 64
Word security, 54
Workers, 48–50, 104, 194
World Bank, 10, 22, 40, 50, 53, 103, 127, 199, 280, 286
World Bank Economic Reports, 9
World Bank Reports, 8, 10

World economy, 48, 97, 312

World trade, 31, 32, 286

World Trade Organisation (WTO),
11, 15, 31, 40

World War I, 103, 179, 202

World War II, 49, 122, 278, 286, 310,
318

Y

"Yom Kippur" war, 6

Z

Zimbabwe, 102, 177, 257, 258, 267, 275

Zuma, Jacob, 275